THE GOOD GOVERNANCE GUIDE TO BOARDROOM DYNAMICS

Jeremy Cross

Chartered
Governance
Institute
UK & Ireland

First published 2021

Published by
CGI Publishing Limited
Saffron House
6–10 Kirby Street
London EC1N 8TS

Typeset by Paul Barrett Book Production, Cambridge
Edited by Benedict O'Hagan
Cover designed by Anthony Kearney

British Library Cataloguing in Publication Data
A catalogue record for this book is available from the British Library

ISBN 9781860728068

As with all legislation, the provisions of the Companies Acts and related legislation are open to interpretation and must be assessed in the context of the particular circumstances at hand, the articles of association of the company in question, and any relevant shareholders' agreement or other pertinent ancillary agreements. While every effort has been made to ensure the accuracy of the content of this book, neither the author nor the publisher can accept any responsibility for any loss arising to anyone relying on the information contained herein.

Contents

Acknowledgements

Figure 8 © Richard Chait (2016)
Figure 9 © Bob Garrett (1995)
Figure 10 © Bob Tricker (2019)
Figure 11 © Chris Rodgers (2007)
Figure 12 © Baddeley and James (1987)
Figure 13 © Kiel and Nicholson (2005)
Figure 17 © Cameron and Quinn (2006)
Figure 18 © Peter Hawkins (2014)

The author would like to thank the following:

My family – Allison, William, Charlie and Florence.

The Chartered Governance Institute team – in particular Saqib Lal Saleem and Ben O'Hagan.

Sue Lawrence for editing and contributing to the text.

All my colleagues, associates and clients for your continued support, challenge, insights and stories.

About the author

Dr Jeremy Cross CPsychol is a Chartered Psychologist, author, educator and leadership consultant. Over the past 20 years he has worked with over 75 organisations across a variety of sectors and has personally coached over 100 senior leaders.

As well as providing online courses to Chartered Governance Institute students, company directors and executive coaches on boardroom dynamics, Jeremy is a regular conference speaker on board leadership topics and a former visiting Faculty Member of Henley Business School.

He lives in Pembrokeshire with his wife and three children.

www.jeremycross.org

About the series editor

Sue Lawrence is the series editor for the *Good Governance Guide to* series. Sue is an experienced independent director having been appointed to a wide variety of board, trustee and committee positions in the UK for over 15 years, including trading companies, operating subsidiaries, start-ups, trustee boards, funding boards, charities and employee-owned trusts. Having been a successful divisional Managing Director in the professional and financial services sectors, she is now enjoying a portfolio career as an independent director and trustee for a diverse range of UK incorporated companies drawing on her past experience, as well as her professional training as a Chartered Director with the Institute of Directors.

In addition, she is the founder of Independent Directors and Trustees Limited, a collective of experienced directors and trustees who share their experience and knowledge with each other for personal development and the benefit of their clients. Primarily focused on the SME and employee ownership sectors, individuals are appointed to main, subsidiary, operating and trustee boards to deliver benefit through sharing this collective experience and knowledge, as well as through their personal contribution.

Introduction

This book aims to act as an engaging, thought-provoking and useful text for any individuals who are interested in the subject of boardroom dynamics. It provides a comprehensive introduction to the breadth of this topic, which is rapidly developing as the study of organisational design and leadership expands. The relevant terms, theories and models used when considering the effectiveness of the board are all considered in detail.

The core message of the book is that the dynamics in play within the boardroom are influenced not only by those appointed to the board, but also by those individuals who work alongside the board, either within their designated role or as individuals aligned to one or more board members. The book introduces the concept of the 'invisible leader' as well as the 'team coach', recognising that a board can be effective not only through its own actions and interactions but also as result of the effectiveness and influence of those around it.

Differing organisational structures and the ways that these differences impact on the effectiveness of the board are covered here. Equally, the personal behaviours and dynamics of the individual are presented, reflecting the impact of individual influence within the collective group that makes up a board.

Overview

Many differing aspects of boardroom dynamics as a theoretical subject will be explored throughout this book. However, as this is a very practical subject, there is a strong emphasis not just on being able to understand concepts and theory, but also on being able to identify and apply them in the real world. All those involved in and around a leadership model in any organisation will benefit from understanding the multifaceted dynamics that are in play within a people-driven environment such as the boardroom. The effectiveness and dynamics of a board is all about people.

The book is split into three parts. Part One will outline the need for a greater understanding and application of boardroom dynamics; Part Two will look at what exactly this involves; and Part Three will delve into the practical side of applying this thinking. Each chapter introduces a different element of the topic of boardroom dynamics and concludes with a thought-provoking question to bring the subject back to personal consideration and plans for action.

Part One

We start by looking at why board dynamics is becoming recognised as important, how it is defined and how it is a better predictor of governance performance than board structures, board demographics and director attributes.

Chapter 1 outlines some of the main reasons for the growing recognition of the role that board dynamics plays in good governance. In particular, it describes how recent corporate failures have led to the questioning of existing corporate governance practice. It also describes how the emerging interest in a range of human factors, the shifts in approaches to leadership and the refocus on ethics more generally are laying the groundwork for a 'psychological perspective' to take its place as one of the ways to approach governance. This is highlighted by demonstrating how the evolution of governance codes and academic research are already acknowledging this. It concludes by outlining an overarching model that harmonises both the existing and emerging elements of governance, which incorporates board dynamics.

Chapter 2 explores board structures – namely board set-up, chair set-up, director set-up and board task considerations. It then reviews each of these structural elements in detail and considers how they may affect board functioning and performance. Despite highlighting the importance of each of these individual structures, it also recognises the fact that, although often necessary for compliance, these are neither sufficient on their own to create the conditions for good governance nor to predict board performance.

Chapter 3 looks at board demographics – including director capacity, capability and connections – and director attributes that may affect board functioning. It explains how the evidence base shows that issues such as external commitment, director independence, technical expertise and professional and social capital are not, in themselves, good predictors of effective governance – despite most board recruitment, scrutiny and commentary focusing on them. The '11 Cs' model, which combines individual and behavioural perspectives of governance, is also outlined here. The chapter also argues that, although the evidence points to some of these behavioural attributes being significantly more predictive of board functioning than structural factors, boards dynamics will always mediate how much individual directors can contribute to board effectiveness.

Part Two

Part One introduces the theory of boardroom dynamics, creating a foundation of knowledge for further exploration of this topic. It establishes the need to recognise and understand the impact of this dynamic and aims to create a broad understanding of and appreciation for the topic. Part Two develops this further, by talking about the 'what' of boardroom dynamics.

Chapter 4 outlines why board dynamics is important as the key predictor of successful board functioning. It serves as an introduction to the psychology of boards and defines board dynamics in relation to this. It introduces the concept of the board as a potentially high-performing team and describes the balance a board needs to strike between the outcomes of cohesion and challenge, along with the potential conflict this may bring. It concludes with a section on what an effective board team process looks like and what happens when the process goes off track.

Chapter 5 looks at the dynamics of board decision making. It emphasises the fact that current thinking sees it less as a process underpinned by pure logical analysis and more as a distinctly human activity that can be inherently, but also predictably, flawed. Consequently, boards should strive for evidence-based practice while acknowledging the predictable cognitive bias inherent in individual director and collective board decisions. The chapter outlines these cognitive biases and a variety of tools to deal with them, concluding with issues and solutions specific to board team decision making.

Chapter 6 introduces a broader systemic perspective to the definition of board dynamics and discusses how all board stakeholders influence, and are influenced, as part of the board's systemic dynamic. The chapter describes what dynamics exist at each of these stakeholder levels, including concepts such as trusting relationships, conversational dialogue and conflict.

Chapter 7 discusses board culture and how it can be understood and influenced. It explains why culture has become an increasingly discussed topic in governance in recent years. It defines culture in general and board culture more specifically. The chapter then describes a variety of perspectives on board culture, concluding with a discussion of how a board may most effectively influence its culture.

Chapter 8 introduces the topic of diversity with a specific focus on diversity in the boardroom. It explores the different types of diversity, with particular attention first being paid to the 'surface' diversity types of gender, race and ethnicity and age; and secondly the less commonly considered 'deep' psychological diversity types of learning style, personality type and team role type. It looks at how this range of diversity types can affect performance and how the board can individually and collectively develop and promote a greater diversity mindset.

Chapter 9 looks at how best to utilise contextual and environmental design factors to influence an effective board dynamic. Specifically, it looks at meetings, describing how research and practice indicates that there are 21 design characteristics that can be separated into temporal, physical, procedural and attendee characteristics. The chapter outlines each of these meeting design characteristics, how they affect meeting outcomes and how a board can best use them to promote an effective meeting.

Part Three

If Part One is the 'why', the rationale for elevating the status of board dynamics and Part Two is the 'what', the description of board dynamics – including how it is influenced and what influences it – then Part Three is focused on the 'how'. In particular, it covers how an individual can most positively influence the board dynamic through an emphasis on the psychological, social and cultural aspects of their role.

Chapter 10 explores the individual as a strategic leader in the boardroom, showing how they might best influence board dynamics through their leadership style and broad influencing skills.

Chapter 11 focuses on an individual's more specific role as a talent manager to the board, exploring how they can best support the cycle of recruitment, induction, development, performance management and succession. This role is increasing; according to a 2018 study by Grant Thornton, a greater focus is being given to supporting board development: for example, up to 54% of those acting alongside the board are now involved in board recruitment.

Chapter 12 provides guidance on the role of a board consultant: in particular, how a governance professional can support an effective board evaluation that goes beyond just ticking the box of governance compliance. This builds on the theories of board culture introduced in Chapter 7.

Chapter 13 focuses on the emerging role of the individual as a 'cultural diplomat', exploring how they can help negotiate the cultural differences in the boardroom, paying particular attention to country and organisational cultural differences.

Chapter 14 explores how an individual can show behavioural agility through their role as team coach to the board. It looks at the various team coach roles that the governance professional may be called on to play, including one-to-one coaching, mentoring, systemic team coaching, facilitation, supervision, mediation and as a board counsellor.

Chapter 15 concludes the book by looking at maintaining personal resilience, reflecting on the governance professional as a 'corporate athlete'. It explores how they can sustain their own performance and, in so doing, support the resilience of others in and around the boardroom.

Acronyms and abbreviations

BAME	black, Asian and minority ethnic
CFROTA	cash flow return on total assets
CEO	chief executive officer
CFO	chief finance officer
CIPD	Chartered Institute of Professional Development
CQ	cultural quotient
ESG	environmental, social and governance
EQ	emotional quotient
FCA	Financial Conduct Authority
FSA	Financial Services Authority
FRC	Financial Reporting Council
GNH	gross national happiness
IAT	Implicit Association Test
IQ	intellectual quotient
IoD	Institute of Directors
M&S	Marks & Spencer
MBTI	Myers Briggs Type Inventory
NHS	National Health Service
NED	non-executive director
OECD	Organisation for Economic Co-operation and Development
PESTLE	political, economic, social, technological, legal and environmental
RBS	Royal Bank of Scotland
SMASH	salmon, mackerel, anchovy, sardine and herring
STEM	science, technology, engineering and mathematics
SID	senior independent director
VUCA	volatility, uncertainty, complexity and ambiguity

Part one
The importance of board dynamics

1 – The emergence of board dynamics in governance

The evolving focus of governance

The Cadbury Commission, which produced the first UK corporate governance code in 1992, defined the four responsibilities of the board as:

- setting strategic aims
- using leadership to implement these aims
- supervising management
- reporting to shareholders

Since then, corporate codes around the world have similarly outlined – with increasing sophistication – what boards are supposed to do, what outcomes they should focus on and what structures they should use to achieve this. This has also been reflected in the more task-focused training offered to chairs, company secretaries, directors (both non-executive and executive) and others who might support board work. This training is often led and delivered through an administrative, legal or accounting lens, focusing on important areas such as compliance and risk.

There is an emerging view that this focus, while important and necessary, is insufficient for boards to achieve their responsibilities in practice. In addition to what tasks boards must do and what outcomes they must achieve, we also need to place attention on how they function, the group processes that underpin them and the behaviours that board members may display both individually and as a team. In short, we need to recognise that boards are made up of human beings, not human doings.

In addition to a thorough grounding in all aspects of corporate governance, a good grasp of evidence-based psychological knowledge (the focus of Part Two) combined with a mature armoury of emotionally intelligent influencing skills (the focus of Part Three) is now the requirement of the modern board member and board influencers.

Organisational failures

Without doubt, the many organisational failures that have occurred over the last few decades are the biggest reason for increasing attention on governance and the ensuing questioning of traditional practices. Although scandals associated with company leadership have always been a feature of organisational life, the last couple of decades have provided us with a never-ending supply of flawed governance case studies. In particular, the stream of large-scale and public governance failures during and since the financial crisis has completely changed the view of what really drives board and organisational performance.

Take the Royal Bank of Scotland (RBS) as an example. The Financial Services Authority (FSA, now superseded by the Financial Conduct Authority) reported in 2011 that their pre-crisis enforcement work into the effectiveness of the RBS board 'did not identify a failure on the part of the Board' as 'the box-ticking affirmation... and evidence base suggests that the RBS Board's composition and formal processes met acceptable standards'. What, then, did the FSA judge its failure to have resulted from? It concluded that the board was making 'multiple poor decisions' suggesting 'underlying deficiencies in RBS management, governance and culture'. Apparently, as far back as 2005, an FSA review team had brought up the issue of increased risk due to chief executive officer (CEO) dominance and was consistently unable to interview non-executive directors (NEDs) one-to-one in order to understand the extent of appropriate boardroom challenge to test this potential risk.

Large private companies in the US have also contributed to the examples of significant governance failure. In the early 2000s, the trio of Enron, WorldCom and Tyco were the headline scandals, which eventually sparked changes in US governance regulation. Enron was a Houston-based commodities, energy and service corporation, whose CEO Jeff Skilling and former CEO Ken Lay, among others, held back large debts from their balance sheets. This led to shareholders losing $74 billion, thousands of employees and investors losing their retirement accounts and, of course, many employees losing their jobs. The directors were eventually caught out in 2001 by an internal whistleblower and high stock prices, which had fuelled suspicions, but this was only after *Fortune* magazine had named Enron America's 'most innovative company' for six years preceding the scandal.

Just one year later, WorldCom, a telecommunications company, also imploded. Its CEO, Bernie Ebbers, inflated revenues by as much as $11 billion using fake accounting entries, leading to 30,000 lost jobs and $80 billion in losses for investors. Ebbers was sentenced to 25 years in prison for fraud, conspiracy and filing false documents with regulators. After the fraud was uncovered by internal auditing, the CFO was also fired, the controller resigned and the company filed for bankruptcy.

Tyco, a New Jersey-based blue-chip Swiss security systems company, similarly hit the headlines in 2002. The CEO and CFO stole $150 million and inflated company income by $500 million by siphoning money through unapproved loans and fraudulent stock sales. The money was smuggled out of the company disguised as executive bonuses and benefits. At the height of the scandal, the

CEO, Dennis Kozlowski, apparently threw a $2 million birthday party for his wife. Kozlowski and his CFO, Mark Swartz, were sentenced to up to 25 years in prison and the company was forced to pay nearly $3 billion to investors.

Following these three high-profile cases (and numerous others around the same time), the US Congress passed the Sarbanes-Oxley Act, which introduced the most significant set of new business regulations since the 1930s. These included the requirement for top management to certify individually the accuracy of financial information, greater penalties for fraudulent financial activity, greater board director oversight and increased auditor independence. These legislative mandates, while potentially costly for institutions to implement and contrasting sharply with, for example, the UK's more regulatory approach, increased transparency and have even been praised for nurturing a more ethical culture due to the protection of whistleblowers.

At around the same time, other large-scale and high-profile scandals were emerging around the world. In Europe, Parmalat, an Italian multinational dairy and food corporation, collapsed with a €14 billion hole in its accounts (still Europe's biggest bankruptcy). Its CEO, Calisto Tanzi, was sentenced to 10 years in prison for fraud. On the other side of the world in Australia, companies such as One.Tel, HIH Insurance, Ansett Airlines and Harris Scarfe failed, leading to legislative reforms known as the CLERP 9. Perhaps echoing some of the dynamics of the RBS boardroom, One.Tel's CEO and executive directors were cited as having had excessive influence, dominating the board (there was no chair) and subcommittees. This subsequently led to poor monitoring and enforcement of due diligence. HIH also had a charismatic CEO who was highly competitive and pursued aggressive strategy positions, leading to a weak cash position. This may not have been as impactful an issue in isolation; however, some of the directors lacked true independence and the assertion was that the risks were poorly managed. Ironically, HIH had previously won awards for its monitoring model which ultimately failed in practice.

Unfortunately, leadership failures are not confined to the finance sector and large competitive corporates, but extend throughout all sectors, including those you might hope would have more ethical and moral underpinnings. One recent example of an organisational failure from the not-for-profit sector charity was Kids Company, founded by Camila Batmanghelidjh in 1996. This charity was set up to provide support to deprived inner-city children in the UK. Originating in one drop-in centre in south London, it expanded over a couple of decades to be a prominent children's charity operating 11 centres, mostly within Greater London but also in Bristol and Liverpool. One reason for the media interest in its collapse was that the charity had received some high-profile support from businesses such as Credit Suisse, Morgan Stanley and John Lewis, as well as media celebrities such as J.K. Rowling and the band Coldplay. The charity's collapse also became a political issue, most notably due to Kids Company receiving a £3 million emergency grant from the UK government following warnings that its reserves were inadequate in

2009. It is suggested that at board level, even within the context of being mission-orientated rather than financially orientated, risks were, again, not appropriately managed, financial procedures were not rigorous and internal controls were not consistently followed. Instead, the exuberance and charisma of the organisation's founder was said to have misrepresented the reality of the financial situation. The official reason behind the closure was cited as lack of funding, followed by rumours of financial mismanagement, as well as allegations of failure to safeguard young people. This led to a withdrawal of donations and the decision by the government not to make further grants. However, the dynamics around the boardroom and, in particular, perhaps, the lack of challenge of a charismatic founding CEO, may have been the initiating and underlying reasons for the failure. This was even the case within a unitary board structure which included clear division of the CEO and chair roles (this has, historically, not been the case in most US governance models) and with a well-known chair, the former BBC1 Controller Alan Yentob, who was an experienced leader and trustee.

There have even been scandals in the most trusted of organisations with the most independent of governance structures. One such example is Volkswagen who, with its supervisory board structure, had long enjoyed a strong reputation rooted in their reliable product range and Germanic cultural heritage. After the company's new product lines won environmental awards and tax breaks, its 2015 diesel emissions cheating scandal led to the company initially spending $7.3 billion to cover costs, a further $4.3 billion in penalties and the ongoing costs of compensation claims. Beyond this, ex-CEO Martin Winterkorn was indicted on fraud and conspiracy charges as well as six other senior executives and other senior leaders. The members of the board apparently only found out about the dishonesty just before the media and wondered why they had not been informed earlier, thus revealing a lack of appreciation of their ultimate accountability for the cultural failure that the misguided incentivisation of technical staff had created.

The recounting of the above failures is not intended to suggest that the central tenets of governance are wrong or unhelpful. Instead, the contention is that they are often diluted, or just outright thwarted, by human behavioural factors. As The Chartered Governance Institute report on Boardroom Behaviours suggests:

> Although further regulation, particularly in the banking sector, appears inevitable, an emerging view is that the system of governance for companies is not inherently 'broken', but rather that its effectiveness has been undermined by a failure to observe appropriate boardroom behaviours.

The ultimate impact of the spate of recent high-profile failures is that individuals, both in governance and more widely, are questioning not whether the more structural elements of compliance are correct, but rather whether they are enough. And, if they are not enough, what other factors might play a key role in appropriate governance.

Interest in human factors

In July 2008, the Himalayan nation of Bhutan was the first to introduce the measurement of gross national happiness (GNH) in addition to gross national product (GNP). The term was first coined as far back as 1972 by the then-King Jigme Singye Wangchuck, who was quoted to have said 'gross national happiness is more important than gross national product'. More recently, many countries and regions, such as Victoria and British Columbia in Canada, Seattle and Washington in the United States, Sao Paulo in Brazil and the United Arab Emirates, have employed the concept and used versions of a GNH index with their populations. Even the UK's Office of National Statistics now attempts to measure happiness and wellbeing.

This national and political level shift beyond the economic and financial also represents the growing broader acknowledgement of the human elements at play in societies' core institutions. Headline examples of such concepts that are gaining increasing attention and are bubbling up to the board include human capital, talent management, culture, diversity, resilience and wellbeing, amongst others. However, it is unlikely that directors, governance professionals and corporate commentators will have been schooled in these approaches. It seems imperative that this education now becomes more widespread. As Robert Armstrong, a senior economics writer at the *Financial Times*, said following the VW emissions scandal:

> I will confess I understand little about how corporate cultures work or how to improve them... I think I understand money pretty well; culture puzzles me. But culture is there and it matters. And if we ignore it, there will be more Dieselgates in the future.

Human capital

Organisational stakeholders are becoming more aware of the impact and value of company's intangible assets. One key intangible that is gathering particular attention in both human resources and financial communities is that of human capital, defined as 'the sum of knowledge, skills and experience and other relevant workforce attributes that reside in an organisation's workforce and drive productivity, performance and the achievement of strategic goals' (Chartered Institute of Professional Development (CIPD), 2005).

In 2003, the Accounting for People Task Force was set up to provide best practice guidance for organisations on how they can account meaningfully for human capital as assets as opposed to costs. A key finding was the clear need for better human capital management reporting, to support more effective people policies and practices, in order to benefit organisations and their stakeholders.

The investor community in particular is one stakeholder group that is pushing for more effective human capital reporting. Although there has historically been inertia between organisations and investors – investors have not used people metrics, so company executives have not been asked to proactively create and measure them – there is now a growing market interest in non-financial information such as environmental, social and governance (ESG) disclosure scores and measures such as employee engagement and satisfaction. There is a shift from financial capitalism to a more inclusive capitalism. The Maturity Institute, a UK-based not-for-profit professional development body, talk about investors becoming interested in understanding and measuring 'Human Governance' and uses Toyota's engaged and purpose-infused workforce as a benchmark employer to do this. More specifically, the human capital in the boardroom, in terms of both skillset and, perhaps more importantly, mindset, is most often the starting focus for investors as their proxy to assess investment risk and reward.

Talent management

If human capital can provide an overall insight into the quality of the whole workforce, talent management is a concept that focuses more on the 'bench strength' of an organisation's most strategically important roles. Talent management is now often seen as the most important leadership issue on the corporate agenda. For example, in some recent research conducted by the consultancy Deloitte, when asked 'What is your biggest business issue?', senior executives most often answered 'Attracting and retaining talent'.

The origins of talent management as a discipline go back to the McKinsey and Company concept of the 'war for talent', coined in 1997. There are a variety of definitions, one being 'the systematic attraction, identification, development, engagement, retention and deployment of those individuals with high potential who are of particular value to an organisation' (CIPD, 2007). The assumption is that if the board members are of 'particular value' and can make a 'significant difference to organisational performance', they should therefore be the focus of 'systematic' talent management.

These considerations around board and organisational talent are even more important in light of the recent attention on diversity, both from an ethical and a performance perspective. Modern workplaces are those that should take better account of diversity practice and the boardroom should be no different.

If those in governance positions might scoff that a human factor such as talent management should be one of the pre-eminent considerations of leadership, one argument is to consider talent in light of risk. A report from EY's corporate governance team showed that of the risks recorded in the risk section of company annual reports, 63% of them were associated with people risk. Of those that were not, most had a people and cultural underpinning to them. For example, take cyber security. Although this is more frequently thought of as a key external risk that is mitigated by significant spending on technology infrastructure, most security threats (recent studies suggest over 90%) emanate from internal staff through simple negligence, accidental disclosure, lost or stolen devices and specific digital skills shortages. Alongside this, it should be remembered that the employees are most frequently the single highest financial cost to any organisation, so their maintenance, input and development as a resource, both collectively and individually, should be of the highest consideration.

Culture

One of the other key shifts to the more intangible and human factors associated with organisations and boards is the increased interest in corporate culture. This has accelerated in the governance world since the financial crisis. Beyond the idea that it is always simply one or a minority of bad apples that are to blame, commentators are now ready to appreciate more fully that scandals are much more likely due to a (sometimes unintentionally created) bad barrel. Although it is often easier for our brains to ascribe blame to individuals, it is perhaps more appropriate to inquire into the culture created by the leadership such that the behaviour is seen as systemic – that is, it is generated through the system rather than solely located in one or a small number of 'evil' individuals. Regardless of whether the specific failure was ethical in the case of the Royal Bank of Scotland, whether it was around health and safety in the case of BP, or indeed related to reporting as in the recent problems highlighted at Tesco (see case study on page 12), there is an increasing recognition that the leadership and, most significantly, the board, is ultimately accountable for the culture that has been created and perpetuated.

The first basic question that is being asked is: What is a corporate culture? This is now recognised in the boardroom as important but is still not well understood beyond the basic idea of culture just being 'how things just get done around here'. In contrast, those involved with organisational development are well-versed in the theory and practice of culture and have been studying it for more than 60 years. Culture is understood academically as not just something you can see in the artefacts when you walk around an office or visit a boardroom setting, it is also what people say (the talk) and, perhaps more importantly, it is evidenced more by what they do (the walk) as an expression of their underlying core beliefs and values. There have been various attempts to measure and quantify culture using some of these variables.

A more recent question asked in relation to governance has therefore been: What constitutes a boardroom culture? In particular, what leadership styles, practices and processes might best influence the culture within a boardroom? Although boards have not, perhaps understandably, always wanted to open their doors to observation, this is a growing area of interest.

Equally, the most significant consideration has been around to what extent a boardroom culture might then influence the corporate culture; this is what is often known as the 'tone from the top'. Although many board directors are aware that they do have an influence, and increasingly so, they may not be completely aware of how this influence is represented in the board and then disseminated throughout an organisation. One recent trend has been for boards to create a 'culture committee' as a mechanism for monitoring and influencing corporate culture. Although this intervention may create an increased focus on key details and assurance of non-financial risk, it may also have the potential to dilute the board's overall responsibility. This is in line with the suggestion that culture is not something that can be delegated, but is as much about the behaviours we role-model as the organisational interventions we action.

Other human factors

What other broader organisational trends influence how we now view the performance of corporate boards? Stress-related illnesses are now the biggest cause of sickness and absence in the workplace. It is not just people's physical health that is suffering but also, perhaps more importantly, their mental health. As well as absenteeism, there is also a jump in 'presenteeism': the situation where people, for whatever reason, choose still to come to work even though they are unhealthy enough to be absent. This often leads to a chronic lack of employee engagement, productivity and performance. At work, the consequences can be serious and far reaching – such as health and safety breaches – while out of work this epidemic of burnout and stress-related illnesses often comes at the expense of relationship quality, family life and personal growth. A 2018 Gallup survey of 7,500 full-time employees in the US found that over two-thirds reported feeling burnt out at work (23% were burnt out 'very often or always', while an additional 44% felt burnt out 'sometimes'). The financial impact of this burnout, in health care spending alone, was estimated to be $125–190 billion.

In addition to the working population as a whole, there are many high-profile cases of senior executives burning out. One of many examples is Arianna Huffington, the former president and editor-in-chief of the *Huffington Post* media group, whose personal wake-up call came from breaking her cheekbone as a result of a fall brought on by exhaustion and lack of sleep. Soon after this moment of personal crisis, Huffington left her role and became an author and advocate of considering life beyond the traditional metrics of success, money and power. Unfortunately, like the frog in slowly heating water, perhaps the majority of leaders are not 'fortunate' enough to experience such an acute jolt and so meander into low-level chronic burnout without noticing.

According to a recent McKinsey report, 'Mental health in the workplace: The coming revolution', perhaps COVID-19 has gone some way to providing that 'jolt'. The report suggests that 'pre-existing mental health challenges have been exacerbated by the impact of the COVID-19 crisis' citing a worrying potential 50% increase in the prevalence of behavioural health conditions. Statistically, this makes workplace stressors as harmful to health as second-hand smoke. Stress is also a diversity issue: minorities suffer more symptoms and consequences than their majority counterparts. With diversity in all its forms being widely accepted as an important aspect of a positive boardroom, the alleviation of stress for boardroom members must also be a key boardroom consideration.

As a response to these increasing levels of stress throughout organisations, particularly at senior levels, people have embraced a variety of concepts and methods associated with 'coping'. 'Personal resilience', the ability of individuals to bounce back and positively withstand strain over periods of time, has become a watchword in organisations. Teams can also become more resilient so that they are able to weather the volatility and uncertainty that the violent change inherent in recent years has wrought. Boards can and may need to develop both individual and group resilience. To work at their best, directors need to be mindful of both their mental and physical health and capability, especially as the decisions that they make are likely to have broad stakeholder ramifications.

There are a variety of human factors that are gaining wider recognition in the workplace. If we turn the lens of recent interest onto the boardroom context, we can conclude that governance has perhaps been slow to appreciate their importance. Boardroom thinking will need a shift in perspective which includes a detailed consideration of the directors as a human resource, in order to maximise their individual and collective governance potential.

Shifts in approaches to leadership

There has also been a recent shift in our understanding of how best to lead in the modern workplace.

Ideas about leadership began with the 'Great Man' theory, which proposed that leaders were born and not made (and were mostly male) or, at the very least, required a privileged education and fast-tracked organisational trajectory. This sensationalised heroic leader, who swoops down to rescue organisations single-handedly, is still the media archetype and what we often expect from senior leadership. The media likes to use human stories, and it is often easy to portray a turnaround as being the sole mastermind of a charismatic, talented individual. Unfortunately, even though these heroic leaders do exist, they usually only generate short-term disruptive change and are less successful at nurturing organisational cultures for longer-term sustained value.

Jim Collins, the originator of the term 'good to great', describes the heroic type as a 'Level 4' leader. These leaders are often those whose books adorn airport bookshop shelves and who leapfrog from one failing organisation to another. However, Collins also contrasts these with the aspirational 'Level 5' leader, who guides organisations from being good to sustainably great, characterised by both their extreme tenacity, but also their excessive humility. Most of those organisations that have become great in Collins' research have CEOs who rose internally and were often reluctantly pushed forward by others, rather than being externally appointed through aggressive self-promotion.

Case study: Tesco and John Lewis – a tale of two leaders

One vignette that perhaps highlights the shift in leadership perspective can be seen in the recent comparative history of UK retail giants Tesco and John Lewis. Although Tesco's former CEO, Sir Terry Leahy, was viewed as a paragon of leadership and the prime architect of Tesco's dominance, the unintentional overreliance on one charismatic leader may have created a relative vacuum of responsible leadership lower down the organisation. This may have been a key contributing factor to the culture of inappropriate reporting that led to later corporate scandals.

At the same time, John Lewis, which is often held up as the leading example of great sustainable retailing, had a less visible CEO in Andy Street, whom few on the high street could name. Interestingly (especially in light of the Collins Level 4 versus Level 5 leadership research mentioned above), Tesco now has an externally appointed CEO who came from the consumer goods company Unilever, while John Lewis has its first female CEO – who joined as a graduate trainee.

The skillset of humble leaders is their ability to build multiple positive stakeholder relationships over time, rather than leaving a group of antagonists in their wake. It is about employing the art of humble inquiry rather than ego-filled advocacy. It is about appreciating and consolidating the strengths of those around them, rather than putting oneself on a pedestal and depreciating others to maintain one's own (often fragile) ego.

This approach is captured in the principle of authentic leadership that has been the focus of much research in recent years. The London Business School research on 'The Future of Work' rated 'transparent and authentic leadership' as the most critical factor for the future of organisations. The NHS King's Fund 'The Future of Leadership' research noted that there should be 'no more heroes' along this theme; conversely, the COVID-19 pandemic has created a focus on all NHS workers being heroes which aligns well to a democratic organisation.

There is a shift in mindset around leadership theory and practice away from traditional authority-based, command-and-control, hierarchical methods to more authentic, democratic, relational and systems-based leadership. A leader becomes a person who is able to articulate or embody an idea compellingly enough for others to choose to follow. Along with humility, this is often made possible when the leader creates meaning for followers by connecting an idea to an understanding of their own life story.

This shift from a 'me' focus to a 'we' focus requires leaders to give up their egos and the traditional individualistic definitions of success to become part of a high-performing (increasingly virtual) team. Leadership is less about a particular person and more about leadership behaviours that can be exhibited by, and be the responsibility of, everyone in the team.

In the boardroom, an understanding of team dynamics becomes increasingly important so that directors know how and when to step forward and, equally, that the chair and CEOs know how and when to leave space for the contribution of others to maximise their board's collective performance. This idea of shared leadership is not just helpful but is increasingly necessary. For example, UK governance and company law is based on the structure of the unitary board, a single board composed of both executive and non-executive directors and the concept of collective responsibility.

Focus on ethics

There has also been an increased focus on corporate ethics and reputation in recent years. This has significant implications for our understanding of, and approach to, boardroom behaviour. The Institute of Business Ethics is becoming an increasingly influential voice and the focus on ethics has been well represented in the latest iterations of governance codes globally.

For example, the South African King Code explicitly lists ethics in its first two principles. Principle 1 states that 'The governing body should lead ethically and effectively' and Principle 2 that 'The governing body should govern the ethics of the organisation in a way that supports the establishment of an ethical culture'. This shows an appreciation of corporate ethics as a primary governance consideration.

However, even with a governance code focus on ethics, there is no guarantee that organisations will actually behave more ethically, gain greater public trust or be the recipients of an enhanced reputation. Bob Tricker, one of the founding fathers of modern corporate governance, recognised in the late 1970s and early 1980s that ethics is inherent to the work of boards and that trust in businesses would only be rebuilt through boards handling ethical risks.

Case study: A crisis of trust

Every year, corporate reputation rankings that reveal the world's most reputed companies are calculated and published. However, in recent years the average company rating in the top 100 has declined by 1.4%, meaning that the public now do not trust around two-thirds of organisations that are currently measured. This has led some commentators to suggest that we now have a crisis of trust in global corporations. What, then, enables those top third of companies to be trusted, even against the bleaker backdrop of overall decreased public trust?

The global competitors Apple and Samsung are interesting recent cases in point. In 2017, Samsung improved by 44 points, jumping to number 26 in the reputation rankings. However, this was not achieved through the absence of media controversy, as it had a couple of these during the year. But its response, which involved significant efforts to increase transparency and fairness, was seen to be key in enhancing consumer trust. On the contrary, over the same period, Apple plummeted 38 spots to number 58 in the 2018 global ranking. This has been explained by reference to a range of incidents such as an encryption conflict with the FBI, tax evasion and long-rumoured battery tampering, in addition to disappointing sales. The company was profitable, but the rankings reveal that this, along with less-potent ethical responses compared to its rival Samsung, had little to no impact on the overall perception of its reputation (which is an indicator of longer-term sustainability).

Therefore, in order to develop more ethical boardroom behaviour and to role-model an appropriate culture to the rest of the organisation, there is a growing appreciation that ethics does not, again, come from simply ticking boxes. Instead, it is inherently psychological. One of the leaders in the burgeoning field of corporate ethics is Professor Roger Steare, the Corporate Philosopher in Residence and Professor of Organisational Ethics at Cass Business School. He has argued that governance failures have occurred not because of a failure to understand financial risk or too little technical knowledge, but because of a lack of moral integrity and courage.

There are a tiny minority of leaders whose behaviour is clinically flawed, including those who may be labelled psychopaths and narcissists. However, most ethical misjudgement arises out of a leadership context of wilful blindness and/or cultural reinforcement that amplifies minor natural human errors. The common view that the dishonesty is in the person is true to a limited extent, but this view is now expanding to recognise that ethical misconduct arises out of the culture around them for which the company leadership is responsible.

In addition to the negative impact of poor ethics, there is a growing recognition that good ethics can be positive for a company as well as its stakeholders. The binary concept of 'ethics or profit' is giving way to the perspective that 'ethics and profit' is not only possible but necessary for success across the corporate world.

Case study: Driving sustainability at McDonalds

Bob Langert led McDonald's corporate social responsibility and sustainability efforts for more than 25 years before retiring in 2015. Since his retirement, he has written extensively on his journey at McDonalds, particularly after he was appointed to lead sustainability in 2006. His contributions spanned sustainable fish, coffee, palm oil, beef, packaging, animal welfare progress, protecting the Amazon rainforest, nutrition strategy and CSR reporting, measurement and accountability. He speaks frequently on the importance of sustainability and the ability to match this with maintaining corporate profits.

The maturation of corporate governance

The evolution of codes

In 2009, the Chancellor of the Exchequer, the Secretary of State for Business, Enterprise and Regulatory Reform and the Financial Services Secretary to the Treasury announced the initiation of a review to recommend measures for improving the corporate governance of UK banks. The review was chaired by the former financial services regulator, Sir David Walker. The Chartered Governance Institute contributed to the review by conducting research on boardroom behaviours. This 2009 review used a questionnaire sent to its members and the company secretaries of the FTSE 350, as well as a series of discussion workshops. Some of the broader findings will be discussed in Chapter 4, but one headline finding from the report was that:

> It is remarkable that there is practically no guidance in the Code on the main drivers of, and factors affecting, boardroom behaviours... Encouraging best practice boardroom behaviours are critical aspects of corporate governance, but seem currently to be a neglected area.

Taking the UK Corporate Governance Code as an example, there has been some movement in the appreciation of the more human aspects of governance. There have been four revisions of what was then called the Combined Code since 2010, culminating in the 2018 UK Corporate Governance Code which took effect from 1 January 2019. As one broad indicator, the word 'culture' is used seven times in the latest code compared to just once in the 2010 Code. This single mention in the 2010 Code is tucked away in a Supporting Principle in section A.3 on page 10. This compares against the latest edition which mentions culture on page 1 in the Introduction and also twice more within the headline five principles in section 1.

Similarly, following the The Chartered Governance Institute's Boardroom Behaviours report recommendations, the Financial Reporting Council (FRC) published a 16-page paper entitled 'Guidance on Board Effectiveness' in 2011. Its updated 2018 version is significantly expanded, weighing in at 47 pages and providing more rigorous and practical advice on culture (37 mentions), behaviours (26 mentions) and even dynamics (two mentions).

Another example of how the UK Code has already evolved to include psychological elements is in how it makes provisions for boardroom evaluation (detailed at more length in Chapter 12). In 2010, the provision only included the requirement to evaluate the 'balance of skills, experience, independence, and knowledge on the board'. In the 2018 version, not only is diversity an additional consideration, but 'how effectively members work together to achieve objectives' is also included (in Principle L). Similarly, Principle J, which relates to board composition, mentions the need to account for 'cognitive and personal strengths' when considering appointments and succession.

Shift in board research away from structural factors

In the same way that governance codes are showing signs of responding to the wider trends already mentioned in this chapter, research literature is also developing. It is worth noting that boards are not always an easy subject to study: they are, by their very nature, often closed to external scrutiny. This has led to an overall lack of board research. The historical literature on boards that has been undertaken has mainly looked at structural factors such as size, composition and leadership structure as the main correlates to tests against board and organisational performance. These structural factors have been used as they follow the prevailing agency theory models of governance and are often easily visible and disclosed in annual reports.

However, since the early 2000s, as a response to the very public corporate failures from around that time, there has been a growing recognition that more research attention needs to be paid to the attitudes and behaviours of directors and the board as a whole. Rather than assume that companies will survive because they have adopted optimal governance structures, the research community (in addition to practitioners) is recognising that there are additional human factors that influence how governance predicts performance.

Case study: Ticking the structure box is no guarantee of board performance
In 2013, qualitative research undertaken involved interviewing governance experts on their opinion of what factors most influence board performance. From over 20 hours of data, 112 answers emerged. Of these, only nine were grouped under 'governance structures'. This reflected the commentary from the more recent governance literature which argues that, although making up the bulk of governance code requirements, the structural elements of evaluation are not the key predictors of board performance. As one interviewee summarised: 'You frequently find companies where the board didn't work properly but they tick all the boxes in terms of structure.'

So, if not structure, what did the interviewees say does predict board performance? Overwhelmingly, the two areas that were most frequently cited were individual director competency (48 answers) and board dynamics (42 answers). Within these two areas, the individual competency answers consistently mentioned the importance of the chair's leadership ability (24 answers) and the need for directors to have a capability in thinking strategically (11 answers), while the board dynamics theme highlighted cohesive team working (10 answers), a culture of openness (12 answers) and a culture of asking challenging questions (4 answers).

A broader model of corporate governance

The preceding sections of this chapter have led us to a point where we can now propose a broader model of corporate governance. This model takes into account both structural and behavioural factors, as well as individual and board group level factors.

The model is an adapted version of the work completed in 2013 mentioned in the above case study and is shown in Figure 1. The two axes – 'technical versus behavioural' and 'individual versus board' create four specific areas of corporate governance focus, each of which comprise a list of components. These components can be summarised into 11 areas, all beginning with the letter 'C', hence the model's name: the '11 Cs' model of corporate governance. The framework of the model is also useful in providing the structure for the following chapters of the text and for individuals to orientate the newer behavioural areas of governance into existing knowledge of the traditional technical considerations. The four areas of the model are described as follows.

Figure 1 The 11 Cs model of corporate governance (adapted from Cross, 2013)

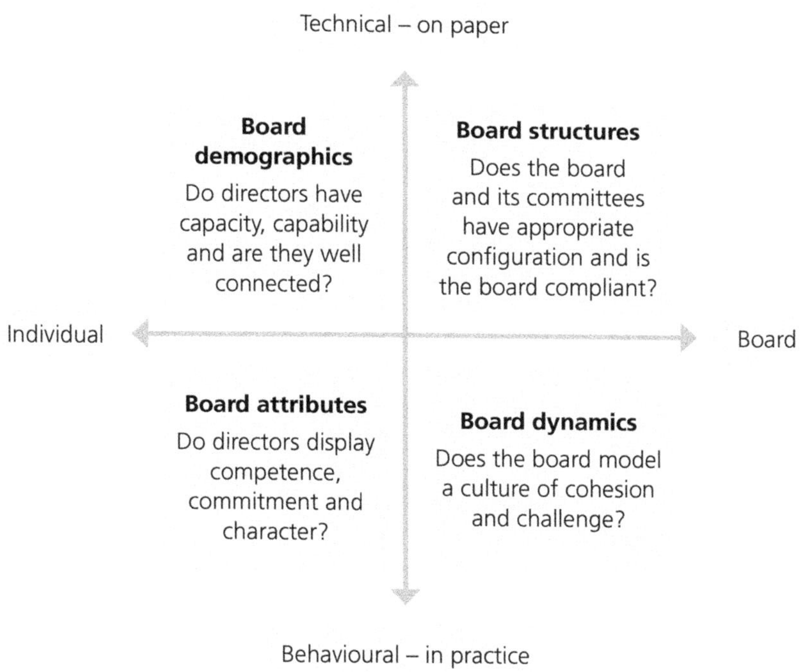

Firstly, the dynamic interaction between the technical and board level axis is labelled 'board structures'. This quadrant is the traditional area of focus of corporate governance. The key question that this area asks of boards is: 'Does the board and its committees have appropriate *configuration* and is the board *compliant*?' This question (and its subsequent answers) are a vital starting point from which to approach corporate governance. However, as we have seen already in this chapter, they are not enough if we are aspiring to better quality governance. Effective answers to these questions are necessary but not sufficient.

The second area on the model is the dynamic interaction between technical and individual factors and is named the 'board demographics'. This term has been selected as 'demography' originates from the Greek *demos*, meaning 'the people' and *graphy* implying 'writing or description'. It is the basic register of minimal 'name, rank and serial number'-type facts and information. The board demographics factors are those that one would usually find in a corporate curriculum vitae or indeed the brief pen portrait from the annual company report under the 'directors and senior management' section. They are the high-level technical expertise and, potentially, professional network aspects of one's career which pertain specifically to someone's board role. This is what is known as professional capital and social capital. The broad question, therefore, that this quadrant asks of a board is: 'Do directors have *capacity*, *capability* and are they well *connected*?' As the answers to this question are usually within the public domain, they are often used as the proxy for board potential and performance by interested stakeholders such as investors, regulators, headhunters, the media and the public more generally. However, we know that a track record can contain significant bias and does not always predict future performance (hence the rise in popularity of tools such as competency-based interviews, psychometric tests, blind auditions and anonymous resumes in recent years).

This leads us to the third area in the model, which is the dynamic interaction between behavioural and individual factors, labelled 'board attributes'. Whereas the 'board demographics' captures some of a director's surface characteristics, the 'board attributes' dig deeper into the psychological and emotional competencies of a director's personality as they play out in the boardroom and beyond. These are also sometimes known as their 'behavioural capital'. The key question that this quadrant asks of the board is: 'Do directors display *competence*, *commitment* and *character*?' For a board to be high performing, these attributes need to be true for all its members. However, there will also be some specific competencies required depending upon the role that each director is taking in the boardroom.

The fourth and final area of this broader model of corporate governance is the dynamic interaction between the behavioural and group level boardroom factors, labelled 'board dynamics'. This factor is the 'black box' of corporate governance because it is the area which, even though largely responsible for shaping boardroom culture and performance, has been largely under-researched and under-acknowledged until now. The main question that this quadrant asks of the board is: 'Does the board model a *culture* of *cohesion* and *challenge*?' This question is one of many versions that could be asked to capture the essence of board group and team working to ensure appropriate cultural role modelling, prudent risk management and effective decision making.

For simplicity, the model can be summarised by the 11 Cs of corporate governance being:

- configuration and compliance (board structures);
- capacity, capability and connections (board demographics);
- competence, commitment and character (board attributes); and
- cohesion, challenge and culture (board dynamics).

Figure 2 goes into these 11 Cs in more detail and provides a structure for the following chapters.

Figure 2 The 11 Cs model of corporate governance (adapted from Cross, 2013), including detailed components for each quadrant

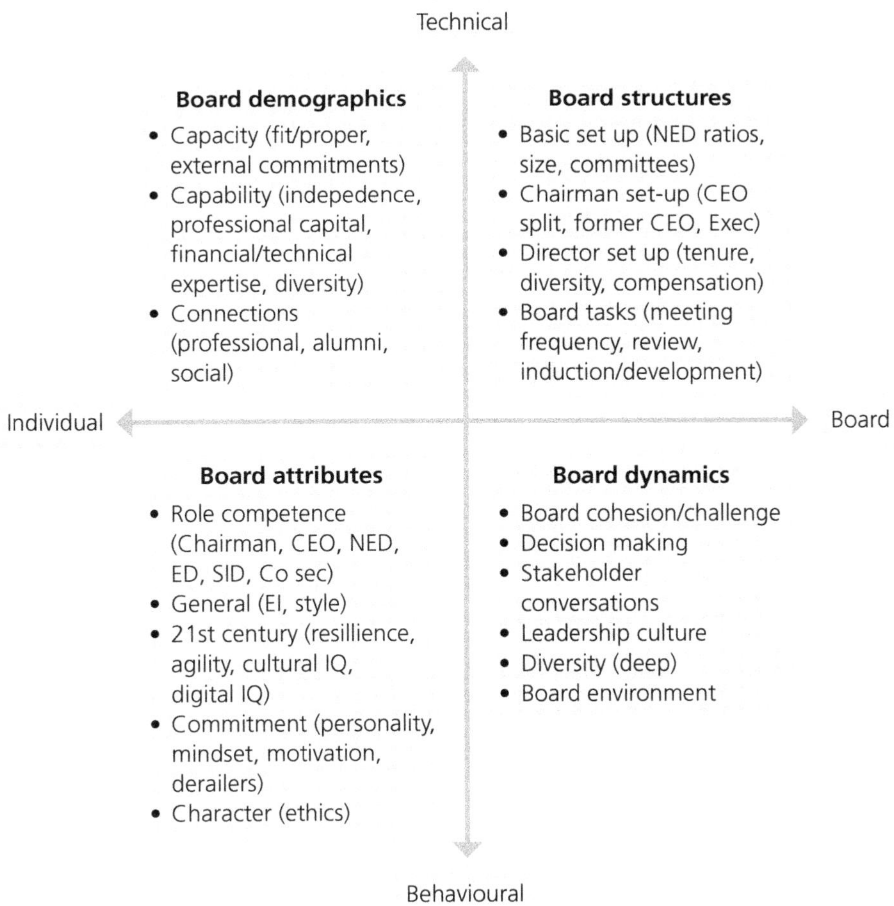

In Chapter 2, we will look in more detail at the board structures quadrant, including:

- board set-up (including non-executive/executive ratios, board size and committee structures);
- chair set-up (including CEO/chair split, chair as former CEO and chair as executive or non-executive);
- director set-up (including tenure, diversity and compensation considerations); and
- board tasks (including meeting frequency, board review and board induction/development).

Chapter 3 will explore the two individual-focused quadrants of the model together. Within board demographics we will consider:

- director capacity (fit and proper tests and the extent of external commitments);
- director capability (including the extent of their independence, their professional capital, their financial and other technical expertise and their diversity); and
- director connections.

Within the quadrant of board attributes, we will consider the impact on board functioning of:

- director competence (in their specific roles as leaders in general and in the modern business environment);
- director commitment (through the lenses of personality, mindset, motivation and derailers); and
- a director's ethical character.

Chapters 4–9 will go into detail into the areas of the fourth quadrant: board dynamics. However, before outlining these chapter areas, it may be useful to provide some initial definitions of the term board dynamics.

Defining board dynamics

People often use the term 'board dynamics' without having a specific idea of what exactly this refers to. Here are some definitions of board dynamics that may help in defining the concept in terms of corporate governance.

Following the 11 Cs model, board dynamics as a noun and as an area of academic study is:

> The theory and application of the behavioural aspects of board functioning.

As an adjective describing the dynamics of boards, board dynamics are:

> The psychological processes that influence how boards function.

Figure 3 The 11 Cs model of corporate governance (adapted from Cross, 2013), including which components feature in each chapter.

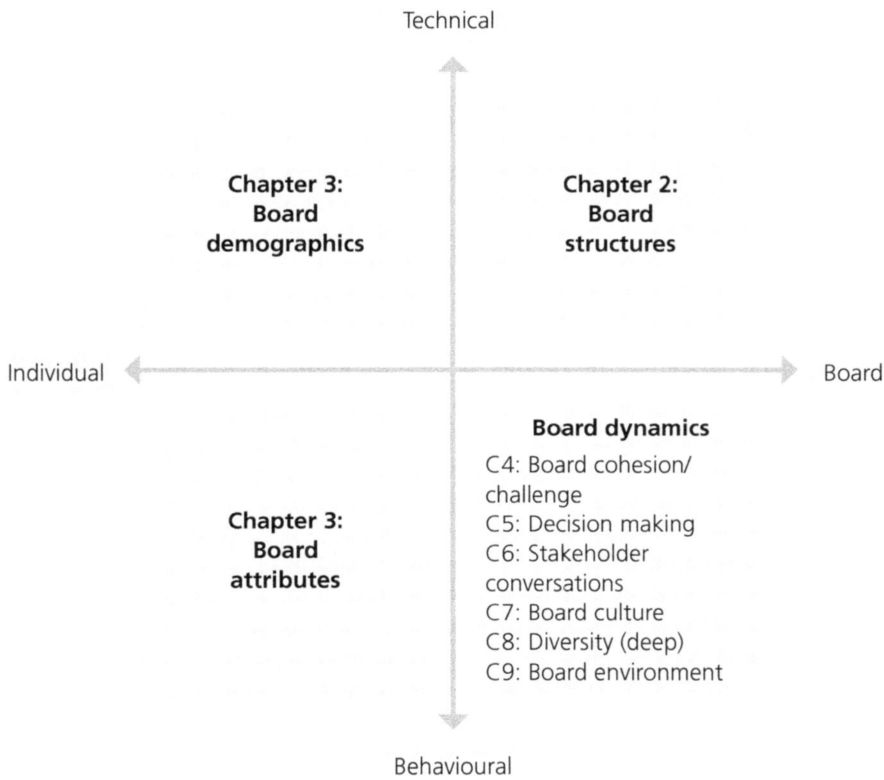

If we combine these first two definitions, a slightly more technical definition is that board dynamics are:

> The psychological processes that moderate structural and individual inputs to board functioning.

Furthermore, if we recognise that psychology is fundamentally about how people and groups relate to each other and that what happens in the boardroom can reverberate outside of it, then we reach this most complete definition of board dynamics as:

> The interactions between board members individually and collectively, and how these influence, and are influenced by, their wider stakeholder system.

Dinally, here are two additional, less technical definitions that add explanatory colour following the themes that have been discussed in this chapter so far:

1 Board dynamics opens the black box of the boardroom behaviour to see how things actually play out rather than what is supposed to happen on paper.
2 Board dynamics is about *how* boards behave and, indeed, about how they misbehave, rather than about what tasks they do. It is about *how* they discuss issues rather than what issues they discuss.

Chapters 4–9 will explore some of the concepts behind these definitions chapter by chapter, following the 11 Cs model as shown in Figure 3.

Chapter 4 provides an introduction to the psychology of the board. This chapter uses the perspective of the board as a cohesive group and/or team as a lens to make sense of board dynamics. It considers what the differences are between the board as a group or as a team and when it can function as one or the other. The chapter asks what constitutes a high-performing team and explores the building blocks of mission, vision, values and role clarity among others. It looks at the structure and psychology behind meeting cycles and processes and shares some of the latest thinking on collective intelligence and team psychological safety.

Chapter 5 on board decision making considers the decision-making dynamics that exist in the boardroom. It outlines an evidence-based methodology to boardroom decision-making conversations. However, taking a psychological approach, it also considers the unfortunate but predictable cognitive biases that we all share as individuals and that can plague us when we come together to make decisions in groups. The chapter discusses the different individual types of decision-maker style that directors may exhibit and shares an array of tools that may support higher-quality and less biased board decision-making.

Chapter 6, on stakeholder conversations, introduces the importance of relating well through its discussions of what constitutes quality in stakeholder conversations, both internally within the board and externally with key external stakeholders. It describes the increasing importance of including multiple stakeholder voices in boardroom conversations and how this may be done. It considers the key concept of trust in creating generative dialogue rather than destructive debate and illuminates how to create appropriate challenge through collaborative tension rather than through disruptive, personal and unresolvable conflict.

Chapter 7 looks at culture in the boardroom and considers the leadership culture that is created by the board dynamic. It discusses what culture actually is, how it is measured and how culture is created. It also details what types of board culture have been mapped and describes how boardroom culture may be influenced.

Chapter 8 considers diversity in the boardroom. It introduces and discusses the recent history of the concept of diversity in governance. It looks at the different types of diversity that have been described in the literature and their impact on performance. Most importantly, it considers how the board, both individually and as a collective, can develop and promote a greater diversity mindset.

Finally, Chapter 9, which covers the effect of meeting design on boardroom dynamics, looks at how best to use contextual and environmental factors to influence an effective board dynamic. Factors including structuring an appropriate meeting process, the intelligent use of physical space, the creation of an appropriate learning environment and the judicious use of digital technology are all considered as mechanisms by which to enhance or moderate the board dynamic.

The evolving role of board influencers

In 2014, The Chartered Governance Institute published research led by Andrew Kakabadse, a Professor of Governance & Leadership at Henley Business School, that investigated the role of the company secretary. Professor Kakabadse and his team interviewed and ran workshops with over 200 company secretaries, chairs, executive and non-executive directors across the UK and Ireland and gathered input from other overseas territories. The research produced a number of findings, which will be considered in greater detail in Chapter 10. However, the general conclusion was that individuals who sit outside the board but influence it, such as company secretaries, are now being expected to – and have the opportunity to – fulfil a much broader role.

As Kakabadse noted, company secretaries are often ideally placed to function with a wider remit due to their independence and longevity, among other reasons, and that, 'while the NED has been the focus of much of the attention in the post-financial crisis period, it is now time for the company secretary role to come to the fore'.

Equally, other organisational leaders – such as the chief of staff, head of strategy or other senior executive functions – have a direct influence over the board in addition to their formal role and associated reports and recommendations. These influencers are often 'invisible' from a hierarchical perspective but can exert significant influence depending upon the trusted network they are able to build.

It should not be forgotten that the non-executive directors themselves are potential key influencers. This was not always the case, given that they have no day-to-day delivery responsibilities, but they can have a significant impact through their contributions both in and outside the boardroom, rather than being perceived as mere 'trophy symbolism'. With influence comes responsibility, and hopefully also awareness, that NEDs can be both positive and supportive, as well as negative and disruptive.

Throughout the chapters of this book, the various invisible influencers should be considered in addition to the company secretary. The dynamics between these influencers, as well as between themselves and the board, can have a direct impact on the organisation. Hence, following the definition of board dynamics above, whilst we are considering the dynamics in the boardroom, we should also be mindful of similar dynamics in play outside and around the boardroom.

If Chapters 1–3 of this text focus on justifying why board dynamics is important and Chapters 4–9 explore in detail what board dynamics is, then Chapters 10–15 are focused on how to influence board dynamics from the perspective of the invisible influencer. These later chapters acknowledge this evolving role and focus on the behavioural interventions that individuals might choose to employ. The chapters will focus on the following content.

Chapter 10 looks at the role of the governance professional in influencing the board. It focuses on the individuals sitting alongside the board, including the company secretary, as strategic leaders. It considers the internal and external facing aspects of these roles, explores the correlated dichotomies of being strategic versus being tactical and being a manager/administrator versus being a leader. The chapter includes theory and practice on how to influence individual behaviour under a number of different conditions. These conditions include leading through change, how to function in a political environment, how to develop networks and broader stakeholder relationships and how a leader might choose to communicate, with a particular focus on the art of storytelling.

Chapter 11 covers effective talent management. It focuses on an influencer's role as a *talent manager*, defines talent management and considers some of the assumptions underlying it. It explores in detail the cycle of effective talent management, which first includes defining board competencies and then includes the practices of recruitment, induction, performance management and ongoing director development.

Chapter 12 provides guidance on how to conduct an effective board evaluation' in the role of board consultant. It considers how board evaluation has evolved in recent years, why it is important beyond a compliance rationale, what kinds of things a board might consider important to evaluate and, critically, how one might run an effective board evaluation process.

Chapter 13 looks at cultural differences in boardroom dynamics, focusing on the emerging role of individuals as a cultural diplomat. Initially focusing on country cultural differences, this chapter also explores sector and company cultural perspectives and how to respond to these differences effectively. It introduces the concept of cultural intelligence and shares how an individual might develop this key competence.

Chapter 14 looks at developing behavioural agility and explores the role of the individual as team coach. It describes a variety of key coaching skills, especially the art of questioning and humble enquiry, which can be used with directors in both a one-to-one and systemic team coaching context. It describes a range of interventions that can be used as a board matures and also explores the related skills of facilitation, mentoring, supervision, counselling and mediation, as well as the opportunities that an individual has to influence through appropriate support and challenge using these modes.

The final chapter, Chapter 15, is about maintaining personal resilience. This chapter explores the role of the individual as a corporate athlete. It acknowledges that, with these increasing responsibilities, effective individuals also need to look after themselves to be able to perform continually at a high level. This chapter will define resilience, explore its key components and suggest methods to develop resilience in oneself and support the resilience of others.

As we will see in more detail in Chapter 10, one powerful method of influencing is through leadership storytelling. If we are able to change the stories and metaphors that we tell ourselves and others, we can create changes in behaviour way beyond simply sharing facts. With this in mind, here is one summarising case study story from a different sphere of performance that may help illuminate some of the main themes of this first chapter.

Case study: The Ryder Cup and the power of a cohesive team

Boards can sometimes take lessons from the most unexpected places. Take sport and the unpredictable storylines of the Ryder Cup, the biennial men's golf competition between teams from Europe and the US, as a case in point.

The 2018 edition was played in late September at Le Golf National, France and the Americans were the outright favourites on paper. The US team of 12 players had 31 major championship wins between them, compared to Europe's lowly eight. It comprised 11 of the top 20 players in the world rankings, while Europe only had six. However, over the three days of competition, it was the Europeans who prevailed, thrashing the Americans 17½ to 10½. The US team that was as good, by most estimations, as any they had ever sent overseas, lost by the third-biggest margin in the competition's history. Two of their star players, Tiger Woods and Phil Mickelson, who had 19 major championships and 20 Ryder Cup appearances between them, could not even win a single match of the six they played. 'On paper' didn't seem to matter very much.

But if the selection of the individuals on the team sheet wasn't predictive of the outcome, what was? Perhaps two things. Firstly, the hosts had played a cumulative 232 rounds of competition golf on the fairways of Le Golf National. The US team as a whole had played it just eight times (half of them by one player, Justin Thomas, who won four points from five). More than a glittering track record and current form, the European team had each come furnished with the specific skills needed to perform under those unique course conditions. Secondly, and perhaps most importantly, they turned up as a team. This was no more epitomised by what was described by Europe's Rory McIlroy, as the 'love-in' on the team's WhatsApp group, even though some of the players didn't even use it before the week began, 'That was a big part of it,' said McIlroy afterwards. 'People questioned the picks and quality, and we showed this week our cohesiveness and togetherness.'

The US team was less cohesive. Commenting on his captain's selection during the weekend, America's Patrick Reed (ranked number 15 in the world) complained that 'for somebody as successful in the Ryder Cup as I am, I don't think it's smart to sit me (out) twice'. However, his reflections to the *New York Times* after the event contained greater insight: 'Every day (in the team room) I saw "Leave your egos at the door". They (the Europeans) do that better than us.'

So it is with boards. On paper, their structures might comply with all the latest governance regulations and the directors might tick all the boxes in terms of previous experience and purported expertise. However, this same board may be unable to function as an effective team. The gap between the potential quality of dialogue and decision making, and their actual group performance may be significant.

This book is about that gap and how boards, supported and challenged by knowledgeable supporters, can learn how to fill it.

Conclusion

Corporate scandals and their high-profile headlines have led to commentators increasingly questioning the existing structural focus of corporate governance practice. This – aligned to an emerging interest in a range of human factors, shifts in approaches to leadership and a new focus on ethics – is encouraging governance professionals to embrace a more psychological perspective when considering the role of the board.

The formal evolution of governance codes, as well as academic research, have made moves to do this already, but there is more work to do in applying this knowledge to practice – especially by board and governance professionals. As has been documented, the 11 Cs model harmonises both the existing structural and emerging behavioural components of board governance and can be a useful foundation for application by practitioners and their advisers.

What is 'board dynamics' and how does the area fit into other aspects of governance? Board dynamics is defined most formally as 'the interactions between board members individually and collectively and how these influence, and are influenced by, their wider stakeholder system'. Less formally, it can be thought of as how boards behave and, indeed, about how they misbehave, rather than about what tasks they do. It is about how they discuss issues, rather than what issues they discuss. Board dynamics offers a group and behavioural perspective on governance rather than a technical or individual perspective, which is depicted by the 11 Cs model of corporate governance.

There are a number of new roles that individuals working alongside the board, such as the company secretary, can and must now play due to this expanded understanding of the behavioural drivers of effective governance. Creating and maintaining an effective board is not just the role and responsibility of the chair and the board members. Having a supportive team that takes on the subtle invisible role of guiding, supporting and encouraging the board to be the best they can be, as individuals and as a collective, can greatly benefit the organisation as a whole.

Whether through conscious or unconscious influence, the individuals working alongside the board can have as great an impact on the board as the directors themselves. The aim of this book is to enrich the understanding of what this support may look like, enabling it to be consciously applied to its greatest impact. Those siting alongside the board, as well as the directors themselves, will benefit from a greater understanding of the various dynamics in play within and alongside the board. This book will share both the theory and practical application, with the intention that it can be applied across a variety of organisational contexts in a way that is most appropriate for the organisation at the specific time.

Board dynamics heavily influences the effectiveness of a board and, as a consequence, the success of the organisation through leadership, strategic focus, organisational culture and stakeholder engagement. What is the culture of your organisation? How can this knowledge be used to enhance the effectiveness of your board and leadership team?

2 – Governance structures

Governance theory related to board structure

It may seem strange for a book on board dynamics to focus on structure. However, in order to present an effective case for the importance of dynamics, we must first turn our attention to the first quadrant of the 11 Cs model outlined in Chapter 1. In doing this, we can begin to recognise the limitations of the prevailing approach to corporate governance with its historical overemphasis on this quadrant.

The term 'board' evolved as a notion in the Italian nation states and describes the table around which the direction-givers did their work. In the first code of corporate governance, the 1992 Cadbury Report, stated that:

> Corporate governance is the system by which companies are directed and controlled. Boards of directors are responsible for the governance of their companies.

This role articulation is built on a number of theories of board behaviour which have been debated over a long period, dating back to the eighteenth century. The core of these, agency theory, recognises that boards are the fiduciaries that resolve the agency problem inherent in a separation of ownership and control of public enterprise. An agency relationship is a contract under which one or more persons (the principles), engage another person (the agent) to perform some service on their behalf. This will involve delegating their authority to the agent.

Agency theory holds some key assumptions about the agent's behaviour – in our case executive management – being that it is inherently self-interested and therefore prone to moral hazard and strategically blinkered. The theory therefore regards the board of directors as essentially an instrument of control. In order for this to happen, the board must strictly ensure its independence from management, something it relinquishes at the company's peril.

Another model of governance, stewardship theory, holds that there is actually no conflict of interest between managers and owners and that, to be successful, an organisation instead needs a structure that allows coordination. In contrast to agency theory, stewardship theory recognises that managers are also non-financially motivated, for example in their need for recognition and progression, intrinsic job satisfaction, and sense of belonging to a larger group and meaningful purpose. A board structure that can best provide leadership with a more fluid non-executive and executive boundary (for example, with the chair also being the CEO) may therefore be preferred.

A final theory, stakeholder theory, has recently emerged. This has been prompted by the increasing recognition that the boardroom needs to take into account the wider views of society. It rests on the premise that an organisation has relationships with many constituent groups that affect, or are affected by, its decisions. It holds that each stakeholder interest is of intrinsic value such that no set of interests is assumed to dominate. Therefore, the board structure also needs to take this into account in its membership and committee structure. This will have implications for the board's size (that is, it may be inefficiently large due to the number of non-executive directors representing different stakeholder voices), aspects of diversity, tenure, remuneration and other board tasks.

The different board theories will each guide different decision making around what structure is most appropriate for a board to take. However, regardless of which theory you subscribe to, each assumes that the structure will be the main predictor of board performance. As agency theory has historically been the dominant perspective, most boards, researchers and governance bodies have taken for granted that board governance structures that maintain independence will naturally lead to better outcomes. However, as we have seen in Chapter 1 and will lay out in more detail in this chapter, this central assumption is now being challenged.

While it is important to have appropriate structures, the argument goes that they are not enough to ensure good governance. However, they must exist as the building blocks of strong and compliant board practice, so understanding them is nonetheless important.

Defining structural elements of boards

What exactly do we mean by 'board structures' and what do they consist of? First, imagine that you are setting up a board from scratch. Where do you start and how are you going to begin to decide how to set it up in a thoughtful way? The 11 Cs model asks: 'Does the board and its committees have appropriate configuration and is the board compliant?' This is a good starting point. There will obviously be a need to be compliant with whatever code of governance is relevant to your organisation based on size, sector and/or country. But beyond this, what will inform your configuration?

Depending on your theory of boards, you have a variety of choices for how to develop more or less board independence. Boards logically can fall into one of four types. Firstly, there is the all-executive board, which is often found in start-up and family companies where the founder is the major shareholder, the chair of the board and managing director/CEO. Similarly, corporate subsidiaries, where the parent company has devolved strategic authority, often have this structure.

Secondly, there is the majority executive board, which is made up mostly by executives from the company's top management positions as well as some external non-executive directors. The conventional wisdom during much of the twentieth century was that, because external directors could play an important role, there should be more than one but never as many as there were internal directors, so as not to interfere with the running of the company. However, this changed with the UK Hampel Committee's 1998 recommendation that listed companies should have at least a third of the board from outside the company.

This move to greater external control has now extended further with the stipulation in the latest UK Corporate Governance Code (FRC, 2018) being that 'at least half the board, excluding the chair, should be non-executive directors whom the board considers to be independent'. So, the third broad configuration is the majority independent non-executive board which is found in the UK, US, Australia and South Africa, among others. The power balance is shifted to the external with the aspiration of ensuring organisational accountability and compliance.

Taken together, these first three board configurations make up the 'unitary board' structures – that is, regardless of composition, there is one overall board to oversee the organisation. The unitary board contrasts with the fourth structure, the two-tier board. This consists of two separate boards:

- a supervisory board made up of external directors, shareholder representatives and stakeholder representatives to govern, supervise the management board and take long-term, more strategic, decisions; and
- a management board comprised solely of internal personnel to manage the business, handle tactical issues and make operational decisions.

This approach is the basis for governance in non-profit organisations and is most often used in Germany, Austria and Holland. It is permitted in France (and therefore often called the Continental European approach).

The assumption of these different board set-ups is that they will, by their very nature, engender an appropriate compliance dynamic. However, as we will discuss in some detail from Chapter 4 onwards, this deterministic structural viewpoint does not take into account how individual and group psychology can make all this redundant under certain conditions. It is not true to say that the structural set-up of a board is irrelevant, as it will provide the theatre boundaries within which the board actors are asked to perform. Beyond the four broad types of board just described, the different structural elements are those that are located in the technical/board group quadrant of the 11 Cs framework and themselves break down into four categories (see Figure 4).

Figure 4 Board structure elements from the 11 Cs model

Board structures

- Basic set-up (NED ratios, size, committees)
- Chair set-up (CEO split, former CEO, Exec)
- Director set-up (tenure, diversity, remuneration)
- Board tasks (meeting frequency, review, induction/development)

Basic set-up

Ratio of executives to non-executives

Following the discussion above concerning the unitary versus two-tier board structures and the three different configurations that are available to the unitary board structure, the first consideration is the ratio of internal executives to external non-executive directors that comprise the board.

For some, such as those in the FTSE 350 and in the charity sector, there will be compliance guidelines that provide boundaries for this ratio. More broadly, the ratio will depend upon a range of factors including organisational life cycle, sector type, country, company culture and various practical constraints.

Board size

Boards must consist of at least one director in a private company and two directors in a public company. There is no maximum limit on board size but there is an often an assumption that there is a sweet spot within which effective board functioning will occur. However, is this the case? Board size will have an impact on the functioning of the board and it will also be affected by the particular requirements of the board and organisation.

Committee structure

Boards use committees as a method of expanding their work, increasing their efficiency and investigating important issues in more detail. The standard committees include audit, remuneration and nomination committees. The size, meeting frequency and functioning of these committees is likely to vary beyond these basic committee requirements such that there are a variety of other themed committees that may be useful to consider.

Chair considerations

Chair and chief executive officer split role

The chair, as the leader of the board, has perhaps the biggest influence on board functioning and is therefore the role that has received most consideration in terms of structural set-up. Whether the same person holds the roles of chair and CEO at the same time has been an issue of considerable debate in governance over the past few decades. It is perhaps the most defining structural feature which indicates whether the board set-up is attempting to ensure external independence (a chair/CEO split) or management leadership (chair and chief executive officer are the same person). Again, codes have evolved over recent years to emphasise a split role. Whether this is the case in practice can be determined by variety of factors. Regardless, the question remains: does a joint role or a split role have a significantly different impact on the board?

Chair as a former chief executive officer

Following on from the issues concerning the chair and CEO split role, whether the CEO goes on to become the chair is also a key consideration. While perhaps not as overtly conflicting as a joint role, this succession is also subject to compliance, is assumed to reduce independence and therefore has an impact on governance.

The chair is either executive or non-executive

Even if the chair is not also the CEO, they can sometimes act in a quasi-management fashion as an executive chair. This role is often created at certain times within an organisation's life cycle, such as a period of significant transition, and is also assumed to reduce the level of independence of the chair's role.

Director considerations

Average tenure

Beyond the chair's role, there are some considerations that will inform how the roles of both non-executive and executive directors are structured. The average tenure – the amount of time that a chair or other director has been part of the board – is considered to be an important factor. The assumption is that directors will, like political presidents, become less independent and perhaps more conflicted over time.

Board diversity

The diversity of a board has received a significant amount of interest in recent years, especially around gender and ethnic diversity. Age or generational diversity is also most often recognised as a potential factor in board performance. Taking a superficial reputational and compliance perspective, a board may need simply first to comply with certain codes or sector expectations to ensure there are appropriate levels of gender and ethnic diversity on the board. Beyond this, boards may also be interested in reflecting their stakeholder diversity within the boardroom's membership.

Director compensation

Whether and how much directors are compensated is a key basic consideration within board structures. This may include to what extent they are remunerated for their work on the board, any time spent chairing or participating in committees, whether they are part of any incentive scheme and what percentage of equity they hold.

Board tasks

Board meeting frequency

It is generally assumed that boards and their committees will need to meet relatively frequently to do their work. However, how frequently will very much depend upon a variety of factors, including practicalities relating to the size and location of board membership, current business requirements and external environmental factors.

Board review

The board review, or board evaluation as it is often known, is becoming an increasingly important aspect of a board's structural calendar. FTSE 350 boards are required to review themselves every year and be reviewed externally at least once every three years. Increasingly, non-listed boards are also now embracing evaluation as a key practice to support board performance.

Board induction and development

Ideally, every director will commence their board directorship with an appropriate induction and will continue to be developed in the role throughout their tenure.

The above list details some of the more common board structure directives and processes that historically have been seen by board commentators as a proxy for good governance. As we have discussed, they are all based on an assumption and hope that if these structures and practices exist, they will have a positive impact on board functioning.

Impact of board structures on performance

This section will discuss how each of the common structural configurations listed in Figure 4 actually plays out in practice. Unless otherwise indicated, the board statistics quoted in each section are taken from Spencer Stuart's Board Index 2017 report on the UK's top 150 listed companies (the FTSE 150). Even though the FTSE 150 only represents one tiny (albeit high-profile) sample of organisations globally, the figures are readily available and may be useful as leading indicators of trends.

Basic set-up

Ratio of executive directors to non-executive directors

The latest UK Code stipulates that:

> The board should include an appropriate combination of executive and non-executive directors (and, in particular, independent non-executive directors) such that no individual or small group of individuals can dominate the board's decision taking.

It also states that 'at least half the board, excluding the chair, should comprise non-executive directors determined by the board to be independent'.

Guidelines about the composition of the board differ between countries. The King III Code, for example, recommends that the majority of directors should be non-executive directors and the majority of non-executive directors should be independent, but also adds that there should be at least two executive directors on the board – the CEO and chief finance officer (CFO). In practice, the number of non-executive directors on boards in the FTSE 150 is 72.7% on average at the time of writing (excluding chairs).

The research and practice evidence is contradictory on the best ratios between executives and non-executive directors, and whether independent and non-executive directors make a greater or lesser contributions. Indeed, there is also a suggestion that there is no link at all to corporate performance. There will be times when outsider-dominated boards may be better – for example, during restructuring decisions, when creating diversification strategies and during the strategic decision-making process. However, there are also times when insider-dominated boards are more positive too – such as when driving research and development intensity and other entrepreneurial activities of the company. Moving beyond the formal definition of independence as 'free from conflicts of interest' to 'having the right attitude' may shift the focus from the structural to the psychological and, perhaps, from a compliance mindset to one more akin to stewardship.

Board size

The chosen size of an effective board will depend upon a variety of factors. The UK Code does not prescribe any particular size, but does suggest that:

> The board should be of sufficient size that the requirements of the business can be met and that changes to the board's composition and that of its committees can be managed without undue disruption, and should not be so large as to be unwieldy.

In reality, the average size of FTSE top 150 company boards is around 10.1, which is trending down from 2014, when it was 10.4. As a comparison, the UK's Charity Governance Code suggests the following:

> The board is big enough that the charity's work can be carried out and changes to the board's composition can be managed without too much disruption. A board of at least five but no more than twelve trustees is typically considered good practice.

These Codes suggest that for every organisation, at any particular time in their evolution, there is a sweet spot that may enable the board and its individual members to fulfil its role most effectively.

It is therefore up to each board to ask what might be the most appropriate size of membership, based on some of the following factors:

- the current size of the company;
- the type of industry or sector the company operates in;
- the current 'life stage' of the organisation (for example, is the company in growth, decline or steady state and what transitions/crises is it going through?);
- the focus and requirements of current organisational strategy;
- the time, skill and knowledge requirements of the various board committees; and
- practical factors such as the ability to recruit and retain appropriate and diverse board talent.

However, the UK Code also points to the fact that a board can sometimes be too large. What might this mean in practice? Some considerations in relation to how board size may affect board effectiveness may include:

- the skill of the chair in managing effective, efficient and inclusive dialogue of a larger group of directors;
- the time, commitment and ability the chair has to develop relationships with directors outside of the boardroom; and
- the practicality of managing and securing consistent attendance of often very busy senior individuals.

Beyond code recommendations and best practices, the research evidence is itself similarly inconclusive on whether board size improves or reduces board effectiveness, or indeed whether it is associated with board performance at all. Although smaller boards are often found to be more efficient, larger boards are seen to be more effective in monitoring managers. A more nuanced finding from research is that when a board has too many members, it inevitably takes on a purely symbolic role.

Case study: Size matters

Italian-listed banks have larger boards when compared with listed non-financial firms. Since the nature of the agency problem and monitoring instances are more complex in banking organisations, a greater benefit may derive from larger boards compared with a smaller board size in non-financial firms.

> When considering the overall lack of consensus in the management and banking literature on board size, one group of researchers has concluded that 'the problem for banks is not to identify an ideal size, but an adequate size for their boards' (Carretta et al., 2010).

When looking at effective board size, it is useful to consider the wider literature on high performance teams. Stanford Professor Bob Sutton summarises much of this research in his article 'Why Big Teams Suck: Seven (Plus or Minus Two) Is The Magical Number Once Again'. The title harks back to psychologist George Miller's famous conclusion about how many digits people can hold in their short-term memory, after which the cognitive load takes too much toll. If we are to draw conclusions from this in relation to board size, we might surmise that performance problems and interpersonal friction can exponentially increase once membership rises over nine.

We may all have had the experience of needing to spend more and more time on what are known as 'coordination chores' as well as hand-offs between board members (which create opportunities for mistakes and miscommunication) and less time actually talking usefully about the agenda items. Equally, as each director must divide their attention among a wider number of people, the board's interpersonal trust and social glue will decrease – consequentially heightening the opportunity for destructive conflict. We will look at these issues in more detail in Chapter 4.

Interestingly, when we take a look at the average board sizes of the global listed companies, the majority are composed of between nine and eleven directors (2017 figures). The highest average size outliers are Italian boards at 11.5, French boards at 13.9 and German boards at an extremely large 16.3 directors on average; the lowest averages are found in Finland, the Netherlands, Norway and Poland, all at around 8.0 directors per board on average. The UK and the US come in at 10.1 and 10.8 directors on average, respectively.

Board committee structures

It is accepted best practice in multiple corporate governance codes that certain aspects of board duties are delegated to specific, focused committees and their activities should be disclosed in board reporting. The 'standard' requirement is for an audit committee, a remuneration committee and a nominations committee (the latter two are sometimes combined). Around 80% of companies in the FTSE 150 currently have between three and four committees.

The range of committee types and names is testament to the fact that committees are created for whatever the current strategic need may be. For example, within the FTSE 150 there are committee names including 'brand and values', 'corporate responsibility' (around 22% have these, often in consumer-related organisations) and 'health, safety and security' (around 9% have these, often in natural resources, industrial and transport companies). There are also some more specialist committees one might not expect, such as 'Galaxy' (TUI's committee to oversee their 'Project Galaxy' merger), 'geopolitical' (BP) and 'clinical performance and sustainability' (Mediclinic International).

In certain sectors, specific committees may be necessary – for example, finance sector organisations will often choose to create some version of risk committee (in fact, this is the most likely fourth committee: around 20% of the FTSE 150 boards have a risk committee). In recent years, the recognition that this risk is not just financial has also led to a growth in committees that oversee the related issues of governance, conduct and values, reputation and, increasingly, company culture.

In terms of the number of meetings that a committee may undertake each year, this is also extremely variable and will depend on a variety of factors pertaining to the function of each particular committee. FTSE 350 audit committees, for example, meet 5.3 times a year on average, remuneration committees similarly meet 5.5 times a year, whereas nomination committees meet slightly less often, at 3.9 times a year.

Taking into account all of the above information on how board committees are configured, one would imagine the quantity and type of appropriate board committee structure should show a clear and positive relationship with company performance. However, there is surprisingly little explicit and conclusive evidence as to whether it actually does. One study of 134 boards from a variety of sectors concluded that 'it may be of some consolation to regulators that the prescription of Audit and Remuneration committees appears to have no visible impact, beneficial or otherwise, on company performance' (Dulewicz and Herbert, 2004).

In the absence of following industry or country compliance mandates, a strategic and evidence-based approach to decision making on board committee structures and meeting frequencies that works best for each individual board would, again, be the best advice.

Chair considerations

Chair and chief executive officer split role

The UK Code is clear in its 'Division of Responsibilities' section that the chair and CEO should not be one and the same person. The Main Principle states:

> There should be a clear division of responsibilities at the head of the company between the running of the board and the executive responsibility for the running of the company's business. No one individual should have unfettered powers of decision.

In addition, the Code Provision notes that 'the division of responsibilities between the chair and chief executive should be clearly established, set out in writing and agreed by the board'.

These principles are based on the agency theory proposal that company management may, due to their close knowledge of the organisation, be tempted to follow their own rather than the ownership's interest. Therefore, an independent monitoring function is required to protect shareholders' interests. If there were to be chair and chief executive duality, this monitoring function would not be possible.

Splitting chair and chief executive roles is the norm not only in the UK but also through most of Europe as well as Canada, Australia, New Zealand and South Africa, among other nations.

However, in the US, this principle is not deemed as significant a governance issue. At the time of writing, only around one-quarter of the Fortune 500 employ a fully independent chair (although this has increased from around one in 20 a decade ago). Even in many of the large banks, such as JP Morgan Chase, Citigroup, Morgan Stanley and BNY Mellon, the same person is both chair and chief executive. This approach aligns more with a stakeholder theory perspective, assuming that company managers are inherently trustworthy and not prone to misappropriating corporate resources. The potential benefit of this, stakeholder theory argues, is that the superiority of the amount and quality of information may lead to better evaluation of top managers.

Case study: JP Morgan Chase – rejecting calls to split the chair and CEO roles

In 2013, JP Morgan Chase's directors recommended the rejection, for the second year running, of an investor proposal to separate the role of chair and chief executive. In their statement in preparation for the annual meeting of shareholders, they felt that the board was functioning effectively in its existing form and that separation of the roles of chair and chief executive may cause uncertainty, inefficiency and confusion.

Their existing structure was such that over 90% of the board and 100% of the committees, were comprised of independent directors and that there was a 'Presiding Director' (somewhat similar to the UKs Senior Independent Director) to create further oversight through convening and leading meetings only attended by the independent directors.

All of this leads to the question: Which model is the right one? Obviously, the requirement to comply with the code of one's country is the first consideration but, beyond that, which structure might be selected if there is a choice? Although governance logic may nod towards the UK model over the US, the many recent high-profile failures show that duality does not guarantee effective board governance.

While an independent chair may focus more on ensuring open debate than simply accomplishing an agenda, and running the board rather than running the company, the splitting of the role may create confusion about who is actually leading the company. In the US model, it is very clear who has accountability and, although uncomfortable, may enable more things to be done at pace. Furthermore, there may be times, such as during a CEO transition or a period of organisational crisis, where individual strong leadership may be warranted.

The research evidence is similarly contradictory on whether the chair also being the CEO affects board and organisational performance. Some research has found correlations between financial outcomes and dual roles but others have found no such relationship. In general, however, the research again tends to suggest that the relationship between duality and performance is perhaps mostly contingent on organisational characteristics and the business environment.

Chair not being the former CEO

A second structural principle concerning the chair of a listed company is that, as a general rule, they must be independent when first appointed. The UK Code lists independence criteria and stipulates:

> A chief executive should not go on to be chairman of the same company. If exceptionally a board decides that a chief executive should become chairman, the board should consult major shareholders in advance and should set out its reasons to shareholders at the time of the appointment and in the next annual report.

There have been several cases in the UK when the chief executive has gone on to become chair without any significant protest from shareholders or investors. For example, in 2005, the Group Chief Executive of HSBC, Stephen Green, became the Chairman of HSBC Bank plc (the group's UK clearing bank subsidiary) and then Group Executive Chairman in June 2006. In addition to such case examples, the research evidence is similarly inconclusive compared to the compliance mandates.

What should also be considered if a chief executive progresses to becoming the chair, is the standing of the new chief executive and their ability to function independently when their predecessor is now the chair.

Chair as an executive versus non-executive

One final configuration of the chair is for them to be more closely aligned with management (either with a chief executive in place, but often not) and act as executive chair.

Case study: M&S – the argument for combining chief executive and chair

This close alignment between chair and management was the case in 2008 when Sir Stuart Rose, the then Chief Executive of Marks & Spencer (M&S), was named as Executive Chairman in addition to this role. The major City shareholders were extremely concerned at the news. Legal & General, the second biggest shareholder, was the first to raise questions about the decision:

> As set out in the Combined Code we believe strongly in the separation of the roles of chairman and chief executive, believing this provides a much needed balance in the boardroom and prevents the potentially damaging concentration of power. As such we believe today's announcement from M&S is unwelcome.

For its part, M&S commented that the appointment was made to avoid succession planning becoming an 'unwanted distraction' as it had in the past and which had been associated with its decline in the late 1990s.

History suggests that this decision and rationale was correct, as a successful Chief Executive, Marc Bolland (previously COO at Heineken and CEO at Morrisons) was later appointed in late 2009. After rolling out a raft of changes, Bolland was named the 'Most Admired Leader' in a *Management Today* award nominated by his FTSE 100 peers in 2011, staying on as Chief Executive until April 2016.

Director considerations

Tenure

What impact does the amount of time a director spends serving on a board have on its performance? Director tenure will fluctuate significantly depending on country, sector and industry type. However, the average length of service of FTSE 150 directors is currently 4.3 years. This amount of time spent on a board has trended down by around 5% between 2014 and 2019.

As the nation that has arguably led on corporate governance (certainly in terms of being both the first and most prolific producer of corporate codes of practice) this average length of service is unsurprisingly low, compared to average board tenure in other countries (only Poland is lower, with an average of 3.4 years). Perhaps also unsurprisingly, Canada (at 7.8 years) and the US (at 8.2 years) have the highest average tenures, reflecting the North American board emphasis on directors being closer to management rather than independent (also reflected in the more common duality of chair and chief executive roles discussed above).

The latest UK Code states that 'the chair should not remain in post beyond nine years from the date of their first appointment to the board'. This rule exists due to the assumption that the longer the chair, or indeed other non-executive directors, is in place, the more likely it is that their independence will be eroded. However, the Code goes on to state:

> to facilitate effective succession planning and the development of a diverse board, this period can be extended for a limited time, particularly in those cases where the chair was an existing non-executive director on appointment. A clear explanation should be provided.

There is a recognition that there should be limits as an extended board membership may be problematic, but that having exact deadlines may also create different problems (the Higgs Review recommended six years for non-executive directors, for example). Although these considerations seem intuitively plausible, there is no valid evidence to suggest that longer tenures are inherently negative and lead to impaired judgement and poorer governance. Some research has tested this and found no link to performance. On the contrary, longer service equates with increased age, which has been correlated with increased wisdom and job-related decision making.

Diversity

The topic of board diversity has been the focus of vigorous debate in governance over the last decade or so. There is no one single argument that one can turn to when making decisions about how to compose an appropriately diverse board.

From a board structure perspective, the two main arguments for diversity are ethical inclusion and stakeholder voice. A good board should include in its membership directors who represent their constituent stakeholders because it is the right thing to do and because it helps improve board decision making. With that in mind, how do we know when a board structure is diverse?

The primary answer over recent years has been that it has an appropriate mix of men to women and an appropriate number of ethnic minority directorships. In the UK, successive reports such as the 2010 Davies review, the 2016 Hampton-Alexander review and the 2017 Parker review have all provided aspirational diversity targets for boards to hit in regard to gender and ethnicity. This has been having an effect.

For example, in relation to women's participation in FTSE 150 boards, as of 2018 female directors accounted for 25.5% of directorships (up from 10.6% 10 years previously). This compares globally with Scandinavian outliers such as Norway (45.4%), Sweden (38.3%) and Finland (33%), similar figures from Germany (28.7%), the US (22.2%) and Canada (26.8%) and the more male-orientated nations such as Turkey (11.1%) and Russia (8.1%).

Unfortunately, of these UK directors, many more are non-executive than executive (women account for 34.7% of non-executive directors, but only 8.9% of executive directors) and only 4.6% of chairs and 5.4% of chief executives are women. Even if these figures show more work to do and greater velocity to attain, the overall movement is positive based on five-year and 10-year trends.

In terms of ethnicity, the DiversityQ FTSE100 Board Diversity Report 2020 noted that there is still some way to go with board composition across this group being only 6% male black, Asian and minority ethnic (BAME) and 3.8% female BAME. It noted that there are just 99 senior BAME people at board level, comprising 19 executive directorships and 80 non-executive directorships. Further, there are seven CEOs from an Asian or minority background, but no black CEOs and 49% have no BAME representation on their board, so there is still some way to go to meet the 2017 government target of having at least one BAME board member by 2021.

Conversely, the number of 'foreign directors' (defined as those who are not from the nationality of the company country) on FTSE 150 boards is relatively healthy, currently at 32.3% (up 31.8% over the last 10 years). Again, taking a global perspective, this figure is similar to Germany (31%) and Belgium (31.2%), compares favourably to the more inward-looking US (7%) and Italian (9.4%) board averages, but poorly to the Netherlands (57%) and Switzerland (59%).

Beyond the 'male' and 'pale' monikers used to describe boards lacking gender and ethnic or cultural diversity, 'stale' or older boards are also denigrated. The average age of FTSE 150 non-executives is currently 60.3 years and that of executives 53.4 years. These averages have been steadily increasing over the past 10 years.

The larger question then is, beyond clear ethical inclusion reasons, does an increase in diversity consequently enhance board functioning? In general, homogeneity is assumed to be more likely to produce 'group think'. There are a raft of studies showing that gender diversity, for example, has positive outcomes, including the following:

- firms with more gender diversity on boards hold more board meetings;
- firms with more volatility in their stock returns have fewer women on their boards; and
- firms with more gender diversity on their boards give their directors more pay-for-performance incentives.

As we shall discuss in more detail in Chapter 8, greater diversity is not simply about surface characteristics such gender, race and age, but also about 'deep' characteristics linked to one's personality type and 'diversity of thought'. Furthermore, greater diversity can actually lead to poorer outcomes in groups if not effectively included and managed. How the raw ingredients of diversity themselves need to be effectively led will also be discussed in Chapter 8.

In summary, there is no one tick-box diversity configuration of a board that confers better board performance and governance.

Director remuneration

Base pay

The issue of director remuneration is one of the more contentious topics in relation to compliance and the public perception of boards. The basic assumption around director remuneration, which aligns to the various theories of boards including agency theory, is that directors will be rationally motivated to perform their board duties in line with the remuneration they receive.

This is immediately problematic, as the first question asks whether directors receive any remuneration for their board and committee membership. Many of those directors in the charity sector, for example, will not be financially compensated for their work on boards. Does this assume that they are therefore not motivated? Obviously, this specific case highlights that motivation arises from many factors beyond simple economics. These will include those more related to internal service orientations and personal development in addition to more external and egotistical 'build the CV' motivations.

Of those that do remunerate, the top end of the scale FTSE 150 average retainer for acting as a part-time chair is currently a significant £384,907 (€434,208). This varies greatly country-by-country, with chairs from Poland receiving a lowly €47,461 on average while Swiss part-time chairs rake in an average €1,913,819. The average retainer for a FTSE 150 non-executive director is £66,655. Both of these chair and non-executive director retainers have increased steadily over the past decade by 13.3% and 9.8% respectively – perhaps representing the greater expectation and commitment now required of chairs and directors. Directors may also often receive separate payments for chairing committees, recognising this extra commitment. Unsurprisingly, there is a strong correlation between the size of an organisation and the size of its directors' fees.

The various country codes have increasingly prescribed principles to follow concerning remuneration of directors. The latest UK Corporate Governance Code has three pages solely focused on remuneration, including some 10 provisions to comply with (or explain) and report on. Some of the key considerations included as regards base pay are that the remuneration policies should be 'formal and transparent' (Principle Q) and that 'directors should exercise independent judgement and discretion when authorising remuneration outcomes, taking account of company and individual performance, and wider circumstances' (Principle R).

In light of all the points made above, there is no evidence that better retainer packages will result in better board performance. Case-by-case discretion in this aspect of remuneration seems the best policy. The issue of reputational impact, especially in light of the ratio of director pay compared to the lowest organisational wage (some have argued that it should not go above 30:1), is one such key discretionary consideration and has recently become a reporting requirement for some companies in English company law.

Incentive schemes

There are a variety of compliance considerations relating to the variable aspects of director remuneration. In line with the agency theory assumption that the most appropriate board structures are those that most align directors with organisational independence and external shareholder return, incentive schemes should:

> be designed to support strategy and promote long-term sustainable success. Executive remuneration should be aligned to company purpose and values, and be clearly linked to the successful delivery of the company's long-term strategy.

Many countries have boards that receive very little of their total compensation from incentive schemes – such as in Germany – for these very reasons. On the other hand, some countries, such as the US, provide for a significant proportion of non-executive fees to be made from performance incentives. For example, last year saw US-listed company non-executive directors taking home an average fee of €370,000 ($450,000), of which only €109,000 ($132,000, 29%) was made up by a basic retainer.

The Basel Committee, in its 2005 report 'Enhancing Corporate Governance for Banking Organizations', warned that the failure to link remuneration schemes for directors and senior management to long-term business strategy can result in actions that run counter to the interests of the bank and its stakeholders. There is some limited research evidence that backs this up, which finds that directors in higher-performing companies by sales tend to receive lower direct rewards but higher equity directors are pursuing sales-maximising objectives for the eventual benefit of shareholders rather than for personal profit.

However, the wider psychological literature on incentives suggests that variable financial rewards have the tendency to transform any useful intrinsic motivation into a less sustainable and, perhaps, even unethical, extrinsic motivation. That is, directing the board for more service-orientated motivations may be unintentionally replaced by a more self-serving money motive if an incentive scheme is introduced. Instead of board incentives being underpinned by the standard rational economic model, we must instead respond to more recent research and practice that uses 'predictably irrational' behavioural economics (and which we will discuss in more detail in Chapter 5).

Equity involvement

The final aspect of remuneration to consider is the proportion of equity ownership available to directors as part of their incentive package. Following a similar logic to the directives on incentive schemes, equity packages are proposed to be an important tool to ensure both that directors are motivated to govern well but also, if appropriately structured to take a long-term perspective, that this good governance be aligned with stakeholder needs and shareholder returns.

A couple of studies have found a correlation between stock ownership and firm performance. However, they were not longitudinal and so are more suggestive than causative. Furthermore, there are many examples of companies whose directors have held considerable stock and failed. There are also no clear directives on how much stock is enough. Again, discretion based on each case seems prudent.

In summary, although director remuneration is a complex area that is fraught with potential issues, taking a wider reputational and psychological perspective will prove helpful over and above the technical or economic lens through which it has traditionally been viewed through.

Board tasks

Meeting frequency

Once the composition and remuneration arrangements of a board are configured, there are some final structural decisions to make concerning board and committee meeting frequency. These are often organised based on a standard schedule of (at a minimum) between once a quarter to (at the most) once every month, with perhaps some short-notice meetings called to deal with particular crisis issues. This reflects the data we have on for the FTSE 150 boards who met 8.8 times on average during 2017 (up from 8.0 meetings on average five years ago).

Taking a broader cultural perspective, most national averages for board meeting frequency are in a similar range – between 7 and 11 meetings a year on average – with Russian (6.8 meetings on average) and German (6.7 meetings on average) listed boards meeting the least. This German board average is perhaps unsurprising from a diarising perspective, based on the average number of German board members being 16.3, but also reflects the two-tier board system such that day-to-day operational matters are not incorporated as part of the meetings of the supervisory board.

Turkish boards are a significant outlier, meeting on average 17.9 times per year (that is, more than once every three weeks on average). We will look at cultural impacts on boards more in Chapter 13; however, the main reason for this high number is most probably due to the combination of the Turkish cultural norms around the importance of building trusting relationships over time (linked to the prevalence of family-owned businesses) and the need to take time over decision making.

There is some evidence that the frequency of meetings is positively correlated to the quantity and speed of decision-making activity and therefore to corporate performance. However, in many cases, board meetings are also found not to result in concrete actions. Similarly, even though measures of attendance are often reported and researched as a proxy of director and board commitment, there are many examples of boards who can boast perfect attendance yet which have failed due to what happened behind the closed doors of the meeting once it began.

Taking both this practical and research evidence together, it seems as though board and committee meeting choices will, again, be idiosyncratic and best tailored to each board's cultural and operational requirements.

Board review

The 'meta' process of boardroom review, which involves the ongoing practice of pausing to look inwardly at one's own performance, is a relatively recent boardroom phenomenon. A recent report from McKinsey highlights that boards that do this regularly, especially with the focus of reducing their decision-making biases, are viewed as the highest performing. In the absence of an ongoing reviewing mindset, the yearly board evaluation has become the first rung on the reviewing ladder for most boards. Over the past decade, compliance requirements have also evolved around board evaluation, with a provision for listed boards to internally evaluate themselves yearly and be externally evaluated once every three years. Unsurprisingly, all but two listed companies in the UK completed, and reported on having completed, a board evaluation in 2017, with 61% conducting it internally and 38% using external facilitation.

As the process is so new, there is no valid evidence yet to confirm that completing a board evaluation, either internally or externally facilitated, impacts board functioning. Anecdotally, of course, there are many positive outcomes but there are also many examples of organisations, such as the Royal Bank of Scotland, that have reported satisfactory evaluations but that have failed soon after. Simply ticking the box of completion is not enough. Board evaluation can be done for many different reasons, underpinned with different motivations and be undertaken in many different ways which will dictate its effectiveness.

Thus, one should not ask whether board evaluation helps or hinders board performance, but rather inquire into what are the characteristics of effective board evaluation. This will be discussed in more detail in Chapter 12.

Board induction and development

For the purposes of this chapter's discussion, the final board tasks are those to do with ensuring that directors are 'match fit' to perform their duties, both at the start of the term of office through effective induction and throughout their tenure supported by ongoing director development. Development needs often arise from an appropriate evaluation process. As the UK Corporate Governance Code stipulates, 'Each director should engage with the process and take appropriate action when development needs have been identified'.

As with board evaluation, there is currently both no evidence linking the existence of induction and development processes to board performance and a wide variety of standards in practice. These range from no formal induction and development at worst, to a strategic and rigorous process that involves not just a focus on providing appropriate knowledge but also developing skill and appropriate mindset. Chapter 11 will detail some of the best practices in these areas.

Board structure and compliance – in summary

Taking into account all of the board structure factors discussed in the last section, we can conclude that there is no clear evidence that certain board structures on their own will lead to good governance – although there are many indications and insights that may guide board configuration decision making. This is the same conclusion that many commentators and researchers over recent years have also arrived at.

What impact might the prevailing pre-eminence of the 'configuration' and 'compliance' board structural approach have on organisations? William Donaldson, the former US Securities and Exchange Commission Chairman, has argued that:

> Such a 'check the box' approach to good corporate governance will not inspire a true sense of ethical obligation. It could merely lead to an array of

inhibiting, 'politically correct' dictates. Instead of striving to meet higher standards, corporations would only strain under new costs associated with fulfilling a mandated process that could produce little of the desired effect. They would lose the freedom to make innovative decisions that an ethically sound entrepreneurial culture requires... (determining criteria for corporate governance) is not a one-size-fits-all exercise... we should go slowly in mandating specific structures and committees for all corporations... There are vast differences in the function, structure, and business mandate of the thousands of corporations struggling with the issues of good corporate governance... there is no one answer to these hotly debated questions.

Conclusion

Setting up a board so that it is well structured is an important first step in the governance process. Ensuring that this structure is compliant is, of course, a vital part of this initial and ongoing process. However, we have shown that the premises of existing board theory, in particular the agency theory approach, do not fully explain what happens in boards in reality. Sound structure is not sufficient in itself to deliver good governance.

Why should a company follow the existing codes of practice at the present time if they are underpinned by incomplete theory and are not reflected in practice? If your company, for whatever reason, is obliged to comply with regulation, these are the best codified principles that exist currently and, more importantly, because it is a matter of principle, ethics and fiduciary duty to do so.

However, as all boards have leeway over their choice of structure, it is important to consider what might be best for the organisation based on its particular organisational idiosyncrasies and external stakeholder context. As the 11 Cs model of corporate governance shows, it is also important to consider how other individual and behavioural factors impinge on the board's functioning. We will discuss these factors in the next two chapters.

Board practice, compliance and research have largely been dominated by the prevailing theories of governance, in particular agency theory. A variety of different structures have been used to inform how boards choose to be configured. What are the different aspects of board structure and how do these affect board performance? Most simplistically, boards can be either unitary or two-tier. Unitary boards can be all executive, majority executive or majority non-executive. Beyond this, according to the 11 Cs model, there are four broad areas to consider when structuring a board: the basic set-up (including NED ratio, board/committee size and committee structure); the chair set-up (including whether the chair and CEO role is split or not, whether the chair is the former CEO or whether the chair is executive or not); the director set-up (including director tenure, diversity and remuneration); and board tasks (including meeting frequency, board review and director induction and development). Although both practice and theory does provide some insight into how the various configurations of these structures and tasks can affect board performance, there is no direct evidence that states unequivocally that a certain structure will lead to better outcomes.

None of these structural directives, on their own, predict effective boardroom functioning with any consistency. Although necessary, board structural elements are not sufficient on their own to create the conditions for good governance. They require an additional broader perspective that considers other more individual and/or behavioural aspects of board functioning. Ticking the box to comply with the required governance codes will provide superficial effectiveness by the board but is unlikely to enhance true effectiveness. If governance is seen as the skeleton of the business, it is important that it works. However, it will be ineffective in isolation and without practical application. The actions and performance of the board and – as will be seen – the dynamics, interaction and delivery of the board will have the greatest effect in setting the tone and creating guidance and oversight of the organisation. The workings of the board and its members are the action that creates a robust skeleton on which the operational workings of the organisation are overlaid. Creating and maintaining successful governance of an organisation can support better leadership and, as a result, more successful organisations.

All leadership teams and boards can benefit from some reflection on their effectiveness; one of the aims of this text is to provide tools and thought-provoking ideas to support this self-reflection.

How can you shape your governance framework and its application more effectively, to avoid it slipping into unchallenged process?

3 – Board director demographics and attributes

Board demographics

While board structures have traditionally been viewed as the main predictor of good governance, board demographic factors have been the second most popular shorthand.

The belief underpinning this focus on board demographics is that a board full of independent and talented directors will most likely guarantee a return in both great governance and organisational performance. The board demographic factors on the 11 Cs model of corporate governance are located at the axis of technical and individual dimensions of the board. They comprise the basic facts and information about individual directors – the more visible, public and often formal artefacts of effective directorship that pertain to an individual director's past and current qualifications and performance. They are what a director looks like 'on paper'.

These director demographics are similar to what you might find in their curriculum vitae or within the short descriptions that are accessible in annual reports, such as in the case study below.

Case study: BP and the Royal Bank of Scotland – the limitations of director demographics

The type of information that we consider within board demographics is often publicly disclosed in listed company reports. Two high-profile examples that highlight how such information is used are presented here for Sir Tom McKillop.

In 2007, McKillop was a director on the boards of two large FTSE 100 companies, BP and the Royal Bank of Scotland. 2007 was a significant year for both firms. At BP, McKillop was part of the 12-director board whom that year appointed Tony Hayward as Chief Executive Officer, who would preside over the Deepwater Horizon oil spill in 2010. Hayward's leadership, especially concerning public relations, was heavily criticised over the crisis and ultimately led to him being replaced. In the year before the disaster, 2009, Hayward was receiving an annual salary of £1.045 million, with a £2.09 million bonus. This is a quote from BP's annual report, providing a board demographic pen portrait of McKillop:

> Sir Tom (64) joined BP's board in 2004. Sir Tom was chief executive of AstraZeneca PLC from the merger of Astra AB and Zeneca Group PLC in 1999 until December 2005. He was a non-executive director of Lloyds TSB Group PLC until 2004 and is chairman of The Royal Bank of Scotland Group. Member of the chairman's, the remuneration and the safety, ethics and environment assurance committees.

We also learn that he attended 10 of 12 board meetings in 2007 and 18 of 19 committee meetings, for which he received a total of £87,000 (£3,107 per meeting).

Perhaps even more significantly, 2007 was also the year McKillop acted as the chairman of the Royal Bank of Scotland. He presided over this board at a momentous time, as this was the period leading up to the financial crash of 2008. Similarly, here is the pen portrait of McKillop from the Royal Bank of Scotland's annual report of 2007.

> Chairman
> Sir Tom McKillop (age 64)
> C, N, R
>
> Appointed to the Board as Deputy Chairman in September 2005, Sir Tom is a non-executive director of BP p.l.c., and president of the Science Council. He was formerly chief executive of AstraZeneca PLC, and was previously president of the European Federation of Pharmaceutical Industries and Associations and chairman of the British Pharma Group. He is a trustee of the Council for Industry and Higher Education.

We also learn from the annual report that, as well as leading all nine board meetings and attending all five of the remuneration and nominations committees, as part-time chairman McKillop was paid £750,000 and received 208,000 shares worth during the year, which at the time was roughly valued at between £800,000 and £1,500,000.

What can we conclude from these brief demographic descriptions? On the positive side, they seem to provide a reassuring level of credibility of McKillop as both a chair and non-executive director based on his significant previous leadership experience in scientific and financial domains. Secondly, this credibility is further enhanced, by the inclusion of his knighthood and by his prestigious professional membership leadership positions. Thirdly, his membership and attendance at two main board and six specific board committees gives an indication of his time and energy commitment to these specific organisations.

However, when we consider this commitment in more detail, we can conclude that he prepared for and attended 31 meetings over the year (nine of which he led) in addition to other trustee commitments (not to mention any other commitments he had external to these two board roles). Therefore, he was exceptionally busy. In light of all this, and knowing what happened in the following years, we can see that being credible on paper does not guarantee a successful non-executive directorship, or indeed a successful chairship.

The traditional board theories , including agency, stewardship and stakeholder theories (see Chapter 2), underpin how the board demographics factors are perceived and used. The assumption of these theories is that recruiting capable and independent directors to a board will give you the best chance of successful governance outcomes, particularly if they function as part of compliant board structures. As we shall see, although retaining highly talented individuals to the board may indeed be a basic requirement, it is not sufficient to produce successful governance outcomes.

What are the individual technical components that are most often used and researched that comprise the board demographics quadrant? They are broadly captured by the three Cs of capacity, capability and connections. These three areas and their detailed components are visualised in Figure 5.

Figure 5 Board demographics elements from the 11 Cs model

Board demographics

- Capacity (fit/proper, external commitments)
- Capability (indepedence, professional capital, financial/technical expertise, diversity)
- Connections (professional, alumni, social)

Capacity – should the individual be allowed to be a board director?

Fit and proper test

The fit and proper test is a measure of whether a director is legally allowed to function on a board, whether they are of good mental and physical health and whether they actually have the appropriate qualifications necessary to function in their board role.

External commitments

The capacity of a board director is also often predicated by the number of other board-level commitments that they currently maintain. This might include a role as chair, a role as a non-executive or indeed a role as a company executive on another board. Directors have increasingly been required to commit more time and energy to their roles in recent years – such that their level of external commitment to other boards has come under greater scrutiny.

Capability – is the individual capable of being a director on this specific board?

Independence

A key tenet of agency theory is that non-executive directors remain independent during their tenure, so that they best represent shareholders' interests. There are various criteria of independence that compliance regulation asks of directors which may affect this.

Professional capital

Professional capital is a concept that captures all those attributes that point towards a director's work-related credibility. Specific demographic factors such as years of industry experience, number of boards served on, current leadership roles, cumulative number of years on boards and highest level of education achieved are just some aspects that have been used to approximate professional capital.

Financial expertise

The specific requirement for financial expertise has been the subject of debate in recent years, especially since the financial crash of 2008. The contention here is that all directors must have some good grasp of finance for them to fulfil their monitoring role of executive management appropriately.

Technical expertise

For directors to be useful, there is also an argument that they must have some specific technical expertise relevant to the current organisational strategy. This is either in addition to, or perhaps as an alternative to, more generalist abilities covered by one's professional capital.

Diversity

Although diversity is also part of the board structures quadrant in relation to the diversity of the board as a whole, diversity here refers to the number of different areas of diversity that one individual director may themselves inherently bring to the board. This may be a contributor to the particular value their board membership brings.

Connections – what social capital does the director bring?

This final area encompasses a director's professional network, their potential alumni network and the networks associated with their social class. This area has been described as a director's 'social capital' and is of particular interest when viewing a director's contribution through the lens of their role as an external resource (often important in early-stage start ups, for example).

The next section will explore each of these aspects of board director demographics in greater detail. It will provide some relevant recent background information on each factor, associated examples of code compliance regulation and explore the evidence base for how the individual demographic may or may not influence board functioning.

Capacity

Fit and proper

The fit and proper persons test, also known as the director's test, was first introduced in 2004 for owners and directors of major British football clubs. Its aim was to prevent corruption or untrustworthy people from serving on boards within the Premier League.

Since November 2014, it has also been used by the National Health Service (NHS) in England for directors of NHS Trusts under the Health and Social Care Act 2008 (Regulated Activities) Regulations 2014. It is also a staple part of the Financial Conduct Authority's (FCA) assessment for its authorisation process for senior management.

In the case of the Premier League regulations, there are six disqualifying events that will result in an individual failing the test. These include filing for bankruptcy, being prohibited by law from being a director and other specific football-related financial failings and conflicts of interests. Within the NHS system, potential and current directors of NHS Trusts are considered unfit if they have been involved in 'serious misconduct or mismanagement'.

A trust must also be satisfied that directors are of good character (through a consideration of any previous convictions and/or removals from professional registers), they must have appropriate qualifications and experience and they must be physically and mentally healthy enough to perform the tasks of being a director.

Case study: Trump: the healthiest President ever?

An equivalent physical and mental health test is performed each year on the US President to ensure that they continue to be fit to remain in office. This test was the subject of media attention in early 2018 when, after a three-hour examination of physical and cognitive abilities, President Trump was declared to be in 'excellent' overall health.

The BBC reported that, when asked by the media how a man who purportedly consumes fried chicken and Diet Coke and does not exercise could be in great shape, the White House doctor replied, 'he has incredible genes'. This was in addition to the pre-election assessment that Trump received from his own long-time doctor that he would be the 'healthiest individual ever elected to the presidency'.

External commitments

As we saw in the example above of Sir Tom McKillop, it is often the case that directors hold significant commitments on various other company boards. In 2017, this was certainly true of directors of FTSE-listed companies. Of the 150 chairs listed, 71.7% held at least one additional listed company directorship and sat on an average of 1.8 additional external boards. This is broadly comparable to the commitments of non-executive directors in the UK, and chairs and non-executive directors in other countries, with Italian chairs and directors being the outliers at an average number of quoted board directorships of 3.4 and 3.8, respectively. The percentage of CEOs who held an outside board directorship has decreased from 47% in 2012 to 34.5% in 2017, perhaps indicating increased pressures in recent years.

According to recent research by Henley Business School, the maximum number of board-level positions should be no more than four. The argument made in every country they assessed was that three or four directorships is the maximum capacity one person can manage in terms of the time required to consider and attend to complex issues appropriately. However, the research also found that, in practice, up to 13 directorships in the US and 14 in South Africa were not uncommon. It suggested that this would necessarily lead to a director simply turning up at committee meetings, looking at papers in front of them for the first time, debating on them, making a decision and walking away.

Different studies have suggested various figures for the average amount of time required for directors to fulfil their board duties appropriately, ranging from 100 hours up to 320 hours per year (between 12.5 and 31.25 days). Obviously, all boards are different and hours expectations will differ from board to board depending on a number of factors; however, these numbers were indicative for part-time directors (chairs would do more) and for when organisations were not in any moments of crisis. High-performing directors, however, as one McKinsey study found, give more commitment on average (up to 40 days per year) compared to moderate or lower-performing boards, whose directors averaged only 19 days per year. Interestingly, all directors in this study gave equal time to compliance (around four days), but better directors also invested an extra eight days on strategy.

The number of directorships and increasing time expected has led to the issue of 'overboarding', where directors are too stretched in their boardroom commitments. The 2003 Higgs Review offered a solution through their sample retainer letter for non-executive directors. The letter stipulates the number of days per month of work required and asks that directors confirm they are able to meet such requirements before undertaking the role.

In some countries including, but not limited to, offshore jurisdictions, this maximum number of board directorships can take on a completely different character with some directors being nominal trustees of multiple – often hundreds – of trust company boards. However, based on recent legislation passed by the EU Code of Conduct Group, these 'vehicle' company structures that are set up for a specific purpose, including holding assets or undertaking a single purpose in a ring-fenced structure to limit liability or to ensure maximum tax efficiency, will now need to prove they are actual companies of 'substance' such that profits 'reflect real economic activity in the jurisdiction'.

It is specified within the 'substance' scope requirements and guidance notes that directors need to be physically present at board meetings and have the necessary knowledge and expertise, so this may challenge the practice of excessive board directorships being held by inexperienced directors. It is this definition of substance and whether a legal entity has any operational activities that can drive the level of time commitment and board experience that is reflected in the number of director appointments. For the purposes of our discussions, we will define a company as one with operational capacity, formal board meetings discussing both operational matters and long-term strategy and a board composed of executive and non-executive directors.

Capability

Independence

According to agency theory, a non-executive director must remain independent throughout their tenure to ensure that they appropriately represent external shareholders' interests. There are many country code compliance provisions which define what director independence should look like. In the latest UK Corporate Governance Code, for example, Provision 10 extensively lays out the seven considerations for a non-executive director's independence, as follows:

> The board should identify in the annual report each non-executive director it considers to be independent. Circumstances which are likely to impair, or could appear to impair, a non-executive director's independence include, but are not limited to, whether a director:
>
> - is or has been an employee of the company or group within the last five years;
> - has, or has had within the last three years, a material business relationship with the company, either directly or as a partner, shareholder, director or senior employee of a body that has such a relationship with the company;
> - has received or receives additional remuneration from the company apart from a director's fee, participates in the company's share option or a performance-related pay scheme, or is a member of the company's pension scheme;
> - has close family ties with any of the company's advisers, directors or senior employees;
> - holds cross-directorships or has significant links with other directors through involvement in other companies or bodies;
> - represents a significant shareholder; or

- has served on the board for more than nine years from the date of their first appointment.

Where any of these or other relevant circumstances apply, and the board nonetheless considers that the non-executive director is independent, a clear explanation should be provided.

Taking an evidence-based approach to the question of whether an independent board leads to better governance, it is interesting to note a somewhat contradictory conclusion. There are a number of studies of boards that find at best no evidence that director independence leads to positive board outcomes. In fact, on the contrary, boards that are more independent have also been shown to produce worse outcomes than those who are not.

There are many significant advantages to having an independent board; however, it should certainly not be considered a panacea according to the evidence. For example, boards that are made up of mainly executive directors are likely to have more knowledge of their organisation and also may be more motivated to help the organisation succeed than those who are detached.

Professional capital

The criteria that a nominations committee draws up to advertise and then select new board directors is most likely to comprise factors that could be considered under the term 'professional capital'. These are the functional, industry and executive management experience, as well as specific prior board directorship that an individual candidate might bring. Although both previous industry and board-specific experience are deemed preferable, it is not always necessary to have served on a board previously to attain a new directorship. For example, of all the newly appointed non-executive directors to the FTSE listed boards in 2007, 34% had not previously served on any other board. Equally, while relevant industry experience is required across the board as a whole, individual board appointments may seek candidates from different sectors, industry or organisational backgrounds. For example, the board of a creative-based organisation may benefit from appointing non-executive directors from non-creative backgrounds to balance the conversation and bring alternative perspectives.

The research literature has attempted to quantify board director professional capital using a variety of criteria with associated percentage weightings. One study used previous qualitative research with boards to weigh a calculation of professional capital as follows:

1. years of industry experience (30%);
2. number of boards served (30%);
3. current executive management role (including CEO, direct report to CEO, other corporate level, or outside adviser) (20%);
4. cumulative number of years on boards (10%); and
5. highest level of education achieved (10%).

Financial experience

Financial expertise is perhaps the most commonly requested expertise in board applications. The argument for financial expertise is that, from a business monitoring perspective, directors should at least have a good grasp of the basic mechanics and key financial reports provided by executive management. This argument has gained significant momentum in light of the financial crisis, during which time many directors were identified as perhaps having less grasp of the basic company financials than they needed to perform their duties and challenge management effectively. Good financial directors are unsurprisingly becoming 'hot property' as potential directors of other companies – for example, around 28% of 2017 FTSE-listed finance directors hold an external listed non-executive directorship, an increase from 26% in the preceding two years.

What does the evidence-base say about how necessary significant technical expertise is as a core capability of all board directors? Firstly, it is important to recognise that having a board dominated by financial experts does not expunge risk and guarantee organisational success. The US boards of Enron, Worldcom and Freddie Mac are high-profile cases in point. Enron, for example, failed at a time when their board included an accounting professor, a former Stanford Business School dean, various international bankers, former financial market regulators and current financial service firm leaders. In these cases, something else was at fault rather than a lack of individual financial knowledge (as we shall discuss later).

Secondly, when we take a broader research perspective, a similar conclusion emerges. For example, one study by Guner et al. (2005) considered the impact of boards with financial expertise on corporate finance and investment decisions. Using the US Forbes 500 as its dataset between 1988 to 2001, the study found that the increased presence of financial experts on corporate boards increases the size of loans to the corporation and the frequency of outside financing and larger public debt issues, as well as poorer stock and earnings performance after acquisitions. The researchers thus concluded that 'financial experts on corporate boards do not necessarily improve shareholder value'. Regardless though, in practice, financial literacy is a prerequisite for any non-executive directors in the modern era.

Technical expertise

Beyond financial expertise, should directors require further specific technical skills or should they be generalists as captured by measures of professional capital? A traditional approach has been to recruit directors against a standard curriculum vitae plus interview process around generalist criteria. However, more recently, there has been a shift in the debate. Similar to the argument for financial expertise, a further reason that banks experienced problems in the financial crisis has also been put down to the fact that non-executive directors were generalists who did not understand the complexities of modern banking and so could not ask the right questions. Commentators argue that members of the board of directors must have a minimum knowledge of accountancy and law, their industry and governance practice, improving knowledge around risk and technology, ideally some years of experience in directing a company and technical expertise relevant to the organisation's current strategy.

This again seems common sense and there is some research to reinforce that specific technical skills can positively affect board outcomes. However, as we shall discuss in more detail later in this chapter and the next, this does not guarantee better outcomes. In fact, when viewed from a team perspective, we find robust evidence that individuals with higher-than-average IQ or technical skill can actually reduce team and board effectiveness due to the weaker team dynamic that their inclusion often induces. For example, one study (Woolley, 2008) found that the greater the proportion of experts a team had, the more likely it was to disintegrate into non-productive conflict or stalemate. As Helen White, the CEO of the Taff Housing Association, recently reflected:

> Make sure that the sum is greater than the parts. I've sometimes been in 'incompetent groups of competent individuals' where, on paper, we were a great board, and yet we made poor decisions together. Lots of big personalities aren't always conducive to good collective decisions.

The general conclusion here is not to imply that these aspects of a director's curriculum vitae are unimportant. Rather, what we can suggest is that they should be viewed as minimum raw materials which the director's personality and the board behavioural dynamics will then moderate.

Diversity

The capability of a director to represent the board's various stakeholder groups, including those minority voices who may often find themselves underrepresented, is dictated by the diversity that each director brings to the board. We have already discussed the group-level diversity that boards have increasingly been asked to respond to in the last chapter on board structures. We will also consider the deeper psychological aspects of board-level diversity in Chapter 8. What we are considering here is the individual diversity that each director represents.

At its simplest, a director will be seen as more capable, and therefore more valuable, if they can represent more types of stakeholders in the boardroom. For example, a younger, 'ethnic minority' female could be seen as a valuable asset compared to the traditional 'male, pale and stale' director demographic in listed firms. However, just because a director technically represents a group (their 'surface diversity'), this does not mean that they either actually represent diverse views or indeed that the board environment will be inclusive enough to enable these to be tapped into.

Connections

A final aspect of an individual director's demographics includes their personal connections, collectively known as their 'social capital'. These might include their professional networks (including their specific board committee membership networks, as well as broader work-related links), their alumni networks (which are often exceptionally strong in the older educational establishments, higher education establishments and professional training cohorts) and their social networks (which may include family, broader acquaintances, sporting or activity connections and those within their class structure).

Case study: *Liberté, égalité, fraternité?*
Taking research on social class as an example, a study of the French corporate elite has found that certain social classes are also disproportionately represented on boards. Perhaps unsurprisingly, those from the upper and especially upper-middle classes tend to dominate.

More broadly, and perhaps as a reaction to our increasingly networked professional existence online through platforms such as LinkedIn, social capital has increasingly become the subject of practical consultancy advice in addition to the interest of theoretical academic research.

In relation to boards, one study has recently measured social capital as a reflection of an individual director's number of connections to other professionals in a relationship capital management database provided by BoardEX (Charas, 2014). This provided a score that represented the number of connections each director had in a database of over 500,000 directors of both public and private organisations. The hypothesis behind the research, and the assumptive value underpinning the consultancy firm that owns the database, is that the more connections one has, the more valuable the director may be.

Following stakeholder theory, this has historically been one of the criteria on which directors have been recruited. However, the researchers found that the predictive power of social capital, in addition to professional capital, was negligible compared to the psychological attributes of board directors, to which we shall now turn.

Board attributes

The board structures covered in Chapter 2 and the board demographics covered in the previous sections of this chapter all take a more 'technical' perspective on boardroom governance. We shall now focus on the behavioural aspects of the board. These have not historically garnered as much attention from governance practitioners and commentators, but are increasingly seen as being vitally important.

The board attributes quadrant of the 11 Cs model occupies the intersection between the behavioural perspective and individual perspectives. This has received less attention than the more technical individual aspects of board demographics. However, living up to the 'formal' standards is not enough. More attention needs to be paid to attitudes and behaviour.

The three Cs that the board attributes quadrant focuses on are all related to what has been called 'behavioural capital' and consist of an individual director's behavioural *competencies* (including those specific to their role, general leadership competences and twenty-first-century leadership competencies), psychological *commitments* and ethical *character*. These are summarised in Figure 6.

Figure 6 Board attributes elements from the 11 Cs model

Board attributes

- Role competence (Chairman, CEO, NED, ED, SID, Co sec)
- General (EI, style)
- Twenty-first century (resillience, agility, cultural IQ, digital IQ)
- Commitment (personality, mindset, motivation, derailers)

In some ways, the list of board attributes reads like a contents page from an introductory text on the psychology of leadership. However, on reflection, this is not a surprise. Boards of directors, and particularly the company secretaries who support them, have focused primarily on technical compliance-related issues. This has perhaps been to the detriment of what actually happens behind the closed doors of the boardroom and may have contributed to some of the negative organisational outcomes recounted in Chapter 1. However, armed with a greater understanding of these more behavioural qualities that the next sections will explore, consistently better governance outcomes are much more likely to be produced.

Competence

A definition for competency is 'a cluster of related knowledge, skills and attitudes that affect a major part of one's job (a role or responsibility), that correlates with performance on the job, that can be measured against well-accepted standards, and that can be improved via training and development'. Although there is perhaps some overlap of the director competencies in this quadrant with the capabilities mentioned within board demographics, the competencies below are more board specific rather than general professional technical expertise.

Specific board role competence

This area of role competence asks directors 'Do you have specific board role competence?' and is very much linked to the role that each individual director plays on the board. The attributes of the chair, the CEO and other executive officer directors, the non-executive directors and the senior independent director are discussed in detail in Chapter 11 and the attributes of those surrounding and aligned to the board are discussed in Chapter 10.

General leadership competence

'Do you have general leadership competence?'

Based on the requirement for directors to function beyond monitoring, but at the same time not to interfere with management, an understanding of board leadership and its related competencies becomes important. Although leadership competence is increasingly important for all directors, it is essential for the chair. As Sir David Walker, in his report on the corporate governance of UK banks, remarked,

> A new chairman of plainly considerable ability but with less than the desired financial industry experience might be assisted through a rigorous tailored induction and training programme to move up the industry learning curve relatively quickly... But what may be characterized as the vital chairman leadership skills, if not already demonstrated at the time of appointment, might not be as readily acquired if a candidate does not already have them. A bank board, the regulator and shareholders in a major BOFI [banks and other financial institutions] cannot afford to rely on a process of learning leadership on the job.

Emotional intelligence

If intellectual quotient (IQ), gets you hired, it is said that emotional quotient (EQ), gets you promoted. There are many definitions of emotional intelligence, but one common one comes from leadership thought leader Daniel Goleman: 'the ability to identify and manage one's own emotions, as well as the emotions of others'.

Emotional intelligence is a collection of various competencies that arise from Goleman's two dimensions of identifying/managing and self/others. These two dimensions, if visualised as two axes, create the four components of emotional intelligence: self-awareness, self-management (also known as self-regulation), awareness of others or empathy and social skill or influence. There is a significant amount of research that suggests that people with average emotional intelligence outperform those with the highest IQ around 70% of the time. Furthermore, 90% of top performers (in work and other domains) have high emotional intelligence; emotional intelligence is also responsible for 58% of job performance. More than this, emotional intelligence is viewed as something that anyone can improve over time with appropriate perspective and practice.

The research on emotional intelligence and leadership is well-trodden. We know that emotional intelligence has some interesting dynamics when related to organisational position. Emotional intelligence seems to peak at around managerial level and then gradually declines in inverse proportion as one climbs the organisational greasy pole through director and senior executive levels, such that CEOs may have the lowest emotional intelligence, on average, of all employees. However, we also know from research carried out on more than 1 million employees that the top performers within all job title categories, including CEOs, have the highest emotional intelligence. Therefore, emotional intelligence is seen to be a highly important trait, not just for successful individual performance but also for successful leadership.

When we look at emotional intelligence in the context of leadership teams, we find some very interesting evidence that can be applied to board directors. Although a board of emotionally intelligent individuals will not necessarily translate to an emotionally intelligent board, the particular emotional intelligence characteristic of empathy – also known as social sensitivity – has been found to be key to high-performing teams. Based on the research of team collective intelligence, if there was one behavioural measure that was the most useful as a key predictor of a high-performing board, it would be the average director empathy of that board. As we also know that at a population level, women have (on average) slightly higher empathy scores than men, this explains why research also finds that boards with more women perform better.

Case study: Jacinda Ardern's emotional leadership

New Zealand's Prime Minister, Jacinda Ardern, represents a great role model of high emotional leadership in action. New Zealand has been widely lauded as having had one of the best national responses to the COVID-19 pandemic, with Ardern (as its chief architect) recently commenting,

> One of the criticisms I've faced over the years is that I'm not aggressive enough or assertive enough, or maybe somehow, because I'm empathetic, it means I'm weak. I totally rebel against that. I refuse to believe that you cannot be both compassionate and strong.

Leadership style

As well as displaying high emotional intelligence in their interactions, especially related to empathic communication, a competent board director will also be defined by their chosen leadership style. The best leadership styles for sustained strategic leadership, based on the large and growing evidence base, are those that are the least 'ego-based' and most 'other-referenced', a perspective perhaps best captured in 1947 by one of the last century's early leadership thinkers, the prescient Margaret Parker Follett: 'Leadership is not defined by the exercise of power, but by the capacity to increase the sense of power among those led.'

This description of leadership has been borne out many times in more recent research. For example, in his study of 'great' companies (popularised by his book

Good to Great), Jim Collins identified five levels of leadership in organisations. Level IV leaders are those who were capable of turning their companies round in the short term but then, upon their exit, these companies were not able to sustain their performance. On the contrary, Level V leaders were those who created and sustained high levels of performance over time. They were characterised by a tenacious attitude combined with a humility and lack of ego not found in Level IV leaders (think conciliatory Joe Biden as the antidote to the narcissistic and provocative Donald Trump).

Similarly, in Daniel Goleman's research with the Hay Group, the two most effective leadership styles are described as 'visionary' and 'coaching', as opposed to the more Level IV-like 'directing' ('do as I say' leadership) and pacesetting ('do as I do' leadership) styles. These more mature leaders are systems thinkers and have a more highly evolved 'strategic action logic' (how individuals interpret their surroundings and react when their power or safety is challenged). Unfortunately, these transformational leaders, who are able to lead in both the short and long term, are also quite rare. In the work of Rooke and Torbert, who have studied thousands of professionals over 25 years, these leaders accounted for only 5% of the profiled sample.

Twenty-first century leadership competence

'Do you have twenty-first-century leadership competencies?'

There is an assertion that we are living in an increasingly challenging working environment, one that combines volatility, uncertainty, complexity and ambiguity (VUCA). This creates the additional requirement for specific leadership competencies that include resilience, learning agility, cultural intelligence and digital intelligence.

Resilience

Resilience is defined by the American Psychological Association as 'the process of adapting well in the face of... threats or significant sources of stress. It means "bouncing back" from difficult experiences'.

The requirement for greater levels of individual resilience is related to (amongst other factors) the need for increasing levels of director commitment and the significant uplift in broad scrutiny. This has made the attribute of personal resilience a prerequisite for sustaining performance in any senior leadership role, an attribute that has only increased in its importance during the COVID-19 pandemic.

It enables us to cope with the increasing demands that organisational life throws at us, the psychological threats that we perceive as part of these demands and also the negative emotional, cognitive or behavioural symptoms that may result as part of our stress and coping response. Fortunately, resilience is a competency that can be built over time through a focus on positive lifestyle factors such as appropriate exercise, nutrition and sleep, cognitive techniques such as gratitude and mindfulness and by having access to appropriate social support networks. Organisations are increasingly providing resilience training as part of their broader development initiatives or well-being strategies, but these have yet to be systematically implemented to support board directors in any significant way in the majority of organisations.

With the ever-increasing demands and professionalisation of the director role, along with the particular short-term challenges faced due to the COVID-19 crisis, the competence of resilience is required now more than ever. We will explore the concept in greater depth, including methods of developing one's personal resilience, in Chapter 15.

Learning agility

Similarly, as the external political, economic, social, regulatory and technological environment changes, and increasingly so during the COVID-19 crisis, there is a requirement for senior organisational leaders to be able to adapt at pace. The ability of an organisation to pivot its strategy to changing conditions is hugely important and it is the competence of 'learning agility' that predicts one's ability to deliver this. However, we often get stuck within our previously successful mental models so that we fall foul to the paradox of 'what has got you here won't get you there'. For example, even though non-executive directors often have access to a vast previous executive experience, they may also need to engage the capacity to unlearn to become successful.

Learning agility is therefore defined as a mindset and a corresponding collection of practices that allow leaders to continually develop, grow and use new strategies that will equip them for the increasingly complex problems they face in their organisations. As this also means that they are also able to jettison outdated modes of thinking and doing to provide space for the new, research has identified four behaviours that enable, and one derailer of, learning agility. The enabling behaviours are:

- **innovating**: questioning the status quo, challenging assumptions and seeing things from multiple perspectives
- **performing**: immersing yourself in the experience, observing, listening and quickly processing data
- **reflecting**: gaining feedback and raising self-awareness (in studies this factor most predicted high-performing leadership)
- **risking**: taking 'progressive' rather than thrill-seeking risk that stretches and where success is not guaranteed.

The derailing behaviour is that of 'defending', which involves being closed and defensive to critical feedback and is a predictor of lower leadership performance.

When looked at from a board director perspective, we can probably map these behaviours onto effective or disruptive directors that we know. Effective directors will be those who are able to challenge effectively, hold multiple stakeholder perspectives, immerse themselves in the workings of the organisation rather than remaining aloof, quickly parse board reports to get to the nub of the issue, continually develop their personal competence, recognise the appropriate boundaries of risk-taking and be open to yearly and ongoing evaluation feedback.

Cultural intelligence

As organisations and stakeholder groups become increasingly globalised, there is a requirement for all leaders to become more culturally intelligent. Although there are overlaps with emotional intelligence, cultural intelligence measures one's ability to empathise not just with other people per se, but with broad groups of others who are part of different national or corporate cultures.

Cultural intelligence has been defined as 'an outsider's seemingly natural ability to interpret someone's unfamiliar and ambiguous gestures the way that person's compatriots would'. It has three measurable sources: one's cognitive quotient, one's physical quotient and one's emotional/motivational quotient. Cultural intelligence and each of these areas will be explored in more depth in Chapter 13.

Digital intelligence

The pace of digital transformation is increasing so that digital intelligence becomes a leadership requirement of all senior leaders, including board directors. However, digital intelligence and digital approaches to leadership are not, perhaps surprisingly, defined by an ability to keep up-to-date with trends in technology and is less of a technical capacity than one might think. Instead, digital intelligence is viewed in the research and best practice as more akin to emotional intelligence. It is defined by a leader's ability to be curious and have a mindset that is open to the changes that digital offers, to be fast-paced, to apply an agile 'fast-fail' mentality, to be open and collaborative, to be experimental, to be well networked and to use social working practices. Board directors, therefore, need to role-model the mindset of digital transformation that will then make it possible to use appropriate skillsets and adopt appropriate technology.

There are a variety of wider benefits of doing this in the current organisational environment. For example, research from Development Dimensions International found that CEOs who are more savvy in their use of social digital tools are 89% more likely to empower others, 52% more compelling in their communications, 46% more influential and cultivated networks 36% better than their non-social peers.

The boardroom is becoming affected more and more by digital factors, such as the increase in virtual working practices, with this being exponentially increased through the impact of the global pandemic in 2020. These will be explored in more depth in Chapter 9.

Commitment and personal disposition

We have thus far explored the various role-specific and leadership competencies that may be required of individual board directors, suggesting that these are more predictive of board functioning than board structures and individual demographic factors. However, just because a director has the 'skill' does not mean that they also have the 'will' to perform.

We will therefore consider the 11 Cs component of 'commitment', looking at the important personality and underlying commitment levels of individual directors and asking the question, 'Do you have the right disposition and motivation?' through the four perspectives of personality, mindset, motivation and derailers.

Personality styles

Our personality is defined as the characteristic set of behaviours, cognitions and emotional patterns that evolve from our biology and our environment. These personality styles are classically broken down into what are known as the Big Five personality traits. These five traits have been defined as:

- openness to experience
- conscientiousnes
- extraversion
- agreeableness
- neuroticism

Not surprisingly, there is some evidence on boards to suggest that director conscientiousness (which can be viewed as a more generic construct of board commitment), agreeableness and openness to experience is positively related to board performance. In the same studies, board director demographics were also measured and found not to correlate with performance.

Mindset

Similar to some of the concepts discussed in learning agility, the orientation of a director's overall mindset and how being what is known as 'fixed' or 'growth' orientated, has a significant impact on personal performance.

The concept of mindset, which was first studied by Professor Carol Dweck of Stanford University, can describe one's attitude to many things, but is especially informative in describing one's attitude towards intelligence. If somebody has a fixed mindset around intelligence – that is, they see intelligence as a static trait – this will lead to a desire to look intelligent and therefore a tendency to behave in certain ways. These behaviours will include the tendency to:

- avoid challenges;
- to give up easily when faced with obstacles;
- to reduce effort as effort is seen as fruitless;

- to ignore useful, negative feedback as this would be perceived as criticism; and
- to feel threatened by the success of others.

As a result, a person holding this fixed mindset may plateau early and achieve less than their full potential. Having a fixed mindset will ultimately therefore confirm the determinist view of the world that this person holds.

On the other hand, a growth mindset – that is, having the belief that intelligence can be developed – leads to a desire to learn and therefore a tendency to a variety of more positive outcomes. These will include:

- the likelihood of embracing challenges when they occur;
- persisting in the face of setbacks;
- seeing effort as the path to mastery;
- learning from criticism rather than ignoring it; and
- finding lessons and inspiration in the success of others, rather than feeling threatened by it.

These outcomes create a virtuous circle and even higher levels of achievement, ultimately reinforcing the person's sense of free will agency to improve their skills and standing.

Case study: Enron's systemic failure

In his *New Yorker* article series, Malcolm Gladwell unpicked the rationale for the failure of Enron in 2001. The judgement of Jeff Skilling, Enron's chief executive officer during the scandal, was that he was personally responsible for the failure due to his greed and moral corruption. However, Gladwell paints a compellingly different picture, asking whether perhaps Enron's failure was more due to an organisational fixed mindset which led to a culture of internal competition, the covering up of mistakes and, ultimately, a systemic failure. This therefore invites a broader spread of blame rather than simply castigating its chief executive officer.

The culture of a fixed mindset, Gladwell argues, came from their management consultancy firm McKinsey and Co who had introduced Enron to, and schooled them in, the concept of the 'war for talent'. This concept was premised on the belief that successful companies are successful because they recruit the most prestigious intellect from the best business schools and then create performance management practices that enable this talent to flourish.

Many of the companies that used this principle and the various practices that it entails – for example, 'the rank and yank' system whereby the bottom 10% are fired each year (General Electric, Microsoft, Accenture, Adobe, Motorola and Ford, to name a few) – have paradoxically experienced significantly reduced performance and have now changed these methodologies.

Fortunately, mindset can be changed through persistence and training. One study found that, before training, leaders who adopted a fixed mindset were worse at recognising real changes in their team members and were less likely to help those they were leading. However, after training, the same leaders were able to give more and better suggestions to their employees during appraisals and were more likely to notice improvements.

Motivation

Even the best directors are prone to dips in commitment and 'social loafing' (exerting less effort when part of a team than when alone). This means that sustainable self-motivation is a key attribute of successful, committed board directors. However, contrary to what you might think, the latest research on motivation suggests that it is not the *quantity* of your motivation that predicts your performance, but more the *quality*. The quality of your motivation is, using thought-leading self-determination theory language, either more 'intrinsic' (that is, driven by your own values, beliefs and enjoyment), or 'extrinsic' (that is, driven by what others would want or are coercing you to do). When people are driven by a more intrinsic motivation because they either enjoy the process of doing something for itself, or because it is aligned with their values, better outcomes will ensue.

We are all motivated by four basic fundamental human needs:

- **autonomy**: the need to feel that you have personal control of your destiny
- **belonging**: the need to feel a connection with others
- **competence**: the need to feel that you are improving and playing to your strengths
- **meaning**: the need to feel a broader purpose for the behaviours that you are performing

Although we each have slightly differing requirements for these four needs, our actions must be buttressed by some or all of them for us to feel sustainably motivated.

Derailers

Much of what has been discussed so far has focused on the positive aspects of director attributes, that is, on what it takes to be a successful board director. However, there are also serious consequences for boards when the darker sides of a director personality emerges.

The bad news is that the estimated base rate of management failure due to these overplayed strengths is, according to a meta-analysis of 12 studies, around 50%. Some of the literature's key derailment behaviours are certainly those that are often seen in the boardroom and include:

- being overly tactical (and therefore not being strategic enough);
- leading too forcefully (and therefore not asking, involving or empowering others);

- focusing too much on the logic of the task in hand (and therefore having bad working relationships); and
- sticking to a failing strategy (and not stopping to reflect and adapt).

It is possible to assess the darker side of our personality both non-clinically through scales such as the Hogan Development Survey (the test's 'mischievous' scale overlaps with psychopathy and its 'bold' scale overlaps with narcissistic personality disorder) and clinically through the Diagnostic and Statistical Manual of Personality Disorders. One useful test to assess for narcissistic personality disorder is the acronym SPECIAL:

- Special (believes he or she is special and unique)
- Preoccupied with fantasies (of unlimited success, power, brilliance, beauty, or ideal love)
- Entitlement
- Conceited (grandiose sense of self-importance)
- Interpersonal exploitation
- Arrogant (haughty)
- Lacks empathy

From a company leadership perspective, we know that narcissistic chief executives are likely to manipulate company finances at some point as they over-identify themselves with the organisations they lead and expend considerable resources to achieve their own personal goals – potentially including engagements in unethical behaviour. (The novel method that the research uses to assess whether the chief executive officer has been showing narcissistic tendencies is their frequency of the use of 'I' instead of 'we'.)

These individual traits of derailed leaders do not necessarily create problems by themselves. They also require susceptible followers (who are either 'conformers' with unmet needs, low esteem and low maturity, or 'colluders' with ambition and similar worldviews) and a conducive environment that is lacking in the appropriate governance structures. Together these three elements create a 'toxic triangle' within which destructive leadership can flourish.

Character

The ethical character of directors is an area that has been gaining in interest in recent years, post-financial crisis and with each sector's new scandal. The 11 Cs model asks directors: 'Do you have sufficient ethical character?' Even furnished with all the competencies and commitment that have been described above, evidence suggests that directors cannot deliver effective governance if they do not have a clear moral purpose and cannot model core ethical values.

One thought leader in this arena is Professor Roger Steare, the Corporate Philosopher in Residence and Professor of Organisational Ethics at Cass Business

School. His MoralDNA profile research on directors and senior leaders clearly demonstrates why failures in character lead to high-risk behaviours and ethically dubious decision making. It finds that there is a significant difference between the ethics of these leaders at work compared to how they are in life more generally.

Specifically, leaders make decisions at work significantly more through an ethic of obedience while suppressing their ethic of care. In the boardroom, this translates into being robotically compliant with dehumanised decisions which, as we have seen, can lead to disastrous consequences. However, the results have a more positive side too, in that the average ethic of care in life outside of work in these leaders was actually higher than the global average. This indicates that the vast majority of leaders have good values and have the potential to do the right thing, especially when working within the right environment and culture. How the behaviours that director's role model can influence the creation of such an ethical culture, will be discussed further in Chapter 7.

Conclusion

In section 91 of its Guidance on Board Effectiveness, among some 11 sections of other detailed guidance, the Financial Reporting Council points out that the role of the nomination committee is to select directors with a diversity of personal attributes and that the committee:

> will want to ensure the board is comprised of individuals who display a range of softer skills, such as… sources of intellect, critical assessment and judgement, courage, openness, honesty, tact, ability to listen, ability to forge relationships, ability to develop trust, (and) strength of character.

This chapter has provided descriptions, insights and an evidence base underpinning what these attributes actually are. One key conclusion is that, of the individual quadrants in the 11 Cs model, it is the personal attributes that are much more likely to predict effective director behaviour and successful board outcomes than the board demographic factors, even though the latter are usually used to recruit directors.

However, even a board with the right mix of highly competent and committed individuals, all with congenial characters, can be less productive than we might expect. This is due to the presence of a limiting board dynamic – the fourth, final and most important quadrant, which we shall turn to in Chapter 4 and beyond.

We have seen that director demographics and director attributes comprise the individual elements of the 11 Cs model. What are some of the most relevant demographic characteristics that are prerequisites of modern board members and do these lead to better board performance? Three of the most likely prerequisites for selection onto a modern board are not having too many existing board commitments, showing evidence of financial expertise and representing diversity. However, these do not in themselves lead to better board performance. Rather, how a director is committed, whether they are facilitated to apply their financial expertise and what specific diversity in relation to the rest of the board and stakeholder requirements they express will ultimately make the difference. It is not whether the board director membership ticks the boxes on key aspects of professional and social capital, but more how these play out within the board dynamic that will affect performance.

Although often used as a proxy for good governance, the elements of capacity, capability and connections within the board demographic quadrant are not, by themselves, good predictors of effective governance.

Director attributes – the individual and behavioural element of the 11 Cs model – include role-specific and leadership competences, commitment and personality attributes and director character. These attributes have significantly more potential to influence board governance outcomes; however, overall, a board's dynamics will always mediate how much individual directors can contribute to board effectiveness. It is the combination of all board members as a whole that can make a board effective: the lack of cohesion between individuals can equally make it ineffective. Having all the attributes identified and included, while a good indicator for success, will not in and of itself create a perfectly functioning team.

This chapter has provided a foundation of knowledge of individual attributes that should be identified and enhanced in board members. It serves as a starting point for the dynamics that will be in play between individual board members – both in meetings and in their interactions, or lack of, outside of the formal board.

With this in mind, it's important to question: What are your own and your board members' mindset, attributes and characters? How do these impact on the dynamics of the board?

Part two
Understanding board dynamics

Part two
Understanding board dynamics

4 – Psychology of the board

The importance of board dynamics

The overarching rationale for this text is that there is an increasing recognition of the mismatch between what behavourial science knows about people and what companies do around governance.

The preceding chapters have discussed the technical and individual aspects of governance. We have now reached the point where we can immerse ourselves in the behavioural and team-level aspects of the board: the board dynamics. Most of the commentary from regulators, the investor community, from academia, from the media and from others in the broader governance community focuses on the areas that the preceding chapters have shown do not consistently equate with governance outcomes. Why has this been the case for so long? One reason is that it may be because our brains find it easier to attribute success and failure to individuals than to groups.

Similarly, we may have relied on a rational economics perspective for too long, encouraging compliance that only takes into account the 'logical' solutions. However, things are not always simple and logical whenever people are involved, so a different perspective may be useful. In practice, it is probably true to generalise that directors have always known that boardrooms are not necessarily always rational places and that human factors such as trust, power, influence and relationships are going to be key to performance. As Karl George, the managing director of the Governance Forum, said:

> Bad board behaviour is the thing that scuppers good governance every time. The people element of governance is so essential. It's the number one reason companies fail.

If practising directors know this, but the broader governance community does not also hold this opinion, a perspective shift may be needed. Dr Tracey Long, an expert in board evaluation, wrote in 2006 that:

> There is an assumption (that) ... companies survive because they have optimal governance structures. However, for practitioners and scholars alike, corporate governance and board performance are inextricably linked but little understood... We need to know more about behavioural dynamics.

The problem with understanding board dynamics is that it has historically been hard to get into the 'black box' of the boardroom to study it and produce evidence-based research. There is a great deal of data from more mainstream team literature to show that team dynamics are the key to performance, which we will discuss later, but to date very little board-specific research on team dynamics has been done.

Some attempts have been made to fill the void of board dynamics research. One such attempt was conducted by Richard Leblanc, a Canadian researcher at York University's business school. In a study where he interviewed 194 directors on 39 boards, as well as directly observing board and committee meetings of 21 of those boards, Leblanc found that board process was the most important factor in predicting board effectiveness and corporate performance. Board membership, that is, director characteristics, were the next important, with board structure trailing in a distant third. Leblanc concluded that 'clearly, board structure is not as important a factor in determining board effectiveness as is normally believed'.

More recently, in 2017, Solange Charas, a board veteran and researcher at Case Western Reserve University, sampled 182 directors from 166 unique organisations with an average revenue size of $2.2 billion across all industries. She found, like Leblanc, that demographic factors did have an impact on profitability, but, also like Leblanc, noted that the impact was extremely small, explaining less than 0.5% of performance. Dynamics and the impact of the board working well together as a team had an 800% – eight times greater – predictive positive impact on profitability. More than this, this impact was also negatively predictive, such that board dynamics accounted for an 8% swing in performance measured by profitability. With appropriate expertise, and a relatively small time and budget impact, working on the board dynamic provides an excellent return on investment. As Charas concluded: 'Organisations in our study with boards that have healthy dynamics consistently outperformed organisations with boards that are dysfunctional.'

In short, understanding board dynamics is vital if we are to do a better job at corporate governance. A starting point is to develop a clearer understanding of what board dynamics actually is, what its components are and how we might influence these for the better.

Defining board dynamics

Chapter 1 provided a number of definitions of board dynamics. The most complete definition for our purposes here is the following:

Board dynamics: definition
Board dynamics are the interactions between board members individually and collectively and how these influence, and are influenced by, their wider stakeholder system.

There are two aspects to this definition. The first part relates to the boardroom interactions that we might notice if we were a fly on the wall, sitting in on a board meeting. This is usually what people think of when we use the term board dynamics, but it is probably more appropriately described as the boardroom dynamics. This chapter and Chapter 5 (on board decision making) will focus mainly on this initial part of the definition, that is, the interactions between board members individually and collectively in the boardroom.

The assumption underlying this first part of the definition is that the behaviours that emerge from the board are more than the accumulation of what board directors might individually bring. It is like pack behaviour in dogs; you may spend all your life with just one dog, observing and becoming familiar with how they act in different situations so that you feel very confident that you can describe everything about them. However, when you put that dog in a pack, completely different behaviours emerge that you could not have predicted from having experienced the dog only as an individual. As Aristotle said: 'The whole is greater than the sum of the parts.'

The second part of the definition of board dynamics, regarding how the internal boardroom dynamics influence and are influenced by their wider stakeholder system external to the board, is perhaps a newer conceptualisation of the term 'board dynamics'. Although there is a focus on the board as a unit in later chapters, Chapters 6–9 will also focus on how the dynamics within the boardroom are shaped by and, importantly, are also able to shape, the culture and behaviour outside of the boardroom.

Our definition of board dynamics employs the words 'interactions' and 'influence', hinting at their underpinning in the more human aspects of governance. Over the last 150 years or so, the science of psychology has emerged as a field that studies such behavioural interactions, so it is perhaps useful here to have a brief historical introduction to the various psychological lenses that have evolved that will aid our understanding of dynamics.

Psychology is the scientific study of the mind and how it dictates and influences our behaviour – for example, how we communicate, how we think, how we are motivated and how we feel emotion. During the twentieth century, a number of psychological theories emerged which each took a slightly different perspective on this scientific study.

The most dominant early theory of psychology is the field of psychodynamics. This is characterised by the study of our unconscious drives and our inner conflicts that are, the theory suggests, most strongly developed through our early childhood experience. Psychodynamics originated in the early twentieth century, led by the iconic Sigmund Freud and his successor Carl Jung. Although perhaps superseded to some extent by later theories, it still provides some useful commentaries and practical approaches to boardroom behaviour, especially when this goes wrong. The Tavistock Institute in the UK has a strong heritage in the psychodynamic approach as it applies to boards, which we will discuss later in this chapter.

The behavioural approach to psychology, known as behaviourism, emerged in the 1930s as a reaction to the highly subjective, quasi-scientific and largely unfalsifiable methods inherent to psychodynamics. Behaviourism rejects the concept of introspection as a unit of scientific data and instead only values and measures observable behaviour. Behaviourism emerged as field of psychology through the leadership of B.F. Skinner and his classical conditioning work with rats and pigeons. Skinner introduced the concept of stimulus and response: where, if you give an organism a particular stimulus,you will naturally get a particular response. This was also a feature of leading behaviourist Ivan Pavlov's earlier work with dogs. In behaviourism there is no room for free will; instead, behaviour arises from the conditioning of our involuntary reflexes.

In the 1950s, post-World War II, human mental processes such as attention, memory, language and perception came back onto the map of psychological research. Cumulatively, the work on these processes has been labelled cognitivism and has evolved in step with the development of computers and artificial intelligence. The personality and mindset theory that we discussed in Chapter 2 comes mainly out of the school of cognitive psychology.

The final waypoint on our brief tour of twentieth-century psychology is that of humanistic psychology, which emerged in the mid-twentieth century as a reaction to the limitations of psychodynamics and behaviourism. It has hence been called the 'third force' in psychology. This approach acknowledges and studies the whole person and their healthy potential and focuses on topics such as creativity, motivation, empathy, motivation and meaning. The founding father of humanistic psychology was Carl Rogers, who reacted to the emotional poverty and lack of acknowledgement of the more vital aspects of humanity in behaviourism. He extended psychotherapeutic research and created counselling approaches underpinned by a person-centred approach and a fundamental belief in potential he called 'unconditional positive regard'.

Abraham Maslow is also a key figure in humanistic psychology who created his theory of self-actualisation (influenced itself by Eastern philosophy and psychology), which is positioned at the peak of his 'hierarchy of needs' model. Topics such as emotional intelligence and mindfulness, as well as the leadership practice of coaching, have more recently emerged from, and are underpinned by, a humanistic approach to psychology.

While much of the above focuses on the study of how individuals think, feel and behave, psychology has also focused on groups and systems behaviour; based on our definition of board dynamics, this is highly relevant to the work of boards. The area of social psychology, where psychology meets sociology, is the body of work that has done much of the research on the attitudes, identity and behaviour within and between small groups. Social psychology describes the phenomena of social influence and group dynamics and has been applied to arenas such as the military, education, sport and the arts. As a discipline, it emerged following World War II through people such as Kurt Lewin, who fled Nazi Germany for the US.

More recently, the field of systems psychology has emerged. This looks at human behaviour as a complex system. This has been influenced by ideas from systems thinking in computing, ecology, environmentalism and even politics. Systems psychology has been applied to ergonomics (the psychology of object, task or environmental design) and organisational or work psychology, which includes the study of organisational leadership.

A broad overview of the psychological topics that relate to board dynamics covered in the following six chapters is captured in Figure 7, from the board dynamics quadrant of the 11 Cs model. The three Cs that relate to this quadrant are those of *cohesion* and *challenge*, which pair together to describe what effective boardroom dynamics are like, and *culture*, which captures the theme of how the board's behaviour influences and is influenced by external stakeholders. The key question that the board dynamics quadrant therefore asks of the board is: 'Does the board communicate a culture of cohesion and challenge?'

Figure 7 The board dynamics quadrant of the 11 Cs model

Board dynamics

- Team cohesion/challenge
- Decision-making
- Stakeholder conversations
- Leadership culture
- Diversity (deep)
- Board environment

Characteristics of boards and board meetings

As function usually follows form, we must look at what makes boards special and different from any other unit of study before we can consider the functional dynamics that exist within the boardroom. Forbes and Milliken have defined boards as, 'large, elite, and episodic decision-making groups that are networked to perform complex tasks in the realm of corporate strategy'. If we unpick this definition in more detail, there are perhaps 10 specific characteristics that make a board different from any other group or team.

1. A board will only meet episodically and at a low frequency. It is common for boards to meet on average 10–12 times a year, which is equivalent to only two weeks per year.
2. Boards have a duty to solve complex and strategic challenges. Often the dilemmas that they are faced with will not have a right answer but will have significant consequences that only transpire over the long term, meaning that it is extremely difficult to assess how effective any given solution was.

3 Boards operate within severe time restraints. Their meeting time is often extremely limited. Although there may be opportunities for board members to connect with each other individually and with employees outside of meetings, their face-to-face time together is usually very limited.
4 The board is always working with imperfect information. It is often comprised of indicators of past performance rather than predicted future success, may not be fully representative of all key stakeholder views or indeed may be a partial truth that has been carefully massaged to fulfil one particular group's agenda.
5 The board includes outsiders, the non-executive directors, who are not employed full-time and so have limited firm exposure. This often leads to the phenomenon of information asymmetry, whereby the executive members may hold significantly more key information than the non-executive directors.
6 Board members can have high public profiles and, often associated with this, strong personalities. As boards exist at the peak of organisational life, directorships can be roles that ambitious people aspire to. As we discussed in Chapter 3, there may also be a disproportionate percentage of flawed personality types in the boardroom.
7 Linked to the above, board members often have other board or senior leadership role commitments. This may be an issue simply due to the constraints on their time or may create other conflicts that can affect board functioning.
8 Board members are expected to represent a particular stakeholder group but are also members of the board unit as a whole. This potentially conflicting dual role can often create role ambiguity, with board members individually wondering which 'hat' they should be wearing when. This individual ambiguity may also be mirrored in the board as a whole, as the board is expected to fulfil a variety of functions at any particular time.
9 Boards are typically larger than senior management teams. Increased size means a higher number of relationships to develop, greater diversity to manage and more personalities to handle, all within a context of less airtime to share.
10 Board meetings have a specific, often lengthy, compliance process that they must follow based on a governance mandate prescribed for boards. This dictates the board meetings themselves and also means that a board will be preceded by specific board committees as well as meetings of the non-executive directors in the absence of management.

The process of meetings often follows some version of what Henley Professor Peter Hawkins has described as the 'three gears' of board meetings that also make boards different from other groups: monitoring, strategising and decision making. When done well – and based on the evolving role of non-executive directors to become partners rather than police – the first gear is more than just monitoring; it

also comprises mentoring to provide the appropriate balance of challenge and cohesion between non-executive directors and executive directors.

The three gears model is similar to the more general three modes of governing framework created by Richard Chait, a professor emeritus at the Harvard Graduate School of Education. The first mode of governing, Type I, is fiduciary governing. Within this mode, the board's responsibility is to see that resources are used efficiently and responsibly. Budgets are often the focal point of this conversation so that boards can focus on oversight and accountability, reports and approving, rather than discussion. The second mode, Type II, is strategic governing, whereby strategic thinking and planning are the primary focus. Within this mode, a balanced budget is no longer sufficient if resources are dedicated to the wrong purpose. Therefore, the key questions in this mode are 'what business are we in?', 'what do our customers want?', 'do we have a comparative advantage?' and 'what are our core competencies?' The final mode, Type III, is generative governing, which focuses primarily on framing problems and issues and making sense of them, so that goal setting and decision making are then possible.

In summary, these particular characteristics of boards make working together a challenge. There are many opportunities for interference with the board fulfilling its potential. Managing the social psychological dynamics within boards therefore becomes particularly important.

Boards as high-performing teams

Defining boards as teams

One way to make sense of the dynamics that exist as a consequence of a board's unique characteristics, as discussed above, is to appreciate the difference between the board functioning as either a group or as a team. This section will make the case that effective boards, which advocate and display great corporate governance, function not only as a team, but as a high-performing one.

However, this is a contentious issue. There are numerous ways that boards have been conceived. Some argue that the board is not a team but, in fact, is always a group. Many definitions and types of group have been studied within social psychology; however, for our purposes a group can be defined as 'two or more people who interact with one another, share similar characteristics, and collectively have a sense of unity'.

This definition will certainly be the starting point for boards: they will always consist of two or more people, a board will always interact (even if sometimes in a very limited fashion), members will share at the least the characteristic of being directors and, as a group, they will share the identity of being the board of 'X organisation'. The argument is made that boards can never function as teams because there will always be two sides (in terms of unitary boards) – the executives and the non-executives – who always have conflicting motivations, meaning that the group will never be able to work jointly towards a shared goal.

Others argue that boards can be teams but only at certain moments in their functioning – for example, when they are in the third gear of decision making. The assumption in this chapter, and also in this text more broadly, is that a board may function as a group or as a team for limited periods, but they should aspire to become a continuously high-performing team. Moreover, boards that are already role-modelling great governance are exhibiting the characteristics of high-performing teams. This assumption is somewhat anti-agency theory, which squarely positions the non-executives as a group necessarily independent from management in order for them to oversee and monitor executives effectively, under the assumption that management's internal focus will always conflict with shareholder requirements. However, the reality and recent commentary is that directors have a shared leadership responsibility, which is a characteristic of high-performing teams, as we shall see below.

The starting assumption that boards can function as teams opens up a significant body of evidence-based research that boards can use to inform their practice. It is to this research base that we shall now turn.

There is a modern assumption in organisations that working as a team will always be better. This is not always the case, but is often, as a variety of research shows. Patrick Lencioni, the author of the influential book *The Five Dysfunctions of Teams*, for example, forcefully argues the case for the pre-eminent competitive advantage of teams in organisations.

This provides an impassioned answer to the first question which must be asked of a board group: 'Why become a team in the first place?' One particularly potent example of the benefits of being a team comes from the NHS Leadership Centre's 2004 research, conducted by Dr Carol Borrill and Professor Michael West. This looked at the impact of various human resource practices on patient mortality. One headline result, after studying more than 60 hospital trusts, was that the higher the percentage of staff that worked in teams in hospitals, the lower the patient mortality rate. In short, more teamwork equals fewer deaths. On average, in hospitals where over 60% of staff worked in formal teams, mortality was around 5% lower than would be otherwise expected. There are many other studies that show the positive outcomes of working in teams on factors such as sales performance, market share and financial performance; however, this study certainly makes the point and is a stark example to sell the benefits of working in teams. In contrast, there is evidence through publicised cases that a lack of teamwork and/or the negative influence of a dominant or respected individual, such as a surgeon, can lead to failings – including patient deaths.

If we have sold the benefits of a board becoming a team, how, actually, should we define what a team is? One of the most common definitions is from Katzenback and Smith who, in their seminal 1993 book *The Wisdom of Teams*, defined a team as:

> A small group of people with complementary skills who are committed to a common purpose, performance goals, and approach for which they hold themselves mutually accountable.

How does a board stack up against this definition? Firstly, the definition mentions a 'small group', which is often considered to be seven plus or minus two people. In Chapter 2, we saw that the average size of boards globally is around 10 people, with outliers being French boards at 13.9 and German boards at just over 16 directors on average. An overall average of 10 would therefore just about fit into the definition of a team; however, as boards get bigger, as is the case sometimes with representative boards in the public sector, they may find it more difficult to coordinate as a team. In these scenarios, it is common for delegation to committees of the board to be introduced to ensure that sufficient time and resource is given to specific topics.

Secondly, the definition includes the idea of a board having 'complementary skills'. We will look at this in significantly more detail in Chapter 8, but, in short, boards are much more likely to function as teams if they have a diverse and balanced skillset and mindset. Historically, board diversity focused primarily on functional diversity, ensuring that the board had the breadth of composition to represent the organisations' functional operations: finance, operations, sales, marketing, HR, technology, etc. More recently, as the benefit of true diversity has been recognised, this has expanded into diversity of individual expertise and representation. Diversity approaches then focused on surface characteristics such as gender and race, albeit for sound ethical and stakeholder representational reasons. From a team perspective, a board will also benefit from considering the deeper complementary skill sets, such as Belbin team roles (see Chapter 8) and personality styles to create true diversity.

Thirdly, the definition uses the phrase 'committed to a common purpose'. As we discussed in Chapter 3, a key attribute of effective directors is their level of motivation and commitment. Even a highly competent director, both in terms of technical expertise and career track record, may not maintain their initial level of commitment to a board common purpose due to their own value set conflicting with that of their board, but also due to the board culture not engendering shared purpose.

Fourthly, teams are also committed to specific 'performance goals'. As we have seen, boards have a range of gears, modes, roles and therefore performance goals at any one particular time. Those boards that work as teams regularly reflect on the appropriateness of their performance goals and ensure that all board members are on the same page at all times.

Fifthly, the definition uses the term committed to a 'common approach'. As well as shared performance goals, a board will only function as a team when there are agreed group norms and ground rules of appropriate and inappropriate behaviour in place. Again, boards that function as teams are those that spend time discussing what these are and regularly reflecting how to improve them. We will provide some practical ideas for how to achieve this in Chapter 14.

Finally, the definition finishes with the idea that teams hold themselves 'mutually accountable'. Instead of being a group of individuals, boards that function as teams will have a shared identity that comes through in their behaviour within the boardroom, but also at all other times outside of the boardroom between meetings. They support and challenge each other and will not wait for the chair, as the formal leader of the board, to fulfil this function.

Working groups versus teams

How would a board know when it is functioning more as a working group versus when it is functioning as a team? Peter Hawkins, in his book *Leadership Team Coaching*, suggests nine factors that distinguish working groups from teams.

1. Leadership

Working groups are defined by strong, clearly focused leadership whereas teams share leadership roles. Although it is true that a chair's formal role is to be the leader of the board, this does not mean that they are the only person that will exhibit the behaviours of leadership such as articulating vision, providing supportive feedback or voicing constructive challenge. In boards that work well as teams, all directors take responsibility at different times whereas in boards that function more as groups, directors are more comfortable sitting back and following the sole leadership of the chair (and potentially chief executive officer).

2. Accountability

Working groups are characterised by members having individual accountability whereas teams are characterised by members having both individual and mutual accountability. Directors in a board team bring their own unique experiences and competencies to bear on the board and they are able to hold a shared identity as a board member.

3. Purpose

Working groups are characterised by having a group purpose which is the same as the broader organisational mission, whereas a team's purpose is different from both the organisational mission and the sum of individual team members' objectives. It is often assumed by board members that their board mission is the organisational mission. This naturally leads them to be functioning, as described by this factor, as more of working group as there will be no specific shared endeavour to bind the board together. However, boards that work as a team recognise that it is important to spend time defining their own unique purpose that is distinct from the broader organisational mission and to review this regularly.

4. Work products

A working group produces individual work products whereas a team produces collective work products. For example, when a board that functions as a group is in 'fiduciary governing mode', its members' work products will be in head-to-head debate either by competent reporting, if they are an executive director, or through effective scrutinising, if they are a non-executive director. However, if the board is to work more as a team, directors must appreciate that the collective work product of fiduciary governing is not simply reporting and critiquing, but jointly dialoguing in partnership as equal directors to ensure appropriate shareholder accountability.

5. Meeting style

The working group will run efficient agenda-based meetings whereas a team will focus more on creating generative dialogue, with open discussion and active problem solving. The traditional, process-driven agenda styled board meeting is set up so that a board is much more likely to function as a working group than as a team. However, this does not have to be the case. If a board reviews how it runs meetings, aligns this more with its strategic objectives and considers how to implement some team-working good practices, it is quite possible for a board to function more effectively as a team.

6. Performance measures

A working group measures its effectiveness indirectly by its influence on others – such as using the financial performance of the organisation. A team, on the other hand, measures its performance directly by assessing its collective work products. We will focus in the next section on what the collective work products of the board are, which, if they can better orientate their performance measures around, will enhance their functioning as a team.

7. Working together

A working group will define working together as discussing issues, making decisions and then delegating to others. The team will also discuss issues and make decisions, but they will then do 'real work' together. A board is a decision-making unit: this largely cognitive and conceptual process is what constitutes its real work. This has significance when we consider how boards use and delegate work to their committees. When boards function more as working groups, they will ask their committees to do the heavy lifting and come up with proposals simply to be rubber-stamped. However, when a board acts as a team, they will use a committee to accelerate effective evidence gathering so that the board can then do the real work of thoughtfully considering what options are actually possible.

8. Working boundaries

The working group will only exist when its members are together, whereas a team member will still be part of the team when they are not together. This aspect has huge ramifications for boards, as many directors believe their role as a board director only exists when they are physically at a board meeting. This will certainly be the case for those directors who are 'overboarded' with too many board commitments to do any of them justice. However, when a board functions as a team, a board member will see themselves as part of that board team at all times. This will amplify their opportunity to engage more fully with stakeholders between board meetings and to communicate and role-model better in order to consciously to influence the culture of the organisation.

9. Board focus

The working group is simply task-focused, whereas a team is task-focused *and* process and learning focused. We know that lower-performing boards simply go through an agenda of task issues, whereas high-performing boards also create space for what is known as meta-practices, such as discussing *how* they are focusing on these issues and reflecting on their practice through ongoing and yearly evaluation and development.

Defining high-performing teams

One final piece of the puzzle from the research on teams is to share a definition of high-performing teams. If the aim of a board is to shift initially from being a working group to team, the next shift is for them to become a high-performing team. One useful definition of high-performing teams is from Salas et al. (2006), who advocate that a high-performing team:

> possesses unique and expert-level knowledge, skills, and experience related to task performance... and adapt, coordinate, and cooperate as a team, thereby producing... superior or at least near-optimal levels of performance.

This definition has three aspects to it. Firstly, it has a membership aspect, which suggests that high-performing teams are chock-full of experts. We know from the discussions in Chapter 2 on director demographics and director personal attributes that the expertise that contributes to board success is less likely to be demographic in nature and more likely to be competency, commitment and character-based.

However, we also know that this is not enough to produce effective board outcomes and this is reflected in the second part of the definition above, which is that the high-performing team must also adapt, co-ordinate and co-operate as a team. This definition is certainly in line with what we have considered so far, that is that the dynamics of the board and how its members work as a team, are the mediating factors which can either interfere with or catalyse the full potential of the board. The characteristics of the individuals that compose the board and the interaction of these individuals when working as a team is covered in more detail in Chapter 8.

Before considering what these effective board team processes might be, we will now consider the third aspect of the definition: what performance outcomes the board should be looking for in order to be a high-performing team.

Board team outcomes

In light of the high-performing team definition above, which includes the mention of performance outcomes in terms of task performance, what key outcomes is a board attempting to achieve? One indirect measure of a board's teamworking dynamics will be its organisation's performance: there are certainly many studies of boards and leadership teams which show that enhancing board dynamics has an impact on overall organisational performance. However, this influence has many intermediary steps and one of those is how board dynamics influences board performance.

In their 2004 study of the priorities and performance of UK public companies, Henley Business School's Professor Victor Dulewicz and Peter Herbert produced some innovative work that defined and measured 16 tasks of the board, which cluster into four areas of performance:

- vision, mission and values
- strategy and structure
- supervision of management
- responsibility to shareholders and other stakeholders

Although all these tasks are important board team outcomes, it is interesting to note which are most predictive of organisational performance. The researchers found that, of the four performance areas, board chairs rated the 'vision, mission and values' factor as more important in order to be high-performing than the other three factors (although all were deemed important) and the one that most frequently underpinned their potential for high organisational performance measured by cash flow return on total assets (CFROTA). Further, of the 134 chairs surveyed, the highest rated of the 16 specific tasks by some margin was also one from the 'vision, mission and values' area being whether their board was able to 'determine the company's vision and mission to guide and set the pace for its operations and future development'. Ninety-one per cent of chairs rated this as vital to the performance of the board.

What, though, are the broad behavioural outcomes that lead to these board task outcomes? The 11 Cs model lists two key behavioural outcomes: cohesion and challenge. We will define these briefly and then explore them in further depth here and in further chapters, including sharing what these look like in practice and what boards can do to enhance them.

Cohesion

There is a significant body of social psychological research on the concept of cohesion, also known as 'group cohesiveness' or 'social cohesion'. Cohesion is defined as 'the tendency for a group to be in unity while working towards a goal or to satisfy the emotional needs of its members'. It is dynamic in nature and may change in strength over time, depending upon a range of factors. Various components create cohesion in groups and teams such as:

- a social element, such that a group likes each other and will want to work together;
- a task element, such that the group approaches a challenge with the same mindset and information; and
- a utility element, such that a group will be will jointly gain meaning from working together.

Team cohesion is often viewed as a key asset in boards. Cohesion has a number of benefits. It can enhance decision making by encouraging earlier and more extensive dialogue around alternative options. This enables what is known as a 'team mind' or 'team cognition', an emergent team dynamic that is neatly captured by American basketball Hall of Fame recipient Bill Walton: 'Winning is about having the whole team on the same page.'

Having a cohesive team mind has been found to be highly influential to team performance. High levels of board cohesion reduces 'information asymmetry'. Information asymmetry is a key concept in effective decision making; it essentially means that those who make the decisions and that those who have the information to make the decisions will hold similar information. Ensuring information symmetry has been held as a key way for boards (as the agents of decision making) to optimise value creation in organisations (where the information is held).

Cohesion will also enhance motivation, team commitment and team member satisfaction. In turn, having high levels of these characteristics is much more likely to engender higher levels of innovation, the feeling of being able to apply one's strengths and higher time spend on board tasks and higher sustained energy levels (useful for long board meetings!).

Group cohesion has also been found to significantly reduce levels of stress and anxiety, which is highly relevant to the modern and post-pandemic board context with increasingly greater demands and scrutiny. Teams with lower levels of stress also exhibit positive outcomes such as higher creativity, higher levels of sustained performance and board members feeling able to express challenge.

There is also significant evidence to show that team cohesion can improve the team's ability to learn from its performance. Taken together, all of these benefits show significant performance outcomes of increasing levels of cohesion. The literature advocates many principles for increasing cohesion, such as enhancing the frequency of interactions, improving the quality of relationships, providing more opportunities for team members to notice each other's similarities and also decreasing group size.

Challenge

Although we have just argued that higher levels of team cohesion provide a host of positive outcomes for the board dynamic, overly high levels can prove detrimental to the quality of the board's decision making. Highly cohesive boards can sometimes be distracted by too much banter and personal exchange. More significantly, though, cohesiveness is the most frequently noted cause of groupthink. This was a term that emerged into the organisational lexicon in the 1980s and gained in prominence through the work of Yale psychologist Irving Janis through his study of American foreign policy disasters such as the Bay of Pigs invasion, aspects of the Japanese attack on Pearl Harbour and the Vietnam War. Groupthink is defined as 'a dysfunctional mode of group decision-making characterised by a reduction in independent, critical thinking and a relentless striving for unanimity among members'.

For boards to function as close as possible to their optimal potential, two things need to be true. Firstly, boards do need to have a moderately high level of team cohesion for all the beneficial reasons cited in the last section. However, secondly and, in order to protect them from the dynamic of groupthink, cohesiveness must also be accompanied by an appropriate amount of challenge amongst members. This challenge is often termed in psychology as 'cognitive conflict', which refers to task-orientated differences in judgement among team members. It is not that people are making personal attacks; instead, cognitive conflict is about disagreements in terms of viewpoints, ideas and opinions. If a board has selected a diverse range of directors who have complementary skill sets, cognitive conflict is both likely to happen and to be encouraged. George Patton, the US Army General during World War II, put it well: 'If everyone is thinking alike, then somebody isn't thinking.' However, for the board dynamic not to descend into relational conflict between board members, enough cohesiveness also needs to be present.

Case study: Theranos's paperweight board

You can have a perfect board on paper but in practice it may lack the ability to work effectively either through lack of clarity of purpose or an inability to challenge. The US case of Theranos shows how well-respected leaders in their fields acting as non-executive directors can fail if they lack the expertise to challenge as a director or are too trusting of the executives they are working with.

Founded in 2003 by Elizabeth Holmes, Theranos was a privately funded startup touted as a breakthrough technology company in the medical sector. It raised more than $700 million with a peak valuation of $10 billion in 2014. Its showcase board included many politically connected figures such as former US Secretaries of State Henry Kissinger and George Schultz, two US Senators, Army General James Mattis, Navy Admiral Gary Roughead and former CEOs of Bechtel Corporation and Wells

Fargo. It is very easy to notice here how none of these people had any affiliation to medical science. One of the US senators was a heart transplant surgeon, but he was spending more time on policy than medicine at the time of his appointment to the board of Theranos. Furthermore, Theranos maintained extreme secrecy in the name of protecting their proprietary technology and also seems to have maintained this secrecy when discussing the business with the board.

The company was eventually shut down and liquidated with its founder indicted for wire fraud and conspiracy. The board was publicly criticised for being composed mainly of directors with diplomatic or military backgrounds but limited board experience and an inability to challenge the day-to-day operations and reporting of the company. Their lack of diversity was also noted, being all male and with an average age of 80. Even as an advisory board, as they later claimed to be, there was an expectation that there would be at least some challenge or understanding of the business itself and the public claims that were being made.

The need for balance

The key dynamic that must exist within the board to enable it to achieve its tasks, and thus positively influence organisational performance, is a balance of cohesion and challenge.

It is therefore essential that a board can facilitate processes that engender a team mind so that the directors can trust each other to share information but also enables them to express high levels of cognitive conflict to enable appropriate challenge. Although there has been little direction on these team dynamics topics from governance governing bodies until recently, the following is now in the 2018 Financial Reporting Council's Guidance on Board Effectiveness:

The boardroom should be a place for robust debate where challenge, support, diversity of thought and teamwork are essential features. Diversity of skills, background and personal strengths is an important driver of a board's effectiveness, creating different perspectives among directors and breaking down a tendency towards 'group think'.

Case study: Google's effective teams: safety in numbers?

In 2012, Google's 'People Analytics' department (human resources) embarked on an initiative, code-named Project Aristotle, to attempt to answer the question: 'What makes a Google team effective?'

After two years, 200-plus employee interviews and crunching data from more than 250 attributes across 180-plus active Google teams, it released its findings. Although it had assumed that the key factors would be the qualifications, track-record and mix of team members, it was, in fact, the dynamics of how the team interacted that was found to be by far the most important.

Specifically, it found that effective Google teams are underpinned by a culture of 'psychological safety' – that is, their team members feel safe to take risks and be vulnerable in front of each other without feeling insecure or embarrassed. The researchers found that individuals on teams with higher psychological safety were less likely to leave Google, more likely to harness the power of diverse ideas from teammates, brought in more revenue and were rated effective twice as often by their leaders.

Following this, a short intervention was designed that included a 10-minute dynamics pulse check and report, a team conversation to discuss results and then some tailored development resources. The pulse check included the following questions (scored out of seven):

- If you make a mistake on this team, it is often held against you (reverse scored).
- Members of this team are able to bring up problems and tough issues.
- People on this team sometimes reject others for being different (reverse scored).
- It is safe to take a risk on this team.
- It is difficult to ask other members of this team for help (reverse scored).
- No one on this team would deliberately act in a way that undermines my efforts.
- Working with members of this team, my unique skills and talents are valued and utilised.

Some of the general advice from the resources included ideas such as to:

- frame the work as a learning problem, not an execution problem;
- acknowledge your own fallibility; or
- model curiosity and ask lots of questions.

The result? Over the following year, teams from Dublin to California improved their psychological safety by 6% on average.

Board team processes

This chapter has discussed the rationale for, and benefits of, the board functioning as a high-performing team and the key board outputs of cohesion and challenge. What are the more tactical processes that a board can adopt to enable it to achieve these outputs? The following three sections will begin to provide some answers to this question and we shall continue adding flesh to these bones over the following chapters.

Best practice processes for senior leadership teams

Although it seems somewhat missing the mark to consider best practice processes from senior leadership teams in a book on board dynamics, there is actually much transferrable learning that boards can take from the research on senior leadership teams. Although boards have historically been under-researched, it is quite the opposite for senior leadership teams. Further, they share many of the ten identifying characteristics discussed earlier in this chapter.

Unlike boards, senior leadership teams are not bound by a director mandate and are probably composed only of full-time 'insiders'. However, senior leadership teams, like boards, often meet episodically with severe time constraints; they need to solve complex and strategic challenges with often significant long-term consequences; they are under significant scrutiny both internally and externally to their organisation; they often work with imperfect information as more junior staff may not always want to tell them the reality of a situation; they often have high-profile members with strong, ambitious and potentially derailing personalities; and they have a role conflict issue of simultaneously being required to represent both their departmental silo and the collective senior team.

Some of the most compelling, well-regarded and practically useful research on senior leadership teams comes from Ruth Wageman et al. which is summarised in the 2008 book *Senior Leadership Teams: What it Takes to Make Them Great*. In a nine-year collaboration, Wageman's team researched more than 100 senior leadership teams from around the world, finding that only 21% of these teams were outstanding, with 37% being graded mediocre and a significant 42% being rated as poor. The research was distilled into six conditions that were required to be present for a team to be classified into this outstanding category. These six conditions included three 'essentials' and three 'enablers', which are the signature processes of the outstanding leadership teams.

The research also uncovered six key challenges that arise when a chief executive officer is contemplating their leadership. We will work through these below, noting as we progress how these challenges and conditions might also inform the development of an outstanding board process. Firstly, the three essentials.

Condition one: a real team

The first challenge for a chief executive officer is to answer the question, 'Do I want a team?' Our contention for boards is that they should always aspire to be a real team as there are significant performance benefits in being so. The research found that three things needed to be true to be a real team. Firstly, the team need to be 'bounded', that is, members must be clear who is, and who is not, part of the team. For a board, this should be relatively straightforward as a board is usually one of the most formalised group memberships that exist in organisations. A real team also needs to be stable: the team membership needs to be kept intact for some period of time. This may or may not be true of the board, depending upon the environment within which that board exists, notwithstanding compliance guidance on term lengths. However, it is useful to reflect that high-performing leadership teams are those that are more stable. Thirdly, a real team needs to be interdependent: members should share accountability for a common purpose. This finding reflects the Katzenback and Smith definition of teams discussed above. This requires the board to recognise that it is possible for non-executive directors and executive directors to work interdependently for a common purpose rather than assuming that they must be, by definition, adversarial.

Condition two: a compelling purpose

The second challenge the research found that chief executive officers face is in answering the question, 'What is the purpose of the team?' In the same way that a leadership team's purpose is not the same as the purpose of the organisation, boards must also articulate a purpose that is different from their organisation. A board must ask itself how it can express the unique added value that it may be able to bring to the organisation on behalf of the stakeholders. Therefore, the second condition that the research found needed to be true of high-performing leadership teams is the requirement for a compelling purpose. To be compelling, a purpose needs to be:

- **clear** – the purpose can be easily imagined and envisioned;
- **challenging** – it must stretch capability in order to achieve it, but not be impossible; and
- **consequential** – it must have an important impact on the success of the organisation and on the lives and work of others.

Interestingly, the researchers found that in the teams they studied, most purposes were consequential, possibly as a result of them being senior leadership team purposes at the apex of their organisation, but some were less challenging and, most significantly, not often very clear. The researchers suggested that, in order to construct a compelling purpose, senior leadership teams must make a very short list of key decisions only they can make to express their unique added value to execute the organisational strategy.

Moreover, they also concluded that it is a myth that great top teams only deal with strategic issues . Instead, they found that top teams deal with mission-critical issues, including tactical ones. As boards have a long shopping list of potential options to discuss in board meetings, but severely limited time, it seems prudent that a board similarly reflect on their compelling purpose, which will hopefully also include an associated very short list of key decisions that only they can make.

Condition three: the right people

The third challenge that a chief executive officer has, according to the findings, is to answer the question, 'Who should be on my team?' This leads to the third condition of outstanding senior leadership teams, which is to compose the team of the right people. The research indicated that well-composed teams include people who can take an enterprise-wide perspective and people who have the ability to work collaboratively, but did not include people who exhibit derailing behaviour (defined as those who undermine others, those who bring out the worst in others, those who exhibit a lack of integrity and those who are unable to see others' perspectives). These findings are very similar to those we discussed in Chapter 3, from the board director attributes quadrant, and the three Cs of competence, commitment and character.

Once the three essentials of becoming a real team – one with a compelling direction composed of the right people – are created, a senior leadership team should focus on three enablers to push them towards outstanding performance.

Condition four: solid structure

The fourth challenge that the research uncovered for senior leadership teams was that members think meetings are a waste of time. They found that this often happens when the senior leadership team is too large, the meeting purpose is ill-defined, what is on the agenda is too much and too trivial, when the process of agenda setting is simply 'What you want to talk about?' and when the meeting time is poorly structured. These issues are often very true of poorly run board meetings.

Therefore, the fourth condition for outstanding senior leadership teams is to create a solid structure. This is defined by having a senior leadership team that is the right size (quite small), having meaningful team tasks (the work members do together is vital and connected to the strategy) and there being clear norms of conduct (members understand what must always be done or not done). The research found that, although there was a small difference between poor, mediocre and outstanding teams in terms of size and meaningful tasks, ensuring the existence of a process to clarify norms was significantly higher in outstanding teams compared to the rest. This will be also true of boards, such that the board must have clear and regular processes for articulating and role modelling its collective norms and ground rules. Board meeting design characteristics and processes to ensure a solid board meeting structure are described in detail in Chapters 9 and 10, respectively.

Condition five: a supportive context

The fifth challenge that the research uncovered for chief executive officers was that their team was not always productive when working together. They found that what often gets in the way is a combination of poorly designed information systems, such as what they called the 'three-inch binder'; rewards that undermine collaboration and that provoke feelings of unfairness or a lack of trust; and a working environment that creates obstacles, such as having little workspace and time.

Therefore, the fifth condition of outstanding leadership teams is to create a supportive context. The research found that outstanding teams created rewards appropriate for team excellence that, at best, were not negative; they provided the right information in a form that could be used; they provided training and technical education to build expertise; and they provided the appropriate space, time and general environmental conditions for working together on difficult decisions. These issues are extremely relevant to boards as director reward packages are under increasing scrutiny. Furthermore, as we shall discuss in Chapter 11 on talent management, aligning rewards appropriately with collaborative organisational outcomes can be hugely important. Similarly, in this age of information overload combined with poverty of time, directors require board packs that carefully and succinctly distil the signal from the noise. Finally, as we shall discuss in detail in Chapter 9, the board working environment is also an undervalued and underused factor in influencing the board dynamic.

Condition six: team coaching

The final challenge the research found was encapsulated in their phrase that 'the team is stuck'. With all other conditions being in place, for some reason there is still no shift in performance. Outstanding teams therefore recognise the value of putting in place condition six – expert team coaching. As CEOs generally spend much of their time either structuring their team or focused on external activities, there is less time for coaching senior leadership team members, either as individuals or collectively as a team. An external coach then becomes a useful addition to the mix.

Applying this condition to boards, there is an increasing recognition that the chair of the board also needs to display the competencies of an effective team coach to help the board when they are stuck. However, it is sometimes difficult to be both a member of the board who needs to participate in discussion and also to see what is actually happening within the dynamic of the team. This is where an external team coach can be useful and may be a role that an internal individual, such as the company secretary or a senior influencer, can take to add value to the board. Similarly, a board team coach from outside the organisation could also be employed to support the board, either working with the board directly, or as the coach supervisor to the chair and/or company secretary. The skillsets and mindsets of an internal influencer acting as board team coach are discussed in detail in Chapter 14.

Wageman et al.'s research is very useful in providing a template for senior leadership teams to follow in their path towards being outstanding. In summary, if a senior leadership team follows these six conditions, including the essentials of being a real team with a compelling direction composed of the right people and the three enablers of a solid structure, supportive context and team coaching, they are much more likely to create the appropriate dynamics for high performance. As we have also discussed, the model can be translated, with the appropriate caveats, to provide guidance to boards in their journey to becoming a high-performing board team.

Best practice processes for resilient teams

A second arena of effective team process that boards can learn lessons from are high-performing teams from sport. There have been some interesting findings from research on resilient teams that have come out of Loughborough University in the UK in the last few years, which are especially relevant to boards in light of the increasing demands on board directors. As we discussed in Chapter 3, one of the twenty-first-century board director competencies that is likely to become increasingly required is resilience. Research from Morgan et al. in 2013 and 2015 dissected a sample of 31 elite sports team members over five team sports and found that there are consistent characteristics of highly resilient teams.

Although the findings do share some similarities with individual resilience research, which we shall discuss in detail in Chapter 15, resilience at a group level seems to be more than the sum of a collection of resilient individuals. Three themes emerge from the data. Firstly, resilient teams all spent time articulating clear team vision, purpose, values and norms. Secondly, resilient teams have high levels of 'social capital' – that is, they have a strong and cohesive identity which facilitates high levels of social support and interaction. Interestingly, the research didn't find that they have equal levels of mutual team challenge, probably as the external adversity and challenge was such that this didn't need to be amplified internally within the team. Finally, an overarching theme was that learning orientation and team resilience are intertwined such that resilient teams regard the role of learning as being vital.

Reflecting on these results, in light of effective processes that boards may use, it is again clear that resilient boards will also be those who (like both the Dulewicz and Wageman examples mentioned earlier) spend time on the tasks of defining a compelling and shared vision, purpose and norms, as well as building cohesive relationships within an environment where continual learning is taken for granted.

Case study: Resilience on the rugby pitch

One resilient high-performing sports team that the research studied was Sir Clive Woodward's World Cup-winning English Rugby Union team. His testimony suggests that the cultivation of team resilience processes are pivotal over time in protecting teams from a broad range of negative consequences that they may encounter. As Woodward revealed in an interview as part of the research:

> Our success has not been a continual series of victories. We have had a number of devastating setbacks; how these are handled is the mark of a great team... It has been against all odds, but winning does not happen in a straight line.

Best practice processes for board teams

The last two sections provided some detail around the behavioural process best practices from the theory and practice of teams. This section will now turn its attention specifically to the information that currently exists on what boards need to focus on behaviourally in terms of their dynamics. It is important to note that there is not much information currently available to chairs, directors, company secretaries and others to inform them on what board dynamics best practice looks like. However, interest is developing. Here we will provide a flavour of the information that does exist across different sectors and industries including a Chartered Governance Institute report, some quantitative academic research and some more qualitative observation research from the NHS.

In June 2009, The Chartered Governance Institute prepared a report called Boardroom Behaviours for Sir David Walker who was leading the Walker review of corporate governance in the UK finance industry following its collapse two years earlier. This report gathered a range of expert views from their colleagues and advisers operating in the boardrooms of major UK companies, including a significant contribution from company secretaries operating in the financial services sector, as well as representatives from other sectors.

Effective boardroom behaviours

One overall key conclusion through the consultation was that boardroom best practice is characterised by the following behaviours:

- a supportive decision-making environment;
- a clear understanding of the role of the board;
- a common vision;
- the questioning of assumptions and established orthodoxy;
- rigorous debate;
- the appropriate deployment of knowledge, skills, experience and judgement;
- independent thinking;
- challenge which is constructive, confident, principled and proportionate; and
- the achievement of closure on individual items of board business.

It is interesting to note that the first three behaviours all contribute to increased team cohesiveness and identity, whereas the final six behaviours arise from expressed cognitive conflict and are more challenging. Not surprisingly, perhaps, as the report was compiled just after some significant corporate failures, the ratio of challenge to cohesion in the list is 2:1.

Just after the Institute report, which focused on listed companies, came out, some academic research on unlisted companies, led by Duncan Neill and Victor Dulewicz from Henley Business School, was also published in the 2010 *Corporate Governance* journal.

This research, entitled 'Inside the black box: the performance of boards of directors of unlisted companies', used a board effectiveness questionnaire to gather views from 67 directors across a range of sectors. The research synthesised data on how directors perceived how their board currently operated and how they thought it should operate, thus providing both information on the boardroom behaviours that directors would most like to see and also the biggest gaps in behaviours which have an impact on board effectiveness. The top five strongest preferences for aspirational board behaviours were as follows:

1. Directors are keen and free to ask questions.
2. Board is willing to take tough decisions.
3. Shared ownership, a vision, mission and values
4. Personal relationships are harmonious.
5= Board knows exactly how it adds value to the business.
5= The board operates as a cohesive team.
5= High level of candour and openness.

Further, the behaviour with the highest ranked gap between current and future board performance, the greatest 'process loss' for board performance, was found to be the quality of team relationships.

A final resource worthy of mention here is the NHS Confederation's 2005 report, entitled 'Effective boards in the NHS? A study of their behaviour and culture'. This study was based on extensive interviews with board members and observations of 12 board meetings from a cross-section of NHS organisations. The research identified four characteristic dynamics of effective boards in terms of their behavioural processes. These were:

- a focus on strategic decision making;
- board members who trust each other and act cohesively and behave corporately;
- constructive challenge by board members of each other; and
- effective chairs who ensure meetings with clear and effective processes.

Unfortunately, the research and observations of board meetings also revealed that 'boards often fall short of members' expectations and ideals'. For example, although there appeared to be high levels of trust within many of the boards, they suggest that some of the boards they observed had arguably too high a level of trust. This meant that 'executives rarely challenge each other in public board meetings and often kept their contribution to their functional responsibility'. However, the report also observed that, when challenge did occur, it was unfortunately often done in an ineffective way and then 'overlooked or dismissed in subtle ways – often by simply moving the agenda on without fully responding to the points raised'.

Although not directly part of this research, the NHS's National Leadership Council has produced a useful guide on improving board performance entitled 'Governing the NHS: A Guide to NHS Boards' (2003).

Reflecting on all the information presented from both the board and broader team evidence base on best practice behavioural processes, we can see that there are many repeating patterns. Governing well clearly requires for a cohesive and challenging boardroom dynamic underpinned by a number of behavioural processes.

Firstly – and as we shall cover in more depth in Chapter 6 – the dynamic will include trusting board and stakeholder relationships as well as effective challenging, but not conflicting, dialogue. Secondly, as we shall discuss in Chapters 7 and 8, there must exist a board culture of learning and inclusion. Thirdly, as we shall discuss in Chapter 9, a supportive context must be put in place. Finally, as we shall now turn to in the next chapter, the board also needs to attend to how it manages itself in order to support better board decision making.

Conclusion

Board dynamics is the most vital aspect to understand and positively influence for successful governance outcomes. It can be defined and understood through a psychological lens.

What is the difference between board dynamics and boardroom dynamics? Boardroom dynamics refers to the interactions between board members individually and collectively in the boardroom and, in particular, what the balance is between them being cohesive and challenging. Board dynamics, meanwhile, includes this definition but also considers how the internal boardroom dynamics influence and are influenced by their wider stakeholder system external to the board. Thus, board dynamics also incorporates the broader topics of culture and systemic stakeholder engagement.

A key concept to understanding dynamics is using the idea of boards as teams. Boards are a specific type of group with unique characteristics and the potential to function as high-performing teams. They have tasks and outcomes that will ultimately require them to balance the opposing forces of cohesion and challenge. Boards can learn how to improve their dynamics through understanding the processes of well researched high-performing senior leadership teams and resilient sports teams, in addition to recent board specific guidance.

There now exist many providers of team assessments that enable directors to understand the dynamics at play within their board, the role that they may be playing and the best way to enhance their interactions with fellow directors. This can counter the egocentric perspective that one individual is greater or better than the board as a whole – a characteristic that is all too frequently seen at board level. This heroic leadership style may work in limited contexts, such as in particularly entrepreneurial businesses, but certainly does not support the development of an effective team-orientated board of directors delivering longer-term sustainable success.

Does your board function as a high-performing team?

5 – Board decision making

Board decision making: an overview

Boardroom decision making is the ultimate outcome and measure of boardroom dynamics. In The Chartered Governance Institute's July 2018 Guidance on Board Effectiveness, the section on decision making begins with the following:

> Well-informed and high-quality decision making does not happen by accident. Many of the factors that lead to poor decisions are predictable and preventable. Boards can minimise the risk of poor decisions by investing time in the design of their decision-making policies and processes, including the contribution of committees and obtaining input from key stakeholders and expert opinions when necessary.

As mentioned in Chapter 4, the third and final gear in Hawkins' framework for boardroom meeting conversations after scrutiny and strategising is decision making. Similarly, in Pick's (2007) research on boards in action, decision making was recorded as the fourth but most important type of board activity, revealing most about board dynamics compared to a board's other activities of learning, evaluating and advising. If this gear of decision making ultimately decides the output of board conversations, then how much do directors actually know about, reflect upon or indeed spend time improving the psychological processes underlying it?

In recent years, the research and popular literature following after it on decision making, especially in the management genre, has exploded. Much of this has focused on individual decision making, but there is also a significant amount that relates to teams and groups which is highly applicable to the boardroom context.

Historically, the field on decision making was underpinned by the idea that the best decision making was done logically, linearly and rationally. For example, the early thought leader in the field, Herbert Simon, argued that decision making had three phases:

- **intelligence**, defined as 'searching the environment for conditions calling for a decision';
- **design**, defined as 'inventing, developing and analysing possible courses of action'; and
- **choice**, defined as 'selecting a particular course of action from those available'.

However, a significant shift in decision-making science occurred through the Nobel Prize-winning work of Kahneman and Tversky as applied to economics. Their work highlighted the difference between the rational decision-making models of economics and what has come to be known as 'behavioural economics': an economics that works practically in the real world with real people in real populations, one that is predictably irrational and hugely impacted by both individual psychology and group social dynamics.

Directors now need to appreciate boardroom decision making through this more modern behavioural lens. The psychological challenges of making good governance decisions, and the potential solutions on offer, are those that we all face as decision-making individuals which multiply across a group. However, there are also emergent collective decision-making issues, such as groupthink (which we touched on in Chapter 4), that are specific to the board as a whole.

It is interesting to note that it is possible to analyse boardroom decision making in terms of either its process or its outcome. For example, it is quite possible to have a good decision-making process that leads to a bad governance outcome. Equally, it is possible to have bad decision-making processes that lead to good governance outcomes. The focus here, however, is more on the process, as the outcome is often the result of wider, perhaps less controllable, systemic forces (which we shall consider in Chapter 6). One practical application of this in relation to boards is in the Delaware Court, which is the setting for most US corporate trials. IT relies on something called the Business Judgement Rule to make rulings about board outcomes. This rule evaluates not whether boards have made the right decision but whether they are seen to have taken the appropriate steps and demonstrated a reasonable process that facilitated good business judgement.

Evidence-based boards

In research that looked at the top 20 CEO competencies, as judged by other directors, 'decisiveness' was ranked a clear number one (Dulewicz and Gay, 1997). This finding is similar to what the rest of the workforce, or indeed the rest of modern society, might commonly value in organisational leadership. At the top of our organisations, we expect, and are drawn to, leaders who are able to make many decisions quickly and with confidence. Speed and conviction are often more important than quality. We believe that confidence and certainty are the same thing, whereas the best leaders, and the best decision makers, are often capable of being both confident and uncertain at the same time. In the above research, 'critical faculty' and 'problem analysis' were (worryingly) ranked last and next-to-last in the list.

One of the key leadership criteria in decision making, however, is the ability to say the words 'I'm not sure', or even, heaven forbid, 'I don't know'. Those leadership skills that we often overvalue such as charisma, expertise, speed and control are actually those that lead to problems in decision making on boards. However, the more undervalued skills such as humility, collaboration, empathy and listening are hugely important for developing more able decision making.

An important recent approach to decision making is that of 'evidence-based practice'. The assumption behind this methodology is that decisions about important problems or opportunities and their likely solutions should be based on the best available evidence. We all use evidence in decision making but the contention of evidence-based practice is that we often limit ourselves in the attention paid to the quality and relevance of evidence and also the amount of evidence sources. Using evidence in general is not the same as adopting an evidence-based approach.

Evidence-based practice originated in the early 1990s in medicine with the recognition that all practice should be as up-to-date and rigorous as possible. When we visit our GP, for example, we would not want them just to rely on their original training, perhaps undertaken decades ago. Nor do we want them to rely solely on any test results that they had observed on our condition. We would also want them to use the latest research evidence, their years of professional expertise, their understanding of our particular health history and their knowledge of the incidence of local illnesses, as well as a variety of other factors. An evidence-based practice approach has increasingly been used in education, the probation service, in housing policy, in social care, in criminal justice and, more recently, in management. In parallel, a number of think-tanks and organisations have emerged to support this practice, for example, the Centre for Evidence-Based Management (www.cebma.org).

One definition of evidence-based practice is the 'conscientious (effort), explicit (clarity) and judicious (critical and quality) use of the best available evidence from multiple sources to increase the likelihood of a favourable outcome'. As mentioned above, it is about a process rather than about a certain outcome (or, as is unfortunately often the case, cherry-picking evidence to support a particular outcome) and it is about reducing uncertainty given a particular context.

The first step is to recognise the multiple sources of evidence that we are (or are not) drawing from. Evidence-based practice defines four sources. Firstly, it acknowledges that professional expertise is not to be ignored and should indeed be drawn on. Although this is sometimes the only thing that board members might draw upon, it is a key primary resource. However, rather than acting upon just one voice, we know that forecasts or risk assessments based on the average professional experience of many people are more accurate than those based on one person's personal experience.

Secondly, an increasingly recognised and used source of evidence is internal organisational data. In this increasingly digital world, the opportunities to collect and apply data to decision making are expanding rapidly. Terms such as 'big data', 'artificial intelligence' and 'machine learning' have found their way into more boardroom conversations in recent years. This is important, as we know that professional judgements based on data, for example, are more accurate than judgements based solely on individual experience.

Thirdly, research evidence provides an often underused and vital source of information to bring into the boardroom. Sourcing the most up-to-date scientific or academic evidence is important, as a large number of studies indicate that this is more accurate than the opinions of multiple experts. More broadly, a decision based on the combination of critically appraised experiential, organisational and scientific evidence yields better outcomes than one based on any single source of evidence.

Case study: The pitfalls of financial incentives

There are many cases of knowledge based on 'best practices' that just don't work, have no impact or completely backfire in real life. One such example is the universally held belief that financial incentives, such as generous stock options, drive company performance – a belief which an avalanche of research evidence simply does not support. Rewards can be used to provide recognition and to share the company success with its employees, but when used to drive performance, can incentivise wrong, and often unethical, behaviours.

In one large retail organisation, the sales force had historically received individual bonuses for selling more products. This had created a culture of infighting, low morale, poor innovation, inappropriate customer service and ultimately poor sales figures. After some soul-searching, the organisation decided to move to a more team-based reward structure, which led to a number of resignations from the 'best' (read: most aggressive) salespeople. This initially led to the change being reconsidered; however, after sticking it out for a few more months, overall morale and employee engagement increased significantly, and overall sales also followed suit.

On the other side of the coin, at senior executive levels, there are many examples of incentive schemes that have ultimately been the downfall of an organisation. The classic case of Enron, for example, could in some ways be put down to an ungoverned incentive scheme that promoted systemic unethical shortcuts. Instead of their rewards being large enough to reinforce, celebrate and recognise the behaviour rewarded, or indeed for them to enable employees to share in successes, they became so large that they began to drive, control and therefore distort behaviour.

The fourth and final source of evidence to be drawn from in the evidence-based practice approach is that of the local context, more specifically the key stakeholders and their values and concerns. This is vital as decision making is not, as has already been discussed, simply a conceptual exercise. It is a process which is inherently practical and must be based in the real world. An approach may be backed up by all the organisational data, may be a best practice that has worked elsewhere in a variety of other organisations and may be in line with the latest cutting-edge thinking, but it might still not work in the current context. Understanding the answer to what will work in this situation, at this time, under our particular circumstances, is a key final piece of the puzzle with which to make an effective evidence-based decision.

Evidence-based practice also recommends a six-step process which provides a lens through which to make decisions using the four evidence sources. These steps are:

1 **asking:** translating a practical issue or problem into an answerable question;
2 **acquiring:** systematically searching for and retrieving the evidence;
3 **appraising:** critically judging the trustworthiness and relevance of the evidence;
4 **aggregating:** weighing and pulling together the evidence;
5 **applying:** incorporating evidence into the decision-making process; and
6 **assessing:** evaluating the outcome of the decision taken.

Following this evidence-based process will therefore lead to an increasing likelihood of a favourable outcome.

Cognitive bias

If we know that an evidence-based board will perform better on decision making than a less evidence-based board, why do individual board members and boards as a whole struggle with the decision-making process?

The Financial Reporting Council's Guidance on Board Effectiveness (2018) recognises that 'most complex decisions depend on judgement, but the decisions of well-intentioned and experienced leaders can, in certain circumstances, be distorted'. One could go one step further and suggest that 'in certain circumstances' could read 'in most circumstances'.

Many studies in recent years have illustrated the difficulty of assessing evidence and arguments objectively. For example, research shows that our brains often treat opinions we agree with as facts; that many of us (especially in senior leadership positions) overestimate our knowledge (the 'Dunning-Kruger effect'); that we often see our own theories as accurate and as 'the truth'; and, unfortunately, that when the facts appear to contradict our current beliefs, we turn to the use of unfalsifiable arguments. Why does this happen? Simply put, as both individuals and groups, we are evolved to be biased.

This is a significant issue for boards, as Oliver Manet from Exeter University Business School has researched. In his article entitled 'Bias in the boardroom: effects of bias on the quality of board decision making', Manet (2010) concludes that:

- bias in the boardroom is inevitable and frequently underestimated;
- bias plays a significant role in board decision making;

- bias particularly undermines the perceived benefits of independent directors; and
- governance regulation needs to emphasise the effects of bias on decision-making and mandate the use of de-biasing procedures.

What exactly is bias? Bias arises due to the two different ways that we think, described as System One and System Two thinking. System One thinking is fast, emotional, low effort, automatic and unconscious. This is the method of thinking we use to brush our teeth, to drive our usual route home and to joke with our friends. System Two thinking, however, is slow, effortful, conscious and deliberate. We engage this system when we learn a new skill, talk in a second non-fluent language and when we park in a tight parking space. We are hardwired to make System One decisions, which is useful for most everyday decisions, but unfortunately not so good for larger, more complicated and more important decisions such as those that are often expected within a board context. The very benefit of System One thinking – that is, its ability to make up contextual stories to provide an energy-efficient and constant representation of the world around us – is its ultimate flaw. Unfortunately, there are notable exceptions to the mental shortcuts that System One thinking uses. In the literature, these have been termed 'cognitive bias'.

Types of bias

More than 180 biases or heuristics are known to influence our System One thinking. Some of the most well-known biases and how they may affect board director decision-making are as follows:

- **Groupthink:** coined by Janis (1982) – and very pertinent to boards – as the 'overriding desire for consensus and unanimity, leading to poor decision making, in cohesive groups due to suppression of internal dissent and consequent inadequate evaluation'.
- **Confirmation bias:** our tendency to interpret and search for information consistent with our prior beliefs, discounting contrary evidence.
- **Anchoring effect:** our tendency to rely too heavily on, or to overemphasise, one trait or piece of information (often the first piece of information presented to us).
- **Hindsight bias:** our tendency to see past events as being more predictable than they were before the event occurred and therefore to believe that events in the future are more predictable than they are.
- **Availability bias:** our tendency to make decisions influenced by events or experiences that immediately come to mind or are easily accessible.
- **Loss aversion:** our tendency to prefer avoiding losses rather than acquiring gains.
- **Sunk cost fallacy:** our tendency not to accept our decisions as wrong and therefore to throw good money after bad.

- **Framing effect:** our tendency to draw different conclusions from exactly the same information presented in different ways – for example, would you prefer an 85% fat-free meal or a 15% fat meal?
- **Metacognitive bias:** our tendency to believe we are immune from all the above biases.

A full list can be found online as part of what is known as the Cognitive Bias Codex.

> You have five seconds to answer the following:
>
> A bat and ball cost one pound and ten pence. The bat costs a pound more than the ball. How much does the ball cost?
>
> Take a quick moment to think about your answer before you read on...
>
> Many people answer that the ball must cost ten pence. Was this the answer that you came up with? Although this is an answer that rapidly and intuitively springs to mind, it is not correct. The correct answer is that the ball costs five pence and the bat costs, at a pound more, £1.05p for a grand total of £1.10p. This is an example of how our System One fast thinking can be led astray.

Mitigating bias

The question therefore arises: what is to be done about these biases? It is inherently and paradoxically difficult to notice bias in yourself as it is emerging from your unconscious System One thinking.

The power of decision making in groups is that it affords us the opportunity to notice and point out flaws in thinking in others. Kahneman, Lovallo and Sibony, in their *Harvard Business Review* article 'Before you make that big decision', propose that executives should spend as much time reviewing the process of decisions as they do in reviewing and discussing the content. In order to do this, they walk through a 12-question checklist to quality control any decision-making process in order to unearth defects in thinking (you may notice some of the biases in the list above being referenced). The checklist breaks down into three categories: questions decision makers should ask themselves; questions they should use to challenge those proposing a course of action; and questions to evaluate the proposal. These are as follows.

Category one: ask yourself

1. Check for self-interested biases.
   Is there any reason to suspect the team making the recommendation of errors motivated by self-interest?
   Remedy – review the proposal with extra care, especially for over-optimism.

2. Check for the affect heuristic.
   Has the team fallen in love with its proposal?
   Remedy – rigorously apply all the quality controls on the checklist.
3. Check for groupthink.
   Were there dissenting opinions within the team? Were they explored adequately?
   Remedy – solicit dissenting views, discreetly if necessary.

Category two: ask the recommenders

4. Check for salience and bias.
   Could the diagnosis be overly influenced by an analogy to a memorable success?
   Remedy – ask for more analogies and rigorously analyse their similarity to the current situation.
5. Check for confirmation bias.
   Are credible alternatives included along with the recommendation?
   Remedy – request additional options.
6. Check for availability bias.
   If you had to make this decision again in a year's time, what information would you want and can you get more of it now?
   Remedy – use checklists of the data needed for each kind of decision.
7. Check for anchoring bias.
   Do you know where the numbers came from? Can there be unsubstantiated numbers, extrapolation from history, a motivation to use a certain anchor?
   Remedy – re-anchor with figures generated by other models or benchmarks and request new analysis.
8. Check the halo effect.
   Is the team assuming that a person, organisation or approach that is successful in one area will be just as successful in another?
   Remedy – eliminate false inferences and ask the team to seek additional comparable examples.
9. Check for some cost fallacy, endowment effect.
   Are the recommenders overly attached to a history of past decisions?
   Remedy – consider the issue as if you are a new CEO.

Category three: ask about the proposal

10. Check for overconfidence, planning fallacy, optimistic biases, competitor neglect.
    Is the base case overly optimistic?
    Remedy – have a team built a case taking an outside view; use war games.
11. Check for disaster neglect.
    Is the worst case bad enough?

Remedy – have the team conduct a pre-mortem; imagine that the worst has happened and develop a story about the causes.

12. Check for loss aversion.

    Is the recommending team overly cautious?

    Remedy – realign incentives to share responsibility for the risk or to remove risk.

The contention is that using this checklist of questions will raise awareness of any inherent System One bias, so that it can be minimised within a group and organisational decision-making context.

Although this list may be a useful tool in general with boards, there are some specific considerations that boards may consider to minimise bias in decision making. The FRC recommends some key steps (as summarised by Brendan, 2013).

- Executives should put their case at earlier stages, well in advance of the point of decision, so that directors have the opportunity and the time to share concerns and to challenge assumptions.
- Inform boards of the pre-boardroom processes adopted to arrive at management proposals.
- Inform boards of the pre-boardroom processes to challenge management proposals.
- Commission independent review of management proposals.
- Seek advice from experts.
- Take large decisions in stages. For example: firstly concept, secondly proposal for discussion, thirdly proposal for decision.
- Introduce processes that allow time for reflection.
- Consider the possibility that it might be the wrong decision.
- Find reasons not to agree with management's proposals.
- Allocate different roles within boards.
- Deliberately introduce a devil's advocate to provide challenge.
- Introduce automatic stops in decision making in the form of circuit breakers, mental breakers or calling timeouts (an increasingly common feature of surgical theatres).
- Establish a sole purpose committee; convene additional meetings.
- Record the pros and cons of the decision in the meeting minutes
- Remove management more quickly after problems emerge.

Individual differences in relation to decision making

In addition to an appreciation of the various cognitive biases and how to remedy them in a board context, it may also be useful to understand individual personality differences in styles that emerge within any group environment. Over the last 100 years, psychology has invested great efforts in categorising individual behaviours and there are various methodologies and tools that have been used to do this. For example, the Big Five personality traits, mentioned in Chapter 3 and also known as the Five Factor Model, are a classic taxonomy for describing why people do what they do. The five factors have been defined as openness to experience, conscientiousness, extroversion, agreeableness and neuroticism. How an individual scores on each of these personality traits provide some information on their approach to decision making. For example, those with low scores on openness to experience are characterised as pragmatic and data-driven, but can sometimes be perceived as dogmatic and close-minded. A higher score on conscientiousness reveals that someone is more likely to be efficient and organised, show self-discipline and act dutifully. High agreeableness, although having a tendency to be compassionate and co-operative, traits useful in any group setting, may be evidenced by a lack of comfort with, or confidence in, challenging others.

There are many personality measures that can be purchased in the marketplace. These have varying applications and also levels of validity, so care should be taken and evidence should be considered when selecting one to use. Some of the best known of these are the Myers Briggs Type Inventory (MBTI), the Insights profile, FIRO-B and the various Hogan inventories. The MBTI was developed by Isabel Myers and Katherine Briggs as an application of Carl Jung's theory of psychological types. His theory was that we have opposite ways of gaining energy (extroversion or introversion), gathering or becoming aware of information (sensing or intuition), deciding or committing to a conclusion about that information (thinking or feeling) and dealing with the world around us (judging or perceiving).

The theory proposes that we all use each of these eight parts of our personality, but we prefer one in each area, in the same way that we have a natural preference for using one hand rather than the other. Therefore, our MBTI ends up being one of 16 combinations of our four preferences, such as ESTJ or INFP. The 'thinking versus feeling' preference is especially relevant in terms of decision making. The thinking preference means that one may have a tendency to make decisions mainly using logical, objective analysis, whereas the feeling preference may tend to make decisions to create harmony and by applying person-centred values.

If you know your own score on any the factors, you may then be able to moderate the extremes of your personality traits in a group environment. Knowing the personality traits of others may similarly enable you to moderate your response to someone else's decision making, or, at the very least, become aware and more open to diverse ways of thinking. Rather than thinking that a colleague is being either incompetent or plain awkward, you may be able to recognise that they are just being different due to their preference or style.

Case study: The importance of MTBI diversity

Working with a particular leadership team, it was demonstrated that their 'average' MBTI personality was ESTJ. There was a higher prevalence of extroverts to introverts, sensors to intuitives, thinkers to feelers and judging types to perceivers.

In MBTI terms, this is neither a good nor a bad thing, but is likely to have consequences for how that group will work together. In terms of decision making, out of the group of 12, there was only one person with a feeling preference. In light of the discussion above about System One bias, this might initially seem like a good thing. However, it became clear that over the past six months this one person had been incredibly important, not in their use of emotion in decision making as was initially thought by the group, but in their consideration of how people might feel in relation to some significant decisions that that organisation was making.

In essence, the person had a greater sense of empathy than their peers and this was incredibly useful in bringing key information into their people-related decision making.

There is one personality trait measure that specifically looks at individual differences in decision making, called the Decision Style model. This tool uses two distinct preferences that individuals may show. Firstly, the preference for either a uni-focus or a multi-focus in terms of solution finding, that is, those with a uni-focus typically come up with one specific solution that they feel is best or most feasible whereas others, faced with the same situation, quite predictably will generate a variety of alternatives for dealing with the situation.

Secondly, the model distinguishes between what are known as 'maximisers' and 'satisficers'. Maximisers are those who prefer to know almost 100% of the information possible before making a decision and taking action. They are often perfectionists and when, for example, they read a restaurant menu, they will need to know everything that is on it, including the specials for that day. Satisficers, however, are happy reaching conclusions with relatively fewer facts. They will make a decision when they have reached a certain threshold of information: for example, using the restaurant situation, if they fancy fish for dinner they will be happy picking the first fish dish that they come across.

The Decision Styles model combines these characteristics into four decision-making types: the 'decisive' (uni-satisficer) who is fast, action-orientated and efficiency minded; the 'flexible' (multi-satisficer) who is fast, action orientated, yet adaptable; the 'hierarchic' (uni-maximiser) who is an analytical, methodological, logical and focuses on quality; and the 'integrative' (multi-maximiser) who is analytical, exploratory and creative. A fifth type, the 'systemic', who is a maximiser combined with both a uni-dimensional and multi-dimensional focus, is also part of the model. This person is analytical, comprehensive and prioritises solution strategies. Again, like the MBTI, one can measure one's type using commercial online questionnaires. There is no one best style, as each has its own merits depending upon the circumstances.

For example, it has been noted that maximisers tend to struggle when there are multiple options. In a novel and now-famous experiment in consumer decision-making theory, researchers placed a selection of new jam products at the end of the supermarket aisle. On one day they offered a choice of 24 different kinds of jam and then another day, at the same place at the same time, people were given only six different types of jam to choose. It was found that, while the table display with more choice generated more interest, people were much less likely to buy a jar of jam compared to the display with the smaller range of choice. Incredibly, the smaller display generated about ten times the sales of the larger display, highlighting that, for many of us, choice often paralyses decision making, especially for maximisers for whom wide choice can be incredibly stressful.

Thus, in the boardroom, there is a balance to be struck between providing enough options for a nuanced director debate with the likelihood that individual directors, let alone a whole board, will be able to agree confidently on one option over others in a timely manner.

Decision-making tools

As mentioned at the start of this chapter, there are many resources that can aid better decision making. Here are three approaches out of many that are evidence-based, acknowledge human bias and fallibility and are also very practical. These may be approaches to try out in a boardroom or committee setting, or at the very least, to educate directors in some of the common approaches to improve decision-making.

The WRAP framework

This framework is a summary of the extremely accessible 2013 book on decision making entitled *Decisive: How to Make Better Choices in Life and Work* from Chip and Dan Heath, two US researchers, teachers and best-selling authors who have consulted for Nike, Philips, Microsoft, Ideo and the American Heart Association among others. The book includes many stories of decision making, bringing the latest research to life and includes questions to ask, discussions to lead, exercises to try and thought experiments to conduct. Their WRAP framework is an acronym summarising their approach, which includes the following:

Widen your options

The aim of this set of seven tools is to break out of a narrow frame and expand the set of options that are being considered.

For example, there is the simple technique of finding someone who has solved your problem previously. The authors suggest spending 20 minutes doing an internet search using three to four keywords that relate to a particular decision.

They appreciate that this sounds simple but cite a study in medicine which found that 58% of diagnostic cases in the *New England Journal of Medicine* (which were selected because they involved difficult clinical diagnoses) were solved using this methodology.

Reality-test your assumptions

The aim of this set of eight tools is to fight confirmation bias and ensure that, when you are assessing options, you are gathering information that you can trust.

For example, use the tool of asking what the authors call 'disconfirming questions'. So instead of asking for advice using questions such as 'What do you think?' or 'Do you like the idea?' ask a disconfirming question such as 'What is the biggest obstacle you see to what we are trying to do?' or 'If we failed, why do you think it would be?'

Attain some distance before deciding

The aim of this set of six tools is to resist the disrupting influence of short-term emotion and ensure that you make a decision based on your core priorities. For example, the authors cite the 10/10/10 rule to enable people to obtain a short, medium and long-term view on any decision. This technique involves considering the decision and asking three questions about it:

- How will we feel about it 10 minutes from now?
- How about 10 months from now?
- How about 10 years from now?

The perspective gained, especially from the second and third questions, enables the decision maker to notice how much emotion is invested in the decision and to evaluate how important this is.

Tangentially, this is also why the sale of all retail financial products have to incorporate a cooling-off period and the ability to cancel with no penalty after further consideration.

Prepare to be wrong

The aim of this set of six tools is to avoid being overconfident about the way our decisions will unfold – instead taking the opportunity to plan for both good and bad potential scenarios.

For example, the authors suggest running a pre-mortem and a pre-parade. The idea of a pre-mortem is to imagine a future, perhaps a year from now, in which the decision has become a disaster. The decision makers are then asked individually to brainstorm why this disaster has occurred and then to share ideas. Then decision makers are asked to imagine the opposite scenario within which the decision has led to a huge success. Again, they are asked individually and then collectively to consider why that had been the case. This type of polarised thinking often helps groups surface some initially unconsidered key issues.

Complex decision making

In his 2016 book *Managing in the Gray*, Joseph L. Badaracco, a professor of business ethics at Harvard Business School, approaches the difficulties of decision making at very senior levels in organisations. He describes how the complex decisions that are encountered by senior leaders do not have clear right or wrong answers or consequences. They are essentially 'gray area' problems. To make decisions within this context, he suggests five key questions that are distilled from his research on great decision making over the ages. These questions are visualised as a funnel, which includes greater options at the top of the funnel with the initial questions, but narrows over time as you reach the final questions in his checklist. The questions to manage complex, grey areas are as follows:

1. **What are the consequences of all our options?**
   This question is about analysing the winners and the losers of the decision and essentially taking an evidence-based view, as described earlier.
2. **What are my core obligations?**
   This question is extremely apt in relation to boardroom and director duties. To what extent are decision makers aware not only of their governance and fiduciary duties, but also their duties as agreed in their particular role as either a non-executive or executive member of the board?
3. **What will work in the world as it is?**
   The wording from this question is actually taken from the writings of Machiavelli and considers how practical the options may be. Within this increasingly volatile, uncertain, complex and ambiguous world, what will work?
4. **Who are we?**
   This question asks decision makers to consider the core values of the organisation and even perhaps the core values of the board more specifically. The recognition of core values in relation to organisational culture is becoming increasingly important within governance thinking and this question is a useful simple check to remind decision makers of this.
5. **What can I live with?**
   This final question highlights the fact that the five questions start by considering a decision very much from an organisational director role perspective, but ultimately concludes with the need to resolve it as a human being. It reminds us that great decision making is not just about applying an algorithm, but also about carefully and judiciously harnessing judgement.

Gender differences in decision making

The topic of diversity is obviously a significant one in governance and boardrooms (see Chapter 8), especially in relation to the ratios of women on boards. In terms of boardroom decision made with this perspective in mind, one general conclusion from the literature is that men and women are essentially similar in how they make good and bad decisions.

However, there is one key difference on the continuum of decisiveness versus collaboration. On average, research suggests that male senior leaders are more decisive decision makers – that is, they make quicker decisions and are more confident in articulating and implementing them than women. However, women are, on average, much more likely to involve others in decision making, which may naturally slow down decisions but equally enhance both their evidence base and the engagement of those who are to implement them. All the commentary so far in this chapter points to the benefit of taking a more collaborative approach both to increase analysis and to reduce bias.

This would suggest that there is a performance benefit, certainly in terms of effective decision making, of women being involved with, or indeed leading, decision-making processes at senior levels in organisations.

Case study: Gender bias laid bare

While the characteristics that are on average associated with female leaders may be of benefit in making decisions at board level, women are unfortunately much more likely to be harshly judged when involved with decisions that have gone wrong. For example, a Yale School of Management study of gender stereotypes evaluated how women were viewed when they made mistakes in traditionally male occupations.

Participants were given a fictional news story about a police chief who was preparing for a large protest rally. In one version of the story, the protest got out of hand and not enough police cars were sent, leading to 25 people being injured. When asked how they would rate this police chief, it mattered to participants whether this person was male or female. In the male example, the leader ratings dropped by around 10%; however, in the female police chief example, who made exactly the same mistake, competence ratings dropped by almost 30%. Participants also wanted to demote the female police chief but did not want to demote the male police chief.

In another version of the story, enough police cars were sent to quell the protest so that no one was injured. In this version, both male and female leaders were given equally high marks. This was taken as evidence that the issue was not that female leaders are not perceived to be unable to lead well in traditionally male environments in general but were instead only perceived to be incompetent when they experienced failure.

Beyond these actual or perceived differences in male versus female decision making, both men and women can benefit from a similar toolkit to help them make better decisions. Here are seven recommendations made by Therese

Huston, author of the 2016 book *How Women Decide: What's True, What's Not, and What Strategies Spark the Best Choices*, that arise from her research:

1 **Increase the options that are considered:** Often decisions are taken between what seem to be only two options, shall we do something or not. This is in fact only one option. Instead, increasing the actual options to three or more will significantly improve the quality of decision making.
2 **Increase one's distance from a decision:** Doing some simple things like sleeping on a decision, making it after lunch rather than just before when you are hungry or simply waiting 15 minutes may change the quality of thinking in an individual decision. For example, in one somewhat worrying study it was found that a parole board was much more likely to grant parole to inmates after lunch, compared to before lunch when they were rushing due to being hungry.
3 **Moderate your confidence:** Recognise that it is possible to moderate your confidence levels and that it is prudent to do this. For example, in general it is useful to turn down your confidence before and during decision making (to reduce the likelihood of bias and increase the chances of collaboration) but, once a decision has been made, it is then reasonable to ratchet up one's confidence in order to ensure that the decision is clearly communicated and effectively executed.
4 **Take time to explore assumptions:** Ask the question, 'What would have to be true for this option to be the best choice?'
5 **Recognise and counter the reasons for individual or group indecisiveness:** Indecisiveness can be linked to things that are happening in the moment, for example stress levels. If this is the case, recognise this and put in place coping mechanisms to reduce the stress and create psychological safety. However, if indecisiveness is linked to personality traits, then recognise that it may not be about creating a solution as much as compensating for this by recognising and balancing personality traits within a group setting. Indecisiveness as a trait can be useful – for example, in conversations regarding risk – but it is obviously important not to become paralysed by this personality style.
6 **Step out of your own shoes:** Find some mechanisms to look in on your decision from the third person to create greater objectivity. For example, ask the question, 'If I was advising a friend on this decision, what would I suggest to do?'
7 **Enhancing group decisiveness:** To improve decision making in a group context, get clarity on the core purpose of the meeting (which part of the meeting to discuss ideas, which parts are to consider decisions, etc.) and set clear time limits using prompts when a halfway point is reached.

As you may have noticed, the previous few sections of practical resources to support decision making overlap somewhat. This is because they are all based on the emerging research on decision making and the paradigm=shifting assumptions that decision making, although starting from a rational evidence-based perspective, is inherently riddled with irrationality and bias.

We will now turn to more specific factors in relation to board decision-making and tools that can help improve their dynamics.

Board team decision making: key factors and tools to contribute to a better process

Many factors can influence team decision making. The research is quite extensive in this area, so what factors and advice would it be useful to summarise here in relation to boardroom decision making?

Five areas, including board structure, board diversity, board leadership culture, board stakeholder conversations and board country cultural aspects, are outlined below. It should be noted that there is a lot of crossover in terms of the dynamics involved in boardroom decision making and those factors considered in detail in other chapters.

Board structure

Board size

The Walker review (2009), commissioned to review corporate boards following the collapse of the finance industry, acknowledged that psychological research on effective groups shows that smaller boards are more effective than large boards. The review authors found that the optimum size for a board is within the range of eight–twelve people; when this is exceeded, the number of psychological phenomena can compromise boardroom competence. These include the 'span of attention' (the ability of people to deal with complexity), the ability to maintain effective interpersonal relationships and the reduction of director-level motivation. The report also finds that the optimum size of a subcommittee is between five and nine people. This reflects Miller's classic 'seven plus or minus two' study which, in a board context, means that below five there is a reduction in the quality of diverse input, while beyond nine the cognitive limit of the group is exceeded.

Quantity of board and committee meetings

There is, perhaps, an assumption that the more frequently a board or a committee is able to meet, the better. Obviously, the frequency of board meetings is largely constrained by formal processes and by the practical difficulties in regularly bringing together a group of senior people. However, the number and/or frequency of board committee meetings may lend itself to being increased due to the reduced number of people needed.

One trend of American boards is that more and more work is being shifted to committees rather than being considered on the main board. However, this may be a dangerous precedent: while committees may be more efficient and more able to specialise, they may take away the core ability of a board to offer a 'helicopter view' of the organisation and the issues it faces. This means that decisions may not be made with information fully shared, such that the 'board mind' becomes fragmented and group decision making becomes impaired. Therefore, if committees are used, it is important to have clear and robust liaison between the committee and main board, with delineation between roles, deliverables and where decision making ultimately lies.

Board diversity

The subject of board diversity is discussed in more detail in Chapter 8; however, it is useful to touch on it here especially in relation to boardroom decision making. Boardroom diversity has historically focused on the diversity of type, often that can be seen visibly, such as gender, race and age.

However, the focus of diversity is more about the output of that diversity rather than the input. It is perhaps unlikely, but quite conceivable, to have a younger female director who has the same information and the same perspective as an older male director. This is one of those situations where the structural component of governance, that a board should balance its gender diversity for example, is necessary but not sufficient for the diversity to enhance the dynamics and therefore quality of boardroom conversations. So, what are the most relevant outputs, or aspects of 'behavioural diversity', to consider in relation to decision making?

For our purposes here, there are two. Firstly, it is important that diverse information is shared in a boardroom context. That is, boards should spend their time discussing and weighing up information that is initially unknown to the group if the diversity in the group is to be maximised. In a meta-analysis of 72 studies, involving 4,795 groups and over 17,000 individuals, it was found that groups tend to spend most of their time discussing information shared by members, which is therefore redundant, rather than discussing information known only to one or a minority of members. This causes the dynamic of 'information asymmetry' that we introduced in Chapter 4. This is a key finding because we know that those groups that actually do share unique information tend to make better decisions. The study also found that the amount of time spent talking was less of a predictor of good decision making than the rarity of information discussed. In short, what a board talks about is more important than how much the board talks about it. One thing that enhances this type of discussion is a focus on using a clear and highly structured discussion methodology.

Secondly, a diversity of thinking styles is important in the boardroom. We know that individuals have different preferences for types of thinking style (as discussed above in terms of personality traits) and this is also true of teams. Unfortunately, this may mean that, although the team may be strong in one area of decision making, this may lead to blind spots in other areas and increase the likelihood of decision-making bias. It may be helpful to use some kind of methodology to overcome this. One such methodology, which is reasonably well known in organisations, is De Bono's 'Six Thinking Hats'. Although it is quite possible (certainly in a training room) for individuals to actually don different-coloured hats, the more conceptual idea of the method is that the coloured hats are used as a metaphor for different ways of thinking such that all natural modes of thinking are used in a conversation. The hat colours and their associated group thinking styles are as follows:

- Blue – What is the bigger picture? What are we thinking about? What is the goal of our decision-making?
- White – What are the facts that we need to bring to this decision?
- Red – What are our instinctive gut reactions or emotional feelings that we are bringing to this decision?
- Black – When we think practically and realistically, and when considering the key risks, what logic can we bring to this decision?
- Yellow – What are the benefits, what are our best hopes, how can we look on the bright side of this decision?
- Green – What if anything was possible? What creative innovations might be possible as a way of breaking through in this decision?

In practice, a chair might introduce this methodology to focus on one type of thinking – for example if the board seemed overly enthusiastic and needed to perform a more thorough risk assessment of a particular option, through a suggestion such as, 'Let's look at the possibility with our black hats on'. Alternatively, they might take an option and methodologically work through each hat to ensure that all perspectives have been considered.

Board leadership culture

The style of leadership and the way that this leadership plays out in terms of methods and processes, that is, the leadership culture, is a key factor in terms of determining the quality of decision making in a boardroom. This topic is covered in detail in Chapter 7, but we will focus on three particular areas here that are particularly pertinent to supporting better decision dynamics.

As we have discussed, better quality decision-making processes arise from teams who are able to harness diverse, and potentially conflicting, evidence-based perspectives and synthesise them with awareness of probable cognitive bias. As has also been mentioned in other parts of the book, the basis for this often lies in a team that shares high trust. One of the key components in trusting relationships is the lack of ego in those leaders that are working together. Unlike the perspectives on leadership that praise the heroic leader with all its associated personality characteristics (decisiveness, challenge, command and, at its extreme, ruthlessness), a trustworthy leader is one that is eminently humble and does not try to force their opinions onto others. What does this look like in a boardroom leadership culture?

Simply put, better decisions emerge from senior leadership teams and boards when the chair or CEO shares their opinions last. When leaders provide their thoughts first, they narrow the decision agenda and this stops others contributing potentially useful ideas that they would have otherwise shared if given the chance to speak first. In order to do this, the skill of drawing on others' opinions and promoting collaborative dialogue becomes important for the chair. The question for the board directors then becomes: can you separate your own ego from the decision-making process in order to support the group outcome rather than any individual agenda?

However, having said that a humble leadership culture in general leads to better decision-making, this is not always the case. It very much depends upon what kind of problem the board is trying to solve. For example, if the board consists of a group of experts (that is, a group where the members are, on average, going to be right more than half the time), a more collaborative majority rule is best. However, if the board is dealing with a specialist subject within which most board members are likely to be wrong, it is better to rely on whomever is most likely to get the decision right.

Equally, it may be useful to turn up the team pressure at some point within meetings, especially when the team has simple tasks that need to be accomplished quickly. For example, sprinting through the initial acceptance of minutes and other administrative matters under clear timed deadlines may be entirely appropriate. Similarly, for a decision where creativity is not required, diversity of thought can actually become detrimental, so tightening the reins with some ruthlessness may be appropriate.

However, when decisions requiring a more strategic 'zooming out', which actually should entail much more boardroom conversation, a pressurising leadership culture can backfire and is more likely to engender groupthink. One has only to consider some of history's most famous examples of flawed military decision making – such as the US rushing into Vietnam or the charge to declare war in Iraq – to recognise the importance of a leadership culture that can alleviate pressure and anxiety on the group's decision making in order to reduce group bias.

The board's leadership culture may also be affected by its explicit country culture. As we will discuss in more detail in Chapter 13, there are hugely varying cultural differences on many dimensions of organisational leadership behaviour. One of these dimensions is around decision-making, that is, whether the decision-making is culturally consensual or culturally more top-down. For example, countries such as Japan, Sweden and the Netherlands have very consensual decision-making systems, whereas China, India and Russia generally rely on a strong leader making the ultimate decision (the US, UK and Germany are somewhere in the middle). These country culture differences are becoming important to appreciate and respond to as boards become increasingly culturally diverse and geographically disparate.

Board stakeholder conversations

A final consideration, which we will turn to in more detail in the next chapter, concerns which stakeholders have been included in the decision making and the quality of stakeholder conversations that the board engages in through the decision-making process. For example, executive directors in particular need to strike a balance between their functional representation and their role representing the board in general as a director among equals. There is an expectation that they bring some functional knowledge and experience to inform a decision, but then they are expected to tread a fine line between ensuring the information holds appropriate weight while having empathy with, or even being able to argue for, other perspectives during the discussion and decision-making phases of board conversation.

Furthermore, we know that boards are better if they actively search for areas of stakeholder disagreement early in discussions and then resolve these into a consensus decision. Ineffective boards are those that simply average stakeholder opinion to reduce conflict. The FRC's Guidance on Board Effectiveness (July 2018) notes this, suggesting that 'where more than one part of the business is affected, integrated and joined up information is likely to aid decision making'. One very clear example of this is NASA's move to formally include one of their key stakeholders in important decisions: the astronaut. One can only imagine that including astronauts in group decision making, especially concerning decisions of flight 'go or no go', significantly amplifies the stark human impact, and thus the quality, of high-level decision making.

However a board attempts to enhance its decision making to reduce its bias, it should be clear on its decision-making remit and whether its primary focus is on decision making based on oversight and ratification of decisions made by others (such as those made by an executive or leadership team) or decisions made based on expert input from others, such as that which may be received from a board committee. If the decision making is different across topics or based on set criteria, it is important that these are documented at board level so that there is both an audit trail and an easy reference document.

Where delegation is given to a committee of the board this should be documented in the approved terms of reference of that committee which should be reviewed on a regular basis. Where operational matters are delegated to an executive or leadership team, the criteria for escalation to the board for approval or discussion should be clear, including where relevant any *de minimis* amounts relating to financial decision making or pre-approved actions in relation to delivering against the company strategy.

Conclusion

As we have seen, decision-making theory has shifted from its classic rational economics model to one that is underpinned by the understanding that people and groups are predictably irrational. To limit this irrationality, boards – like many other forums composed of individuals – may benefit from a decision-making approach that utilises evidence-based practice to drive consistent and clear decision making wherever possible. However, in order to be more evidence-based, directors must become aware of, and put into place, processes to mitigate the variety of individual and group biases to which we are prone.

There are specific issues associated with boardroom decision making to consider (which, unsurprisingly, overlap with other aspects of boardroom dynamics covered elsewhere in this book) such as the size of the board, quality of board and committee meetings, board diversity, board leadership culture and board stakeholder conversations.

Specifically, a board should be clear on how it seeks to make decisions. What evidence it will use? What input will board members use from non-board experts and advisers and to what extent will they rely on it? There may not be one clear answer to this as the nature, extent and quantum of each decision will influence whether the board is the ultimate decision maker or whether its decision can be a direct result of presented evidence. No matter what route is taken, the ultimate responsibility will rest with the board, even if decisions are delegated or made based on evidence produced by non-board members. However each decision is reached, it is important that these are documented, incorporating how and why the decision was taken if it adds clarity to why it was made, so that there is both an audit trail and an easy reference document if the decision is ever challenged.

How can boards make better decisions? They can attempt to become more evidence-based and minimise decision bias. Ways to reduce bias might include educating the board on how cognitive bias affects us all; evaluating and discussing the individual director's personality and decision-making preferences; applying decision tools to board decision-making process; and considering how to respond to board specific issues such as board size, board and committee meeting quality, board diversity, board leadership culture and board stakeholder conversations.

One final point: whatever process is taken to make a decision, or evidence used to underpin that decision, nothing paralyses a board (and as a result the organisation itself) as much as indecision, a lack of clarity and discussion with no outcome.

Are your boards and other forums suffering from indecision that diminishes effective leadership and hampers progress? Is there clarity about the basis on which decisions are made?

6 – Stakeholder conversations

Introduction to stakeholder systems

From boardroom dynamics to board dynamics

In Chapter 3, we explored how individual director characteristics – both demographics and behavioural attributes – have been used as proxies for good governance. The emphasis on these individual elements reflects our standard assumption that leadership is inherent within individuals rather than in groups. It is the temptation of reductionism over holism, that goes back to seventeenth-century Cartesian rationalism and Newtonian mechanics, which has taught us to break things down to their fundamental parts in order to diagnose and then repair. However, Chapter 3 also concluded that although somewhat useful, board performance does not equal the sum of these individual parts.

In Chapter 4, we introduced the emergent team dynamics that arise in the boardroom which have a much stronger impact on performance. This shift in perspective was captured by Dr William Tate at the Centre for Progressive Leadership, London Metropolitan University Business School:

> Wise owners do not blame the fish for their poor appearance or performance. They do not take the fish out from time to time to give them a spot of training, tell them to smarten up and look more lively, and then plop them back in the same dirty water. Instead they clean the tank.

What constitutes the 'fish tank' for our purposes? So far, we have considered the boundaries of the tank to be the boardroom, where face-to-face director interaction occurs. This chapter encourages us to see the broader systemic factors that impinge upon the board's performance. We have shifted from director attributes to boardroom dynamics: we now continue that shift from boardroom dynamics to board system dynamics. This is reflected in the original definition of board dynamics that we introduced in Chapter 1:

> Board dynamics are the interactions between board members individually and collectively, and how these influence, and are influenced by, their wider stakeholder system.

The board is shaped by the stakeholder system it is part of; this stakeholder system, in turn, is also changed by the dynamics that exist within the board. Therefore, an appreciation of board dynamics must go beyond individual psychology – which focuses on personal cognition, emotion and behaviours – and also beyond social psychology – which focuses on the group interaction – and extend to systems psychology, which pulls heavily on the theories and concepts of systems thinking.

In fact, company law has evolved to recognise this very issue, such that one of the seven duties of a company director is enshrined in section 172 of the Companies Act 2006 as follows:

> A director of a company must act in the way he considers, in good faith, would be most likely to promote the success of the company for the benefit of its members as a whole, and in doing so have regard (among other matters) to—
> (a) the likely consequences of any decision in the long term,
> (b) the interests of the company's employees,
> (c) the need to foster the company's business relationships with suppliers, customers and others,
> (d) the impact of the company's operations on the community and the environment,
> (e) the desirability of the company maintaining a reputation for high standards of business conduct, and
> (f) the need to act fairly as between members of the company.

The success of the company, and the requirement of each director to promote that success, is not a duty to deliver increased financial profits in isolation of wider benefit.

The board as a system

Systems thinking focuses on the patterns, relationships and independency between systems. It is guided by the notion of interdependency – that every system is dependent on the subsystems within it and the systems within which it is nestled. Therefore, the understanding of board dynamics is similar to the metaphor of a Russian doll. There is always another doll that exists inside or, indeed, another that can be placed around the doll that is in your hand. Systems theory also implies the concept of co-creation – that is, that the organism is shaped by its environmental niche but can also change and shapes this niche. This is the constant ever-changing dynamic dance that is happening at all levels of the system.

There is a phenomenon in therapy called the 'parallel process' that describes how the therapist recreates, or parallels, their client's problems when they, in turn, discuss the problems with their counselling supervisor. This mirrors what happens within the boardroom. Behaviours that exist in the boardroom do not just emerge from the contributions of an individual's psychology or from the collective group functioning. In addition, boardroom behaviours can also be understood as representative echoes of the wider stakeholder systems that the board members and the board itself are located within.

What might this look like in practice? Although not a true story, the following is a narrative of a systemic process, based on a combination of different interventions that have been experienced over recent years, that highlights the six different systemic lenses through which one can view board dynamics.

Imagine that a chair asks their company secretary for some help sorting out a problem with a relatively new non-executive director. This director has been ruffling feathers in the boardroom with their approach to particular topics. At face value, this looks like an individual issue to do with them being young and vigorous and wanting to share their specific expertise to make a difference on the board too quickly without first getting to know other directors and understanding the organisational context. The chair assumes that this is due to a lack of emotional intelligence or perhaps governance experience and so asks if the company secretary, who has already developed a bit of a rapport through inducting the new director and who is also independent, can have a 'quiet word'. At this stage in the narrative, both the chair and company secretary are seeing the situation through the first systems level, the *individual* lens.

However, after speaking to the new non-executive director, the company secretary comes to understand that this might be a symptom of a broader issue. It seems as if the new joiner has a particular conflict with one of the more established non-executive directors. As the company secretary has some understanding of personality types, and as both directors have been previously assessed with the same psychometric tool, the company secretary decides to use this as a way of mediating a three-way conversation to discuss personality styles. A meeting is set up. The company secretary is now viewing the issue through the second system perspective, the *interpersonal* lens.

After this conversation, the two directors are glad to have spoken, and they appreciate that their clashing in recent meetings is nothing personal, they just have different communication preferences. However, through the conversation, it becomes clear that their conflict is also mirrored in other relationships in the board. After the company secretary talks this insight through with the chair, it is agreed that it may be useful for all board team members to attend an 'away day' to go through a similar process. The board spends a productive day (facilitated by the HR director) and evening meal together getting to know each other better before the following day's board meeting. As well as understanding personality styles, they do exercises on their personal values and share the story of how they came to be on the board in the first place. The board members all agree that they now feel part of a much more cohesive group. This intervention is working at a third system level through the lens of *team relationships*.

Although all directors now recognise that any conflict that has existed is not personal, there is still a frustration in the camp. As a function of their newfound ability to speak more openly about their problems, some of the directors' have voiced that this frustration stems from the fact that the board does not have real clarity over its current purpose or direction, resulting in varying levels of commitment being shown by different board members. Some longer-standing members, including the chair, see the executives as highly competent and thus the non-executive's role is only about superficial understanding, light monitoring and encouraging rubber-stamping. These same directors have sometimes left meetings early or not attended meetings at all due to other commitments. Other directors are worried that the management may be missing things and these directors are spending more time in the business talking to executives. It turns out that this is why the new non-executive director was perceived as impatient and overly enthusiastic, as they were not enamoured by the more *laissez-faire* approach of some of the more tenured non-executive directors. With this new appreciation, and with some behind the scenes influencing of the chair by the company secretary, the board commited to a further session (this time facilitated by an external consultant) to help them define their shared purpose and joint endeavour. After this session, the board has agreed and is committed to a clearer and more compelling vision, purpose and objectives; members now feel more of a team rather than just being a cohesive group. Based on this raised level of commitment required, one of the longer-standing directors decides to resign but does so on good terms. This episode has employed the fourth systems lens, focusing on *team tasks*.

In the next meeting, however, the chief executive reports back on progress and it seems that some of the strategic requirements of the new board purpose jar with the expectations of a key customer group. The board discusses this issue, having not fully considered this customer in the previous team tasks session. There emerges a growing realisation that other stakeholder needs may also now be being neglected. After a short break in the board meeting and, following a huddle over coffee between the chair, the chief executive and the company secretary, the board flexes the agenda to provide some time to identify key stakeholders and begin to map their needs. It is decided that a stakeholder project team will be formed to gather data from these stakeholders and reconvene to share the results at a future board meeting. The project team will be led by the new non-executive director, as they used to work with these customers directly and so has many personal contacts. The board, and stakeholder project team, are now using the fifth system lens, looking at the *stakeholder interfaces*.

It emerges that, through the stakeholder consultation process, some new regulatory changes in the industry are likely to have a significant impact on the industry as a whole. The new non-executive director was very aware of these changes, hence their impatience as they were concerned that the organisation would be put on the back foot. After a difficult but ultimately evidence-based and richly considered dialogue, it is decided that the board purpose be tweaked and the stakeholder project be turned into a formal committee. Further, the major regulatory change will become a standing agenda item for the next four board meetings.

This will enable the board to work through what this key issue might mean for them over the coming months and years in order to make the most of any opportunities and also to mitigate potential threats to the organisation. This final lens through which the board is now considering the issue is the *wider systemic context*.

A week later, the chair pops in to see the company secretary. The two reflect on how far they have progressed as a board since that first conversation, both acknowledging that, in retrospect, things were not as simple as they had initially seemed.

Hopefully, the above narrative provides some insight into the importance of holding a systems perspective. To recap, the six lenses of board dynamics (adapted from Leary-Joyce and Lines, 2018) are as follows:

1 the individual director;
2 the interpersonal director relationships;
3 the board team relationships;
4 the board team tasks;
5 the board's stakeholder interfaces; and
6 the board's wider systemic context.

What if the chair, board members, company secretary and those individuals around the board had simply stopped at the individual or their own boardroom team relationships level? Although board functioning might have improved somewhat, it might not have achieved the level of co-ordination, sophistication and enhanced outcomes that it did by working through all of the systems perspectives. As Professor Peter Hawkins of Henley Business School writes: 'No longer do the main challenges in organisations lie in the people or in the parts, but in the interfaces and relationships between people, teams, functions and different stakeholder needs.'

Although a board systems perspective hopefully makes sense in light of the explanation and narrative above, it can initially appear somewhat strange or threatening. This is because it is different to how we are schooled, through the media and mainstream societal beliefs, to conceive of organisational and board leadership. In social psychology, there exists a cognitive bias known as the fundamental attribution error. This describes how, in contrast to interpretations of our own behaviour, we tend to emphasise internal characteristics unreasonably (such as competency, commitment and character) rather than broader systemic factors in explaining other people's behaviour. This effect has also been described as the 'tendency to believe that what people do reflects who they are'.

This bias, combined with the standard worldview of either heroic or flawed leaders propping up or single-handedly pulling down organisations, can lead to resistance to a systemic perspective. People may consider that it gives board members an excuse as they can blame the system, for example. Similarly, it may be considered to take too long or be too expensive to consider all of the different perspectives and it may feel like it is constraining to those board directors with more activist and pragmatic leadership styles. However, if the system as a whole is ignored, it is often the case that problems will crop up further down the line, so any time taken up front to consider the broader systemic dynamics will, in the long run, be richly rewarded.

The systems inside the board

Individual director lens

Although we argued in the introduction to this chapter for a broad systemic perspective to understand board dynamics, appreciating what is going on for each individual director is still important. What key aspects, then, must we understand within the individual system that is each individual director?

Biology and personality

Firstly, each director can be seen as a biological system. Although this seems slightly nebulous and strange to consider in a text on how boards function, the physical wellbeing of individuals is often neglected in the cognitive-heavy corporate lifestyle. There is a growing recognition of the importance of physical factors such as appropriate nutrition, sleep, exercise and stress management to enable sustainable functioning in our modern working world. We will discuss this area in more detail under the topic of resilience in Chapter 15 and also share ideas for how to influence biology positively through the boardroom environment in Chapter 9.

Secondly, each individual director is also system of sub-personality types. This area was touched on in Chapter 3 on individual director attributes. We have noted, in particular, that unlike expertise and intellect, the emotional intelligence-related aspects of directors are often neglected but are ultimately the key attributes for team functioning.

Life roles

Thirdly, we can also understand an individual director's behaviour through an understanding of how their director role fits into, or indeed conflicts, with their other life roles. This perspective has been the domain of research called 'work–life balance', which includes the key concept of role conflict. Role conflict can be defined in terms of:

- time conflict – the extent to which the amount of time spent on one role interferes with significant other roles in people's lives;
- strain conflict – the extent to which the amount of stress that is created by one role leaks over to another role (for example, not being able to focus at home with one's family due to the pressures of work or vice versa); and
- values conflict – the extent to which what one is expected to do as a board member misaligns with what one believes based on one's life values.

Values alignment, such that one's role aligns most congruently with one's core personal values, is perhaps the most key antidote to role conflict. As the saying goes, 'With a strong enough why, you can bear almost any how'. However, when a board member feels a conflict between their director role and what they believe, or indeed what competence they believe they have, then psychological difficulties and stress can occur.

For example, one might begin having feelings that are described by the term 'impostor syndrome', defined as a psychological pattern in which an individual doubts their accomplishments and has a persistent fear of being exposed as a fraud. Interestingly (especially in light of the current preoccupation with board gender diversity), while the early research on impostor syndrome focused on the prevalence of high-achieving women, the condition has been recognised to affect both men and women equally.

Director roles

As well as understanding that the above research that describes the issues that can occur due to conflict between work and other life roles, individual directors also have a sub-system of diverse identities within their director role. We shall discuss the cultural aspects of board identity in Chapters 7 and 13 and other aspects of director diversity in Chapter 8. However, as we saw in the narrative story above, how directors perceive their role as a director in general, their role as board member of the particular company and their role in the particular board team, will have an impact on how they behave. As Dr Katharina Pick at Harvard noted in her 2007 observational research of the inner workings of five boards:

> Director self-construal influences process because it informs how directors think they should contribute in board meetings, how they explain their behaviours to themselves, and how they interpret responses from other directors. I find that directors are first and foremost interested in bringing their professional expertise to bear on board activities.

This view that board members are eager to make a positive contribution, look good and strengthen their personal brand is backed up by interviews conducted with non-executive directors by Dr Sabine Dembrowski, Managing Partner of Better Boards. Here are some quotes from her research that show how strongly board members believe that their role is about bringing their expertise.

> 'I love the intellectual challenges of being a non-executive director. It is so rewarding to see that you can use your expertise and brain.'
> Non-executive director

> 'I would not like to be back in the rat race, but being part of various boards is just great. I can use my brain and stay involved and, above all, I know that I am contributing to something big and important.'
> Trustee of a major charity

> 'For me it is all about the feeling of having an impact. I am now for three years, a member of this board and it has been incredible to see where the organisation was when I started, and seeing it now. It makes me ever so proud to being part of this board.'
> Non-executive director

If a director believes and is motivated by bringing their expertise to the board, what effect will this have on the boardroom dynamic? As we have discussed in previous chapters, a level of challenge is required at the boardroom, which will arise from the diversity and cognitive conflict that director expertise is likely to bring. However, unique expertise may silo a board director if they cannot also integrate their expertise into their role of being an equal member of the board team.

How a director thinks about themselves as a board member of the particular company that they are on is an important contributor to their internal dynamic. Directors often join a business that excites them; this creates an initial 'honeymoon' level of commitment. They like being associated with people they respect and this will create a level of cohesion and personal connection. They may have joined through a personal connection with another board member, which may create a level of informal accountability towards their role. Of the 31 directors that Pick observed in her research, 26 joined their board due to a personal connection with another board member. The two boards that were the most socially connected to each other in the study were also the most pleased with their own performance.

On the other side of the coin, the board that had the most crippling problems with divisiveness, a history of mistrust and high conflict around important decisions, was the board that was assembled by executive recruiters. This led her to suggest that social ties may be contributing something to more sustainable and effective board process. Conversely, this may be because external recruiters were bringing diversity to the board which can, at least initially, create discord until the engagement with this diversity becomes a positive. Directors may have also joined the particular company board because they were interested in contributing to a larger goal, as mentioned in relation to the word 'impact' in a couple of the non-executive director quotes above. Finally, and more financially, directors may take up board positions as they have a psychological or monetary stake in the company that they have joined.

A final director identity perspective is how directors think of themselves as a member of the particular group of directors on the board. To what extent does a director feel that they are contributing personal expertise, contributing process, skill, or contributing to effective governance? We know that a director will feel that their contribution is valuable if it is unique, regardless of what they contribute. When there is too much overlap between one director's perception of their contribution with another's, their engagement and commitment may wane, which will naturally have consequences to how they show up in the boardroom conversation.

The overemphasis of the individual lens

Having mentioned all of the above influences on how an individual director's internal systems may contribute to how they turn up at a board meeting, we must also recognise that this individual impact has been overemphasised. As mentioned in the introduction to this chapter, the historical adoration of heroic leadership combined with our fundamental attribution error bias means that we overplay the individual level in our understanding of board dynamics. Research also suggests that this is amplified in individualist societies, such as the US. In the same way that genetics and the unravelling of the human genome was thought to reveal everything about our destiny, but has been superseded by recent thinking in the field of epigenetics, organisational thought leaders now believe that individual behaviour only affects organisational systems between 5% and 20%. This is not a modern thought, but it is certainly a modern realisation. As the prescient organisational thought leader Mary Parker Follett wrote in 1918,

> The individual is not a unit, but a centre of forces... and consequently society is not a collection of units, but a complex of radiating and converging, crossing and re-crossing energies. Society is a dynamic process rather than a crowd or a collection of already developed individuals.

Case study: The 'rogue trader' scandal – an individual or systemic failure?

The classic case of derivatives 'rogue trader' Nick Leeson, whose unauthorised and fraudulent actions brought down Barings Bank in 1995 (the UK's oldest merchant bank) is an interesting case study in systems thinking. The focus on his personal psychology through the lens of the system was such that a film was made of the story, with Ewan McGregor playing Leeson. Leeson is still widely interviewed and even appeared on the television programme *Celebrity Big Brother*.

However, to what extent was the Barings Bank disaster the fault of one individual trader going rogue? Should the fault actually be seen as more of a management issue due to the freedom afforded to superstar traders? Was it a board failure due to allowing and role-modelling a culture of risk deficient in appropriate safeguards and challenge? Was it a wider financial industry or government failure to not regulate more tightly? Or was it just a zeitgeist of wider society and something like that was bound to happen at some point?

It may have been all of these things, but we tend to punish the individual and not learn the wider systemic lessons.

The interpersonal board relationships lens

The importance of good relationships to us all as human beings is startlingly significant. A 2010 medical study entitled 'Social relationships and mortality risk: a meta-analytic review', for example, found that the influence of having poor social relationships on the likely risk of us dying is comparable to elevated risks caused by smoking and alcohol consumption and is greater than the influence of physical inactivity and obesity.

The interpersonal board relationships lens looks at the quality of the one-to-one relationships between directors on the board. This is the first aspect of the board dynamics definition that we first introduced in Chapter 1, and also mentioned at the start of this chapter, that is, that board dynamics are the interactions between the individual board members. Taking a group psychodynamic perspective, it has been asserted that 'the relationship precedes the individual' (Leal, 1982). This section will explore the board relationships lens through the concepts of building trust and ego states.

Building trust

The quality of a one-to-one relationship is largely down to the amount of trust that exists between the two people. However, what exactly is trust? Although trust is a human feeling that can ebb and flow from moment to moment, it has been practically parsed out in something called the 'trust equation'. David Maister, Charles M. Green and Rob Galford articulated this equation in their book *The Trusted Adviser* and have even developed an online self-assessment that can measure an individual's 'trust quotient'.

Maister et al. suggest four characteristics that contribute to trust. Three improve one's trustworthiness; the final one reduces it. The first factor is 'credibility', which is defined by what you say and how believable you are to others. Things that might improve one's credibility are one's track record, one's qualifications, the testimonials that one has received from others and how confidently one comes across in one's interactions.

The second component is 'reliability', which is defined as one's actions and how dependable you appear. This is the most tangible of the trust elements and directly links your words and deeds. Reliability is achieved by consistently and repeated allowing the other person to experience the link between one's promises and actions.

The third component is 'intimacy', defined as how safe people feel sharing things with you. Intimacy speaks to your ability to connect with other people and requires vulnerability, honesty and openness. It may also require an investment of time and effort and the appropriate environment within which one can connect.

The equation proposes that trust is the sum of these elements, credibility plus reliability plus intimacy, all divided by the fourth characteristic, the denominator of the equation, 'self-orientation'. This refers to whose interest is going to be put first within an interaction; to what extent will it be the other person's, or will it be your own? The higher that the other person perceives your self-interest in the interaction to be, the less likely it is that they will trust you.

In research by the authors using a 20-question online trust quotient self-assessment test, a number of interesting patterns linked to trust emerged. It was found that women were slightly, but statistically significantly, more trustworthy than men. In relation to trust and age, it was found that at every 10-year age grouping, self-assessed trustworthiness goes up, from age 20 to age 80. And in terms of trust and leadership types, it was found that most people consider the expert type, one that focuses on their credibility and reliability to be trusted, to be the most effective for building trust. However, of the six leadership types that the research identified, the expert type was only placed equal fourth. The most trustworthy types, however, had one factor in common: strong intimacy skills. This mirrors the commentary about board directors in Chapter 3, that emotional and cultural intelligence trumps professional capital in predicting performance. This suggests that intimacy is probably the place to start in terms of improving trusting relationships generally in life but also specifically, for our purposes here, in the boardroom context.

What, then, does high intimacy look like? The Levels of Communications model, created as part of Transactional Analysis theory in the 1950s by Eric Berne, is useful in understanding how intimacy is built. When we begin conversations, we usually start at the level of 'ritual and cliché'. For example, we begin with the usual hello, how are you, how was the traffic, nice weather isn't it, etc., without really expecting or wanting to receive a full answer. We are going through the appropriate conventions and motions of a cultural welcome.

Once we have fulfilled this level of communication, we usually move to the level of 'facts and information'. This is the level of communication at which the majority of business transactions exist in the workplace and boardroom. This is perhaps characterised by going through a standard agenda, reporting finances and largely remaining formal and structured.

The third level of communication is 'values and beliefs'. When we take part in a conversation within which we are able to share our personal values, we are disclosing more information. There is not only inherent risk involved in doing so, but also the possibility of greater trust. Within cohesive teams, conversations about what one actually believes will be put on the table, whereas individuals within working groups may not feel able to go beyond facts and information.

The final level of communication is that of sharing one's 'emotions and feelings'. This does not necessarily mean that one is being emotional, but simply that one is able to feel comfortable expressing a particular personal emotion about a topic. This obviously ups the risk and vulnerability stakes. However, we know that leaders who are able to do this most effectively are those that garner the most trusting followership. If, within a conversation, one person's level of communication is elevated too quickly or significantly higher than another's, trust will not develop. Only when relationships are paced and matched at the same level will trust develop.

The group cohesion literature informs us that relationship quality and trust is also related to the perceived similarity that is found between people in terms of their personality, background, culture, style, beliefs, interests, etc. We also know that people are more attracted to each other (in both a romantic and non-romantic sense) as they spend more time together and interact more frequently. Therefore, we might assume that board members who have been working together longer and who meet outside board and committee meetings, either through other work or socially, are likely to have better-quality relationships.

Case study: How to destroy trust within the board

In 2016, Alison Donaldson and Rob Warwick, in association with Roffey Park, a leadership institute based in the UK and Singapore, conducted some interviews with senior leaders to investigate their stories and reflections on the emergence of trusting relationships. One charity trustee reflected on how the way that management responded to a question in a board meeting was indicative of the level of trust between those two directors. The trustee set up the story as follows:

> 'I was on a charity board where two members of the executive team were very nervous that the board was going to misunderstand their role and make decisions in excess of their responsibility. This created a dynamic in meetings in which what we got from the executives was defensive. There was a lack of trust and a lack of openness.'

When asked to recall a striking moment that brought to life the extent of this mistrust, the trustee described the following:

> 'We were discussing the budget for the following year. It was quite an ambitious one, and there were things that needed to be explored. I wanted to know what scenarios had been considered, for example, a change in government policy or change in income. The FD's response was that what I ought to understand was that was this is an extremely difficult thing to do. So then I felt doubly concerned. Had they said "that's an interesting question, I've done the following and would appreciate discussing it", I would have felt relaxed. And it led to difficulty because my anxiety meant that I asked again and then they became even more dogmatic. So, you can create trust simply by the way you respond to a question.'

Parent, adult child ego states

A useful model to understand how people relate to each other is a framework from transactional analysis theory, developed by Eric Berne. Transactional analysis is a theory of personality as well as an organised method of psychotherapy for personal growth and change. 'Transactions' refer to the communication exchanges between people, and transactional analysis is the method of examining transactions, that is, 'I do something to you and you do something back'.

As well as the levels of communication model described earlier and the drama triangle, which will be illustrated a little later in this chapter, Berne also categorised three different 'ego states' that people can be in when they transact. These are the 'parent' ego state, the 'adult' ego state and the 'child' ego state.

When a person is in the parent ego state, they think, feel and behave as someone who is acting as a parent. The parent can be either critical, using language such as 'why haven't you...?', or nurturing, using language such as some version of 'take care', 'please remember to' or 'I'll help you'. The critical parent ego state is often a characteristic of autocratic leadership whereas the nurturing parent is often the characteristic of more of a benevolent dictator style of leadership. Both have been shown to be useful in a limited number of situations, but in general are highly corrosive and engender lower performance. Not surprisingly, when someone acts from the parent ego state, this invites the person in the interaction with them to go into their child ego state, so that they think, feel and react as a child. This can lead to a passive/aggressive response from those who are communicated to in a parental way. However, being childish also has a more positive side, which enables creativity and playfulness, which may be useful at times to let off steam.

The adult ego state is more neutral and logical, is able to examine data from both the parent and child and often acts as a mediator between the two. This is often the style of interaction required from the chair and professional adviser. The adult state is able to ask questions and seek evidence and also invites those in the parent or child ego states to behave more as adults. This is one theoretical explanation why the chair's behaviour has such an influence on the boardroom dynamic. In role-modelling largely adult behaviours, they will invite other directors to be adult too. However, when the room becomes overly formal and the ice needs to be broken, an effective chair will recognise this and become briefly playful from their ego state.

Considering the relationship between the chair and the CEO, transactional analysis can also provide some insight into the conversational dynamics in the boardroom. Many argue that the relationship between the chair and the CEO is the single most important ingredient in good governance, so one would hope that there is an appropriate adult–adult relationship between these two roles most of the time. However, there are inherent and necessary tensions between the two roles. For example, the CEO is likely to have a bias towards action and what might be perhaps perceived as an impatient need to get on with things and deliver results. However, the chair's role is to think more broadly about the longer-term interests of the organisation. On occasion, this may result in the chair needing to hold back the CEO from immediate action and getting them to rethink their approach. How a chair manages to do this, in terms of the quality of their interaction, may dictate both the tone in the boardroom and also the culture outside of it. From a transactional analysis perspective, the chair may be pulled into the parent ego state and the chief executive may be pulled into their child ego state as a reaction.

On the one hand, taking a system relationship lens, it may be important to support both parties in exploring their personality differences through three-way mediation style conversations or one-to-one coaching support. However, taking a broader systemic lens, it may also be useful to support the chair and chief executive officer to recognise that their relationship together is perhaps more powerfully influenced by forces outside of the boardroom. It may be a parallel process of a wider systemic conflict which, if they are able to transcend the interpersonal lens, their relationship itself can generate material for a rich systemic conversation.

Team relationships lens

When people use the term 'boardroom dynamics', they are probably talking about the team relationships lens and applying it to boards – that is, they are only using the second part of the definition that we introduced in Chapter 1 that 'board dynamics are the interactions between board members… collectively'. This is not an atypical misunderstanding, however. The idea that team building will resolve all the team issues, whereby teams go on an away-day to do some personality profiles, perhaps build and race some rafts and then go for a nice meal, has been the traditional team development paradigm for the last 50 years or so. However, this does not mean that the team relationships lens is unimportant, merely that it has, as is true with the individual lens, been viewed as the panacea to all team ills. When interventions are located as part of a broader systemic perspective though, they can add significant value.

Team development frameworks

There are many frameworks that can help us to analyse the dynamics of the relationships in a board team. One classic model is Tuckman's stages of group development, first proposed by Bruce Tuckman in 1965. This model initially proposed four phases that groups necessarily and inevitably must move through in order for them to grow and deliver results. The first stage is the *forming* stage where a team meets and agrees on initial goals. The team will be task focused and team members may behave quite independently and may tiptoe on eggshells around any potentially threatening topics to avoid conflict. The aim here is to build initial cohesion around a task.

The second stage of development is the *storming* stage, where people begin to voice their opinions, which may result in task, process and relationship conflict. The assumption of this stage is that any differences in personality clashes must be resolved before the team can move on. The original research suggested that, through a lack of skill or will to resolve potential conflicts, some teams never emerge from this stage. However, those that do, emerge stronger and more able to work effectively.

The third stage of the development is the *norming* stage, within which teams begin to resolve differences and coalesce around a common goal. This is the shift from being a group to a team such that all members are able to take responsibility and accountability and a sense of joint leadership emerges.

The final stage, the *performing* stage, is characterised by establishing mission, vision, roles and norms such that team members can focus completely on achieving their common goal. This stage will also be characterised by the potential for high levels of performance.

In later iterations of the model, Tuchman added a fifth stage, what he termed the *adjourning* stage. This is also known as the mourning or transforming stage and is characterised by the team completing their task, breaking up and 'turning the lights off' as a team. Although the model is linear, there is no reason why, due to changes either within the team or externally to the team, such as the replacement of the leader or individual members, the team may not relapse into any of the previous stages.

Looking back at the board narrative at the start of this chapter, we might notice aspects of the Tuckman model being played out.

A further model that has gained traction as a useful method of diagnosing team dynamics comes from Patrick Lencioni, who published *The Five Dysfunctions of a Team* in 2002. The framework, and its associated online diagnostic, are widely used to support the development of team dynamics globally. According to the model, the five dysfunctions, with associated team leadership roles for each dysfunction, are as follows:

1. Absence of trust – unwilling to be vulnerable within the group.
   Role of the leader: Go first.
2. Fear of conflict – seeking artificial harmony over constructive passionate debate.
   Role of the leader: Mine for conflict.
3. Lack of commitment – feigning buy-in to group decisions creates ambiguity throughout the team.
   Role of the leader: Force clarity and closure.
4. Avoidance of accountability – ducking the responsibility to challenge peers on counter-productive behaviour which sets low standards.
   Role of the leader: Confront difficult issues.
5. Inattention to results – focusing on personal success, status and ego before team success.
   Role of the leader: Force on collective outcomes.

As you can see, this model reflects both some of the aspects of Tuckman's stages and important concepts such as constructive dialogue, conflict and challenge, which we shall now consider in greater detail.

Team dialogue

High-performing board teams must be able to have constructive conversations such as those described by Niall FitzGerald KBE, when he was Chairman of Reuters (now Thomson Reuters plc):

> We must be prepared to challenge, confront, disagree and probe, but always in a way that is constructive and supportive of the business agenda. Nothing should be left unsaid within a team that is committed to success.

One of the most useful behavioural models for analysing group behaviour, and whether a team is exhibiting constructive and generative interactions, is the 'Four Player' model developed by David Kantor and popularised by William Isaacs in his book *Dialogue and the Art of Thinking Together.* Kantor is an American systems psychologist who initially developed his model in the field of family therapy and expanded it to organisations. In his original research, Kantor studied the ways that families interact and noticed that there are four ways of relating within a group context that must exist for that group to be in what he called productive 'dialogue'. Understanding the four roles and how they interact provides a useful frame to study team interactions and to identify effective ways of working and blocks to high performance. It can also be used to raise awareness of the positive intentions and possible misinterpretations associated with each role.

The first role is the *mover*, who provides direction. This is often the role that a chair will need to play at the start of meetings. However, an effective chair will also quickly and artfully encourage others to step into the mover role. The positive intentions of the mover role are not only direction but discipline, commitment, perfection and clarity. But these may be misunderstood on occasion as omnipotence, impatience, indecisiveness and being dictatorial, especially if one gets stuck in this role.

The second role is the *follower*, who provides completion. This is the role played by a director when they support a point, agree with a suggestion, or take accountability for a decision. In addition to completion, the positive intentions of the follower role include compassion, loyalty, service and continuity. This is a service role which, not surprisingly, those supporting the board or acting as a professional adviser, including the company secretary, may find themselves playing. However, the role can be misinterpreted as one that is placating, indecisive, pliant, wishy-washy and perhaps over-accommodating. These are misinterpretations that individuals need to be mindful of in case they, or their role, is perceived as inconsequential or irrelevant.

The third role is the *opposer* role, who provides correction. This role is vital to counter any overly risky proposals by a mover and can also be important in preventing groupthink. In the boardroom, this may be seen, for example, as a key task for non-executive directors in their role of representing shareholders. The positive intentions of this role, in addition to correction, include courage, protection, integrity and survival. However, when one gets stuck in being the devil's advocate opposer, one's behaviour may be misinterpreted as being overly critical, competitive, blaming, attaching and contrary. Not surprisingly, this is often how executive directors may feel towards non-executives if the latter exclusively contribute an opposing stance in all boardroom conversations.

The fourth and final role is the *bystander*, who provides perspective. This is certainly another key adviser role and, although sounding relatively passive, is a highly active observation role. The positive intent of the bystander is, in addition to providing perspective, to provide patience, preservation, moderation and self-reflection. However, these behaviours may be misinterpreted as being disengaged, judgemental, deserting, withdrawn and silent. There may be some personality differences at play here in that more extroverted director types may misunderstand the more introverted director who speaks less but, when they choose to, can positively transform the direction of the meeting.

Isaacs overlaid a distinction between 'inquiry' and 'advocacy' onto Kantor's Four Player model. He defined advocacy as the dynamic balance between moving and opposing and inquiry as the dynamic balance between by-standing and following. He further proposed that effective leaders work to find a balance between advocacy and inquiry in dialogic conversations. A number of observational research studies have confirmed the principles of Isaacs' proposal. For example, Losada (1999) observed more than 50 business teams at work, mainly involved in planning activities, and coded the interactions they made according to a number of criteria. These included the ratio of advocacy to inquiry, the ratio of positive and negative statements, the ratio of internally focused statements (self) to externally focused statements (other) and the amount of connectivity or turn-taking between team members. He also assessed the effectiveness of the teams on a number of performance dimensions including profitability, customer satisfaction and 360-degree evaluations. The results were as follows:

- Connectivity – high-performing teams had extremely high connectivity, medium-performing teams had medium connectivity, low-performing teams had low connectivity.
- Advocacy: Inquiry – high-performing teams had a 1:1 balance of advocacy to inquiry, medium-performing teams had a balance towards advocacy, low-performing teams were advocacy dominant.
- Other: Self – high-performing teams had a balance of self to other-referenced comments, medium-performing teams had a balance towards self-focused statements, low-performing teams were self-focused statement dominant.
- Positivity: Negativity – high-performing teams were strongly positive dominant, medium-performing teams were balanced, low-performance teams were negative dominant in their statements.

The positivity-to-negativity ratio that Losada noticed in high-performing teams was that they exhibited at least three positive statements for every one negative statement (strictly a 2.9:1 ratio called the 'Losada Line') and that their performance only dropped off once the ratio went above 12:1.

Isaacs also proposed four conversational skills that can help each of the four roles to be more effective.

1 Learning to voice effectively is important if we are to be heard by others in the conversation.
2 The better we can listen, the more effective we will be in the role of following.

3 Respect for the other participants is key if we are to oppose in a constructive way, keeping the conversational flow intact.
4 It is essential for the bystander that we are able to suspend our own ideas and opinions in such a way that both we and others can examine them and see their strengths and weaknesses.

Some key takeaways from the Four Player model are that:

- it is important that all roles are played within a conversation for it to be constructive;
- individuals should be aware when they are becoming stuck in one particular role and develop skills in all roles;
- high-performing team dialogue will be highly connected, that is, that there will be significant turn-taking such that everyone will be given and take the opportunity to speak;
- a balance of inquiry and advocacy, as well as making one's own points while equally being interested in others, is key; and
- there needs to exist a strong positive feeling in the boardroom, whereby people build on others' points and show encouragement and support, rather than constantly critiquing and negative nit-picking.

Board conflict

An introduction to team conflict

A key issue related to interactions in the boardroom and across stakeholder groups is when tension and challenge turns to conflict. The word conflict itself tends to have negative connotations. However, it depends how one defines conflict. Conflict in teams can come from three main sources:

1 relationship conflict, which involves personal issues such as dislike among group members and feelings like annoyance, frustration and irritation;
2 task conflict, which is related to differences of opinion on how the team should go about the task; it does not have the negative feelings that can accompany relationship conflict (this is also known as cognitive conflict and arises from diversity of opinions and approaches); and
3 process conflict, which is more about using resources, such as who has responsibility for which deliverable.

According to research conducted by Jen and Mannix (2001), higher levels of relationship conflict are likely to lead to problems and a team being less effective. However, higher levels of task and process conflict can be beneficial depending upon when they occur in the team's evolution. The research suggests that it is beneficial for process conflict to occur at the start of a task when the team is forming. However, performance steeply decreases over time if strong team process norms are not quickly resolved. The research also found that high levels of task conflict can be very beneficial to the quality of decision making and discussion up until the midpoint of that discussion. Lower-performing teams are those who continue with high levels of task conflict, such that they are never able to agree and commit to a team decision. Or, indeed, they are those teams who never actually reach any level of task conflict earlier in the discussion to critically test and evaluate alternative ideas. They therefore reach consensus too early and suffer the negative consequences of groupthink.

The extent of conflict currently in boardrooms

What is the current quality and quantity of conflict in boardrooms today? In 2013, the International Finance Corporation's Corporate Governance Group, in association with the Centre for Effective Dispute Resolution, conducted an online survey of 191 board directors worldwide. Respondents came from the full range of organisational types and a wide range of sectors, with nearly half the respondents having over 10 years' experience as a board member. Some of their headline findings were as follows.

- Overall, 29.6% of respondents had experience with a boardroom dispute affecting the survival of an organisation.
- The most common subject matter of board disputes was 'financial, structural or procedural workings of the organisation' (task conflict using the definitions above), closely followed by 'personal behaviour and attitudes of directors' (relationship conflict using the definitions above).
- Respondents stated that the most difficult factors in resolving board disputes were issues related to competing factions on the board and handling the emotions of those involved in separating personal and business interests.
- Sixty-seven per cent reported that they had encountered unresolved issues; this was especially true of small enterprise respondents.
- Some 75% describe training in the ability to deal with different personalities as very useful.
- A gender difference emerged regarding the kinds of training desired; women were far more interested in receiving training in negotiation skills, while men are more interested in training on how to deal with different personalities.

It is interesting to note that, while the above research notes that around a third of directors have experienced task and relationship conflict, it is the relationship conflict that presents the biggest challenge to their boards.

In 2017, The Chartered Governance Institute, in partnership with Henley Business School, published a report entitled 'Conflict and tension in the boardroom: how managing disagreement improves board dynamics'. This study was informed by 35 face-to-face interviews with 11 chairs, 10 chief executive officers, seven company secretaries, three chief financial officers, three non-executive directors and one general counsel. Some of the key findings were as follows:

- Interviewees characterised tension as disagreement, which is often uncomfortable, but can be resolved by healthy debate. Conflict, however, was regarded as aggressive tension that usually escalates to extreme and unresolved unresolvable levels.
- Tension was seen as positive and necessary, while conflict was seen as disruptive and detrimental and fundamentally damaging to the dynamics of the board.
- Tension and conflict are most likely to emerge during decision making, or be linked to people, personality and historic issues.
- Tension is most likely to lead to destructive conflict when disagreements and concerns are left unresolved for too long.
- Board diversity was seen as positive and facilitative of healthy tension, not an issue that was likely to lead to unresolvable conflict.
- Strategies for managing tension and minimising conflict included explicitly acknowledging concerns during board meetings, face-to-face conversations and de-personalising tension by reminding board members of the higher purpose.
- Conflict resolution takes place most effectively outside the boardroom as informal discussion between board members.
- Strategy and decision-making issues are more appropriately resolved inside the boardroom.
- The chair, company secretary and senior independent director are perceived as playing the most important roles in managing tension and conflict resolution.
- Company secretaries play a critical role in conflict resolution, facilitating and maintaining boards ability to function.

As we can see, both of these reports express findings that are congruent with the Jen and Mannix research – that is, that task conflict (or 'tension' as it was labelled in The Chartered Governance Institute research) was largely positive, whereas relationship conflict was universally negative.

Board role conflict

Katharina Pick's research, mentioned earlier, also identified two specific relational tensions on boards due to board members' potentially conflicting roles. Firstly, there is the relational tension that exists between the non-executive directors and the executive directors. On the one hand, non-executive directors are supposed to be independent, fulfilling an evaluating and monitoring governance role. On the other hand, however, they are also supposed to be mentors who fulfil an advising and joint decision-making role. For their part, executive directors are supposed to be in a reporting and perhaps often defending mode while also similarly jointly responsible for those same board decisions. How the non-executive and executive directors relate to each other around these conflicting roles will largely be dictated by the role-modelling of the relationship between the chair and chief executive officer. If their relationship is open and balanced, then the broader non-executive/

executive relationship will follow suit. However, if their relationship is more parent/child and adversarial, then the other directors are more likely to line up behind their particular captain and take sides.

The second relational tension that Pick suggests exists on the board is the tension between the team being comprised of siloed expertise versus the team having a more cohesive voice. While both roles are required, a careful balance needs to be struck between the two ends of these dynamics. If directors overly advocate expertise, there is a danger that the boardroom interaction can lead to concussive debate rather than cohesive inquiry and dialogue. Overplaying one's expertise in the boardroom may also lead to another dynamic described by transactional analysis called the 'drama triangle'. The drama triangle always has three players: the victim, the persecutor and the rescuer. One example of the drama triangle playing out in a boardroom, which highlights the dangers of overemphasising individualised expertise, is when the management presents itself as being the victim of a persecuting stakeholder and a non-executive director weighs in with some expert advice. The drama in the triangle might occur at the next board meeting, when the management reports back that they tried the non-executive's advice and then blames them for it not working. The management has now shifted to become the persecutor and the victim is now the non-executive director who unintentionally disempowered the management. The drama triangle is a game that is played out when we fall into the trap of being overly parental and rescuing others who themselves should know better.

How to challenge well in the boardroom

What do we do when conflict emerges and how do we challenge constructively to stop it appearing in the first place? We have given many pointers over the text so far and there are some in the report findings above. The UK board review organisation Bvalco summarised a number of recommendations for challenging well in the boardroom. Bvalco suggests the following to encourage constructive challenge:

- The chair should never start or finish a discussion with their opinion as this will stifle ownership and collective authority.
- The chair's ability to listen to others, effectively summarise views around the table and encourage equal participation is vital.
- The chair's role is to encourage evidence-based rather than person-centred challenge.
- Notice and raise an overly aggressive approach with the board. Understand whether this is a style or confidence issue and offer support.
- Get to know other directors individually and at a personal level to enable one to adapt one's style and approach to ensure challenge is heard.
- Verbally praise differences and the thorough consideration of options.

- Use empathy and information search in equal doses. If people feel listened to, they will listen more attentively to others' views.
- Encourage directors to agree the single most important thing the board must do.
- Expect input to the agenda, so that directors arrive at board meetings engaged.
- Instil a sense of team authority, not just a board with a collective agenda.
- Thinking and deciding require different types of brain processes and stimulate different behavioural responses: don't let them become intertwined.
- Consciously apportioning time between informing, thinking and decision-making helps to frame expectation and promote effective behaviours.
- Use the 3:1 ratio rule of appreciation versus criticism to promote resource for thinking and engagement rather than justification and rejection.
- In the annual review of board performance, explicitly analyse the quality of constructive challenge using content and behavioural analysis.

The team tasks lens

The team tasks lens is the usual starting point and domain of team leaders, board chair and governance professionals. As we discussed in Chapter 4, there is general agreement around what the key board outcomes are. Dulewicz and Herbert (2004), for example, define 16 tasks of the board, which cluster into the four areas of supervision of management, accountability to shareholders and other stakeholders, strategy and structure and longer-term vision, mission, values and policy formation.

On the flipside, psychologists are sometimes challenged for focusing too much on the relationship aspects of teams and becoming so intrigued by the dynamic relationships that they miss the opportunities for solving problems in the team at their source. Ruth Wageman, for example, suggests that although the team dynamics are vital, sometimes simply tweaking a few task issues, such as her model's three factors of getting the right people, the right vision and the right structure in place, can cut off later relational issues at their source. The argument here in this chapter, though, is that they are both important lenses to recognise.

What is involved in clarifying team tasks? There are many potential things to tick off the list, such as the team addressing purpose or shared endeavour, vision, values, strategy, objectives and targets, systems, processes and protocols and roles and responsibilities. A simple heuristic that is a useful way of summarising team tasks is thinking of them as grouped under the four Ps:

- purpose (mission and values)
- picture (vision)
- plan (strategy, objectives and targets, systems and processes, charter, etc.)
- parts (roles and responsibilities)

It is important to remember that, in the broader context, these tasks will already be clarified for the organisation as a whole. However, to become a team, the board also needs to consider which of these tasks are specific to their team, independently of the organisation. Remember that one of the definitions of a working group was that their goal was the same as the organisation's overall goal. We will explore how an individual outside the board, in a role as team coach, might support the development of these tasks in Chapter 14.

The systems outside the board

External stakeholders lens

We now turn our attention to the systems that exist outside of the boardroom, starting with the external stakeholders lens.

One first point of clarity is that, when people use the word stakeholder, they are usually thinking about external stakeholders. The definition of stakeholder in this chapter is anyone that has an influence on the board conversation. This is in line with the definition of stakeholder from Edward Freeman, who was one of the initial developers of stakeholder theory in 1984. Freeman looked at stakeholders from an organisational perspective, defining them as 'any group or individual who can affect or is affected by the achievement of the organisation's objective'. Stakeholders are usually initially identified as either internal or external. However, with our systemic hat on, we can see that all the interactions with external stakeholders can become internalised into the board dynamic. Thus, strictly speaking, none of them is fully external to the board. Take regulators, for example. As Tate says:

> Regulators conveniently imagine themselves to be objective observers, positioned outside a flawed fishtank, entitled to point fingers and pass judgements. But... (we are not) passive observers of an external world; rather we know our world through interacting with it, and our emotions can limit or enrich that interaction, crossing the divide between subject and object. This analysis clearly locates regulators inside the fishtank, contributing their fair share of toxins, and sometimes having unintended consequences... The way the regulators' involvement is designed cannot avoid their becoming part of the effective hierarchical power structure, ratcheting up all-pervasive and institutionalised 'management by fear'.

A useful tool to understand the external source stakeholder dynamic is through mapping them based on the extent of their influence or power and interest. Those stakeholders with lower interest and lower power/influence are seen as the least important and therefore merit the least consideration in decision-making. However, those stakeholders who have higher power/influence and interest will be key players who the board need to focus their efforts upon and perhaps even involve in their decision making through regular engagement and consultation.

While shareholders are often seen as the stakeholders with the most influence and interest, other stakeholders are becoming seen as just as influential, or even more so in some cases. Consider customers in a retail environment, the environmental lobby in mining sectors, employees in any organisation or students as consumers in the education sector.

Case study: NatWest's stakeholder engagement

In its 2019 annual report, NatWest Group identified not only the key objectives of all their main stakeholders, but also the various activities that the board undertook to engage with these stakeholders and how they were able to bring their voice into the boardroom.

Specifically, the stakeholders listed were its customers, colleagues, shareholders, regulators, suppliers, their community and the environment. Their discussions with these stakeholders provide insight into their board discussions across a number of areas including their purpose, the appointment of their new CEO and distributions of capital.

They also provide a stakeholder engagement diagram (see below) that explains the interaction between the bank and each of these stakeholder groups:

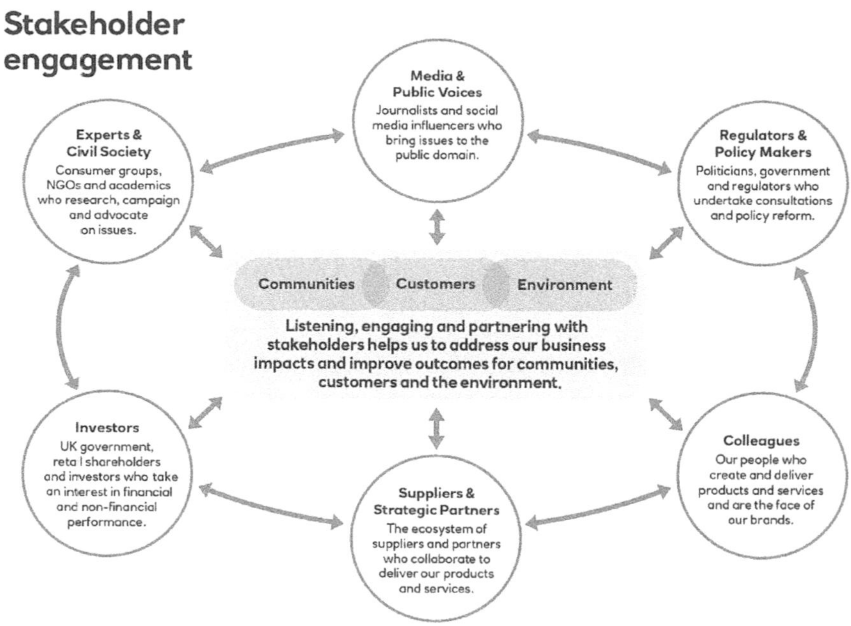

The recognition of the need to understand and engage more fully with key stakeholders is growing within organisations. This is reflected by the extensive section on relations with stakeholders in the Financial Reporting Council's 2018 Guidance on Board Effectiveness. The guidance begins with the following statement (number 34):

> An effective board will appreciate the importance of dialogue with shareholders, the workforce and other key stakeholders, be proactive in ensuring that such dialogue takes place, and that the feedback is taken into account in the board's decision making. How the board approaches this will provide useful insight into the company's culture.

The guidance then provides 12 further pointers on relations with shareholders and other key stakeholders and concludes with the following six checklist questions for boards:

1. Can we describe how stakeholders are prioritised and why?
2. What are the key concerns of our workforce, our suppliers and our customers and how are we addressing them?
3. Does the workforce consider that customers and suppliers are treated fairly and that the company cares about its impact on the environment and community?
4. Have we sought input from enough stakeholders to be comfortable that we have a rounded view?
5. Have we listened properly to the stakeholder voice and what impact has this had on our decisions?
6. Have we considered how environmental and social issues might impact on the business or linked our strategy to a recognised international framework?

To support this guidance, The Chartered Governance Institute produced a report entitled 'The stakeholder voice in board decision making: strengthening the business, promoting long-term success', in 2017. There is a significant amount of detail and further guidance in this report concerning directors' duties, stakeholder identification, board composition, induction and training, board discussion, engagement mechanisms and reporting and feedback, all in relation to greater awareness of a board's key stakeholders. This is all as part of a reaction to new UK secondary legislation requiring listed companies to explain how their directors comply with the legislative requirement to have regard for employee and other stakeholder interests. Ten core principles are outlined in the report.

1. Boards should identify, and keep under regular review, who they consider their key stakeholders to be and why.
2. Boards should determine which stakeholders they need to engage with directly, as opposed to relying solely on information from management.
3. When evaluating their composition and effectiveness, boards should identify what stakeholder expertise is needed in the boardroom and decide whether they have, or would benefit from, directors with directly relevant experience or understanding.
4. When recruiting any director, the nomination committee should take the stakeholder perspective into account when deciding on the recruitment process and the selection criteria.

5 The chair – supported by the company secretary – should keep under review the adequacy of the training received by all directors on stakeholder-related matters and the induction received by new directors, particularly those without previous board experience.
6 The chair – supported by the board, management and the company secretary – should determine how best to ensure that the board's decision-making processes give sufficient consideration to key stakeholders.
7 Boards should ensure that appropriate engagement with key stakeholders is taking place and that this is kept under regular review.
8 In designing engagement mechanisms, companies should consider what would be most effective and convenient for the stakeholders, not just the company.
9 The board should report to its shareholders on how it has taken the impact on key stakeholders into account when making decisions.
10 The board should provide feedback to those stakeholders with whom it has engaged, which should be tailored to the different stakeholder groups.

All of these recommendations will strengthen the stakeholder voice within the boardroom. This will not only create more inclusive, evidence-based and diverse conversations, but the associated increase in cognitive diversity and task conflict will impact the board dynamic. Within a cohesive team, this a potent potential platform to significantly enhance board performance.

Case study: Inviting employees into the boardroom

One practical step to involve a key stakeholder, the employee, is to include them in board meetings. This was a practice encouraged by Ricardo Semler, the chief executive officer of the Brazilian company Semco Partners and author of the management books *Maverick* and *The Seven-day Weekend*.

Semler has stated that he runs his company as an experiment in democracy. In line with this, he offers an open seat at each board meeting for a worker representative to apply for on a first-come, first-served basis. A week before the board meeting happens, an invitation is sent out and the employee who is selected then attends and fully participates as a voting board member.

In Germany, it is a requirement for all companies to have an employee representative permanently appointed to the supervisory board, thus ensuring that the workforce voice is heard at board level. Of course, there are other models of workers' participation than the German one. The Organisation for Economic Co-operation and Development's (OECD) Employment Outlook 2017 shows that other forms of employee participation in the management of private companies are also present in Austria, Denmark, Finland, France, Hungary, Luxembourg, the Netherlands, Norway, Poland, Slovakia, Slovenia and Sweden. In Chile, Greece, Ireland, Israel,

Poland, Portugal and Spain, workers' representatives often sit on boards of state-owned companies. In some of these countries, workers sit on the board of directors, in others they sit on a supervisory board. Further, in some cases, they are appointed by labour unions or are elected directly by the employees, while in other cases they are selected by employee committees. There is no single or dominant model of worker representation to be easily imported from one country to another.

All of the above recent developments around stakeholders in corporate governance are in line with how stakeholder theory is now changing its thinking away from 'managing' stakeholders to 'engaging' with stakeholders. There is a recognition that there is not just a one-way relationship where one can control the thoughts and actions of various stakeholder groups. Instead, there is a bi-directional relationship, which is also acknowledged in our definition of board dynamics, whereby boards may influence the stakeholder environment around them but, equally, may also be influenced back by them. As Andriof and Waddock (2002) have stated:

> Stakeholder theory has moved away from an entirely corporate-centric focus in which stakeholders are viewed as subjects to be managed towards more of a network-based, relational and process-orientated view of company stakeholder engagement.

As the nature of engaging with stakeholders has changed to be one that is more relational, the issue of encouraging dialogue, trust and appropriate challenge across these system boundaries – just as we would hope directors would model inside the boardroom – becomes an important way to engage with stakeholders outside of the boardroom.

One further broad stakeholder theme that has gained ground in governance commentary in recent years is that of 'stewardship'. Stewardship refers to any organisational stakeholder's acceptance of responsibility to shepherd and safeguard the organisation and its assets. One operationalisation of this into governance regulation is the 2010 UK Stewardship Code. This was created by the FRC, following a 2009 recommendation from the Walker Report about the stewardship responsibility of institutional investors. The Code's aim is to enhance the quality of engagement between investors and companies to help improve long-term returns to shareholders and has been updated a few times, including as recently as 2019.

Wider systemic influences

The sixth and final systemic lens through which to make sense of the board dynamic are the wider systemic influences. The COVID-19 pandemic, as a general example, has provided a stark and chastening example of how a wider systemic crisis can significantly influence the dynamic within the board. These wider influences can be summarised by the acronym PESTLE:

- Political – what is changing in the political landscape that may have an effect on your sector, industry and organisation? For example, globally there has been a shift away from 'left versus right' politics to a 'closed' (fear, anger, ignorance, etc.) versus 'open' (curiosity, compassion, courage, etc.) political agenda.

- Economic – what are the economic patterns that may be influencing your wider environment? For example, post-economic crisis there is a recognition that the classic 'market versus government' continuum is incomplete and so the 'GDP versus well-being' co-ordinates are also now part of the global economic conversation.
- Social – what are the societal trends in terms of demographics, consumer expectations, etc.? For example, how will COVID-19 crisis patterns such as remote working influence us and how will wider trends, such as the increasing average age of industrialised countries and plateauing life expectancy due to alarming rises in chronic illness, affect organisations?
- Technology – what are the cutting-edge industry innovations and technological advances that may have an impact? For example, Amazon Echo was the biggest-selling Christmas gift in 2018, so how will an 'audio-first' internet affect how people interact with your organisation?
- Legal – what legal statutes, case law, directives and/or regulations exist or are being introduced, that may have an impact on your organisation? For example, how might you need to respond as equality issues increase, especially around the various diversity types discussed in Chapter 8?
- Environmental – what are the local and global energy, waste, pollution, wildlife impacts and relationships with your organisation? For example, how might the recent growing awareness of global plastic pollution affect your organisation?

It may seem strange to wallow in such a big picture perspective in what often feels like a very tactical and cut-and-thrust business agenda. However, it is often useful to take this big picture view to horizon scan, scenario plan and attempt to limit board 'black swan' blind spots. As we saw in the board narrative at the start of this chapter, taking a wide-angle lens enables the board to acknowledge the changes in their regulatory environment, which may turn out to be at the source of the issues. Thus, recognising that the wider system will also influence the internal dynamic, can present a powerful opportunity to engage in more productive board dynamics.

One final relevance of having this wider perspective as part of the board conversation is how it relates to what is known as the environmental, social and governance (ESG) agenda. This perspective is gaining significant interest, as many material and financial risks are directly related to these broad ESG issues. This agenda has been accelerated by the recent Black Lives Matter movement and the global pandemic. However, recent research on US Corporate Boards by Tensie Whelen at NYU Stern suggests that boards 'suffer from inadequate expertise in financially material ESG matters' and highlights how broad awareness, or indeed specific expertise, in ESG issues should be included in board advertising, recruitment and training.

Conclusion

How do we know when board director relationships are working well? There are two factors that can indicate this. Firstly, the board members will mutually trust each other: they will see each other as reliable and credible and that the relationship is mutually beneficial. Importantly, they will also feel comfortable discussing their personal beliefs, opinions and feelings with a degree of intimacy. Secondly, they will talk to each other as equals, in 'adult–adult' terms rather than talking down (as a parent might do to a child) or being beholden to (as a child might do to an adult) the other person.

Boards must extend their perspective from purely individual attributes, to team dynamics. How do we know when the board is working well as a team? There are many ways of assessing how well a board team is functioning. Using Tuckman's model, we might see that a board has progressed to the 'performing' stage, characterised by it having an established mission, vision, roles and norms such that members can focus completely on achieving their common goal. They will be free of most or all of the team dysfunctions described in Lencioni's framework. Following dialogue theory, they will also be well connected by taking turns to speak, they will have a good balance of inquiry and advocacy and other to self-statements, as well as at least a 3:1 ratio of positivity to negativity. Finally, the board will display a degree of challenge but, when conflict does occur, it will be based on the task and process (when appropriate) rather than on relationships and will be appreciated as directors will have the ability to challenge constructively rather than destructively.

Beyond individual director and board dynamics, relationships must also include their stakeholder network. The whole stakeholder system includes the individual director, the inter-personal director relationships, the board team relationships, the board team tasks, the board's stakeholder interfaces and the board's wider systemic context. Key concepts to understand board dynamics across all these stakeholder lenses include trust, dialogue, conflict and challenge.

While the focus of this text is on the dynamics of the board itself, the collective and individual engagement by board members with their wider stakeholder group cannot be ignored. The stakeholder voice in the boardroom is justifiably becoming increasingly recognised. The board must be mindful of each stakeholder's individual perspective, as well as each stakeholder's interaction, interdependence and impact on the organisation. Ignoring stakeholders is no longer an option for an organisation in any sector.

The stakeholders of an organisation and, by extension, those of the board, are intertwined. The challenge for the board is to balance their differing needs while maintaining their its own effectiveness. Do you consciously consider all your stakeholders or just a few?

7 – Culture in the boardroom

Governance and culture

In recent years, 'culture' has become the watchword in governance. There has been a growing appreciation that boardroom scandals are not simply due to one or a small number of rotten apples – being either those at the very top of the organisational tree or those from the branches where the scandal first hit (such as the engineers who rigged the tests in the Volkswagen emissions scandal). Instead, there is a shift in perspective to question whether the fault was more likely due to a bad cultural barrel in the lead-up to a crisis event.

Similarly, culture is also becoming seen as superseding compliance regulation. The phrase 'culture eats strategy for breakfast' is often used to rally people round to the appreciation of the impact of culture on organisations. However, based on the increasing recognition that tightening up on compliance rules and regulations is not, by itself enough to move the needle in any significant way in reducing the number of governance failures, the adapted refrain 'culture eats compliance for breakfast' now seems particularly apt.

The 2018 Chartered Governance Institute report entitled 'Organisational culture in sport: assessing and improving attitudes and behaviour' captures this tone well:

> Whilst steps to improve governance processes are to be welcomed, there is a growing recognition that rules-based compliance cannot on its own deliver healthy behaviour within organisations. Indeed, the efficacy of rules and processes depends in large part on the integrity of those subject to them: their usefulness is negated if there is a mindset of bypassing them. Across all sectors there is an awareness that behaviour is determined to a significant degree by the culture of the entity concerned.

This shift has partly been a reaction to the financial crisis, which triggered a great number of independent reviews to more rigorously understand what went wrong and where to lay the blame.

Case study: The Bank of England and the financial crisis

The UK's Bank of England is an apt case study when looking at reaction to the 2007–2008 financial crisis. The Bank was the subject of three independent reviews into its operations during the period when it handled the emergency lending to HBOS and the Royal Bank of Scotland in late 2008.

One of the key conclusions of the reviews was that a culture of 'excessive deference and hierarchy' was a major part of what damaged effectiveness during the period. The banker, Bill Winters, who wrote one of the reviews, noted that the bank was too 'centralised and hierarchical' and that, 'there appears to be some tendency for them [less senior staff] to filter recommendations in such a way as to maximise the likelihood that senior staff will find the recommendations palatable'.

This hierarchical, deferential culture meant that the organisation became slow to react, learn and innovate.

The recognition of the importance of culture has also been reflected in recent corporate governance codes. For example, the UK Corporate Governance Code declares that:

> The board should establish the company's purpose, values and strategy, and satisfy itself that these and its culture are aligned. All directors must act with integrity, lead by example and promote the desired culture. (Principle B)

The first sentence of this principle suggests that the board has a responsibility that is rational and formal in the way that it discusses and conceptualises culture. However, the second sentence also recognises that each individual director has the responsibility to behave informally in such a way as to role-model the culture; they must also 'walk the walk'. This importance placed on culture is also reflected in the Financial Reporting Council's associated Guidance on Board Effectiveness. The guidance on culture spans no less than three pages and has six detailed guidance notes associated with it.

However, if we were to ask any board member what exactly the word 'culture' means, we might get blank looks or very differing answers. Most of those answers would probably be associated with organisational culture, as this is what much of the mainstream commentary focuses on. Further, if we assume that the 'tone from the top' is what is most likely to influence organisational culture and that the fish does indeed 'rot from the head', then what do we know about board culture specifically? The following sections of this chapter therefore focus on what board culture is, how well boards are currently doing in terms of their culture, what types of perspectives currently exist that help us look at board culture, and, importantly, what can a board do to develop a more positive culture.

The first thing to do is to go back to basics and take a look at what we mean by the term 'culture' in the first place.

Defining board culture

What is culture?

When considering culture, we can combine the individualist focus from psychology that we introduced in Chapter 3, the group lens that we employed from social psychology in Chapters 4 and 5 and also a more anthropological perspective that we began to consider in Chapter 6.

When people hear the word 'culture', they often assume we are talking about country culture – that is, one's nation state. However, there are many varieties of culture, both to compare differences across individuals but also inherently within the same person. Geert Hofstede, a Dutch social psychologist, former IBM employee and professor of organisational anthropology at Maastricht University in the Netherlands, is a well-known pioneer of research in cross-cultural groups and organisations. He has argued that an individual's culture has a variety of levels, which are:

- national, according to one's country (or countries for migrants);
- regional and/or ethnic and/or religious and/or linguistic;
- gender, having different assumptions and expectations of females and males;
- generational, the differences between age groupings;
- social class, linked to educational opportunities and occupations; and
- organisational, with different organisations having their individual cultures and subcultures.

We touched on social class in Chapter 3 and will cover gender, generational and ethnic cultural differences within the chapter on diversity (Chapter 8). The significant differences between national cultures that might exist on a board and the organisational or corporate culture will be topics discussed in detail in Chapter 13. The focus in this chapter, however, is specifically on the different ways that board culture has been conceptualised, how it is shaped and how to influence this.

What might be a way to define board culture? There are many colloquial definitions of culture that give us a window into a potential definition, such as that a board culture could be:

- 'What's expected when no one says what's expected.'
- 'A unique combination of processes and priorities.'
- 'What actions lead to a person being promoted/getting paid more.'
- 'How we deal with each other and with our customers.'
- 'What happens when no one is looking.'
- 'A by-product of the leaders and what they stand for.'
- 'The worst behaviour the leader is willing to tolerate.'

In addition, perhaps the most frequently used high-level description is: 'Culture is the way we do things around here.'

If we are to unpick what the above phrases are grasping at in more technical detail, we can take our lead from Edgar Schein, a former professor at the MIT Sloan School of Management and another significant thought leader in organisational culture. Schein describes 10 categories of culture which relate to the observed behavioural regularities that exist when people interact, including the language they use, the customs and traditions that evolve and the rituals that they employ in a variety of situations. These categories are as follows:

1 **Group norms:** these are the implicit standards and values that emerge in working groups, e.g. the processes of boards and committees, how board meetings get done.
2 **Espoused values:** these are the articulated, publicly announced principles and values that a group claims to be trying to achieve, e.g. the governance section of an annual report.
3 **Formal philosophy:** these are the broad policies and ideological principles that guide the group's action towards the requirements of their stakeholders, e.g. organisation-specific corporate governance codes of conduct.
4 **Rules of the game:** these are the implicit, unwritten rules for getting along in the organisation, the ropes that a new member must learn in order to become an accepted member, e.g. I must not directly challenge the aggressive chief executive.
5 **Climate:** this is the feeling that is conveyed in a group by the physical layout (discussed in Chapter 9) and the way in which members interact with each other and with outsiders, e.g. a very hierarchical and deferential culture may have a classic imposing boardroom and table on a top floor and stakeholder communication will follow a classic formal style.
6 **Embedded skills:** these are the special competencies displayed by group members in accomplishing certain tasks that get passed onto future generations without necessarily being articulated in writing, e.g. the ability to oppose and challenge another's perspective with respect, tact and care.
7 **Habits of thinking and mental models:** these are the shared cognitive frames that guide our perception, thought and decision making taught to new group members, e.g. that 'an 80% good enough decision taken is better than a 95% decision delayed'.
8 **Shared meanings:** these are the emergent understandings created by group members as they interact with each other, e.g. shared agreement around board discussion priorities.
9 **Root metaphors or integrating symbols:** these are the ways in which groups evolve to characterise themselves, which may or may not be appreciated consciously, but can become embodied in the physical layout and other material artefacts of the group, e.g. the board as the company royalty in the ivory tower office and company jet, or the board as the company servants rotating offices for meetings to ensure all stakeholders are engaged.

10 **Formal rituals and celebrations:** these are the ways in which the group celebrates key events that reflect important values or important passages by members, e.g. the meal the night before the board meeting or how board members are inducted.

Schein has proposed that these categories exist within corporate culture on three levels, in what is sometimes conceptualised as his 'iceberg model' of culture. Firstly, there is a surface level that he calls *artefacts and etiquette*. These are the visible concrete elements such as language, the form of greeting, clothing, physical layout, etc. Secondly, there is a middle level, which he calls the *espoused values*. These are not immediately visible but drive a consistent pattern of behaviours and actions throughout the culture – for example, how decisions are made, how information is communicated and how teams are supposed to interact and work together. Thirdly, there is the deep level, which he calls the *basic underlying assumptions*. These are the culture's unconscious, taken-for-granted values and beliefs, their core ethics and morals which will guide judgements that the group holds about what is right or wrong, fair or unfair. The concept of the iceberg, that is, that only the first surface layer is completely visible, denotes that culture is largely something that cannot be observed or measured directly but that can only be inferred from a variety of more surface cultural markers.

The various distinctions described above led Schein (2004) to define culture, at its most precise technical level, as 'the accumulated shared learning of a given group, covering the behavioural, emotional and cognitive elements of the group members' total psychological functioning' leading to an overall definition of culture as:

> A pattern of shared basic assumptions that was learned by a group as it solved problems of external adaptation and internal integration, has worked well enough to be considered valid and, therefore, to be taught to new members as the correct way to perceive, think and feel in relation to those problems.

This can lead us to the useful conclusion that one simple definition of board culture is therefore 'the repeating patterns of the board dynamic'. As we discussed in Chapter 6, the board dynamic is defined by the visible and behavioural interactions between individual board members and the interactions of the members as a whole group that can influence, and are influenced by, the wider stakeholder environment within which the board exists. Thus, the unseen board culture is created internally by board members' individual internal web of different cultural values (national, organisational, gender, etc.) and also the values and ethics of all their stakeholder system. These jointly emerge in the observable board dynamic. As Hofstede et al. (1990) note:

> The core of culture is formed by values… and feelings that are often unconscious and rarely discussible, that can't be observed as such but are manifested in alternatives of behaviour.

Thus, the behavioural patterns that appear within the boardroom through how board members interact will be markers of the board's core cultural values. The most basic cultural marker in the boardroom is the unit of conversation, to which we will now turn our attention.

Board cultural markers

There are many artefacts and behaviours that provide a window into the culture of an organisation, which we will explore in more depth in Chapter 13. In the boardroom these markers are the patterns of board dynamics, the various interactions and conversations that exist.

Board conversations as a representation of culture

The central unit of culture mentioned in our board dynamics definition is the unit of 'interaction' between board members individually and collectively. This interaction could also be labelled 'communication' or 'conversation' (as we did in Chapter 6). In the field of organisational psychology, there is a recent school of thought that proposes that organisations are just the loose boundaries between systems and can be viewed as simply a set of conversations and, therefore, that organisational change happens, and culture is built, one conversation at a time.

Conversations and interactions are not just words. They include tone, body language and a multitude of other consciously or unconsciously transmitted methods of communication which might include:

- facial expression
- eye contact (or the lack of)
- tone of voice
- pace of speech
- frequency of speech
- whispering and asides
- who speaks to whom and how frequently
- gestures
- angle of body
- choice of clothing
- late or early arrival
- interruptions
- note taking (or lack of) and
- early or late departure

How these verbal and non-verbal interactions cluster to form dynamic patters will create the board culture. Equally, how these can be used or adapted in a virtual setting can heavily influence the culture of the board. The Financial Reporting Council's Guidance on Board Effectiveness defines a healthy culture as one that has the attributes of:

- honesty
- openness
- respect
- adaptability
- reliability
- recognition
- acceptance of challenge
- accountability
- a sense of shared purpose

The quality of conversational interaction was introduced in Chapter 6, particularly around creating a high-performing board team that has trusting relationships and dialogue. This type of board would therefore create a healthy culture reflecting the list above. Unfortunately, however, there is much that can go wrong with conversations that will have an impact on efforts to maintain a positive culture.

What can go wrong with board conversations?

There are a whole host of things that can, and often do, go wrong with conversations on boards. These may denote a negative dynamic which, when ossified, will result in a toxic culture. Many of these issues arise because of the particular characteristics that boards exhibit (discussed in Chapter 4) and generally fit into broad categories (following Merchant and Pick, 2010) such that:

- directors who are expert and well-qualified may cease to be engaged in board conversations and 'loaf';
- the board may be susceptible to group conformity rather than challenge;
- directors, like members of all groups, are likely to discuss information that is already known, rather than novel, causing information asymmetry;
- individual concerns may not be raised;
- the group may make more extreme decisions than any one individual would choose to make;
- the group may become prone to groupthink;
- the board's conversational processes may reflect previously useful but now outdated routines;
- conflict conversations may turn personal, emotional and be destructive; and
- the board may be vulnerable to particular directors abusing their power.

More specifically, what can these problems actually look like in the boardroom? Here is a list of commonly occurring conversational issues that can occur within boardroom interactions that many of you may recognise and empathise with (drawing from Chamber101, 2018; Tavistock/Walker Review, 2009; and Leblanc, 2011).

- An issue is discussed for a whole meeting then left unsettled.
- Personal conflict exists between a director and the board.
- A talkative member takes over a meeting or a quiet member rarely speaks.
- Emotional interactions commonly occur which are draining and negative feelings carry over for a long time.
- Board members fail to signal their concern or disagreement about a significant issue, only alerting the chair after the meeting.
- The board is over-engaged in minor details and avoids addressing more strategic and difficult issues.
- Board members fail to make decisions, or constantly revisit and reopen debates about decisions that have already been made.
- Board members appear remote and uninterested, for example, through erratic board attendance, not reading board papers, getting distracted by phones or side conversations, not carrying out agreed actions, etc.
- One or two individuals dominate the conversation and proceedings.
- People are overly polite and feel that consensus must be achieved. Consequently, there are no dissenting voices or differing views.
- A small group sews up decisions before the meeting.
- The chief executive is aggressive and tries to manage and control the board or committee meeting.
- One or more of the directors: breaches confidentiality, does not support board decisions, acts out of self-interest, says one thing and does another, or speaks on behalf of a stakeholder rather than the best interests of the organisation.
- There is an overall lack of diversity of opinion in the boardroom.
- The chair weighs into topics too early or unduly influences the collective board or, on the contrary, is 'owned' by the chief executive officer.
- The board does not assess itself or its members adequately or at all.
- The board 'over relies' on one particular director.
- The chair seems to favour some directors over others.

Current quality of board cultural dynamics

If board conversations are the unit of cultural dynamics, then what evidence do we currently have about what is actually happening in the black box of boards so that we can take the temperature of board culture more generally?

Of the many sources of evidence that we could cite, three provide a flavour of the current negative picture. Firstly, in Dulewicz et al.'s research in 1993, looking at board standards, it was noted that there was a significant lack of cohesion among many boards. The research found that around 50% of directors stated that they viewed the board as a group of individuals rather than seeing them as a team. This led the authors to conclude that many of the boards within their sample were experiencing a lack of cohesion in their culture.

At the same time as this research, there were many high-profile reviews being undertaken on the public sector, in particular of the UK's NHS failures. These reviews, coordinated by the Healthcare Commission, identified board dynamics as a causal factor in the failures, citing in particular autocratic leadership styles and a culture of denial at board level. This specific finding was also reflected in a review of the evidence on failing health care organisations.

As well as many boards suffering from a lack of cohesion, many have also been found lacking in a culture of appropriate challenge.

More generally, there is research that has provided an overall sense of the cultural dynamic on boards. For example, Tomorrow's Corporate Governance organisation published a report in 2012, entitled 'Improving the quality of boardroom conversations'. This report cited a survey of FTSE 350 non-executive board members that was facilitated by Korn/Ferry and KPMG. When asking their sample if they 'felt valued', only 54% of respondents felt that the boards they served on often really leveraged their expertise and knowledge to maximum advantage. Similarly, only 53% of non-executive directors felt that their executive director colleagues often viewed them as valued and experienced business partners. Worryingly, only 60% felt that their contribution was often valued by their chair. When asked, 'Do their boards actively address the quality of their conversations?', the sample gave even lower scores. For example, only 39% of respondents stated that their board often discussed ways to improve the quality of interaction and debate; while 23% stated this was addressed at the annual board review, 38% said that they rarely or never had that type of discussion. One further finding of note from the report was around the most common reasons given for poor or ineffective boardroom conversations. The top four issues mentioned were:

1. dominant personalities/groups of people among board members (79%);
2. inappropriate allocation of time at board meetings to discuss matters requiring debate (52%);
3. lack of preparation by board members and other attendees in advance of board meetings (50%); and
4. the unhelpful manner of presenting information to the board (46%).

Of these four drivers of ineffective conversations, three seem like simple technical issues (allocating time, preparation and improving presentations). However, just because something seems simple does not mean that it is. Perhaps these boards are stuck in a culture that reinforces existing and ineffective processes, which then negatively influence the quality of board conversations. Perhaps the lack of preparation by board members is aligned to the quality of conversation at the board meeting itself, or there is a failure to address the lack of preparation by individuals which results in all members reviewing board pack contents in the actual meeting. Perhaps invited attendees include those who have prepared part of the content of the board pack and, during the meeting, regurgitate the same information – in which case, why should a board member pre-read an item for it to be presented again at the meeting?

Although the majority of the evidence cited above is more than five years old, there seems to be no reason to believe that the quality of conversations on boards has improved significantly in the last few years. We urgently need a better understanding of why these behaviours occur and what to do about them.

Board cultural dynamics

There are many frameworks through which to analyse board culture. These can help us understand the patterns of shared basic values and assumptions that the board might have. This section will describe and explain a number of models that help make some sense of these basic assumptions, which create the emergent and dynamic behaviours that are the visible evidence of these assumptions.

Bedrock of the board culture model

Richard Chait, a professor emeritus at the Harvard Graduate School of Education, has created a model he calls the 'bedrock of board culture' which draws on more than three decades of observations of small and large boards, largely from the not-for-profit sector. Although the model arose from this sector, its lessons can be easily and usefully applied to boards from all sectors and industries. Chait asserts that two key assumptions dictate a board's culture.

The first assumption concerns the board's dominant presupposition about the director's role. Are directors group members, or are they free agents? Chait uses the metaphor of musical groups to illustrate his point and asks, 'To what extent is a board more akin to a symphonic orchestra or a jazz ensemble?' Members of an orchestra will subsume their individualism and adopt prescribed roles, such that the musicians are literally and figuratively on the same page. Boards that act as orchestras will fulfil the criteria of teams that we discussed in Chapter 4, such that they will play by shared team rules and collaboratively create team norms. However, members of a jazz ensemble-style board will operate on different assumptions. They will play together, but this time more as a group rather than a team, with far more self-direction and improvisation.

The second key assumption concerns the board's role as, in Chait's public sector language, a 'public watchdog' or an 'institutional guardian'. The public watchdog assumption is equivalent to a board that solely focuses on their wider stakeholder interests (which is often a 'taken for granted' assumption that many boards may have). This is the classic agency theory assumption that a non-executive director's role is to represent the stakeholders and act as a counterbalance to an organisation's innate bias towards self-interest. At the other end of the spectrum, boards who are institutional guardians will be much more internally focused, perhaps even more so if the chair and chief executive officer roles are conflated, such that board members will assume that their success is posited in solely fulfilling the institution's ambitions.

When combined, these two assumptions about the board's role generate four cultural archetypes which, although oversimplified, can create diagnostic value. These four types are as follows (see also Figure 8):

- **Type I – 'Orchestra' (group member and institutional guardian):** These boards are highly collegial and cohesive, but are at risk of groupthink and excessive deference to peers.
- **Type II – 'Consultants' (free-agent and institutional guardian):** These boards serve the organisation's best interests, but they only do so with board members adding value as individuals or as subsets rather than as a whole. This type of board engenders strong central leadership, which can risk micro-management and reduced decision-making ability through information asymmetry whereby directors understand parts of the organisation but not the whole.
- **Type III – 'Regulatory agency' (group member and public watchdog):** This culture is more of a compliance and oversight-focused board, which sees its responsibility as monitoring rules, regulations, policies and procedures. The culture in the boardroom is therefore rather formal and bureaucratic and agendas can be long and underpinned by significant reporting. This board may lack an ability to be strategic in issues and be able to generate innovation and insight.
- **Type IV – 'Lone rangers' (free-agent and public watchdog):** This board culture will be weaker, as individual directors will see their role as more about representing their particular shareholder interests rather than functioning as part of a cohesive collective. Directors will have significant expertise and will not be afraid to use this to challenge organisational decisions. There may be a risk of the organisation being continually pulled from pillar to post with a zig-zagging strategy and of non-executive directors/trustees and executive directors/management often working at cross purposes.

Figure 8 Bedrock of board culture framework (Chait, 2016)

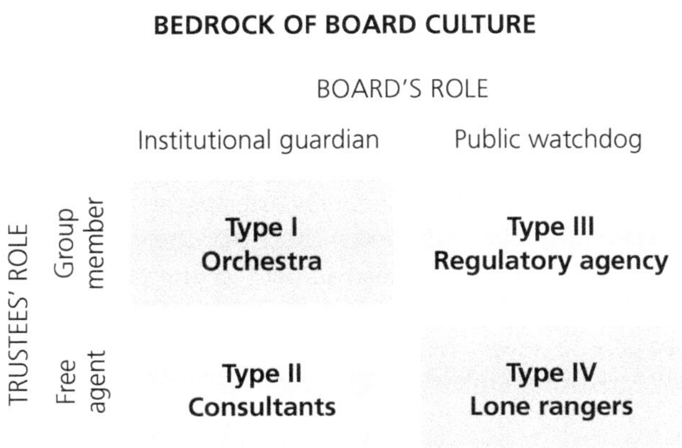

Chait acknowledges that these descriptions are caricatures, but they do provide a springboard for boards to ask a series of important cultural questions:

- Do we have a dominant culture?
- If not, what assumptions do we need to reconcile?
- If yes, do we fit squarely within one quadrant or at the border of two?
- Are we where we want to be and, if not, what assumptions do we need to confront?

Addressing these questions may provoke some uncomfortable conversations. However, they will ultimately help a board to acknowledge its cultural assumptions and address any potential dysfunctions that these might be creating.

Power culture

Another similar framework that provides some insight into how the assumptions of the board can influence its culture is the typology of the relative powers of the chief executive officer and the board of directors created by Pearce and Zahra (1991). Again, using two axes to create four types, this model pitches either 'low' or 'high' CEO power against 'low' or 'high' board power. The first type of board culture that is characterised is the *caretaker* board, also known in the literature as the 'third party' or 'review and approve' board type. This kind of board exists simply out of legal necessity and a leadership vacuum, due to power being shared by the CEO and other key executives. Decision making is largely ceremonial and outsider input may be limited. Unsurprisingly, these boards do not contribute significantly to effective company performance and should be rarely seen in operational organisations.

The second board culture, the *statutory* board, is characterised by high CEO power and low board power. It has also been described as an 'advisory', 'managerial control' or 'ratifying' style board in the literature. This board is the prototypical image of an ineffective board that is there, again, out of legal necessity, only to rubberstamp executive decisions. This may be because the board of directors do not have enough expertise or interest, but equally could be because there has been insufficient attention given to defining roles and responsibilities. These boards may have been the cultural norm in the UK before the 1992 Cadbury Report and may be somewhat still the case in countries where the chief executive and chair roles are held by the same person. These types of boards are also often seen in early stage startups, family businesses or entrepreneur-led businesses.

The third board culture is the *proactive* board, characterised by low chief executive officer power and high board power. More like the supervisory board model seen in continental Europe, this is also known in the literature as a 'strategic/shareholders control' style board. These boards will usually be comprised primarily of outside directors, represent all key stakeholder constituencies and enjoy diverse expertise of members with a primary focus on strategy.

The final board culture is the *participative* board, which is characterised by both high chief executive officer power and high board power. This type is also known in the literature as the 'collegial', 'shared leadership' or normative/strategic style board. It is characterised by discussion, debate and disagreement and distinguished from the proactive board due to the emphasis placed on building and reaching consensus in decision making. As proactive boards rely more on formal powers to resolve disputes, this can lead to more of a culture of antagonistic debate and potentially conflict compared to the dialogue and measured challenge of participative board conversations.

In their study, Pearce and Zahra investigated what the differences were between these four types of board and their composition, characteristics, process and style. They found that there was no difference in composition measures (such as size, number of outsiders and the inclusion of minorities) between the four board types. However, they did identify that participatory boards included significantly more women, had better board processes (in terms of being more efficient, more deliberate and less impulsive, being quicker to make decisions, being more progressive and being supportive of the chief executive officer) and showed overall higher subjective and financial performance. One conclusion from this study was that boards would be well advised to create a culture of sharing power across all directors, both executive and non-executive, in an effort to achieve more favourable results. If nothing else, this also ensures that all directors participate and their individual capabilities, experience and knowledge are used for the benefit of the board and the wider stakeholder system.

David Nadler, Chairman of Mercer Delta Consulting, a global management consulting firm that specialises in corporate governance, similarly proposes a continuum around the question: 'How engaged should a board be?' He suggests five possible board models which fall along a continuum of engagement.

- The *passive* board, similar to the previously mentioned statutory board, functions at the discretion of the chief executive officer and has limited participation and accountability, only existing to ratify management's preferences.
- The *certifying* board confirms to shareholders that the chief executive officer is doing what the board expects. This board type emphasises the need for independent directors who meet without the chief executive officer and who stay informed about current performance. The main role of these directors is in recruiting and replacing management.
- The *engaged* board establishes a partnership between the executives and the non-executives, similar to the participative board in the power framework. This board engages in dialogue and decision making and is comprised of directors who have sufficient competence to add value. This board also allocates time to define roles and behaviours required of directors and boundaries.

- The *intervening* board becomes intensely involved in decision making during a crisis, whereby it convenes frequent and intense meetings common, often at short notice.
- The most engaged board is the *operating* board, which makes all the key decisions that executives then implement and which fills in the gaps in management experience.

Again, like the board culture model from Chait described above, the relative powers and engagement models are useful starting points with which to diagnose, discuss and, if needed, review, board assumptions.

Ethical culture

Ethics, governance and risk

As various corporate scandals have piled up over the years, so too has the interest in better business ethics. This has been reflected in more training in corporate ethics, increased calls for corporate citizenship and social responsibility and, of course, further regulation. However, there has been a fundamental recognition that ethics is a governance issue and therefore something the board must consider.

This board responsibility is reflected in the majority of company codes. For example, the South African King IV Code of corporate governance states (in its first and second principles of 17) that

> The governing body should lead ethically and effectively ... [and] should govern the ethics of the organisation in a way that supports the establishment of an ethical culture.

If an ethical culture is dictated by how a board governs, what will most inform a board's attitude? Echoing Tricker, the Cass Business School's corporate philosopher Professor Roger Steare argues that it is not through a fixation on additional compliance and structural policies. Instead, a board culture that manages all elements well will be based on shared values and an understanding of the 'spirit of the law'. This arises from individual character and integrity – the sum total of our moral values – and will then inform judgement, which in turn creates behaviours of trust, both within the boardroom dynamic and also outside the boardroom between the board and its key stakeholders. Therefore, an ethical culture in the boardroom – one that will be able to manage all elements appropriately – is one that is based on trust.

This conclusion is similar to the argument made from research by the Great Place to Work Institute, a global workplace consulting firm that compiles best workplaces lists in 29 countries. Its research showed that trust is the bedrock of a positive organisational culture and that a high trust culture defines a great workplace regardless of organisational size, sector or country. Therefore, the ethical practice of developing trust within the board team becomes important.

Ethical culture through board team trust

We discussed the dynamics of high levels of trust between individual directors in Chapter 5 which, unsurprisingly, has many overlaps with the overall level of trust within the board team. Trust will bring a higher level of psychological safety (as described in the Google case study in Chapter 4), enabling a team to benefit from higher levels of cognitive conflict. As one of the directors in a recent report from Tomorrow's Company, 'Improving the quality of boardroom conversations', said:

> Openness and straight dealing is key. This does not mean like-mindedness or groupthink, but means that everything starts from a basis of trust and once trust exists the board can move much more quickly and be more effective.

One of the ways that team trust has been conceptualised and measured is through Stephen Covey's work on the 'speed of trust' and his Team Trust Index. His research identifies 13 behaviours that can be measured and benchmarked to high-performing teams. The questions explore the results of self-reported trust in each behaviour – i.e. 'How do *you* typically behave within this team?' – and asks each individual to rate members of the team in each of the behaviours. The behaviours break down into character-based traits (1–5), competence-based traits (6–10) and combined character and competence behaviours, (11–13). They are as follows:

1. Talk straight – communicate clearly so that you cannot be misunderstood. Don't withhold information, manipulate people or distort facts.
2. Demonstrate respect – express genuine care for others and show kindness in the little things. Don't fake respect or only show respect and concern for those who can do something for you.
3. Create transparency – tell the truth in a way that people can verify. Don't have a hidden agenda and pretend things are different than they are. Err on the side of disclosure.
4. Right wrongs – make things right when you are wrong and apologise quickly. Don't cover things up or let personal pride get in the way of doing the right thing.
5. Show loyalty – give credit to others and speak about people as though they are present. Don't take credit, represent people unfairly, or disclose the private information of others.
6. Deliver results – define results upfront, establish a track record and be on time and on budget. Don't overpromise and under deliver or make excuses for not delivering.
7. Get better – continuously improve by being a constant learner and receiving both formal and informal feedback. Don't consider yourself above feedback or assume your knowledge and skills will be sufficient for tomorrow's challenges.
8. Confront reality – tackle issues head-on, even the 'undiscussables'. Don't ignore problems and skip the real issues, even when discussing uncomfortable topics.

9 Clarify expectations – create shared vision and agreement upfront and renegotiate them if needed and possible. Don't be vague about specifics or violate expectations.
10 Practice accountability – hold yourself and others accountable for high performance and be clear on how you will communicate how you are doing you and others are doing. Don't avoid or shirk responsibility or blame others when things go wrong.
11 Listen first – genuinely understand another person's thoughts and feelings before trying to diagnose or advise, and find. Find out what the most important behaviours are for the person with whom you're working. Don't assume you know what matters most to others and therefore speak first and listen last, or not at all, or pretend to listen while waiting for your own chance to speak.
12 Keep commitments – say what you are going to do and then do what you say you're going to do. Don't break confidences or make vague and unreliable commitments or never make them in the first place.
13 Extend trust – demonstrate a propensity to trust by shifting trust from a noun to a verb. Do not withhold trust as a default even when there is risk involved by giving people responsibility.

As you might note from this list, there are many repeating board dynamics concepts in the measure of team trust. The main takeaways are firstly, that team trust exists over and above the sum of individual trust between directors; secondly, that team trust is measurable; and, thirdly, that those teams with benchmarked high levels of team trust will be those that are the highest performing.

A board culture that role-models high team trust according to the above variables will be one that is better able to manage all elements of their roles and responsibilities, and will thus be one that is modelling an appropriate ethical culture for the rest of the organisation to follow.

Performance culture

The extent to which a board is focused on long-term sustainable performance is dictated by whether it is orientated towards learning, as well as the extent it balances its focus on relationships and tasks. This section will explore both of these perspectives on board culture.

Learning culture

As introduced in Chapter 6, Dulewicz and Herbert (2004) define 16 tasks of the board which cluster into four areas. Building on the external versus internal and short versus long-term dilemmas that a board continually faces, Garrett (1995) visualised these four functions while adding a fifth – learning function (see Figure 9).

Figure 9 The functions of a board (Garratt, 1995)

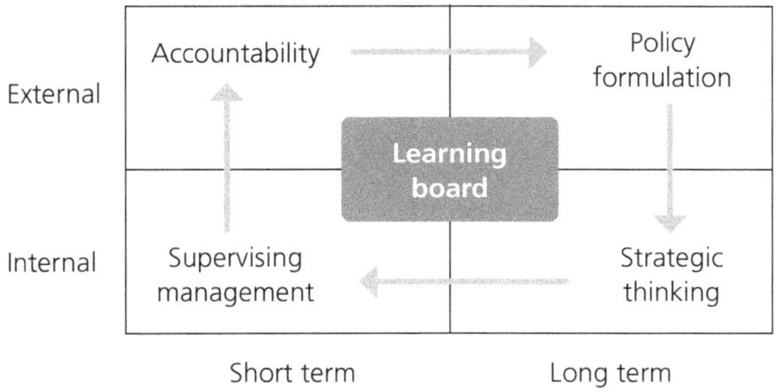

A 'learning board' will certainly place significant emphasis and value on their yearly board evaluation. However, a board which values learning as a key pillar of its performance will understand that learning is more than just a 'once a year' event, building reflection, evaluation and feedback into its meeting process. As we mentioned in Chapter 5 on decision making, a McKinsey (2014) report on high-performing boards found that boards that were functioning at the highest levels were those who were able to look inward and deliberate on their own processes. Practically, this might look like brief reviews at the end of each meeting, the use of dashboards and scorecards, providing peer feedback (as we shall see in a case study in Chapter 9), ongoing team coaching (such as suggested by Wageman and et al.) and a variety of other methodologies to engender greater psychological safety as a platform for learning.

One of the shared mindsets of a learning board will be that of a 'growth mindset', as opposed to a 'fixed mindset', in relation to both individual contributions and the board's joint capacity to improve. We discussed mindset in greater detail in Chapter 3, reflecting that many of the high-profile boards who have been the subject of public scandals were those who had a fixed-mindset culture that did not promote ongoing peer feedback and thus limited learning, growth and development.

Task versus relationship culture

One final perspective through which to consider a board's culture is to ask, 'To what extent does a board emphasise cohesive board relationships versus emphasising that a board is simply a place where one must achieve tasks and challenge, with no need for empathy for others?'

There have been many ways of representing these cultural assumptions in the group and team literature; however, Tricker has famously visualised these dynamics in his model describing how boards have different styles of operation. Tricker defines two axes being the concern for board relationships (high or low) and the concern for the tasks of the board (high or low). These axes create four quadrants with which to diagnose the culture of one's board (see Figure 10).

Figure 10 Tricker's framework of board styles of operation

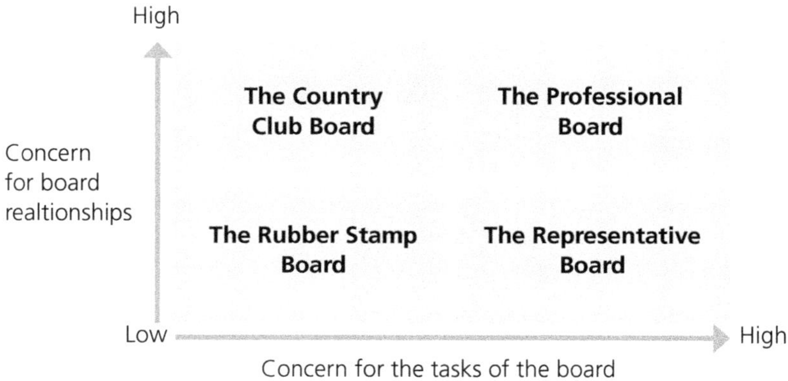

Firstly, with both low concern for relationships and tasks, there is the *rubber-stamp* board. This board rarely adds much value and is largely symbolic. The second type of board, characterised by high board relationships but low regard for board tasks, is the *country club* board. This board probably feels like a nice place to be but is prone to the problems of groupthink and the lack of diversity of opinion.

The third type, the *representative* board, is characterised by a low concern for relationships, but a high concern for tasks. This board is likely to be the largest board of all four types, ensuring that it meets the requirements of as many stakeholders as possible. The consequences of this are that group cohesion will naturally be lower due to the number of relationships and board directors may slip into the role of external experts, such that there is no sense of team.

Finally, Tricker identifies the *professional* board, characterised by high concern for both relationships and tasks, as the highest performing. The culture of this board acknowledges the need for strong team cohesion married with appropriate, well-delivered and diverse challenge to enable the board to develop dialogue and deliver effective decision making.

Again, like all of the perspectives discussed concerning how we might perceive board culture, this framework is a useful tool for a board to open conversations to more fully understand and improve its culture.

How to influence board culture

Bearing in mind that the broader system may have a larger impact, how can a board most influence the impact that it does have? Based on the definition of culture

– that a culture is mostly comprised of the unconscious and thus invisible values and beliefs held by individuals and the board as a whole – this is perhaps the wrong question. We cannot focus on influencing a culture directly, as we can only experience instead the visible behaviours that emerge at the tip of a cultural iceberg. What we can do, is enquire into which core values and assumptions have created these behaviours. To do this, we need to facilitate space for the board to reflect on how they have previously behaved and thus of what culture this is indicative.

For example, you do not change an Enron-style unethical board culture simply by asserting that change must happen and that we must become more moral, or by slapping on extra layers of compliance. You help shift this type of culture by enabling an understanding of the assumptions surrounding a fixed mindset and then acknowledging the behavioural effect that this has in the boardroom. This may then create a mindset shift that will translate into different role-modelling behaviours.

Despite what some people think, you cannot simply roll out a culture. It exists as a function of the shared values, beliefs and assumptions within a particular grouping. However, what one can do is to become more aware of where, externally from the board, the culture has arisen such that the board can have more choice when potential ethical, risk and conflict issues arise.

Roger Steare (2012) argues that many boards currently do not understand their cultures properly and therefore what they are role-modelling to the rest of their organisation. There is an urgent need to create an understanding of joint values and character and to use this to drive a conversation about who the board actually is. As Steare suggests in a submission to the FRC in the 2010 review of the UK Corporate Governance Code (co-authored with David Phillips, a senior corporate reporter at PwC):

> It may also be beneficial for boards to explain the behavioural tone which is established in the way it engages with shareholders and the management team and in the actions it takes. This can be seen as a statement of who we are and what we stand for. In this context, boards may wish to explain what management style and behavioural norms they encourage and what behaviours they will not tolerate.

To enable boards to do this, Steare suggests that boards consider gathering individual director feedback, such as that measured by his 'Moral DNA' test, and by implementing some of the following key actions:

- Question the purpose of your business. Is it meeting the needs of all your key stakeholders?
- Challenge your own values, decision making and behaviours as leaders. Are you bringing your humanity to work?

- Ask colleagues, customers, suppliers and local communities how they really feel about your business. Does it inspire them? Do they love it? Why and in what way?
- When you have the answers to these questions, ask yourself: 'What are we doing well that we need to keep doing?', 'What are we beginning to do well, but need to do more of?' and 'What are we not yet doing and need to begin?'

In a similar vein, the 2017 Chartered Governance Institute report, 'Culture in the charitable sector', provides a number of questions that the board may reflect on to assess to what extent they are role-modelling a positive culture. These include the following:

- Has the board set out a clear set of values for the charity and are these reflected in its business model?
- Do trustees consistently place the interests of the charity, in fulfilling its charitable objects, above their own?
- Has the charity proactively considered its approach to corporate partnerships in general and identified any ethical 'non-negotiables' that support the culture and values of the organisation?
- Do trustees have personal knowledge of how the charity operates and the impact it has on its intended beneficiaries (and wider society)?

Beyond these recommendations to reflect on and communicate the values and assumptions of the board as a group, what more individual approaches are there to influencing the culture of the board?

In a recent report by the consultancy firm Korn/Ferry, looking at what goes into making an exceptional board of directors, the question was asked, 'What are the most important characteristics of boards that have an effect on a culture of quality conversations?' Three characteristics were overwhelmingly mentioned.

Firstly, the report found that the quality of the chair was seen as the most important characteristic, being mentioned by 93% of respondents. The FRC's 2018 Code (principle F) outlines the chair's role in the culture of the board as follows:

> The chair leads the board and is responsible for its overall effectiveness in directing the company. They should demonstrate objective judgement throughout their tenure and promote a culture of openness and debate. In addition, the chair facilitates constructive board relations and the effective contribution of all non-executive directors, and ensures that directors receive accurate, timely and clear information.

In order to do this successfully, a chair will need to display the role competencies that were outlined in Chapter 3 from the 'board attributes' quadrant of the 11 Cs model.

On the more negative side, the Association of Chairs 2017 report, entitled 'Managing difficult board dynamics', lists a number of problem behaviours by chairs that can be markers of poor role-modelling. These behaviours are as follows:

- has difficulty seeking and accepting feedback from others
- fails to make trustees feel their viewpoint is heard and valued, even if it is the minority view
- discourages legitimate questioning and challenge
- offers and defends own decision or opinion too early in discussions, with summing up biased to own views
- tolerates poor behaviour, or is unwilling to stand up to dominant individuals
- dominates discussion
- prone to emotional outbursts, e.g. impatience or defensiveness making it difficult for others to speak up, fails to bring discussion to a decision
- relies on an inner group to make decisions that belong to the board as a whole

It is the responsibility of all the board, but most particularly the senior independent director, the company secretary and other board influencers, to notice and challenge these problem behaviours that can be exhibited by the chair. Developmental processes such as peer feedback, one-to-one coaching and/or mentoring, or a specific developmental training programme may be useful to support a director to better role-model and fulfil their role-modelling mandate. At the extreme, however, the chair's position may be challenged if they are not able to shift their problem behaviours.

The second key driver of a positive board culture from the research was 'directors having a real interest and commitment to the company and its activities'. This was mentioned by 88% of respondents. Therefore, an effective board culture is associated with directors who are there for the right reasons. Although there may be some level of personal gain that arises from board membership, this must not be the main driver for a director's motivation.

The best way of encouraging effective board culture is to select more humble individuals and to deselect those that display more heroic, charismatic and potentially derailing tendencies. Following the early leadership thinker Mary Parker Follett (1924), 'the most essential work of the leader is to create more leaders'.

The third most significant driver of the board culture from the study was to increase the diversity of the board, which was mentioned by 75% of respondents. We will explore this topic in greater detail in the next chapter.

Conclusion

Culture has become increasingly recognised as a key aspect of good governance in recent years, with many varieties including national, regional, ethnic, gender, generational, social class and organisational. It has been defined using an assortment of categories which can be conceptualised in visible artefacts, espoused values and underlying assumptions.

What is 'board culture', how can it be understood and how can it be influenced? Board culture can be defined as the repeating patterns of the boardroom dynamic. These more visible patterns of behaviour emerge from the less visible shared values that have become integrated into how the board works. Some of these shared values and assumptions are around: the board and director roles (for example, whether the board is more of an 'institutional guardian' or a 'public watchdog' and whether directors are more 'free agents' or 'group members'); the relative power of the CEO and the board; the board's approach to ethics; the relative board focus on internal versus external and short-term versus long-term issues; and the extent to which the board focuses on task versus relationships. Boards can influence their cultures by: making explicit their assumptions around these issues so that they can be reconsidered if necessary; role-modelling (especially by the chair); communicating more widely; and by increasing board diversity to reinforce it.

Conversations are important markers or artefacts of board culture. Boards are comprised of a group of individuals and conversations can (and often do) go wrong. Understanding the power dynamics in play within the board is invaluable and there are a number of useful perspectives through which to understand a board's culture. These can raise awareness of assumptions around board role, power, ethics and values and performance. There are also a number of ways to influence board culture from within the board system. Amongst others, these include understanding board identity and values, the influence of the chair, director attributes and identifying and embracing diversity.

Culture is often the topic least discussed in governance, partly because it is just seen as something that exists, can't be changed and is aligned to the wider culture of the organisation. However, as we have seen, board culture covers a wide variety of areas and has a considerable impact on its effectiveness. One question to consider is whether the culture of the board is a reflection of the wider organisational culture or whether the organisational culture stems from the board. In most cases, excluding entrepreneurial startups or founder-led businesses, it is most likely a combination of both. A new board member joining from within the organisation will bring their cultural expectations honed through their time with the business to the board when they join. An external board appointment is less prone to adopt the existing culture of the board, potentially bringing some aspects that may adjust the culture, but they will be unlikely to totally change the existing culture, at least not completely or immediately.

Influencing and nudging the board to recognise the existing culture – building on the positives and marginalising the negatives – can create a board that has greater effect and impact if undertaken consciously. Board members themselves may be too close to the practicalities, discussions and operations to have a clear view of the culture. Therefore, the most insightful observers of organisational culture are often outsiders, as the cultural givens are not implicit to them. Equally, the individual sitting outside or alongside the board, but within the organisation, can also have insight into the culture of the board and can therefore become a positive influence if there is a need for adjustment or change.

Are you consciously aware of the culture in the organisation and board that you work for? What are the most common patterns of conversations in your board? Do they positively influence the culture so as to deliver benefit and encourage effectiveness?

8 – Diversity in the boardroom

Diversity in governance

In recent years, diversity – the concept of valuing everyone as individuals – has become an increasingly hot topic. In our world, where many high-profile governments are becoming less progressive, where borders are being tightened and within which intergroup tension is increasing, diverse views and minority groups are becoming ever more challenged. However, the world of governance reveals a more positive outlook. Taking the UK perspective for a moment, we can see that over recent iterations of codes, the concept of diversity, in its various forms, has steadily gained greater recognition.

In June 2010, the revised UK Corporate Governance Code came into effect. For the first time, this Code included a principle recognising the value of diversity in the boardroom. The principle stated that: 'The search for board candidates should be conducted, and appointments made, on merit, against objective criteria and with due regard for the benefits of diversity on the board, including gender.'

The year 2010 was also when the UK government commissioned Lord Davies of Abersoch to undertake his review of gender diversity on listed company boards. The remit of this review was to identify barriers preventing more women from reaching the boardroom and to make recommendations to government and business on what they could do to increase the proportion of women on boards.

Fast forward to the most recent Code in 2018 and the equivalent principle (Principle J) mentions diversity but also extends it beyond gender as follows:

> Both appointments and succession plans should be based on merit and objective criteria and, within this context, should promote diversity of gender, social and ethnic backgrounds, cognitive and personal strengths.

Furthermore, the Code also requires that the annual evaluation of the board should consider its composition in relation to diversity and that the annual report should describe the work of the nomination committee, including:

- the process used in relation to appointments, its approach to succession planning and how both support developing a diverse pipeline;
- the policy on diversity and inclusion, its objectives and linkage to company strategy, how it has been implemented and progress on achieving the objectives; and
- the gender balance of those in the senior management and their direct reports.

In addition, the FRC Guide to Boardroom Effectiveness (2018) also mentions provisions for diversity and the impact that diversity may have in the boardroom. Section 88, for example, notes that:

> Diversity in the boardroom can have a positive effect on the quality of decision-making by reducing the risk of group think. With input from shareholders, boards need to decide which aspects of diversity are important in the context of the business and its needs.

Guidance notes 89 and 90 also outline the importance of developing a more diverse executive pipeline and the nominations committee's role, working with human resources, to set and meet diversity objectives and strategies for the company as a whole as well as in the boardroom.

This greater awareness in governance mirrors the broader awareness within organisations of diversity and inclusion issues. For example, in recent years, diversity policies, training and training providers have increasingly become part of organisational life.

Although the media and business literature sometimes confuses the terms, equality and diversity have been defined slightly differently. Equality is the moral case for equal opportunities, for equity among groups, and therefore has led to legislation and governance regulation. It is based on the ethical argument for equality that underpins the idea of positive discrimination and percentage targets that have been proposed for male/female proportions. It may be fair to say that most companies initially approach the issue of diversity through an equality and rule-based lens. That is, they are externally compelled to consider other groups and perspectives because they are legally obliged or regulated to do so.

A zoo metaphor is useful to consider how organisations can be initially focused on simply 'housing' a breath of variety compared to an ecosystem of rich diversity. This sanitised entry-point onto the continuum of diversity describes a system that relies more on external input (zookeepers) to carefully manage and limit interaction between groups. Real diversity, on the other hand, is more akin to the metaphor of a rainforest, which has systems that are both co-operative and competitive. These systems welcome disruption as a catalyst for growth and evolution.

While it is vitally important to respond to the moral case for equality, this chapter focuses more on the business case for diversity, which includes an assessment of the impact of board diversity on its internal and external stakeholder dynamics. Managing diversity quotas and including people because it is the right thing to do is a vital necessity, but ensuring that the dynamics of a board actually supports a shift in diversity culture and mindset is perhaps of even greater value.

The role of the effective company secretary and other supporters of the board, both internally and externally (including NEDs), is thus about supporting and promoting variety for its own sake. Company secretaries and others may also be seen as being key guardians of equity legislation and its effective application. This role should be in addition to understanding, monitoring and supporting the appropriate handling of board, committee and strategic diversity to drive better conversations and ultimately better performance.

Types of diversity

Leaders often have difficulty delineating the different types of diversity that are present in their organisations and teams. It is often viewed as a thorny area within which one must tread carefully so as not to cause upset. It is therefore useful to be aware of some of approaches to classifying diversity.

At a broad level, diversity has been described as either 'surface' (for example, the demographic differences that one can often visibly see and that are most commonly first thought of when the topic of diversity is raised) or 'deep' (for example, one's attitudes or beliefs that are not as immediately on show). More specifically, and with more granularity, diversity can be mapped into a number of categories and associated types that directors may not have previously considered.

Table 1 shows some of these which may be relevant to your organisation and board.

Table 1 Categories and types of diversity (Mannix and Neale, 2005)

Category	Type of diversity
Social category difference	Race Ethnicity Gender Age Religion Sexual orientation Physical abilities
Differences in knowledge and skills	Education Functional knowledge Information or expertise Training Experience Abilities

Category	Type of diversity
Differences in values or beliefs	Cultural background Ideological beliefs
Personality differences	Cognitive style Affective disposition Motivational factors
Organisational/community status differences	Tenure or length of service Title (work function, seniority, discipline, etc.) Work-related ties Friendship ties Community ties In-group membership

As you can see from Table 1, when considering diversity, things can get quite detailed and potentially complicated. It is easy to become overwhelmed with diversity considerations when considering all the above categories. However, to simplify things, it is often easiest first to consider what types of diversity from the above menu are most important internally and externally to your board. Does the board have enough diversity in its current membership of individual directors not only to fulfil governance requirements but also to achieve its boardroom dynamics goals of innovative dialogue and effective decision making? Similarly, does this board membership represent all its external stakeholder contexts appropriately so that a variety of perspectives are voiced within board-level conversations?

The impact of diversity on dynamics and performance

The common business case for diversity

Based on the above definitions of diversity, what are the main reasons for having diversity in a board, senior leadership population or in an organisation in general? Simply put, the business case is that diversity generally improves performance. However, this improvement is nuanced and depends on many other moderating factors, such as group leadership capability to minimise losses from potentially increased discord.

The business case for diversity is often positioned at either end of the spectrum, whereby either diversity leads to significant positive benefits, or a lack of diversity leads to a number of negative outcomes. Diversity broadly affects six dimensions:

1 A diverse organisation has a reduction in the cost of integrating new workers, who due to globalisation are themselves taken more increasingly from a diverse population.

2 A diverse leadership group often has the benefit of increasing the reputation of its company, which leads to that company becoming more of an attractive proposition for talented individuals to join. This enables organisations perceived as being diverse as being those that can recruit the best talent, particularly in the type of diverse talent for which they have a reputation. For example, a science, technology, engineering and mathematics (STEM) industry firm which has female board representation sends a clear signal to talented women in their marketplace that this is a place which values and promotes females in a male-dominated industry.
3 Broader diversity enables a better customer strategy due to the increased representation of that customer group within leadership conversations and decision making.
4 A common benefit of diversity within an organisation or team is that the team will become more innovative and creative due to multiple perspectives being considered. This is an increasingly key team competency, especially considering the advances in digital technology.
5 A diverse group membership will increase the impact on problem-solving abilities and enhance decision making. (This has been discussed in detail in Chapter 5 on decision making.)
6 A final benefit is the ability of a board to be seen as flexible, agile and resilient. That is, its ability to 'horizon scan' and quickly pivot to adapt to external environmental conditions is seen to be enhanced through increasing its diversity.

The first three of these benefits are largely external benefits, whereas the final three are largely internal benefits to an organisation's board, board committees or executive leadership teams.

Case study: Jersey's diversity drain

The island of Jersey provides an interesting case in point in relation to board diversity. Jersey cannot fill some 300–350 director positions due to a lack of upcoming diverse board talent in the local population, especially in terms of the number of women, but also regarding neuro-diversity, ethnicity and other differences from traditional director demographics. This has led to significant 'overboarding', whereby local directors often sit on too many boards.

This is an example of how a lack of director-level population diversity can hurt local boards and the island economy in general. As Charlotte Valeur, previous UK Institute of Directors' Chair and founder of Jersey-based not-for-profit organisation Board Apprentice, says, 'That's about £9 million leaving Jersey every year simply because we haven't upskilled our own population. With indirect taxes of 20%, that's like saying goodbye to £1.7 million.'

Gender diversity

Of the much-quoted phrase of 'male, pale and stale' boards, up until recently it is the 'male' aspect that has received most attention in relation to boardroom diversity. This was given significant impetus by the Davies Reports, commissioned by the UK Government, to look at the issue of women on FTSE 350 boards. Initiated in 2010, by 2019 the representation of women on boards had increased to 32.1%, hitting its original target of at least 25%. A new goal of 33% by 2020 was set and the gauntlet taken up by others, including the independent Hampton-Alexander Review body. Although now close to their target, it should be recognised that, while 100% of FTSE100 companies have at least one female director, only 48% have at least 33% female board composition, so there is still some way to go if the gender balance on boards is to reflect the gender balance in the population. It should also be noted that of the 100% appointments, 75% are non-executive director roles rather than executives with a day-to-day influence within the organisation. The Female FTSE Index produced each year by Cranfield School of Management is also a useful resource for the latest movements in female board membership.

What is the evidence that, beyond moral equity, women have a specific positive impact on the dynamics of boards? There is evidence that female directors enhance board independence, take their non-executive director roles more seriously, prepare more conscientiously for meetings and ask more of the awkward questions. Studies going back to Solomon Asch's original work on conformity suggest that three women are required to change boardroom dynamics, enabling them to become more vocal and their voices to be heard.

In terms of broader organisational performance, a McKinsey study of 366 companies from the US, UK and Brazil revealed a significant correlation between gender diversity and financial performance. Those companies that were in the first quartile of gender diversity outperformed those in the bottom quartile by 15%. Similarly, at board level, corporate boards with greater gender diversity have been associated with up to a 16.2% greater return over five years compared to lower economy-wide gender diversity averages. Gender diversity enables organisations to access the widest talent pool, as women account for approximately six out of every 10 university graduates in Europe and the US. Similarly, women now form 51% of the UK population and make an estimated 70% of household purchasing decisions, which creates a necessity, especially in retail organisations, to include significantly more women at senior levels.

The evidence of both the internal and external benefits for greater board gender diversity is therefore overwhelmingly compelling. The recent UK legislation on gender pay gap reporting, requiring organisations of 250 or more employees to report on their gender pay gaps annually, is a broader positive reflection of this evidence for the benefits of gender diversity in addition to the ethical arguments for equality.

What is the mechanism by which greater numbers of women on boards enhances the boardroom dynamic? Most of the reasons cited for the benefits are correlational rather than causational. That is, an argument could be made that, even though gender diversity happens at the same time that benefits arise, this does not necessarily mean that gender diversity is what caused these benefits.

Therefore, in terms of understanding what is inside the black box of effective boardroom dynamics, the key issue is to look for what the mediating mechanisms are between more women and better board performance. The most compelling recent research illuminating this comes from researchers who have looked at the concept of 'collective intelligence'. In the same way that there is a single score, IQ, that measures individual intelligence, researchers looked for a single component to measure team performance. It was found that teams with higher collective intelligence – that is, those that outperformed others consistently over time – had three key components.

Firstly, and most significantly, they had more women. In fact, the more women they had, the higher performing they were. Secondly, they had higher average individual empathy scores (as measured by the 'reading the eyes in the mind' test, developed at Cambridge University and available for free online). This is therefore perhaps the key mechanism by which increasing gender diversity improves the internal dynamic of a board. It is not that women improve decision making and creativity per se, or indeed better represent the stakeholder voice (although they most often do), it is that they are more likely to have empathy for others' views and therefore enhance the quality of dialogue in the boardroom. They are on average, in short, better team members compared to men. This does not mean that men cannot be excellent team members or that men are not empathetic, just that as a population, men are on average less empathetic. Thirdly, teams that were higher performing were those who were more likely to have high levels of turn-taking – that is, they were skilled at both speaking up but also including others when needed. Therefore, while socially skilled directors improve the collective intelligence of teams, this will only be true if the processes of the team enable these individuals to be expressed.

The take-home message for boards, beyond the issue of gender, is to recognise the importance of selecting and training for social intelligence in addition to experience and expertise and to ensure that meeting agendas and meeting facilitation always has an eye on appropriate process as well as content.

Race and ethnic diversity

The second type of diversity that the latest Code requires board membership to take into account is that of social and ethnic background. In the same way that, in the UK, the Davies Reviews were a significant impetus to increasing gender diversity on boards, the more recent Parker Review is aiming to have a similar impact on ethnic diversity.

The Parker Review, which was launched in 2016, has a goal for every firm in the FTSE 100 to have at least one BAME (black, Asian or minority ethnic) board director by 2021 and every FTSE 250 company by 2024. As Sir John Parker, the leader of the review, stated, 'UK companies have made great progress on gender diversity, but there is much more to do around ethnic and cultural diversity.'

As of March 2020, in the UK, only 9.8% of board members in the FTSE 100 were directors of colour. By contrast, 14% of the UK population is from a non-white ethnic group. In total, 49 of the FTSE 100 companies had no directors of colour and only seven have more than 10% of their board members with BAME origins. The key business benefits of ethnic diversity are very similar to those of gender diversity. The internal benefits are cited to be a more inclusive leadership and enhanced corporate culture, whereas the external benefits include brand enhancement, attracting and retaining the best talent and de-risking the supply chain.

In terms of the specific relationship between ethnic diversity and performance, the McKinsey 'Diversity matters' report provides a headline figure that the first quartile of organisations that are ethnically diverse perform 35% better in terms of their financials compared to those in the fourth quartile. When we look at the impact of ethnic diversity, specifically on board-level performance, we find that there is some clear evidence for better performance. For example, a US study found positive correlations between board level diversity and firm profitability in the same way as gender diversity. Similarly, in the UK, studies of FTSE 100 firms have suggested an association between the total value of a company's stock and the appointment of directors from minority ethnic backgrounds. However, there has been no attempt to inquire into the causal impact of ethnic diversity on organisational outcomes.

One conclusion from all the evidence above is that when it comes to the ethnic diversity of boards, context matters. If the society or key stakeholder population that an organisation and a board needs to consider is not represented in the board, then boardroom dynamics and a variety of other outcomes will suffer more than if they are represented.

Age diversity

The idea that many boards are lacking in diversity because they are 'stale' – that is, that they over-represent older generations – is also a working assumption of much boardroom commentary.

Is this assumption correct? To understand this assumption, we must firstly understand what the generations in the workplace currently are. Most classifications suggest that there are five generations to consider. These (with approximate birth-year windows) are:

- the Maturists (pre-1945)
- the Baby Boomers (1945–1960)
- Generation X (1961–1980)
- Generation Y (1981–1995)
- Generation Z (born after 1995)

Each of these generations have different formative experiences. Generation Y, for example, will have a mentality that is informed by the 9/11 terrorist attacks, by the invention of social media, by the invasion of Iraq and by reality TV, to name but a few. It is suggested that these formative experiences, therefore, create differences in the characteristics of the generations such as differences in aspiration and variations in attitudes towards technology, their jobs and communication media and therefore also to communication preferences.

For example, Maturists are said to aspire to homeownership, whereas those from Generation X aspire more to work–life balance. It is argued that older generations generally prefer face-to-face communication compared to the younger generations who will prefer online and mobile communication. What does this mean in terms of workforce or board generational diversity? The assumption is that an organisation and a board should represent its population in order to voice these differences.

At this point we should highlight the impact of COVID-19 on the generational adoption of online communications, given its necessity of use in lockdowns both professionally and personally. Within and across all generations there are 'early adopters' and 'laggards' of online communication tools, although the perception is that generational adoption level still applies, just not as extensively. Increasingly it is a less important factor, however, as Generation X onwards have grown up using technology, even if the pace of innovation has significantly increased.

When we look at the actual evidence for the mountain of populist commentary on generational differences in the work environment, it seems that the stories painted do not actually portray the reality that we have been led to believe. Recent research which took an evidence-based approach (as described in Chapter 5) asked, 'What is the evidence for generational or age differences in work-related outcomes?' Some of the conclusions reached were as follows:

- There are no differences in work ethics between Baby Boomers, Generation X and Generation Y.
- There are only small differences across generations regarding job attitudes.
- Evidence of generational differences in work values is at best mixed.
- The relationship between age and a large number of job attitudes is weak.
- Older workers contribute considerably to non-core performance domains, i.e. other than task performance.
- Older workers are less motivated by training and development opportunities than their younger counterparts.
- Most health-related stereotypes about older workers are not supported by evidence.
- Older and more tenured employees tend to display higher coping strategies against stressors and lower performance declines.

Overall, the general conclusion is that the assumed generational differences in the workplace are not supported by scientific evidence. In terms of boardroom diversity, then, it would seem like generational diversity is less of a concern for boardroom dynamics than is commonly considered in the public media. Age diversity should potentially only be a significant consideration when mapped against a company's community, customers and consumers.

Country culture diversity

With the increased opportunities provided by globalisation and the greater movement of populations around the world, cultural diversity on boards is becoming a necessity for those boards who either have, or aspire to have, some form of an international stakeholder presence. What do we know about the impact of diverse cultures on the dynamics of teams and boards?

A variety of research has shown that highly culturally diverse teams suffer what is known as 'process losses' through task conflict and decreased social integration. This means multicultural teams often tend to work less well because of differing opinions about how to get things done and differences in how comfortable cultural cliques can feel when working together. However, on the other side of the coin, culturally diverse teams show process gains through increased satisfaction and enhanced creativity. They perform better due to the high levels of innovation and increased enjoyment from the stimulus that their differences often bring.

Case study: The United States versus Sweden – gender differences

It is useful to notice how the types of diversity discussed so far interact and coexist. For example, there are significant gender differences when comparing boards across different cultures. One recent example of this that was picked up in the media was when the Swedish Deputy Prime Minister, Isabella Lovin, tweeted a photograph of herself signing a progressive climate bill surrounded by a room of her seven senior female colleagues, including one who was visibly pregnant. The suggestion was that she tweeted this in response to a widely mocked series of photographs of Donald Trump signing executive orders, one of which included a decree barring US federal funding for foreign NGOs that support abortion, as his all-male colleagues looked on.

When we compare the cultural differences between Sweden and the US, one key difference stands out. This is the 'masculinity' score. High scores on masculinity indicate that a group will be driven by competition, achievement and success. Success is defined by being the best – a value system that starts in school and continues through organisational life. A lower, more feminine, score, on this dimension, however, expresses that the group's dominant values are caring for others and quality of life. A feminine society is one where quality is the sign of success and which applauds greater levels of co-operation such that decision making is achieved through involvement and consensus.

On the Hofstede cultural model, the US scores 62 for masculinity while Sweden scores just five.

It is quite possible for highly culturally diverse boards to work well together, but more emphasis needs to be made in pulling them together and working through cultural differences to reap the benefits. The key point about cultural diversity is that, again, it is highly context dependent. If an organisation has significant stakeholders who are working in, or who are from, other cultures, then there is an absolute need to include this cultural voice within the boardroom setting.

For those organisations whose own operations, or their clients' operations, straddle continents and countries, having a board that recognises, embraces, accommodates and reflects this internationalism is imperative to be able to lead the company to success – however that may be measured.

Other 'surface' diversity

The latest version of the Code also refers to the requirement for board membership to attend to diversity of 'social background'. Some of the characteristics of social background include disability, religion, socioeconomic status, sexual orientation and the more recently coined term, neurodiversity (where neurological differences such as autism, dyslexia and ADHD are recognised and respected as any other human variation rather than being seen as inherently pathological). Although there is no direct evidence of the impact of these types of diversity on boardroom dynamics, there are many case studies that show the positive impact of including these categories of diversity, when appropriate, in the boardroom.

The key consideration is that a board has to decide whether each of these diversities is relevant to its effective operation. For example, on any charity board, it would be vital to include individuals with a specific knowledge or, indeed, personally lived experience, of what the charity itself represents. To take one of many high-profile examples, the current Chair of MacMillan Cancer Support, Julia Palca, has herself had cancer.

'Deep' diversity

The final aspect of diversity that the latest UK Code refers to requiring consideration are 'cognitive and personal strengths', often also referred to as 'cognitive diversity'.

There are many ways to consider these factors, most of which have some grounding in psychology. In Chapter 3, we discussed how the so-called 'Big Five' psychological types can each affect the style of director decision making. Further useful examples of cognitive differences to consider include learning styles, personality types and, particularly in relation to a board functioning as a team, role types.

Learning styles

Perhaps the most well-known theory of learning styles is the Honey and Mumford categorisation of four different learning styles. Although all learning is said to arise through a cyclical process using all four styles, we may each have a preference for one or more of the style types in the following categories:

- Activists: people who learn preferentially through experience, e.g. who will want to try something out first;
- Reflectors: people who learn preferentially through reflection, e.g. who will want to think it through first;
- Theorists: people who learn preferentially through theory, e.g. who will want to understand the concepts first; and
- Pragmatists: people who learn preferentially through hands-on trial and error, e.g. who will want to know how to apply something first.

When teams approach tasks, it is perhaps useful to have a good spread of these types of learning styles. It would also be important for all members to understand that there is a need for this spread so that, when a reflector is sitting in the corner looking out the window and doodling, they are not assumed to be loafing but could in fact be actively engaged in the challenge at hand through their learning preference.

In a boardroom context, recognising and understanding these different approaches can be beneficial in understanding differing approaches to preparing for meetings, contributing to discussions and following through on actions. More relevant is the composition of board committees, where tasks and actions delegated from the board may be more defined and their delivery more critical.

Personality types

One example of a commonly used personality type is the Myers Briggs Type Indicator (MBTI). The stereotypical CEO type on this inventory is the ESTJ 'executive type' (the extroverted, sensing, thinking and judging type) who is described as hardworking and thrilled to take charge in organising projects and people. Famous people with this personality type include Michelle Obama, Alan Sugar, Theresa May, Henry Ford and, on the other side of the ethical coin, Saddam Hussein (and even, it has been suggested, Darth Vader!). Not surprisingly, based on this list, we also know that the ESTJ type is the most common type associated with being a politician. There are, for example, twice the number of ESTJs in local government in the UK than in the general population. Again, being aware of the personality types on a board may be incredibly helpful in understanding a board's communication preferences and blind spots.

Team role types

One other example of 'deep' diversity cognitive difference that is highly useful to teams is the Belbin Team Roles framework, designed by Meredith Belbin at Henley Business School in the 1970s. The framework describes what types of team role strengths are required within a team to enhance that team's performance. Teams with a balance of different role types are those that are more successful. The nine team role types (each with unique contributions and allowable weaknesses) are as follows:

1. **Plant:** the creative problem solver, but often too preoccupied.
2. **Coordinator:** the mature chair role, who can often be seen as manipulative.
3. **Monitor-evaluator:** sober and strategic, but lacking drive to inspire.
4. **Implementer:** turns ideas into practical action, but somewhat inflexible and slow to respond.
5. **Completer-finisher:** highly conscientious but inclined to worry and reluctant to delegate.
6. **Resource investigator:** extroverted networker, but often overoptimistic.
7. **Shaper:** challenging and driven, but can offend people's feelings.
8. **Team worker:** diplomatic and listening, but sometimes indecisive in the crunch.
9. **Specialist:** single-minded and highly skilled but often overly technical.

It is proposed that a necessary requirement for boardroom effectiveness is that a board should have a balance of these nine roles. This may be important to consider informally or even to formally assess using a team roles questionnaire. However, it is also important to know that a balanced team can only function well when it is supported by an effective team process: one that involves the whole group, that promotes good communication and that is effectively facilitated by the leader (for our purposes, the chair). It is also important to recognise that individual directors may need to be flexible in their cognitive and personal style to serve the team balance.

The overall conclusion from the above commentary on different aspects of diversity is that, beyond compliance considerations, the organisational stakeholder context is perhaps the biggest driver of diversity considerations in the boardroom. All nominations committees and boards need to consider the most important types of diversity that need representation within boardroom conversations and decision making. Once this diversity is in place, then the second major consideration is how a board's processes, in terms of structures and leadership style, ensure that the represented diversity is valued and heard rather than excluded.

Case study: The Rolling Stones as a superteam

Although unlikely as a case study to highlight the performance benefits of building board role diversity, the band the Rolling Stones have proven to be illuminating as the subject of study as a 'superteam' (Tu, 2012).

There is an argument that it is their combined role diversity that has enabled them to stay together for more than 50 years and, having played to more people in more places than any other band, achieve their stated vision of being the greatest rock and roll band in the world.

Mick Jagger is, in Belbin terms, the Coordinator. He is the lead both on and off the stage, the CEO of the band. Both planful and having clear vision, he was the one who brought in a new financial adviser who helped make them £1.7 billion over their past three tours. Keith Richards has been quoted as saying that 'if Mick is the rock, I am the roll'. More freewheeling but also with a creative leadership spark, Keith is the Shaper and Plant, who has frequently clashed creatively with Mick. What makes the band cohesive through this conflict though is the balance from the other two band members. Ronny Wood plays the role of harmoniser and mediator and is the band's Team Worker. Equally supportive but in a different way is Charlie Watts, the band's drummer, who plays the Monitor-Evaluator role. He is steady, stoic and settles the band's rhythm to diffuse the drama between Mick and Keith.

Diversity mindset

If diversity in all its different categories and types is important in enhancing the internal boardroom dynamics and the voicing of external key stakeholder needs within the boardroom, then how do individual directors and the board as a collective develop a diversity mindset?

This concept has become important, as boards need to recognise that they have to have the right mindset to embrace difference if they want to reap the benefits of diversity. They need to understand that they must move from being different 'from' each other to being different 'for' each other.

The problem here, as we have discussed elsewhere, is that we are all inherently biased. However, there is a difference between people who can accept that we have bias and who are then able to raise this to their conscious awareness and act and those that do not. Cognitive bias, in terms of diversity, has been described as having an attitude or 'implicit association' about a particular group that operates beyond our control and awareness, that informs our perception of a person (or of that person or social group) and that can influence our decision making and behaviour towards the target of that bias. These unconscious biases can be powerful predictors on our behaviour in a variety of ways – for example, they can maliciously affect both quick judgements and decisions that are given more careful consideration. We know, for example, that on standard tests of bias, up to

88% of white people have a pro-white or anti-black implicit bias and that 83% of heterosexuals show an implicit bias in favour of straight people over gays and lesbians. Surprisingly, minority groups are not equally biased towards themselves in the same way. For example, we know that 48% of black people show a pro-white or anti-black bias, 36% of Arab Muslims show an anti-Muslim bias and 38% of gays and lesbians have bias in favour of straight people over gays and lesbians.

How can we get a window into our implicit biases in relation to diverse or minority groups? One well-known method is the Harvard University Implicit Association Test (IAT), which can be taken for free online (see 'Useful websites' at the back of this book). This test has seven different aspects, each revealing the direction and the amount of bias a test taker has towards different types. The tests measure bias in:

- gender (male–female intelligence)
- race (black–white)
- skin-tone (light skin–dark skin)
- age (young–old)
- weight (fat–thin)
- countries, (UK–US)
- sexuality (gay–straight)

The tests use either pictures of people representing each stereotype or words often associated with that stereotype and require a test taken to respond to particular questions, with the time of response being an indicator of bias. Although some have argued that there are methodological issues with this test, it has been taken by millions of people around the world and is probably the test that one would take on any diversity and equality training programme. How people respond to their test results is often a good indicator of how seriously they are willing to consider the idea of unconscious bias affecting their diversity mindset. If one shows a significant negative bias towards a minority group, the initial reaction may be one of denial. However, the very point about unconscious bias is that, although it affects our behaviour, we are, by its very definition, unaware of this. Instead, a more mature response would be to accept the result (and perhaps re-test at a later date) and gain feedback from others on your behaviour in relation to the topic of diversity.

What kinds of behaviour may be exhibited by people if they show relatively biased scores on the various IATs? Essentially, bias can emerge at any moment in any context. However, perhaps the most pernicious type of bias behaviour is what has been come to be termed as 'micro-aggressions'. These are words or actions that, although they would probably not be noticed by the person enacting them, or even indeed by others around them, reinforce stereotypes and thus reduce the likelihood of viewing people according to their individual merits as opposed to the merits or otherwise of their stereotype.

Case study: Tackling micro-aggressions at Google

Google has had its fair share of diversity challenges in recent years. Just one example of this, and a good example of board-related micro-aggression, occurred in the summer of 2016. On a Google shareholder call, Google's CFO, Ruth Porat, answered a question posed to her by a caller. In posing the question, the shareholder referred to Porat as 'the Lady CFO', so making a choice, consciously or unconsciously, to amend her title with a gender designation. In essence, he was the perpetrator of a public micro-aggression. Porat answered the question without reference to the comment. However, shortly after in the same meeting, another shareholder, Danielle Ginach, commented, 'I am sorry to put another shareholder on the spot, but Ms Porat is "the CFO", not "the Lady CFO"'.

Ginach later commented, 'Reflecting on my decision to speak out at that moment, I realise that what angered me most is that one of the most influential people in finance was addressed based on her gender. If someone at her level of success cannot escape the trappings of gender, what hope is there for the rest of us? I was also frustrated that both Porat and her colleagues, who led the industry in improving diversity, didn't find the comment worthy of addressing.' (Note: the board of 14 currently includes three women and two non-white directors, which is representative of its employees but not its customers.)

Following this interaction, social media picked up the baton with a variety of interactions playing with the 'Lady' epithet. Following this, 800 members of Google staff, both men and women, took a stand by adding the word 'Lady' to their job titles in their email signatures and within the Google internal directory.

How to promote a diversity mindset

Promoting a diversity mindset within the boardroom

Ee has discussed the different types of diversity, how these affect boardroom dynamics, what a diversity mindset is, how to measure it and the impact of that through micro-aggressions. How do you promote a diversity mindset both within the boardroom and, more broadly, throughout an organisation?

First of all, some small things may make a large difference. We know that diverse teams work better when they are told that diverse teams work better: simply doing this, as well as sharing some of the information from this chapter, may be an easy place to start. In addition, it may be useful to communicate the following three useful principles to counter micro-aggressions:

- Three things you should never do: ignore it, excuse it, become immobilised by it.
- Two things you should always do: address it, communicate with those involved.
- One thing you need to decide: address it now or address later.

There are also a variety of more concrete actions that each director may consider as action points to develop the diversity mindset beyond the general points above. These may include:

- Measuring one's potential bias using one or more of the Harvard University Implicit Association Tests, starting with those types that are most prevalent within the boards key stakeholder groups.
- Obtaining some feedback on your behaviour in light of your diversity bias results. To what extent have people noticed either inclusive or exclusive behaviour in oneself or other board directors in the past? Monitor this over time.
- Get to know each board director personally beyond board meetings. This is especially important if directors come from different backgrounds to each other and have different perspectives, psychological approaches and mindsets.
- Lead and sponsor diversity initiatives. The dual benefit of becoming involved in organisation-wide diversity initiatives is that taking a leadership role forces one to consider one's own bias and at the same time produces a role-model effect which may have a significant positive impact on the organisational followership. It is counterintuitively much more effective for a leader to stand up and admit their biases and that they are working hard to counter these, rather than to present as someone who has no flaws.
- Avoid making jokes at the expense of particular individuals or groups and do not be part of jokes of others. Instead, be seen to challenge inappropriate humour, even if it does not make you popular.
- Within board, committee, and other stakeholder meetings, notice whose comments get airtime and greater support and then evaluate this information through the lens of potential diversity bias such as gender, race, personality type, etc.
- Review board practices in light of the diversity considerations discussed in this chapter. Although the board may be making good strides in terms of including a diverse membership, it may not be capitalising on this and maximising the diversity's potential due to ineffective boardroom practices.

Directors and those supporting the board may also help decrease the potential feeling of exclusion by some individuals, and increase their feeling of acceptance of themselves in their role and their contribution, by reflecting this contribution in the board minutes. These should reflect the contribution of all members. Too frequently, some individuals, especially those in the minority or who are new to the board, have their contributions ignored, only for them to be subsequently repeated by a representative of the majority. Often the repeater is unaware that they have appropriated another members' contribution. A good chair will ensure that the first comment was received and brought into the discussion, Equally, if the chair themselves failed to acknowledge the contribution, the minutes can reflect it.

For those in the minority, one option if this happens is to discuss the topic with the individual who appropriated the contribution during the meeting by speaking to them one-to-one after the meeting. In this way, a rapport could be created through mutual recognition of the topic and, by doing so, future contributions may be acknowledged through this creation of shared interest.

The actions that a particular director may take will also be dependent on whether they are in the majority or minority grouping within the most pertinent diversity type that exists on their board. Those who are in the majority often suffer from something called 'advantage blindness' which can prevent them from seeing their impact on the de facto less powerful group members. When confronted with advantage blindness, unhelpful director responses would include denying that the playing field is not level, focusing on one's own disadvantages and claiming inequity is justified by the innate superiority of some groups over others. Instead, if one finds oneself in a majority group (and are challenged about the advantages of being in this group on the board) more constructive reactions might include owning your personal prejudice and bias, empathising and connecting with people who are the 'other' and considering how you could put personal advantage to collective good use.

Case study: The 30% Club

The 30% Club is an initiative focused on supporting many projects to develop gender diversity, with a mission to have at least 30% female representation on all boards and C-suites globally.

The first stage of its approach has been to connect with company chairs and CEOs to ask them to pledge their support and commitment to the goal. When asked about the primary characteristic of those (generally male) chairs who were most proactive in pledging support, one is of particular interest.

Many of the chairs who had supported the 30% Club and raised the agenda of diversity also had daughters who were on the initial rungs of their working careers. Sometimes it takes something extremely personal to shift one's diversity mindset.

If you find yourself in the minority on a board, it may initially be difficult to be heard and to be considered as an equal. Rather than being malicious, this is most often due to the unintentionally biased behaviours of others. The particular skillset of negotiation is an important one to consider here as developing yourself as a more competent negotiator has been shown to serve dividends as a minority trying to influence a broader group. Some of the key concepts of negotiation include being consistent, investing yourself in the argument, having autonomy in conversations rather than being tied to a particular party line, being able to be agile in how you respond and using fairness to your advantage. One superb example of minority influence under pressure using all these five negotiation tools can be seen in the Oscar-nominated classic 1958 film *Twelve Angry Men*, in which one juror (Juror 8, played by Henry Fonda) is able skilfully to shift all of the other eleven jurors' mindsets throughout the course of the film.

Promoting a diversity mindset more broadly

What can the board do more broadly to develop an increasingly diverse executive pipeline within senior positions in their organisation? As the FRC Guide to Boardroom Effectiveness notes, 'Improving diversity at each level of the company is important, if more diversity at senior levels is to become a reality.' One initial action is to create, as the guidance suggests, greater transparency about the make-up of the workforce. Understanding what level of diversity exists within an organisation to start with is vital to see how improvements can be made. The difficulty, however, when it comes to measuring diversity, is in defining what diversity actually is for your organisation. Some aspects of diversity are reasonably straightforward to measure – for example, gender, race or ethnicity. However, other types are less obvious. The debate therefore needs to be about what diversity the company needs as a strategic capability and how this can specifically be measured.

The question is whether diversity starts at the top with the board and filters downwards, or starts in the workforce and climbs up. Either way, effective implementation is most important when addressing and promoting diversity. The board, as well as those advising and supporting the board, can influence this implementation – in both mindset and action – at the collective and individual level.

Beyond measurement, there is no one single approach that will guarantee success in promoting a diversity mindset. There are some core recommended principles, however. Best practice quotas need to be approached with care, as they may mask the real cultural shifts needed within the boardroom and beyond. Organisations whose espoused values conflict with the underlying assumptions and mindsets that actually exist can be uncomfortable places. Therefore, approaches to diversity need instead to be both strategic and systemic, rather than ad hoc approaches like simply ticking the box on mandatory diversity training. Some principles and approaches to consider might include:

- clarifying how diversity can be a strategic capability;
- mapping diversity in the company's community and consumer base so it can be aligned with and reflected in the organisation;
- agreeing which specific types of diversity are required and then measuring, monitoring and managing them over time;
- ensuring the nominations committee is clear on the importance of diversity and its place in the boardroom and the workplace, so it can apply it to its actions;

- recognising the associated costs of introducing diversity measures and investing accordingly so that momentum continues;
- considering positive actions to support and encourage diversity in learning and development as a route to leadership and executive roles;
- creating a mentoring culture, especially around mentoring diverse groups;
- implementing evidence-based diversity methods – for example, when recruiting use methods such as standard question lists; processes that reach beyond the organisation's current social network and anonymising CVs; and
- ensuring that the recruitment process and its members includes diversity, even if the final candidate may not be from a minority.

Diversity quotas

We have mentioned in passing in this chapter the use of quotas in creating a diverse board. There are benefits and negatives in the use of quotas: increasingly, they are being seen as a necessity where the mindset of boards cannot be changed and the historical value of board experience, outdated thinking and 'looking the same' goes unchallenged.

Charlotte Valeur, the former Chair of the Institute of Directors (IoD) is a champion for diversity in the boardroom, both in terms of gender and cognitive skills, and has publicly shared her personal diagnosis of being autistic. At a November 2020 IoD Chartered Director conference, she noted that she is 'tired of discussing why and is now focused on the how, as we're running out of time' to make the change. This has made her more open to the implementation of quotas in the boardroom, something that she has been opposed to in the past.

In November 2020, Germany's coalition government voted to introduce a mandatory quota for the number of women working as senior management in the country's listed companies, in a move hailed as a 'historic' step towards gender equality in German boardrooms. Under its terms, management boards with more than three members must include at least one woman, reversing a voluntary system that critics argued had failed to achieve the required shift towards gender equality.

The move came after research found that the representation of women in senior management in German companies was lagging behind peers in rival major economies. Women make up 12.8% of the management boards of the 30 largest German companies listed on the blue-chip Dax index, according to a September 2020 survey by the Swedish-German AllBright foundation. The study stated that the figure compares with 28.6% in the US, 24.5% in the UK and 22.2% in France. The research also stated that Dax companies were losing women in senior positions, citing that there had been a rise in the number of Dax companies without a single woman on the board, from six companies in the previous year to 11 by mid-2020.

With or without quotas, the case for diversity has been studied and discussed for many years. Quotas may be adopted in some countries; in others they may not. However, the heart of the matter is the attitude of the members of the board, their recognition of the benefits of diversity and their adoption of its implementation in a form that benefits their organisation, sector and country.

Conclusion

The concept of diversity has been increasingly recognised in organisational theory and practice and its application in governance is no exception. There is a strong, growing and widely accepted business case for boardroom diversity.

Board members need to decide firstly how they want to embrace diversity, rather than simply ticking compliance boxes on gender or race, then consider how best to manage the associated dynamics to maximise the potential benefits of a diverse board rather than succumb to the potential downsides of increased diversity. With this recognition and acceptance, the mechanics of building a diverse board can then be applied, being mindful of the unconscious bias that will already be in play within the board.

An individual's personal diversity mindset relates to specific and measurable diversity biases they may have, which be expressed in micro-aggressions of which they may be unaware. Visible diversity doesn't necessarily deliver diversity of experience, knowledge or thought and certainly doesn't automatically deliver a high performing board. However, with self-awareness comes knowledge and the potential to address any areas of negativity. Individual directors can develop a variety of approaches to their diversity mindset. These might also be considered more broadly to assist the board and senior leadership team in developing a more diverse organisational culture.

How can a board truly become more diverse? Board diversity is most often assumed to mean simply recruiting more people from minority groups. Although this may be necessary from an ethical equality and compliance perspective, it does not guarantee that a board will become 'better'. More specifically, a successfully diverse board will be one that strategically reflects and, through an appropriately cohesive and challenging boardroom dynamic, can then effectively represent the diversity of their key stakeholder relationships in boardroom conversations and decisions. This should also be combined with a diversity not just of stakeholder demographics, but also of board director psychographics to ensure that diversity of thinking is encouraged and facilitated.

Those supporting the board can positively influence the board recognition of diversity, its benefits and its reflection in a company through their actions and interaction with the board and executives. Acceptance of the need for diversity is the first step. While simple to communicate, due to the academic evidence of its benefits, it is the mindset of the board that needs to embrace the benefits of diversity and to commit as individuals to creating a diverse board. Aligning the purpose of a nominations committee (where there is one) to the need for diversity at the board level is an important step. Alternatively, it must be ensured that the recruitment process (whoever runs it) fully understands the board's expectations in terms of having a diverse membership, and that this recruitment process considers diverse candidates throughout the whole process.

Board members need to be firm on their intention for inclusion. As one CEO in Silicon Valley noted, it is simple to identify the need for inclusion, but it is equally simple to accept the feedback from recruitment agencies that the only available candidates are those already in the pool of known individuals. Forcing a headhunter to look again, with the additional costs in terms of time and resources, is difficult – but it must be done if board diversity is to improve. Eventually, appointments will be made that meet the requirements to create a board that delivers in diversity of thought, experience, knowledge and actions.

Board acceptance of the need for diversity needs to be followed up with actions to achieve greater diversity for the benefit of the organisation. Yes, it may take more time, but the long-term benefit needs to be delivered and difficulties must be overcome to make it happen. Can any board continue to function in a global world without a board composed of differing views, experience, knowledge and outlook? The time for talk has finished; action needs to be taken to make it happen.

Are you and your board open to diversity? Do you recognise the benefits of diversity to your company? Do you believe you have already embraced diversity across all forms or is there still more to do?

9 – The effect of meeting design on boardroom dynamics

Introduction to meeting design

The challenge of meetings

The board meeting is the centre of gravity of all board life and the arena within which board dynamics plays out. The general concept of the meeting, though, does not currently have a good reputation. As Dave Barry, the Pulitzer Prize-winning author, once wrote: 'If you had to identify, in one word, the reason why the human race has not achieved, and never will achieve, its full potential, that word would be meetings.'

The science of meetings also points to the conclusion that they are often unproductive and costly. Surveys have suggested that over 50% of meeting time is wasted and that, in terms of the unproductive meeting cost to American corporations, this equates to over $37 billion in lost time and resources (Mosvick and Nelson, 1987; Sheridan, 1989). One study by Romano and Nunamaker (2001) categorised 1,305 reported problems of meetings, of which the most frequent were 'getting off topic', 'having no goals or agenda', 'being too lengthy', 'poor or adequate preparation', 'being inconclusive', being disorganised', 'starting too late', 'being too large' and 'having no premeeting orientation'. So far in this text we have mostly how considered individual personality and group dynamic behaviours influence the quality of board conversations. However, this list of problems with meetings is more to do with how they are designed, affecting the quality of a board outcome. The impact of these design features is often significantly underappreciated.

In fact, one study by Di Salvo et al. in 1989 showed that 22% of problems with meetings were related to pre-meeting issues. Many of these design factors are quite easily fixable with good preparation. Research looking at what is true of meetings when employees look forward to them, by Allen et al. in 2012, showed that, conversely, *productive* meetings were influenced by factors such as whether 'the information is relevant and/or important', 'the information is interesting and enjoyable', 'the meeting is timely or punctual' and whether people feel they are 'prepared for the meeting'.

Case study: Ray Dalio's meeting principles

Ray Dalio, the American billionaire investor and philanthropist, is the founder of the investment firm Bridgewater Associates, one of the world's largest hedge funds. He attributes his success to clear and recurring lessons that he has learnt through his life, or as he calls them in his bestselling business book of the same name, 'principles', which he applies to his organisation. Some of these principles are about meeting design procedures. He recommends a set of specific principles for effective meetings, most of which are related to the meeting's design in some way, as follows:

- Emphasise the meeting's purpose – clarify and communicate this to meeting participants ahead of time to provide them direction.
- Be as precise as possible in meeting communication – either before, during or after a meeting, in terms of precise agenda items and meeting attendee questioning.
- Establish the type of meeting you are holding – is the meeting to educate, is it to discuss issues from all stakeholder perspectives, is it to make some specific key decisions or is it a mixture of all of these? The meeting agenda will need to be tailored to each of these different types.
- Be assertive and open-minded – encourage, depersonalise and, if needed, reconcile different points of view by reminding attendees of the meeting's objective.
- Keep track of the progress made – although much of a meeting will be about the topic in hand, some of the meeting also needs to be a discussion of how well the attendees are progressing towards the goals of the meeting.
- Try to avoid 'topic slip' – stop random drifting from topic to topic by visualising the conversation on a whiteboard so that everyone can appreciate where the conversation is at any time.
- Remain calm and analytical at all times – challenge feeling statements with questions that ask for evidence to back up claims.
- Be clear in assigning responsibilities – ensure everyone knows who owns which tasks both during and after the meeting.
- Utilise the 'two-minute rule' to avoid introduction interruptions – use this rule to give individuals time to explain thinking before others jump in with their own, to ensure understanding and to give quieter voices a fair platform.
- Reach a conclusion – ensure discussion achieves an appropriate completion, most likely a decision and/or an action.
- Figure out if the meeting was effective – review the meeting in terms of both its effectiveness and efficiency of communication.

Board meetings

When we consider board meetings more specifically as a subset of the meetings that exist within organisational life, we also find that the research and practical evidence paints a similarly dismal picture of overall quality.

As we discussed in Chapter 7 in some detail, the quality of conversations, and therefore the board dynamic, often fails to reach its potential in the boardroom. This is perhaps unsurprising considering the constraints and context that the board as an organisational unit is working under in meetings. As we discussed in Chapter 4, boards:

- only meet episodically at a low frequency;
- have a duty to solve complex and strategic challenges;
- operate within severe time constraints;
- always work with imperfect information;
- include both insiders and outsiders to the organisation, leading to the potential for information asymmetry;
- often include members with busy lives, strong personalities and high profiles;
- have roles that are both cohesive and conflicting at the same time;
- are typically larger than most senior management teams; and
- often have lengthy compliance processes that they must follow.

When we look at what directors mention when they are asked for the most common reasons of ineffective boardroom conversations, we surprisingly find that many are design related rather than personality related. As we saw in Chapter 7, a Tomorrow's Corporate Governance report in 2012 cited that, in addition to 'dominant personalities among board members', the next three most rated reasons for board issues were the more design issues of 'inappropriate allocation of time for discussion', 'poor preparation' and 'unhelpful manner of presenting information'.

Contrastingly, in their study evaluating what constitutes a good corporate board, Van den Berghe and the Levrau (2004) found that the 'quality of the board meetings' was by far the most frequently reported element constituting a good board of directors in their in-depth interviews with 60 board members of Belgium listed companies and that appropriate and well-timed pre-meeting information was a key condition for a quality board meeting in the first place in order for a director to feel well prepared.

Therefore, as the quality of a board meeting is vital to the quality of governance and as the preparation and design features of a meeting can have a significant impact on board meeting quality itself, it becomes imperative for governance professionals to understand more fully what meeting design characteristics exist and how to influence them. Although the chair is ultimately accountable for facilitating a board meeting, the company secretary usually has significant ownership and responsibility for supporting the process before, during and after a meeting to support the chair. Other governance professionals and board influencers, as well as board members themselves, have an important function to play in this pre-meeting period. Equally important is the quality and format of the information that forms the supporting documentation of any board pack and the contributors to these should be mindful of the purpose and use of their reporting into the board. Therefore, understanding and positively influencing meeting design can become a key tool in 'invisible leadership' influence.

Design characteristics

In *The Art of War*, Sun Tzu advocates that 'every battle is won before it is fought'. This is the philosophy behind the idea of meeting design characteristics. Rather than fight hard in meetings to reduce disruption, maintain focus, improve positivity and enhance follow-up, setting a meeting up for success so that participants are naturally drawn towards more positive states and outcomes is much more strategic. Design characteristics usually satisfy three criteria. Firstly, they are generally under the control of the meeting organiser. Secondly, they are related to the meeting's conduct, composition or setting. Thirdly, they can be thought through and planned in advance or initiated at a meeting such that they influence perceptions of meeting quality.

In their 2011 study 'Meeting design characteristics and attendee perceptions of staff/team meeting quality', Melissa Cohen et al. sampled 367 participants across a variety of industries and identified 18 design characteristics that could potentially affect perceptions of meeting quality. These 18 factors were grouped into four categories of characteristics: temporal, physical, procedural and attendee. Based on a review of the literature, three other factors are also important (being time of day, meeting space arrangement and the impact of pre-meeting talk). The full list of these design characteristics, which we will use to structure the rest of this chapter, is as follows:

A. Temporal characteristics

1 Meeting length
2 Promptness of start and end
3 Use of breaks
4 Time of day

B. Physical characteristics

5 Lighting
6 Noise
7 Temperature
8 Refreshments
9 Meeting space
10 Technology use

11 Seating dynamics
12 Meeting space arrangement

C. Procedural characteristics
13 Meeting goals
14 Agenda use
15 Pre-meeting talk
16 Visual displays
17 Meeting agreements
18 Minutes
19 Meeting recorded

D. Attendee characteristics
20 Number of attendees
21 Presence of a meeting facilitator

It is interesting to note that Cohen et al.'s study found that nine of their 18 design characteristics correlated with perceived meeting quality. These were the promptness of the start and end of the meeting, the lighting, adequate meeting space, having complimentary refreshments, appropriate room temperature, having a formal agenda, prior access to the meeting, employing a meeting agreement at the start of the meeting and having fewer attendees. Although having the meeting facilitated did not correlate with meeting quality in the initial statistical testing, it became important and significant when meeting size increased. Thus, having clear facilitation rather than participation becomes helpful with larger meeting sizes. Further, as four of the nine design characteristics were physical factors, the study concluded that physical design factors in particular are crucial to get right to encourage an appropriate environment for meeting effectiveness.

It is important to recognise that cultural norms may significantly affect the importance of specific design characteristics and therefore how much attention is placed on them by a meeting organiser or facilitator. For example, in China, due to a more pronounced power hierarchy, more care and attention may be taken in the process of attendee invitations and the precise positions which people are allocated around the boardroom table. However, the more general point here is that these design characteristics matter and knowing how they matter cannot be ignored if one wants to facilitate an effective board meeting. We will now go through each design characteristic in turn, commenting on how an individual might best make use of their potential to positively influence the outcome of a board meeting.

Temporal characteristics

The temporal characteristics of a board meeting relate to how meeting time is used. The contention is that meetings that take temporal considerations into account will reduce the likelihood of disruption, either by meeting participants distracting each other or self-distraction due to reducing focus and fatigue. These design characteristics will include the meeting length, how prompt the meeting is in terms of start and end time, how breaks are used throughout the meeting and at what time of day a meeting is scheduled.

Meeting length

A 2014 board practices study entitled 'Perspectives from the boardroom', published by Deloitte Consulting and the Society of Corporate Secretaries and Governance Professionals, reported that 75% of boards meet between six and nine times a year. For around half of boards in the sample, the length of these full board meetings (not counting time spent on committees) was found to be around three to five hours, whereas around a third of boards typically spent between six to eight hours in their board meeting.

Obviously it depends on what items need to be discussed and how many people are attending to discuss them, however, good practice points towards the three- to five-hour range as being more likely to produce better perceptions of meeting quality in attendees than a longer meeting. Sometimes a chair may feel the need for a board to meet for a full day to honour the time commitment a board might have made in preparing for, and then travelling to, the meeting. In these scenarios the formal board meeting itself may be a sub-set of the full days' agenda, or may be divided into multiple board meetings with different agenda items and focus areas. This rationalisation for longer meetings is less of an issue with the rise in virtual board meetings – a trend that has only accelerated due to the global pandemic – and is perhaps one of the reasons for the likelihood of virtual meetings being attested to be shorter on average.

However, the key factor in board meetings should be quality over quantity. As Seth Levine, a partner and co-founder at the venture capitalist firm the Foundry Group (whose investments include companies such as Zegna and Fitbit), mentions in his excellent 'Design the Ideal Board Meeting' blog series:

> Substantive board meetings aren't measured by time in the boardroom and I think a (chair's) first and highest priority should be to creating a meeting that is high on substance and information and low on filler. As a general rule for most companies that are reading this, something in the three to four hour range makes sense for how long your board should be meeting. In my experience meetings that run longer than that (and I've been in plenty of seven-hour board meetings over the years) ramble, are not focused, are actually light on substance (much of which gets missed because of all the filler) and tend to devolve into executive team meetings. Less than three hours feels too short to cover substantive issues.

Research also shows that meetings last up to twice as long when materials are distributed during a meeting, which has implications for meeting preparation and timely material distribution.

Promptness of start and end

Cohen et al.'s (2011) research found a clear correlation between promptness at the start and end of the meeting and perceived meeting quality. Being on time was seen as both an example of good temporal courtesy (presumably leading to less frustration from other attendees) and it is also less disruptive in that board members do not feel like they are having to wait on late members to start. There are significant country cultural differences in expectations to do with time and the issue of promptness, which we will discuss in more detail in Chapter 13. There may also be significant corporate cultural expectations around meeting etiquette; however, the cultural formality of a board meeting may supersede the country cultural norms around promptness, thus keeping to time seems an important boardroom default design choice.

Use of breaks

The most obvious benefit of thoughtful scheduling of breaks in (especially longer and or virtual) board meetings is to ensure that all attendees are able to maintain mental performance throughout the meeting. Psychological research shows that one's attention can only be held for around 30–40 minutes, so a good practice process would ideally be to take short breaks after this amount of time. For example, the 'Pomodoro Method' of focused work time-boxing is often recommended to help maintain mental clarity on work throughout one's day. This method suggests a rhythm of 25 minutes work followed by five minutes break for four cycles, followed by a longer break of half an hour. To regain mental clarity and concentration fully, it is recommended that breaks do not include other work, such as the ubiquitous checking email on one's mobile phone (research shows that we often experience a worse mood when we do this in a break), but instead include some light physical movement such as a brief walk, ideally taken socially with others and outside in fresh air. One Danish study as a proxy for this advice showed that when students took a 20-minute break before a test, their scores were substantially higher.

The use of breaks has other functions in addition to rejuvenating mental focus. Breaks are useful as a method of enhancing relationship building through small talk and are thus often experienced as warm hospitality. Further, breaks can be useful when a group conversation gets stuck such that after a break, insight often emerges. One final benefit of a break is following group conflict, to allow emotions to settle so that more rational and depersonalised dialogue can continue.

Time of day

If the ideal meeting length is somewhere in the region of three to five hours, then does what part of the day the meeting is scheduled in have any bearing on meeting outcomes? Indeed it does, as it turns out that there is a significant amount of research and anecdotal evidence showing that we perform at different levels depending upon what time of day it is. Firstly, there is research that shows that different people have different chronotypes. The most simple classification of these splits people into either Larks, who perform better in the morning, or Owls, who perform better later in the day. The former are more likely to be born in autumn and winter, while the latter tend to have birthdays in spring or summer. Another chronotype theory separates people into Dolphins, Bears, Lions and Wolves. Each of these chronotypes has a different pattern which one can discover using online questionnaires developed by sleep expert Dr Michael Breus.

Beyond individual types, though, general patterns have also been noted which highlight different population-wide levels of performance and emotion at different times of the day. In 2011, researchers at Cornell University analysed approximately 500 million tweets posted over two years in 84 countries. They found a clear pattern that, regardless of time of year, positive emotions rose in strength through the morning and then fell markedly in the afternoon, before climbing back up again in the evening. This pattern of an early morning peak, an afternoon trough and early evening rebound is important when considering meeting time. As many other studies show, not just positivity, but also concentration and decision-making quality follow the same pattern. As we mentioned in Chapter 5, one study of parole judges found that inmates had limited chances of winning parole if their hearing was scheduled in the afternoon (however, if the judges had taken an afternoon break, then their mental state was drastically changed such that paroles were far more likely in the afternoon).

Thus, one clear conclusion here is that, unless individual chronotypes are known and are, on average, significantly skewed from a normal distribution, board meetings should be scheduled in the morning. Further, if a board meeting is likely to extend over a longer period, or even a full day, then important discussions and decisions should be scheduled earlier in the agenda. Or, if this is not possible, appropriate restorative breaks need to be built in so that focus and decision-making capacity does not metaphorically fall off a cliff later in the day.

Physical characteristics

Ed Schein, the former professor at the MIT Sloan School of Management and one of the leading thinkers on organisational culture, was famously quoted as saying, 'If you want to shift the culture, move the furniture'. This captures the essence of the *physical* design characteristics, which relate to all aspects of the meeting setting and environment. These characteristics include some of the environmental basics such as lighting, noise, temperature, whether there are refreshments and other factors such as the size and type of meeting space, meeting modality (that is, whether the meeting is face-to-face or facilitated by technology), the seating arrangements and dynamics and the arrangement of the meeting space. Like the temporal design characteristics, these physical characteristics can also have a profound impact on the participants' emotions and feelings as well as their ability to maintain focus over periods of time. The effect of the physical characteristics of space are so profound that they have spawned a science called 'proxemics', defined as 'the study of human use of space and the effects it has on behaviour, communication and social interaction'.

The concept of conversational 'dialogue', which we introduced in Chapter 6, which describes effective group thinking processes as a balance of advocacy and inquiry, includes the concept of a 'safe space'. This concept denotes a setting that encourages dialogue and a mood within which people feel free to be themselves and speak their minds without fear of adverse consequences. As well as agreeing ground rules to reduce social barriers, safe spaces also reduce physical barriers through their design. A broad principle of the safe space physical design is that furniture should not make people feel socially distant and equipment should be flexible to accommodate personal preferences and styles. In addition, seating arrangements should not send signals about roles and status and all other physical distractions should be removed.

In summary, then, the physical design characteristics of board meetings are both powerful but often operate through an unconscious bias. As Weiss and Cropanzano (1996) state:

> Overall, the evidence suggests that a wide variety of environmental factors influence individual affect levels. By and large, these operate in the background, but it seems clear that their consequences on organisational behaviours as mediated by mood states, are likely to be important.

This section will delineate the key physical design characteristics and provide recommendations on how individuals might best use them to positively influence board meeting outcomes.

The basics: lighting, noise, temperature and refreshments

Research identifies a number of physical design basics that require consideration. These include lighting, little background noise, appropriate temperature and access to refreshments. These may be considered as constituting the bottom rung of Maslow's hierarchy of needs for a board meeting.

Although not mentioned in the literature, but certainly of note in our modern digital age, these basics have perhaps been superseded by the even more basic needs for a fast wifi connection and access to plugs so that electronic devices can be recharged. Although seemingly arbitrary, these are important considerations to enable people to feel at home and not distracted by wondering what is going on elsewhere. However, a balance needs to be struck between distraction and maintaining contact: ground rules around being in actual and metaphorical 'airplay' mode during a meeting might be useful agreements to add to one's procedures. One general point to make about these basic design features is that regardless of how much they may influence meeting attendees' emotions and concentration, there is evidence to suggest that the most important psychological principle is to give attendees control over these characteristics. It turns out that, psychologically, for example, it may be better for participants to be in control of their environment than, for example, for it to be a perfect temperature.

In terms of lighting, the simple fact of being neither too light nor too dark was actually seen as important to perceptions of meeting quality in Cohen et al.'s (2011) research. Also, appropriate lighting such that meeting participants do not feel strain throughout the day is important. Obviously, natural light would be better than artificial light in this regard. A niche but significant body of research also shows strong evidence of the positive psychological benefits of having windows in a room or, at the very least, an internal window that creates the effect of having a view outside of one's immediate environment.

The amount of outside noise that might cause a distraction was not found to correlate with meeting quality perceptions. However, temperature, such that a room was neither too hot or too cold, and the presence of complimentary refreshments, did correlate with perceived meeting quality. The issue of refreshments has a number of mechanisms by which it can influence meeting behaviour. Firstly, that meeting refreshments are complimentary is seen as good hospitality and therefore creates better feelings of comfort and positivity. Secondly, as we shall discuss in further detail in Chapter 15 on personal resilience, appropriate refreshments for personal well-being may have a positive impact on participants' ability to focus. Having a variety of caffeinated and decaffeinated options (depending on the time of day) and minimising sugary snacks can have a significant impact on the ability to maintain mental energy levels throughout long meetings. After all, a board meeting is a significant performance event and treating it as such will ensure better performance outcomes.

Finally, enabling participants to consume refreshments during a meeting rather than in breaks may have an unexpected psychological benefit. A famous experiment by Yale University psychologists, published in the journal *Science* in 2008, found that people judged others to be more generous and caring if they were holding a warm cup of coffee but less so if they held an iced coffee. Also, in a second study, it was found that people are more likely to give something to others if they just held something warm and more likely to take something for themselves if they had held something cold. Therefore, if you want to encourage cohesiveness in a group around an important key decision, make sure that warm drinks are served just before that point in the agenda!

Meeting space

The overall meeting space is naturally a key consideration when planning a board meeting location. Ensuring that the space is large enough and uncluttered to minimise distractions is one first consideration. However, more importantly, the overall cultural symbolism needs to be taken into consideration. We all know the feeling when we walk into a room of being able to very quickly get a sense of what the space is like. This is what Edgar Schein (as discussed in Chapter 7) described as the 'cultural symbols and artefacts' that are the visible aspects of an organisation or group culture. Classically, many boardrooms are standard office space design or designed to the taste of the leadership, which may, or may not, be appropriate to the effective functioning of the board in question.

Case study: Make Sainsbury's great again

The walls of the boardroom in Sainsbury's Holborn head office used to be adorned with classical paintings and portraits of previous leaders, mainly the Sainsbury's family over the generations.

However, after a period of complacency and losing ground to Tesco, the new leadership, under the direction of ex-Asda and Marks and Spencer retailer Justin King, made some significant changes to 'make Sainsbury's great again'.

This was reflected in the head office's name change to the 'Store Support Centre' and the more historical, traditional and grand pictures in the boardroom being replaced by pictures of employees working in stores as a subliminal reminder to the board of this previously underserved key stakeholder.

There is research to back up this example, showing the impact of background cultural artefacts on how people think, that highlight the importance of getting this design aspect right. For example, in one study, when people who were completing an analytical task were shown a picture of Rodin's *The Thinker*, their correct answers increased by a startling 41%. Another study found that by placing pictures of prominent women scientists on the walls of an exam room, the grades of women who were sitting science subjects in those exams went up. Therefore, careful consideration of the cultural symbolism in a boardroom should be taken into account. If a board is trying to emphasise cohesion, then pictures of prominent teams could be an option. Similarly, if a board is not particularly diverse or representative, then pictures of its key stakeholders and other important diverse groupings could be strategically positioned in the boardroom. This may seem somewhat Machiavellian or unethical to some; however, the argument made for these types of interventions is that our thinking will be influenced regardless so we might as well influence it in as positive a way as we can.

A broader consideration around meeting space is the office location choice for a board meeting. Where should the board meeting be held? Should the consideration for this be based on stakeholder importance, meeting agenda, rotation around sites or some other symbolic consideration?

Case study: Lego's global board meetings

In an effort to include its various global offices, the then-CEO of Lego, Jorgen Vig Knudstorp, made an attempt to rotate executive board meetings continuously around different country offices. Surprisingly, he received some criticism from the main head office in Denmark that, although appreciating his intent, it was feeling slightly unloved. From then on, the board meeting location rotations were adjusted to include the Danish head office from time to time.

It may be that the best option is not to hold a board meeting at an office site at all, but rather to go off-site. This may be preferable, for example, if the agenda is to be more strategic and future-thinking. In this scenario an off-site location away from the more tactical day-to-day setting would have the function of creating more distance and perspective and could be particularly beneficial for executive directors who would be less prone to being interrupted or pulled back into their day-to-day responsibilities.

Technology use

In recent years, many technological solutions have been applied to the boardroom to help with meeting and governance functioning. For example, companies such as Diligent and Board Intelligence provide secure and paperless solutions for electronic board packs and meeting minutes for directors to access. Similarly, virtual board meetings were already becoming more prevalent due to benefits such as the significant cost and time savings and the potential access to greater global diversity.

The impact of the global pandemic has driven the prevalence of virtual board meetings to new levels, creating an environment where, in most cases, holding a virtual board meeting is the only option. Their use has ensured that board meetings can continue, with the resultant boardroom dynamics being considerably impacted by their use. No doubt, virtual meetings and technological solutions will continue at a greater level than previously, although, they are not perfect solutions in isolation.

Careful consideration rather than blind adoption of the use of technology in board meeting design is important, as there are also many downsides of technology use. For example, we know that virtual teams find it much more difficult to build trust than face-to-face teams. Furthermore, virtual teams suffer when they are required to have conversations that need greater interaction and are more creative and strategic. Therefore, if virtual board meetings are to be employed, the following may be important:

- Directors have face-to-face meetings first to build a personal relationship or, as a minimum, have had an opportunity to hold a one-to-one conversation prior to the meeting to build up a level of mutual understanding and some rapport.
- Virtual meetings are used as an ad hoc addition built around more predictable face-to-face meeting patterns.
- Include some more socialisation at the start of the meeting.
- Ensure video use to be able to see people as well as hear them to emphasise and humanise.
- Agree specific ground rules around virtual meetings that may be different from face-to-face meetings, such as individuals flagging when they want to add to the discussion, ensuring that all individuals contribute, monitoring interruptions and, at the outset, confirming that all attendees are comfortable with the meeting being recorded (if this is indeed going to be the case).

The Chartered Governance Institute published a guidance note entitled 'Good practice for virtual board and committee meetings' in March 2020 at the start of the pandemic. Some of the key advice included the following:

- The choice of the right communication channel is vital.
- Virtual meetings need to be well structured and avoid unnecessary complexity.
- Preparation is key.
- The chair will need additional techniques to run an orderly meeting.
- 'Ground rules' for participants should be circulated to all those joining the meeting.
- Clear instructions on accessing the meeting system or app are essential.
- Good boardroom practices are even more necessary.

More broadly, research shows that simply having technology such as mobile phones on a table during a physical meeting can reduce levels of trust and concentration. Therefore, a general recommendation would be to limit the use and presence of technology on tables and around the boardroom during meetings to enable better team interaction and focus. Good practice is for the chair to ask all participants to put their mobile devices on silent and away from the table and, for any individual that is expecting an important call, to make the chair aware of this before the meeting.

Seating dynamics

Seating dynamics is a subset of the science of proxemics (defined earlier) and is the art of seating people in certain positions according to their purpose in communication. There are some generally agreed principles of seating dynamics to encourage specific outcomes. For example, to encourage participation, one should seat the other party next to you so that they are facing the same direction. To facilitate direct and open communication, the advice would be to seat the other party across a corner of the desk from you or in another place where that person will be at right angles. This allows for the possibility of more honest disclosure. However, if one wanted to take a competitive stand against someone, the advice would be to position that person directly across the table from you. Further, in order to block two meeting attendees from being disruptive, the general advice would be to sit one either side of the chair to block their interactions. However, there is also a school of thought that suggests that the way to stop disruptions is to stop people from having eye contact. As one of the company secretaries in The Chartered Governance Institute's 'Conflict and tension in the boardroom' report said,

> When you've got a meeting with two people who are likely to light the blue touch paper because of each other's presence, make sure they're in a position where they can't have eye contact. I used to sit them side-by-side. It was quite something, and they never had a row.

The question of eye contact is also important for where any non-director boardroom supporters choose to position themselves. As one company secretary observed in the same report, 'I always want to sit where I can make eye contact with the chair, as the odd hard stare or raised eyebrow can be quite helpful in terms of flagging something up.'

A final principle around seating dynamics is around using seating to create different perspectives rather than allowing people metaphorically to get stuck in the same perspective. Different options that board meetings have might be to encourage or even position individuals in different seats each time the board meets or to ask them to shift round in positions after every break. This will enable participants to talk to different people in break small talk, perhaps challenge thinking, symbolically keep them on their toes and mix executives and non-executives to encourage team cohesion. Some boards even keep one or more seats free to represent one of their key stakeholders. For example, some organisations regularly do this to ensure that leadership teams always keep the customer in mind. This technique is taken from psychological therapeutic practice and is known as the 'empty chair'. With its roots in Gestalt therapy, it enables meeting participants to empathise more fully with the stakeholder's feelings, thoughts and behaviours as if they were present.

Meeting space arrangement

The final physical design characteristic to consider is how the meeting space is used dynamically as a way of improving meeting function. One general principle is to ensure that the space is as flexible as possible so that it increases participants feelings of control and enables changes to suit a board meeting's different 'gears' of monitoring/mentoring, strategising and decision making. There is nothing stopping a board meeting moving away from a formal table environment to another particular type of space arrangement at a certain point in a meeting. For example, breaking into smaller groups to sit with no tables may be useful to encourage more discussion, or standing up around a whiteboard may be chosen to increase creativity. Although this might seem radical, we know that 'standing up' meetings are 34% shorter than 'sitting down' meetings but have no measurable decision quality differences. In addition, there is a relational benefit of having no tables, as this reduces the psychological distance that people perceive.

When a table is being used, it is also extremely important, from a meeting design perspective, to consider what shape that table is. The classic idea of a formal board meeting table, for example, is one that is rectangular, such as the extremely long and narrow one used in the Cabinet in the British government at 10 Downing Street. This naturally denotes status differentials, can create adversity and often make it difficult for directors at the longer sides to have eye contact easily with those on the same side as them. Therefore, a recommendation for cohesion and to reduce status would be to have a circular table to avoid the head of the table effect and to ensure equal eye contact. Furthermore, tables with soft and curved lines tend to create a space that feels more pleasant and attractive. The table in the American President's Cabinet Room in the White House is quite traditional; however, it is more oval, enabling better lines of sight around the table.

One point that must be borne in mind, whatever physical format the meeting space arrangement may take, is to enable all attendees to contribute. Having a formal room that is difficult to navigate for an attendee with disabilities will result in their contribution being negatively affected. Remember these disabilities may be in terms of both physical movement but may also be sensory, such as poor or no eyesight, limited hearing or other. As the benefit of diversity is now accepted, the physical environment for each meeting should be able to accommodate all types of diversity, including physical.

Case study: Meeting design at the Northern Ireland peace talks

During the Northern Ireland peace process, the issue of physical design characteristics played a significant part in the proceedings. First of all, the choice of venue was a continually sensitive and symbolic consideration. However, it was the choice of table shape that apparently became even more significant.

In his autobiography, the then-Prime Minister Tony Blair wrote that the final stages of talks in 2007 nearly collapsed over a choice of a table for a key meeting. The Democratic Unionist Party had apparently wanted the sides to sit opposite each other 'to show they were still adversaries', but Sinn Fein wanted everyone to sit next to each other 'to show they were partners and equals'. Apparently, the deal was only done after a Downing Street official had suggested a diamond-shaped table 'so they could sit both opposite and with each other'.

Procedural characteristics

The procedural design characteristics of board meetings concern how each meeting is conducted. These characteristics include:

- whether the meeting has clear goals;
- whether the meeting has a formal agenda and how this is used;
- whether the meeting provides an opportunity for pre-meeting talk;
- whether the meeting uses visual displays;
- whether the meeting includes and is initiated by a meeting agreement;
- whether and how meeting minutes are taken; and
- whether the meeting is electronically recorded.

The evidence base from both research and practice shows that the inclusion of these procedural considerations can enhance meeting effectiveness through better task focus, better assistance in reaching meeting goals and the increased likelihood that agreed action items are followed up on following a meeting.

Meeting goals

Providing goal or theme clarity before, during and in reviewing the meeting can have a significant impact on meeting effectiveness. This will be unique to each board meeting and will be shaped by a variety of factors that are evolving within a board and the company of which the board is part.

There are a number of criteria that shape the 'season' in which a board finds itself which will affect the purpose of any particular board meeting. These include the current performance of the organisation (whether on an upwards or downwards trajectory), the industry type and culture (for example a more mature industry versus a more entrepreneurial start-up) and the board situation (whether the board is in 'crisis' or in more 'normal' times). These may be entirely appropriate although not classically 'best practice' if viewed in isolation. As Katharina Pick's (2007) Harvard research on board function notes,

> A meeting with very little discussion may at first glance, suggest a rubber-stamp board with little involvement and poor oversight. However, if the observed meeting was a strategic review meeting where the primary purpose was to give management a chance to communicate as much information as possible to board members, this impression of board director participation would not seem so egregious.

This quote is an example of a meeting goal that is more a 'discussion' process than a 'decision' process. Thus, being clear on what a meeting, or indeed an agenda item, purpose is in terms of 'decision or discussion' is a key design distinction that will enable better board outcomes.

Agenda use

Cohen et al.'s (2011) research found that having a formal agenda with prior access was correlated with positive meeting evaluations whereas no agenda, or an agenda tabled only at the meeting, was not. A variety of board-specific research backs up this finding, showing that the development of an effective agenda and the usability of accompanying board materials is one of the most important ingredients to an effective board meeting. Board agendas may vary, depending upon the meeting goals or themes as we discussed above, but (following Pick's research) they will typically include:

- administrative matters such as the approval of minutes;
- routine approvals, such as committee assignments or previous meeting actions;
- financial review;
- committee reports;
- chief executive officer report;
- a business review, for example, an operations review or perhaps a review from a specific business group; and
- strategic matters, such as new ventures.

The interactive process through which an agenda is designed in the time leading up to a board meeting can be an act of governance in and of itself. Therefore, the deliberate process that the individual responsible for the agenda, most frequently the company secretary, is usually responsible for can play a key role in effective meeting design. As one director in Pick's study noted:

> I think the establishment of the agenda is important... What is decided to be on there is very important. A good management team and a good chairman of the board go a long way on that. It doesn't limit the conversation to those things, but it certainly is where the focus and the attention is. My feeling is that any director has a right, and in fact a responsibility, to contribute on those matters.

Not only is there a collective responsibility required in the design of a board meeting agenda, but also there is a responsibility for anyone producing information in support of that agenda to do so in as concise and usable way as possible. For example, the CEO's report needs to be a synthesis of issues that they feel are both most important for the board to know and also most appropriate to bring to the board to provide perspective and mentoring support. The report should not simply be a regurgitation of the consolidated executive committee work since the last board meeting. The impact of this design issue is eloquently summarised in a story by venture capitalist Seth Levine in his recent board blog series:

> I was on a board once that consistently sent out 160+ page 'board decks'. I put board decks in quotes because they really weren't – they were essentially Executive Team meetings disguised as board meetings. The ensuing board meetings were long, boring, and consisted of the board mostly listening in to the executive team's discussion about the details of the business (to their credit they changed this after I asked them to consider a different format for the meeting). As the saying goes: 'I must apologize. If I had more time, I would have written a shorter note.' Long board decks may seem like you're being transparent but from my perspective it's just being lazy. Take the time to distil the key aspects of your business so your board can efficiently but effectively understand the business. Your board doesn't operate your business – they provide oversight and guidance. Help them do that with the materials you provide. I'm not going to give you a page maximum but if you're more than about 20 or 30 pages for the reporting portion of your board deck, you're probably too long.

Pre-meeting talk

Creating the time, space and opportunity for pre-meeting small talk is a significant predictor of meeting effectiveness, even while considering further good meeting procedures. One study by Allen et al. (2014) found that the impact of small talk was even greater for those who had an introverted personality type.

This research highlights the importance of punctuating board meeting design with informal conversation opportunities and also designing the process to provide the opportunity for introverts to speak, for example, by employing 'round robins' to gauge everyone's opinion around the table, especially after a break.

Cultural differences of individuals as well as personality type will also impact on effective discussion. In certain cultures, and as a result the potential contribution by individual board members who have worked in these cultures, will conversely value pre-meeting discussion or actively discourage it. In some cultures, the formal meeting is the coming together of pre-discussed and largely agreed ideas, with the meeting formally ratifying them. In others, the purpose of the meeting is to share and discuss all ideas, whether they have been pre-discussed or not. An individual who has been pre-conditioned to the former, either through experience, may find a highly discussive meeting, with no pre-meeting discussions, to be disconcerting or ineffective. It may take some time to recognise, value and contribute to this alternative form of meeting, and vice versa. Chapters 7, 8 and 13 cover cultural diversity in more detail.

Visual displays

Board meeting conversations will never completely follow a logical and linear process. At times, topics may take lateral turns as a variety of stakeholder perspectives are shared. In order to best capture the content and flow of meeting dialogue it is recommended that visual displays be used to allow attendees to organise information and retain collective memories more effectively. This is often done unconsciously through the use of PowerPoint presentation; however, it may also be achieved through collecting ideas on Post-it notes, through using whiteboards and flipcharts, or even a through the employment of a graphic artist.

Individual preferences of attendees should also be taken into account in using alternative use of data and visual displays. A highly numerate, detail-focused individual may struggle with the use of visual materials and may prefer a data-heavy appendix to a board pack than visual displays during a meeting. More visually based individuals may dismiss data-heavy appendices in preference to a more fluid visual discussion at the meeting. Being able to support all attendees and their preferences is a balance to ensure that the full board contributes and is one that the chair, the company secretary and any individual supporting the board, especially those preparing reports for a board pack, should be mindful of.

Meeting agreements

Board meeting 'ground rules', which govern the meeting's allowable behaviours, types of interactions, topics and how the meeting is conducted, are a vital tool to support effective meeting functioning. These agreements form the basis of the outputs of the 'norming' stage of board team development mentioned in Chapter 4.

The skills and tools required to implement effective meeting ground rules are part of a broader facilitation competency, which will be explored in greater detail in Chapter 14. In short, it is important that a meeting agreement is discussed, mutually agreed and committed to (rather than being enforced), formalised, regularly reviewed and, for the purposes of meeting design, repeated at the start of each meeting to ensure that each meeting participant understands the rules of engagement for the meeting. Although spending time upfront discussing and confirming meeting ground rules may seem a luxury within the context of a board's time-poor environment, ensuring that the director behaviours are on the same page from the start of the meeting will likely save considerable time and reduce potential conflict, which can occur later in meetings in the absence of a clear meeting agreement upfront.

One interesting and relevant line of research from Duke University's professor of psychology and behavioural economics, Daniel Ariely, concerns how environmental design factors can influence ethical behaviour. His research shows that there are a number of factors that decrease the likelihood of dishonesty in people, which can be applied to meeting behaviour. Firstly, dishonest behaviour can be reduced when people are asked to provide a pledge or signature to confirm their honesty. Therefore, a board might consider an initial verbal or physical 'signing in' to the meeting agreement at the start of the meeting to provide a reminder of their commitments. Secondly, the research also found that moral reminders at the time they are required can also decrease the likelihood of dishonesty. Therefore, it may be appropriate for a chair or company secretary to voice a director's responsibility as required at a particularly pertinent time during a meeting, such as when a key vote is being made or before an important strategic discussion. Finally, dishonest behaviour is also reduced through supervision. A board could therefore employ tactics such as utilising the 'empty chair' tool described earlier as metaphorical supervision, invite stakeholders to attend meetings, publish minutes as appropriate or even livestream the meeting, as described in the example below.

Minutes

The keeping of minutes is a key procedural design characteristic for meetings in general, but is of course particularly important in the board meeting context. There is a technical best practice process for effective minute taking which is a full topic in itself, however, it is something that an effective company secretary and governance professional in particular will need to be particularly mindful of.

From a board perspective, the preference of the company to have detailed full minutes or brief minutes may be static for all meetings or may be agreed at the outset, or, indeed, be dependent on the type and purpose of the meeting. Each attendee should be prepared to review draft minutes to ensure that their points were captured. This is particularly important for any contentious matters where the dissent of an individual may be required in the future. It should be remembered that board minutes are also an audit trail that may be relied on in future.

One further issue is the use of technology in relation to minute taking and circulation, which will no doubt increase in use over time and is particularly easy to implement when virtual meetings are being held.

Recording meetings

It is not uncommon for a board meeting to be electronically recorded. This may be for use as part of board evaluation or it may be as a record for information purposes for board directors (or for those who could not attend). Further, it may also be for cultural transparency purposes, for example, when an organisation is fulfilling a public service such as with health or education organisations (e.g. the NHS Sussex Partnership Foundation Trust, Public Health Wales and Westminster Schools in Colorado all currently livestream board meetings).

Case study: NHS England – livestreaming board meetings

One further example of livestreaming board meetings is the board of NHS England, who are committed to the values of 'openness and transparency' and therefore have recently attempted to conduct as many of its board meetings in public as part of a live broadcast.

This is accessible from their website and kept in a playback format. The board also holds some aspects of their meeting in a closed session where confidential items of business are discussed.

Attendee characteristics

The final aspect of meeting design are the attendee characteristics, which the literature refers to as the number of attendees and the presence of a meeting facilitator. These can influence the use of time, the amount of participation and the meeting information flow and have also been found to relate to perceptions of meeting quality.

Number of attendees

We have discussed board size norms and issues in various places in this text; however, the research is clear that, as the size of a meeting increases, the participation per director is naturally likely to decrease and more time will be needed to involve all attendees. It is not necessarily the case that board functioning will reduce as a consequence; however, the research does indicate that perceptions of meeting quality do go down when more attendee participation is designed into a meeting.

One way around this issue is to invite participants but also to be clear about why they are there such as whether their participation is more for observation and informational reasons rather than for them to be a full member of interactions. It may be useful, for example, for members of the CEO's senior team to attend board meetings in some capacity. This can help establish relationships between the team and the non-executives which may then be developed outside meetings; it may allow non-executives to see the chief executive officer 'in action' interacting with their team; and it may also enable clear communication back to the team on what the board was discussing as they are hearing it first-hand. However, just because executive members are present does not necessarily mean that they need to be asked for their opinion or, indeed, that they are required to leave when their opinion is not needed. As long as the reasons for their participation are made clear at the start of the meeting, this can be a very useful method of increasing attendee size without the downsides.

It may also be useful to have additional attendees for part of the meeting, especially when meetings are held over a long period, thus enabling the input of external experts to contribute to specific discussion topics. This is particularly useful where the attendee is not an employee of the company, for example a professional expert in a particular topic discussed by the board.

However, the board, and particularly the chair, should be cognisant of the balance of members versus invited attendees, to ensure that board members remain as the driving contributors and decision makers. All invited attendees should have the purpose for their attendance made clear before they attend to ensure that mixed purposes are not seen during the meeting.

Presence of a meeting facilitator

The final design characteristic of note in the generic meeting literature is whether a meeting has a designated facilitator. This role usually falls to the chair in any board meeting as the de facto meeting facilitator to control the meeting flow, to assist in decision making and to allay any significant derailment from the agenda.

However, there may be times when additional facilitation is needed – for example, when the chair wants to take a more active role in discussions, when the board format requires smaller group discussion, as part of an extended strategic away-day board meeting format, or when a particularly thorny relationship issue needs to be discussed. This may be where the company secretary can add value as a co-facilitator or indeed can organise for some expert external facilitation to be brought in.

The added advantage of an external facilitator is that they have no view or connection to the discussion and, as such, can focus solely on the process of facilitating the meeting to ensure the most effective contributions by all attendees.

The board design checklist

We have discussed in detail the 21 temporal, physical, procedural and attendee design characteristics which all function to set a board meeting up for success. Based on these, the below 'board design checklist' provides a timeline to implement these various design characteristics to ensure that the dialogue within a meeting is as cohesive and challenging as possible:

1. Set the meeting date and co-create (initially with the chair but also all directors) the meeting goal/purpose/theme focus and agenda.
2. Select minimum additional attendees to contribute (to minimise time requirement).
3. Brief required personnel on what board pre-information is required, emphasising the need for only concise and relevant details.
4. Select an appropriate meeting space based on purpose, location, symbolism, attendee numbers and technology requirement.
5. Circulate the confirmed agenda and timings (ideally morning, three to five hours long with pre-meeting coffee time and breaks), along with board materials, in good time prior to the meeting.
6. Evaluate and adapt the meeting room facilities including temperature, lighting, visual aids and symbolism.
7. Arrange appropriate refreshments.
8. Assign seating if required and set up recording equipment as necessary.
9. Start of meeting: start on time even if attendees have not arrived; ensure refreshments can be self-served before/during the meeting (for feelings of ownership and so as not to distract others); complete a meeting agreement on the tasks and behavioural ground rules (including ethics and technology use).
10. During meeting: use facilitation and/or physical position changes as required for certain agenda items; record through minutes and electronically/live stream as necessary.
11. End before or on time (having reviewed meeting agreements).
12. After the meeting: circulate the minutes (and recording as appropriate) and detail any agreed actions, ensuring that these are allocated to the agreed individuals/teams.

Conclusion

Meetings have a poor reputation in organisations in general and in boards more specifically. This is often due to the fact that the design aspects of meetings are not consciously considered to set meetings up for success. Research and practice indicate that there are some 21 design characteristics, which can be separated into temporal, physical, procedural and attendee characteristics. Temporal characteristics include meeting length, promptness of start and end, the use of breaks and the time of day. Physical characteristics include lighting, noise, temperature, refreshments, meeting space, technology use, seating dynamics and meeting space arrangement.

The increased use of technology and virtual meetings, accelerated by the COVID-19 pandemic, is an opportunity to also rephrase the content, purpose and benefit of meetings, not just the time spent. One current consideration is how updated technology can therefore be used to create more effective meetings, rather than purely attempting to replicate the format of previous physical meetings.

Procedural characteristics include meeting goals, agenda use, pre-meeting talk, visual displays, meeting agreements, use of minutes, whether the meeting is recorded. Attendee characteristics include the number of attendees invited and the presence of a meeting facilitator. The design characteristics can form a 'board design checklist' to provide guidance on best practice board meeting design to promote an effective board dynamic.

What are the most vital aspects of meeting design to get right to influence a board meeting outcome positively? The theory suggests that some design characteristics may be more important than others to get right. In particular, the physical characteristics seem to be more important in the research than others. However, taking an evidence-based approach requires us to consider not just the research but also one's personal experience, those affected (in your case the participants in your meeting) and one's context. Although the characteristics outlined in the chapter provide a useful guide for consideration, how one chooses to implement them in practice will change depending on personal circumstances and the specifics of the meeting you are curating. For example, your ideal room may be booked out, you may have different country cultures participating (the research was mainly based on US populations) and budgets may be tight, so a 'good enough' rather than 'perfect' approach may be more appropriate.

As we initially opened this chapter, meetings are too frequently seen as poor in terms of practicalities and output. Why is this so when all attendees and those in support can influence their purpose, content and output? If we agree that there is a benefit of having the attendees share their knowledge, discuss the topics and agree decisions and outcomes, surely it is incumbent on those involved to make the meeting more effective. Or is it that attendees are too comfortable with spending time being less focussed, seeing their role as being visible but not necessarily effective, or leaving operational aspects of the meeting to others. If meetings, especially board meetings, can be honed to be more effective and efficient, it may 'set the tone from the top', make best use of the time allocated by expensive resources and can make an organisation more efficient. If governance is the foundation of a good business, board meetings are the evidence that these foundations are effective.

'Meetings for meetings' sake' is a phrase that is often heard in organisations where frequent meetings are held with little or no purpose or outcome. Surely it is the attendees' role to call these meetings out? If all contributors, attendees, board supporters and those that contribute to the board pack recognise how they can influence their meetings, making them focused and effective (or not holding them at all), they may become beneficial supports to a business. Given the time that is often spent in meetings, can anybody afford for them not to be well run, efficient and productive?

The physical environment and activities of a meeting may seem trivial but, as has been discussed, they can have an immense influence on the effectiveness of the meeting itself. Who do you entrust this vital part of your meeting preparation to and how can you ensure that it has sufficient focus?

Equally, all attendees have a responsibility to ensure that they are mentally as well as physically present in meetings of the board. Are there any actions that can be taken to ensure that the members of your board recognise their responsibility in making the mechanics, content and outcome of board meetings effective and productive?

Part three
Effecting change in the boardroom

10 – The role of the governance professional in influencing the board

The twenty-first-century governance professional

The role of the statutory director, whether executive or non-executive, is clearly defined in law. Similarly, the role of the company secretary has a long and rich history, attaining legal status in 1841 and having its current role broadly delineated, following the corporate scandals of the 1980s and ensuing 1992 Cadbury Report, as follows:

> The company secretary is responsible for ensuring that board procedures are complied with, advising the board on all governance matters, supporting the chair and helping the board and its committees to function efficiently.

This role of the company secretary – as an expert on governance matters, supporter of the board and its committees – can equally be applied to other aligned roles, including that of the chief of staff, executive assistant or other functional roles that, while positioned at the top of the organisational hierarchy, do not have a formal seat on the board. In some ways, the role of the non-executive director – when not acting as the chair of the board – is another individual that can have considerable influence within board discussions due to their statutory appointment, but also outside the boardroom as a result of their interactions with others.

One of the few recent studies that has been undertaken into the role of the company secretary, the findings of which can equally be applied to other governance roles in an organisation, was published in the 2014 Chartered Governance Institute report entitled 'The role of the company secretary: building trust through governance'. The study's general conclusion was that the most capable governance professionals embrace a broader role that goes beyond a simple focus on the formal internal board administration and technical governance solutions to having an additional informal, social, external and strategic leadership focus. The study defines three company secretary role characteristics: the requirements to be technical, commercial and social. Being able to flex between all of these areas elevates the company role to being one having both 'breadth and majesty', as the report says. A large amount of discretion is required in the role and the deployment of the characteristics will vary depending upon the company's particular circumstances.

This approach aligns with the new The Chartered Governance Institute Competency Framework for Governance Professionals, published in 2018. This framework notes that:

> Being an effective company secretary and/or governance professional means enabling the board to set and achieve the strategic goals of the organisation. This requires mastery of specialist knowledge, combined with strong values, emotional intelligence and the ability to apply understanding in the particular context of the organisation and its wider environment.

In terms of the more social or people elements, the framework includes the requirement of a core understanding of both 'the psychology of the organisation, the types of behaviours that may be exhibited and the impact of these behaviours on others' and also an appreciation of 'organisational and especially boardroom dynamics, understanding that different people have different motivations'.

A company secretary or governance professional who is excelling in these core understandings will be one, therefore, who 'provides effective support for the chair through deep understanding of issues of boardroom dynamics and the interpersonal skills necessary to be the trusted adviser of all in the boardroom'.

What are the particular personal qualities that this individual must bring to the table to help them excel in their role in this way? The 2014 The Chartered Governance Institute report on 'The role of the company secretary' suggests the following list, summarised from its research:

- learns *in vivo*
- wisdom
- supportive
- facilitative
- integrative
- has a resilient but not forceful personality
- patience
- times their comments/inputs
- deflects tension/disagreement
- has courage to speak out
- takes a broad view
- invisible qualities
- disciplined and sensitive
- operates at different levels: organisationally, emotionally and intellectually

Interestingly, the final catch-all quality identified is that the individual needs to be have similar qualities to those of the chair. As the report summarises:

> In many respects, the company secretary has similar attributes and is closest to the role of the chairman. They require the leadership qualities of humanity, humility, high intelligence, an understanding of agendas, negotiation and a tough resilience to dealing with everyday issues.

The invisible strategic leader

In the 2014 report's key findings, the number one finding is as follows:

> The role of the company secretary is much more than just administrative. At its best, it delivers strategic leadership, acting as a vital bridge between the executive management and the board and facilitating the delivery of organisational objectives.

How does this individual, whether a company secretary or other invisible influencer within an organisation, become more of a strategic leader? An important starting point is to be become the third person in the chief executive officer and chair relationship, as one of the respondents notes:

> The trio of chairman, CEO and [company secretary]... if you're lucky enough to have all three highly effective people, you're likely to have a good board because they'll make sure that the people joining the board are high quality and they'll make sure that the processes of the board and the relationships [are of the standards required].

The shift in a company secretary's role to one that is more strategic is also backed up by the Grant Thornton (2018) research from their 105 cross-sector board and company sector participants. As one housing company secretary respondent agreed: 'the role has become more strategic. I act as a trusted adviser and independent expert'.

This, however, is a double-edged sword. The company secretary has the challenge of balancing the greater focus on regulation and compliance with the increased responsibilities due to their role becoming more strategic.

It is this balance that may also enable other influencers of the board to find their position aligned to the chair, the CEO and the board. These influencers may be appointed to other functional roles. In most organisations, there are a number of roles that are aligned to the CEO, chair or board that fulfil part or all of the roles identified here as being that of the company secretary. Increasingly, the CEO's or chair's executive assistant or chief of staff may fulfil part of the role, and other invisible influencers will also be in place in the organisation: the strategist, trusted confidante, board consultant or external adviser to name but a few.

Developing a personal understanding of the various individuals with influence in an organisation underpins the opportunity to carve out a role as a trusted partner of the board.

Recognising, understanding and aligning with these individuals may be more effective than calling them out or pushing for formal recognition in the organisational structure. Invisible influencers are present in all organisations, built up through networking, interpersonal relationships, collaborative working or other informal touch points. Identifying and developing personal influence requires both recognition of the possibilities for oneself, as well as recognition of this role in others.

What does strategic leadership as a governance professional or trusted influencer look like? To answer the question, we must first take a quick detour into leadership's conceptual history and its current theories.

Leadership and management

Over recent decades, an argument has raged about what difference, if any, there is between management and leadership. The standard model is possibly best articulated by Harvard Business School professor and leadership thought leader, John Kotter, who strongly advocates that there is a key distinction between management and leadership. He argues that management is more about creating order and doing things right with a focus on efficiency and administration, maintaining a focus on systems and structure and relying on compliance and control. Management therefore usually takes a more short-term, tactical view and asks 'how' and 'when'. Leadership, on the other hand, Kotter argues, is about producing change and doing the right thing. It is focused on effectiveness, innovation, development, and leaders spend time with people building their trust and alignment with the directional vision and values. Leadership often has more of a long-term view and asks 'what' and 'why'.

The Chartered Governance Institute's 2014 company secretary report records an interesting trend:

> The majority of public sector company secretaries emphasise social or people skills over more technical abilities. The study findings conversely suggest the private sector may be moving from technical towards more social behaviours.

This seems to be in line with Kotter's distinction and suggests that public sector company secretaries are already emphasising leadership while private sector company secretaries are playing catch-up, but also beginning to emphasise the strategic aspect of the company secretary role.

There is a competing view that, in fact, the difference between leadership and management is actually illusionary. One of the leading proponents of this contrary view is Henry Mintzberg, a Canadian professor of management studies based in McGill University in Montréal. In his observational research of board members and senior leaders across organisations, Mintzberg argues that people are constantly required to flex their role from moment to moment across different activities and that a senior individual is not someone who is constantly in 'visionary change mode', as Kotter would have us believe. Instead, Mintzberg identifies 10 managerial roles across three categories that senior people flex between over the course of any given day. These categories and roles, with associated example activities, are as follows:

Category one: informational

1 Monitor – seek and receive information scan papers and reports, maintain interpersonal contacts.
2 Disseminator – forward information to others, send memos and reports.
3 Spokesperson – transmit information to outsiders in speeches and reports.

Category two: interpersonal

4 Figurehead – perform ceremonial and symbolic duties, greet visitors, sign legal documents.
5 Leader – direct and motivate subordinates, train, counsel, advise and influence.
6 Liaison – maintain information links in and beyond the organisation.

Category three: decisional

7 Entrepreneur – initiate improvement projects, identify new ideas, delegate news of business development to others.
8 Disturbance handler – take corrective action during crises, resolve conflicts among staff, adapt to external changes.
9 Resource allocator – decide who gets resources, schedule, budget, set priorities.
10 Negotiator – represent department during negotiations with stakeholders and generally defend interests.

Evolution of leadership theory

As well as understanding the debate between leadership and management, it is also useful to comprehend the history of leadership theory and how definitions of leadership have evolved over time.

The earliest theories of leadership revolved around the concept of the 'Great Man', with its roots in military leadership and the idea that leaders are 'born and not made'. Leadership in organisations was then influenced in the late 1970s by the concept of transactional leadership, which held that it is possible to influence followers through the transactions of reward or punishment. In the 1980s and 1990s, this was replaced by the concept of transformational leadership which emphasises the need for charismatic leaders to inspire others to do great deeds through communicating a clear vision. Perhaps as a reaction to the more egotistical versions of transformational leadership, ideas and concepts such as authentic, ethical and servant leadership emerged at the turn of the millennium, emphasising the importance of leaders having high levels of self-awareness and a strong moral compass.

More recently, conceptions of complexity, distributed, adaptive and connected leadership have emerged, which recognise that leadership may not be a quality of an individual, but more a practice that emerges through the relationship between people, such that anyone at any level in an organisation can show leadership behaviour, not just the formal leaders. The 2016 Henley Business School research report on 'Tomorrow's leadership' summarises this recent shift in leadership theory, suggesting that we have moved from heroic to collective and collaborative leadership – where the focus shifts from 'leading my people' to 'orchestrating business ecosystems', such that leadership needs to be driven by purpose and value creation for all stakeholders.

Leadership based on purpose and value then also aligns to the increasing expectation that organisations and their leaders recognise, identify and deliver against an appropriate set of environment, social and governance (ESG) measures that underpin the company, its setting and its stakeholders.

It is interesting to note that this emerging leadership approach seems to be reflected in the 2018 The Chartered Governance Institute Competency Framework for Governance Professionals. For example, the behaviour statements for influencing and enabling list the core practice that a governance professional:

> Builds and maintains effective relationships with a wide range of internal and external stakeholders in order to influence governance and compliance and develop the appropriate skills, behaviours and understanding in the board and across the organization.

Leadership styles

One final aspect of leadership to understand is the associated question of what the main leadership styles are. There are many approaches in the literature to this. However, one useful framework is presented by Daniel Goleman, whose research with the Hay Group uncovered six specific leadership styles. Their research found that the style a leader takes can account for up to 70% of the variance in organisational climate, which in turn accounts for 30% of variance in organisational outcomes. Therefore, the leadership style that a leader chooses to enact can have a significant impact on organisational outcomes. The six styles are as follows:

1 **Directive** – this is about getting immediate compliance by giving lots of directives, controlling tightly, relying on corrective feedback and motivating by stating the negative consequences of non-compliance. It is most effective when applied to relatively straightforward tasks, in a crisis and when deviations from compliance will result in serious problems. However, it is least effective when applied to tasks that are more complex than straightforward, when used over the long term and when used with self-motivated and capable employees.
2 **Visionary** – this is about providing long-term direction and vision and explaining the 'why' in terms of a follower or organisation's long-term interest.

It is most effective when a new vision, clear direction and standards are needed and least effective when the leader is not perceived as credible.

3 **Affiliative** – this style is about creating harmony and is most concerned with promoting friendly interaction, placing emphasis on personal needs than standard, and therefore will avoid personal confrontation. It is most useful when used as part of a broader repertoire, and when getting diverse, conflicting groups to work together harmoniously. It is least effective when performance is inadequate, in complex situations where clear direction and control are required and when followers are uninterested in personal friendship.

4 **Participative** – this style builds commitment, generates new ideas and invites followers to participate in the development of decisions. It is useful when followers are competent or if the leader is unclear about the best approach. It is least effective in crisis, when employees are not competent, lack crucial information or need close supervision.

5 **Pacesetting** – this style is about accomplishing tasks to high standards of excellence through leading by example. The pacesetting leader will be apprehensive about delegating and has little sympathy for poor performance. It is most effective when employees are highly motivated and competent and when they can make individual expert contributions and when followers are similar to the leader. It is least effective when the leader cannot do everything personally and when employees need direction and development.

6 **Coaching** – this style supports and challenges followers to complete tasks while also developing their long-term potential. It focuses on helping employees to identify strengths and weaknesses through providing ongoing feedback and building trusted relationships. It is most effective when followers are interested in their own learning and development on the job and least effective when the leader lacks belief in their employees and lacks expertise in questioning and empathy, as well as in an immediate crisis.

Unsurprisingly , the older transactional theories of leadership are more associated with directive and pacesetting styles where the leader is asking followers to 'do as I say' or 'do as I do'. Although useful in a limited number of situations, these two styles have repeatedly been found to be corrosive and have a negative impact on organisational culture and performance. Interestingly, the directive and pacesetting styles, along with the visionary style, are the three most commonly found among male leaders. The three most common styles among female leaders are the visionary style combined with affiliative and participative styles. In general, the two styles that outperform all the others are the visionary and coaching styles of leadership. Therefore, if you were to excel at only two, these would be the two to choose.

How do these styles relate to the role of the invisible influencer? They may find themselves often having to police compliance, and therefore may naturally take on a more directive style which may contribute to a negative perception of their role. Their strategic role may be best served by a formal platform to use a visionary style; however, they are more likely to encounter informal leadership opportunities which would best suit the coaching style.

Recognition of these styles in an organisation and their effect on the culture of the business will enable individuals to understand and then adapt their own style. This recognition of the dominant styles of the leaders in an organisation will also be beneficial to the invisible influencer in how to interact with these leaders. It should be noted that most organisations do not have a single dominant style in their boards and most individuals will evidence more than one style in their approach, behaviours and actions. Having noted this there are always exceptions.

The individual as an 'invisible leader'

In light of this more general appreciation of aspects of leadership theory, how then can we conceive of the invisible influencers' strategic leadership in practice?

In the chapter entitled 'Leadership on the board: the role of company secretary' in the 2017 *Routledge Companion to Leadership*, Kakabadse et al. from Henley Business School introduced the concept of the company secretary as an 'invisible leader'. They suggest that individual leadership capacity in the boardroom is most commonly observed through the use of words as an expression of IQ (intelligence) and PQ (political acumen). However, invisible leadership is more associated with the subtle actions of higher-order EQ (emotional) and MQ (moral) skills in leadership decision making. This, they contend, is more often than not, how the company secretary enacts their strategic leadership role with the board and, unfortunately, why the role is often not appreciated to its full extent.

In a commentary defining the location of a company secretary's power and influence on the board, the authors also introduce Luke's (2005) conception of third-dimensional 'smart power'. First-dimension power is also known as 'hard power', which is defined similar to the directive leadership style in Goleman's framework. It is coercive and is power over someone to tell them what they must do and often derives from one's formal position. Second-dimension power, also known as 'soft power', is defined as the power that arises from convincing followers through an appeal to what is right and aligned with what society values, such as a governance code. It is power based on what one should do.

Third-dimension power, or 'smart power', is the most potent type, as: 'the supreme exercise of power is to get others to have the desires you want them to have'. Smart power is concerned with influencing others to change their perception so that they then intrinsically choose to do something emanating out of their own motivation.

We will discuss later a variety of influencing techniques which leverage smart power and enable a company secretary to transform what might initially be seen as a task-based role into a position of considerable influence. Although not formally observable in the boardroom, a competent company secretary's smart power influence may be seen, for example in setting the agenda and thus influencing boardroom priorities.

In fact, the nature of the company secretary's role actually positions them as the person who is ideally placed to align the interests of different parties around a boardroom table, facilitate dialogue, gather and assimilate relevant information and thereby enable effective decision making. They are often the only people to know first-hand how holistic decision-making outcomes have been arrived at.

Thus, not surprisingly, the new The Chartered Governance Institute Competency Framework's recommendation for a company secretary who excels at influencing and enabling is as follows:

> Exerts subtle influence, often behind the scenes, drawing on accrued respect of peers to get issues addressed fully and fairly.

The best company secretaries are highly regarded by their chair often through unconsciously benefitting from this invisible leadership and smart power. Research by the consultancy firm Better Boards (2018) found that this invisible leadership and smart power was a highly prized competency. For example, when chairs were asked, 'What are the characteristics of the best company secretaries you have worked with?', a couple replied:

> She knows the characters, knows how to handle them and alerts me to any issues.
>
> Chairman, FTSE 250

> The best company secretaries I work with provide me with information that helps me manage the dynamics of the board.
>
> Chairman, FTSE 100

But this invisible and informal influence is not just useful in the boardroom; it can also be used externally with stakeholders. Finding six of The Chartered Governance Institute's 2014 company secretary report suggests that: 'the role is changing: it is increasingly outward focused (incorporating investor engagement and corporate communications) and not just about internal administration'.

As one company secretary reflected: 'consultation with shareholders is an enormous part of the job now... I must've done 60 to 70 meetings with shareholders in the last four months in the run-up to the AGM'.

> As can be seen, the role of the company secretary is merging and aligning with other external-facing roles in an organisation such as relationship management, investor reporting and marketing, as well as internal roles such as HR and internal communications. Equally, these other roles, depending on the individual post holder, can also be trusted board partners and invisible influencers.

Leadership influence

We have acknowledged that governance professionals can play an important strategic leadership role, and that this role will be much less the classical outspoken, heroic and directive style and much more likely to be the coaching and invisible leadership influence on the board. The question now to ask is: what techniques and perspectives might be best used to accomplish this role? The Chartered Governance Institute's 2014 company secretary report suggests that:

> Many experienced company secretaries explain that it can take up to 18 months to become comfortable in their role, and it is at this point that they are able to engage more strategically in a leadership role.

As one respondent said: 'Things like influencing, listening, negotiating, collaborating... getting the board to work better... actually what you learn on the way up, it doesn't come naturally.'

What follows are a number of good practice approaches and tools to accelerate the process of developing 'comfort' in the influential strategic leadership role.

Approaches to leadership influence

There are a variety of approaches that we could detail around leadership influence; however, below are four frameworks that can raise awareness of particular criteria to help get one's message across effectively.

The first of these is the acronym SUCCES (with the last S intentionally omitted) popularised by Chip and Dan Heath in their 2007 book *Made to Stick: Why Some Ideas Survive and Others Die*. Each letter of the acronym refers to a particular characteristic that can help make an idea 'sticky' as follows:

- Simple – understand what the core of your message is and then communicate it with an analogy.
- Unexpected – make your idea memorable by grabbing people's attention through surprise and violating what the standard norms for your communication might be.
- Concrete – use concrete and sensory language to help the person paint a mental picture.
- Credible – link credibility from outside authorities to your idea, including statistics or vivid details.
- Emotional – appeal to people's human values as this influences them more than through rational numbers. Ensure that you include what's in it for them.
- Stories – share your idea through a narrative story to bring it alive.

A second approach is the combined 'persuasion' and 'pre-suasion' approaches popularised by Robert Cialdini, a professor of psychology and marketing at Arizona State University and adviser to Barack Obama's presidential campaign in 2012. In his seminal 1984 book *Influence: The Psychology of Persuasion*, Cialdini summarises his evidence-based research that influence is based on six key principles: reciprocity, commitment and consistency, social proof, authority, liking and scarcity. In 2016, he added a seventh principle called the 'unity principle', such that the more we identify with others, the more we are influenced by them. His latest book, *Pre-suasion* (2016), makes the point that often the best way to persuade is not at the moment of communication, but in artfully setting up the moment so that influence naturally follows the course intended by the persuader. The meeting design factors explained in Chapter 9 are examples of some of the pre-suasion techniques that are available to the company secretary as smart power in the boardroom.

A third approach that is relevant to the invisible leadership of any professional is the concept of 'currencies of influence', which was popularised by Cohen and Bradford in their 2005 book *Influence without Authority*. The authors identified five types of currency that are most often valued in organisations around the world. Understanding each currency and flexing one's approach appropriate to the needs of what would work best for any individual or particular stakeholder group will enable governance professionals to deliver change more effectively. The five currencies of influence they identified are as follows:

- **Inspiration-related currencies** – these are related to inspiration, vision and morality. People who value these currencies want to find meaning and purpose in their actions and they may go out of their way to help if they know that something is the right thing to do or if it contributes in some way to a valued cause. One can appeal to these people by explaining the significance of the request, by illustrating it is the right thing to do and appealing to their sense of integrity and virtue.
- **Task-related currencies** – these currencies relate to the task at hand and to getting the job done. They are often highly valued in new organisations where supplies and resources may be scarce. One task-related currency is challenge, so one can appeal to people through this currency who want to test or expand their skills, or work on challenging tasks and projects.
- **Position-related currencies** – people who value this currency focus on recognition, reputation and visibility. They value increasing status and can be appealed to by a public acknowledgement of their efforts.
- **Relationship-related currencies** – people who value relationships want to belong and will value being included as part of a cohesive team. They can be influenced by creating a personal connection, being actively listened to and being offered support and understanding.
- **Personal-related currencies** – one can appeal to this currency by showing a person sincere gratitude for their assistance. Further, this type of person appreciates having freedom, so creating options within your idea will help influence them.

A final framework for considering how best to influence is the Leadership Communication Grid (see Figure 11).

Figure 11 Leadership communication grid (Rodgers, 2007)

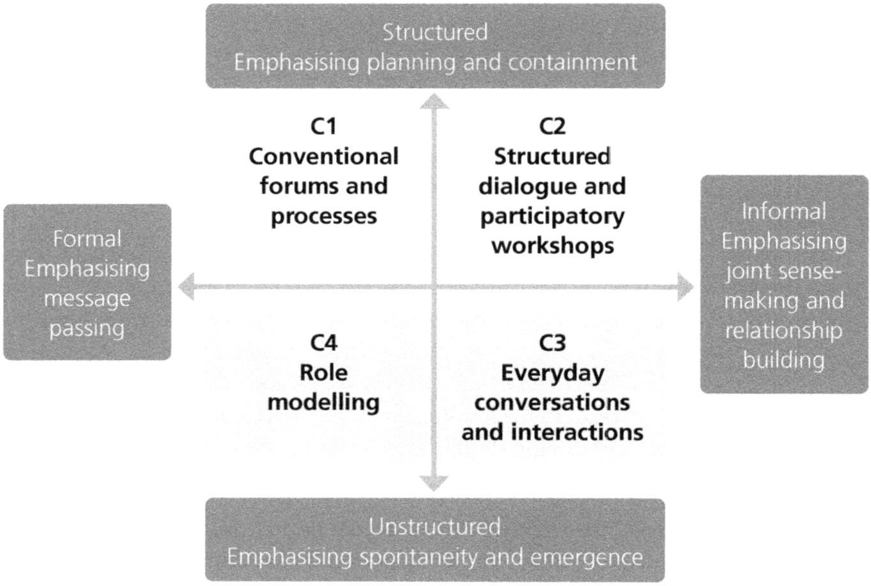

This framework is a four-box model created by the two axes of either formal communication (which is one-way and has an emphasis on message passing) versus informal communication (which has an emphasis on two-way joint sense-making and relationship building) and either structured (planned and contained) versus unstructured (spontaneous and emergent). The classic traditional methods of leadership communication are the more structured and formal types such as one-way platform speaking, reports and updates, as well as structured informal events such as meetings and workshops. These are often characterised in leadership, whereas the framework characterises the more unstructured types that those outside the board are more likely to be involved in influencing. For example, how the governance professional role-models appropriate leadership behaviours is defined by the formal and unstructured quadrant. Finally, the informal and unstructured box, the everyday conversations and what the model defines as 'informal coalitions' are the 'quick word' opportunities before and after more formal or structured conversations have occurred and where the influencer can make a real impact.

The importance of these informal opportunities is characterised by the company secretaries who commented in The Chartered Governance Institute's 2014 company secretary report to such an extent that finding four noted that:

> It is vital that company secretaries have both direct and informal access to board members – executive and non-executive directors (NEDs), CEOs and chairmen.

Two examples of respondents' perspectives around the importance of the 'informal coalitions' quadrant of the leadership communication grid can be seen in the following quotes from the research:

> 'Your ability to influence the outcome of any particular decision is governed much more by your informal chats.'

> 'They add value in terms of being formal, but also informal, routes for board members to make general enquiries... you can always feel very free to ring them up about anything.'

When seeking to influence the board these frameworks should be applied in a way that suits the individual. Adapting theoretical frameworks to personal preference, behaviours and attitude ensures that they are authentic to the individual. They should also be applied in alignment to the board members themselves and to the organisation in which influence is being wielded. Having knowledge of these frameworks and their underlying principles may support and assist individuals in their practical application.

Leadership influence tools

Beyond the four leadership influence frameworks, there are a number of tools which the invisible leader might use to wield smart power in the boardroom and beyond. These tools include building relationships, networking, acting politically, storytelling and challenging.

Building relationships

We have discussed building relationships in some detail in relation to a cohesive board team and developing effective stakeholder relationships. We will also touch on building one-to-one director relationships in Chapter 14 as part of effective coaching and mentoring so there is no need to go into much further detail here, apart from to emphasise the foundational importance of building relationships in terms of leadership influence. The power that a competent individual has is largely dictated by the role the chair gives them and this agreement will be significantly influenced by the quality of the trust in the relationship between the chair and the individual. As we might remember, trust can be defined by the equation 'credibility plus reliability plus intimacy, all divided by one's projection of self-interest': these are all factors that an individual can influence in the relationships with the chair and the rest of the board. One final piece of the puzzle to mention here is the concept of a radical collaboration coined by Judge Jim Tamm, who advocated managing one's own defensiveness.

Therefore, working on reducing one's ego, perhaps through mindfulness exercises described in Chapter 15 in relation to personal resilience, may be key in maintaining the humility required to work diligently in the background as an influencer.

Networking

According to the 2018 Chartered Governance Institute Competency Framework for Governance Professionals, to excel at 'influencing and enabling', a company secretary must use 'internal and external networks effectively, leveraging relationships and exchanging knowledge'.

Although the concept of networking as a method of influencing often has a bad reputation, caricatured as a skill for extroverted and pushy ladder-climbers, it can actually be characterised in a much more understated and win–win manner. The London Business School professor Hermania Ibarra has described three types of networks. The first type, personal networks, are about exchanging important referrals and beneficial outside information as well as developing professional skills through coaching and mentoring. Advice to build a larger personal network is to participate in alumni groups, clubs, professional associations and personal interest communities.

The second network type is the operational network, whose purpose is to help you get your work done and to get it done more efficiently. The recommendation to build this network is to identify individuals who might block or support the project. Thirdly, there is the strategic network, which supports an individual to explore future priorities and challenges and get stakeholder support for them. The recommendation to build this strategic network is to identify relationships outside of 'one's immediate environment or control who might help one determine how one's role and contribution could fit into the overall future picture'.

Corporate anthropologist Karen Stevenson suggests that networks operate based on the quality of trust:

> The critical information that makes organizations functional is transferred not through established channels within the formal hierarchy but instead through informal relationships. And the medium of exchange is not just the authority of transactions but, significantly, the trust within relationships.

Therefore, the quality and trust of an individual's internal and external stakeholder network could arguably be the most important component in their ability to exert informal strategic leadership on the board dynamic. Stevenson, in her description of what constitutes the DNA of a network, defines three types of person: 'hubs', who know the most people; 'gatekeepers', who know the right people; and 'pulse takers', who know the most people who know the right people (it is possible to complete an online test to see which type one is within one's organisational network). Based on their organisational longevity, but combined with a natural reticence to be highly visible, the invisible influencer may often find themselves as a pulse taker within the board network. To further raise awareness using these network DNA types, here are some questions that are useful:

- To hubs – how can you introduce your network to another area to encourage innovation?
- To gatekeepers – are you creating a bottleneck of information?

- To pulse takers – how can you connect to and influence new hubs to stimulate change?
- Who are the powerful pulse takers relevant to you? How can you build trust with them?
- Who are the gatekeepers? How can you form alliances with them?
- How can you strategically position yourself within the hubs?

More broadly, though, here are some practical tips to develop one's network:

- Have coffee – the organisation NESTA used a coffee trial experiment, whereby one has a random 30-minute coffee with a colleague each week and found it to significantly enhance collaboration, knowledge sharing, engagement, productivity and innovation in organisations. They have created a spin-off company called Spark Collaboration, which now sells the process to companies as a product.
- Ask questions – in speed dating, research showed that those who ask more questions got more dates and an equivalent non-romantic conversational question asking will similarly greatly improve relational trust.
- Be genuinely interested in someone with no other agenda – this equates to the low self-interest denominator in the trust equation.
- Build your external as well as internal relationships – we often neglect relationships external to the organisation, especially if we have worked there for some time.
- Use digital as well as face-to-face networking – for some, LinkedIn, Twitter and other digital platforms may not seem relevant. However, they can be strategic ways to create larger and more diverse networks than one can access simply face-to-face. This has been considerably tested during the various pandemic lockdowns when digital connections were the only way to work. Digital networking has created a greater opportunity for those who may shun physical gatherings but could shine in a smaller, less visible, medium.
- Be free with your time and resources – people respond well to altruism and usually pay back in greater amounts.

Acting politically

In a 2013 study by Snell et al., political skill was found to be more important than any other traditional management skill (including technical, administrative, human and citizenship skills) for predicting overall managerial effectiveness. In the sometimes volatile board environment at the apex of an organisation, being politically skilful is an important tool to support informal strategic leadership. Ferris et al. (2005) have developed a Political Skill Inventory, which measures political skill along the four dimensions of networking ability, interpersonal influence, social astuteness and apparent sincerity. They define overall political skill as: 'the ability to understand others at work and to use that knowledge to influence others to act in ways that enhance one's personal or organisational objectives'.

Unsurprisingly, they also find that political skill predicts both performance evaluations and career success. This may be an inventory to test on oneself so that one can build on strengths, mitigate weaknesses and create an action plan for developing politically.

Baddeley and James' (1987) political skills model is a useful tool to reflect on one's political acuity. This is a four-box model which memorably characterises each quadrant as a different type of political animal (see Figure 12).

Figure 12 Political skills model (Baddeley and James, 1987)

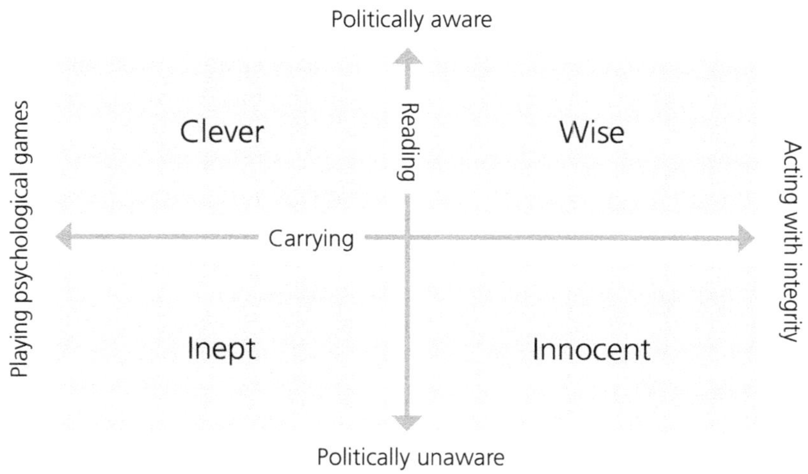

Across the two axes are either 'playing psychological games' versus 'acting with integrity' and being 'politically aware' versus being 'politically unaware'. The unaware game player is the 'inept donkey', whereas the politically unaware individual who acts with integrity is the 'innocent sheep', a type with which many early career individuals may empathise. The psychological game-playing and politically aware animal is the 'clever fox' and is the type that a savvy corporate individual will need to be most mindful of at board level. The clever fox will often be the charismatic and egotistical director who seems charming at first, but ultimately is only out for themselves. The final quadrant, the person who is acting with integrity and who is politically aware, is described as the 'wise owl'. The owl type can be defined as being 'politically wise' due their combination of the following (adapted from Baddeley and James, 1987):

- aware of purpose;
- interested in direction in association with power and purpose;
- can cope with being disliked, good interpersonal skills;
- personal values/ethics, thinks before speaking, assertive, tactful, emotionally literate, plans actions, checks gossip/rumour;

- excellent listener, is aware of others' viewpoints;
- takes account of other people personally;
- sees realities, knows how the formal processes work;
- non-defensive, learns from mistakes, reflects on events;
- can make procedures work for them;
- sense of loyalty;
- capacity for friendship;
- knows the formal and informal organisations;
- open, shares information;
- in tune with the grapevine;
- recognises who knows, who cares, who can;
- gets support;
- negotiates/co-operates; and
- likes win–win situations.

Each of the above benchmark points should be considered against one's own attitudes and actions when reviewing how well one works politically in terms of leadership influence in the boardroom.

They should also be considered in respect of the organisation's culture and the changing wider environment. As a need to align to all stakeholders – not just a small group of shareholders – increases, and focus on ESG and company purpose gains more traction, the political skills may become more blended. The traditional self-contained 'clever fox' may struggle in the new world, while aptitudes of integrity and teamwork are becoming more highly valued. It is interesting to note that the aptitudes of the politically wise are so long and broad. Each of these attributes may equally be aligned to individuals in the other three categories. The combination of the many, whether consciously or unconsciously, by an individual, is what supports political aptitude.

In many large organisations, playing 'politics' is often seen as negative or self-servicing. This reflects the clever fox personality who drives for personal gain, often openly identifying themselves with what they see as clever game-playing. Where there are too many of these in an organisation, the need of the individual can take over from the need of the collective organisation and the culture of the business will be shaped by this collective of thrusting, self-serving individuals.

Playing 'politics' can, and should, be considered as a part of all individuals' career paths in an organisation. Having the knowledge to assess when, and in which scenarios, to apply this knowledge and the attributes is invaluable for any career-focused individual.

Storytelling

One influencing technique that has gained in recognition in recent years is the power of storytelling. Stories are more likely to be remembered than facts or figures alone. When you tell a story, your audience slows down to listen.

The story is a highly effective way to move people to action and is one main way we project our personal brand and credibility out into the world. Great storytelling follows the story structure defined by 'Freitag's pyramid' (Freitag was a playwright who defined his pyramid in 1863.) A story will always start with an initial exposition and then include rising action, a crescendo in climax, followed by falling action and a final resolution. In order to apply storytelling in terms of leadership influence, it is useful to follow the following six steps:

1 Identify your audience.
2 Determine the one key message you want your audience to hear from you.
3 Think of a story that represents this.
4 Plan the initial scene-setting, the rising action, the crisis and the resolution.
5 Plan exactly how you will deliver the story (tone, pauses, emphasis, movement, etc.).
6 Practise with feedback.

Remember to start with identifying your audience, and not just their area of interest, background, experience or functional responsibility. Also consider their time, willingness to list and attention span and adapt your story length to the audience. A long story, while it may be highly relevant and interesting, may have a negative effect in a time-pressed environment, while a short story may not sufficiently deliver the key message.

Case study: London winning the 2012 Olympics bid

It is 6 July 2005, 10.30am British Standard Time. The world is watching, your whole nation crosses its fingers and your Prime Minister, who has just flown in from hosting the G8 summit, is counting on you. As leader, this is your last throw of the dice in a bid to sneak past an old rival and win the biggest prize in global sport...

This was the situation facing the Chair of the London Olympics Games Organising Committee, Lord Sebastian Coe, as he prepared to make his final speech in an attempt to win the right to host the 2012 Games. It is widely agreed that the personal story Coe told, of how he had been inspired to 'choose sport' as a 12-year-old after watching grainy pictures of hometown athletes – hurdler John Sherwood and his wife, the long jumper Sheila Sherwood – compete at the 1968 Mexico Games, then linking this to his legacy vision for 2012, was the masterstroke that convinced the swaying International Olympic Committee voters to choose London over Paris.

Challenging

Although the company secretary may require expertise in informal and invisible leadership behind the scenes, that does not mean that they cannot also be challenging of the formal leadership represented by the chair, chief executive officer and other senior stakeholders. However, as Kakabadse et al. (2017) note in relation to this:

> The company secretary's challenge is to resolve tension between being the invisible *power behind the throne*, i.e. in the shadow of the chairperson, and knowing how to diplomatically challenge individual board member effectiveness towards higher collective board performance.

What tools are there available to guide how one approaches diplomatic challenge? Firstly, one might consider the Thomas Kilman model, created in the 1970s by Kenneth Thomas and Ralph Kilman, which describes five methods of conflict handling, including:

- **avoiding** – sidestepping the conflict;
- **accommodating** – trying to satisfy the other person's concerns at the expense of your own;
- **compromising** – trying to find an acceptable settlement that only partially satisfies both people's concerns;
- **competing** – trying to satisfy your concerns at the expense of others; and
- **collaborating** – trying to find a win–win solution which completely satisfies both people's concerns.

The model challenges us to notice our intention when we enter a potentially conflicting situation. If we are able to take both a co-operative and assertive intent, then we are much more likely to find a collaborative solution.

A second more recent tool for challenging effectively that has gained significant current attention is the idea of 'radical candour', popularised by Kim Scott in the book of the same name. Radical candour is the top right behaviour in a four-quadrant framework delineated vertically by whether we have high 'personal care' for the person we are challenging and the horizontal axis of whether we are 'challenging directly' or not. This matrix therefore creates four potential behavioural responses, with only radical candour truly being an effective method of challenging.

Scott uses the humorous example of somebody noticing a colleague with their trouser zip undone and then wondering what to do having noticed. The bottom left quadrant, where one challenges indirectly but does not care about the person, is labelled 'manipulative insincerity' which, in our example, will result in silence and worrying about one's own feelings. The top left box, where one is scared to challenge but does care about the colleague, leads to 'ruinous empathy'. In our example, this will mean ineffectually tiptoeing around the issue, perhaps throwing knowing looks downwards but not actually saying anything, while constantly worrying about the other person's feelings.

The bottom right quadrant, where one does challenge directly but does not have empathy or care for the other person, is labelled 'obnoxious aggression' and in our example would entail someone shouting, 'look, his zip's undone!' This is often the classic army-style masculine approach to leadership. However, the top right quadrant, the quadrant of radical candour where someone cares personally and is able to challenge directly, would in this case enable someone to be effective and whisper, 'your zip's undone', ultimately saving the person's blushes.

The aim with radical candour is to be confident in challenging but also to do it in a way that shows empathy for the other person. In the boardroom, this is the balance of support with challenge and it is the ability to advocate and voice while respecting another's opinion.

Ethical dilemmas

We have discussed the role of the individual as strategic leader and how this is most often performed behind the scenes with smart power and also described a variety of frameworks and tools with which to enact this influence. As The Chartered Governance Institute's 2014 report on company secretaries notes:

> There are numerous ways ...[individuals]... can exercise influence... it can be quite powerful to observe and then have a quiet word on the side... [individuals] can add value by precisely observing dynamics, how people are behaving, how it's affecting their decision-making.

However, in tandem with these many opportunities to influence comes an equal number of potential ethical dilemmas that the report summarises. These dilemmas include:

- The requirement for the individual constantly to defend their independence.
- An often unclear delineation in role, resulting in a conflict in values.
- Increasing stakeholder demands which build the compliance load, often with no further team to support.
- Straddling both the board and an executive function.
- Both one's role and one's profession being taken for granted, such that the role is understated, under-recognised and often underutilised.

Even though a highly competent company secretary is able to adopt these additional higher-order influencing skills when they are relating to their leadership role, the understated nature of how they enact leadership means that it often goes unnoticed. In addition to being able to shift with agility from the technical to the behavioural, from the internal to the external, from the tactical, reactive and short term to the strategic, proactive and long term, and from being a solution provider to being more of a collaborative partner, perhaps the aim of both each individual company secretary and the governance profession as a whole should now be to increase the profile of the company secretary to enable them to move from a more covert leadership role to one that is more overt. This will require significant trust building at both an individual and a governing body level.

This is echoed by the positive conclusion of The Chartered Governance Institute's 2014 company secretary report, which contends that: 'while the NED has been the focus of much of the attention in the post-financial crisis period, it is now time for the company secretary role to come to the fore'.

Conclusion

Those supporting the board or sitting alongside it require the ability to be a strategic leader as much as those sitting around the boardroom table. As an invisible influencer, they can influence the strategic focus of the board and thus the organisation through their actions, contributions and facilitation, often bridging the communications between strategic forums, leadership positions and others. This individual is now required to embrace the psychological, social and cultural roles associated with being an effective governance professional.

One of the most important of these roles to understand is that of being a strategic leader. What is meant by an individual being a 'strategic leader'? The role as a strategic leader of the board does not mean that they are expected to be out front, barking orders and setting the direction. Rather, due to their unique position alongside the board plus the respect they can engender and their independence, they have the opportunity to lead 'invisibly' through 'smart power' and informally facilitate, relate and connect with directors one-to-one as much outside the boardroom as within the boardroom environment.

There are a number of leadership tools that an individual can employ in order to influence key stakeholders informally outside the boardroom environment. These include: building collaborative and trusting relationships through selflessly and non-defensively developing credibility, reliability and confidentiality with others; developing one's personal, operational and strategic network through connecting with hubs, pulse takers and gatekeepers either face-to-face or digitally; acting with political savvy combined with integrity; telling effective stories to communicate and convince; and challenging with radical candour.

Having an awareness of the invisible influencers around you and your organisation can be invaluable in understanding the power dynamics of the organisation. Often those individuals that wield this invisible influence are unaware of it themselves, or do not consciously use their position and network to influence. There are individuals who wield this power consciously, sometimes for their own benefit, though more often for the benefit of the organisation which has a knock-on benefit to themselves in terms of perceived value, personal satisfaction, career progression or other benefits.

Invisible influencers will be present in all organisations: think of senior political leaders such as Theresa May who frequently consulted her husband, Philip, on matters of policy and personnel when she was British Prime Minister. Too frequently individuals identify them as negative influencers and seek to remove the influence in some way instead of recognising it for what it could be – a positive influence for individual leaders, the board, its members and the organisation as a whole.

Are you an invisible influencer or invisible leader yourself, or do you recognise those that are in your organisation? How will you use this knowledge to the greatest benefit for your organisation?

11 – Effective talent management

Board talent management overview

The board adviser as talent manager

This chapter takes a detailed look at an individual's role as a board talent manager. This is not to say that an individual with a broader board advisory role, such as a company secretary, is directly accountable for managing the board talent. The broad remit for board talent management falls under the accountability of the chair, with the nomination committee responsible for providing the board support and recommendations on any board personnel issues.

However, as one broad theme of this text has been that a competent modern governance professional needs to move beyond the technical to the more behavioural elements of their role to be effective, and those individuals that are the most successful are the ones who are most competent at softer skills, then supporting the thinking, processes and decision making around talent management naturally emerges as part of the role.

What effective board talent management is, and how an individual sitting alongside the board might then effectively support board talent management, will therefore be the focus of discussion in this chapter, beginning with some introductory background on how the concept of talent management has evolved.

Introduction to talent management

The origins of talent management as a discipline go back to the McKinsey and Company concept of the 'war for talent', coined by Stephen Hankin in 1997 and popularised in the 2001 book of the same name. Much has been written about talent management since then and a plethora of organisational surveys generally find that it is a pressing business issue with which senior leaders in organisations continually must grapple.

For example, an Accenture report during the 'war for talent' era of talent management (2005) assessed the top 10 current business issues for senior executives and found that 'attracting and retaining skilled staff' topped the list, with 35% of respondents selecting this issue in the top 10. Similarly, following the financial crisis, a 2011 Chartered Institute of Professional Development (CIPD) study reported that at that time, 41% of organisations saw that the economic situation had led to an increased focus on talent management, while 52% felt that competition for talent was even greater now, with the pool of available talent having shrunk sharply.

More recently, a 2017 international study by the Association of Executive Search and Leadership Consultants found that this talent challenge has morphed into a talent diversity challenge, such that the top issue for their 196 global senior leader respondents was a lack of talent that reflects the diversity inherent in the society and the customers their companies serve. The study also highlighted that the composition of diversity in the organisations they researched varied depending on the strata of the workforce such that diversity (in terms of gender, ethnicity, nationality and diversity of thought) 'dropped off' as one moves up through the organisation. This led them to pose the challenging question: 'Does your leadership and your board reflect the market, your employees at large and your customers?' This theme of incorporating stakeholder diversity in talent management is a key idea that will run through the content of this chapter.

Although there is a general agreement that talent management is important to organisations, especially at leadership levels, there is surprisingly little consensus on a clear definition or approach. In looking for a clear definition of talent management, it is noticeable that there are various differing perspectives throughout the literature and in practice. As the CIPD concluded in its 2006 learning and development survey:

> Only 20% of respondents specifically had a formal definition of talent management and, although 51% of respondents said they undertake talent management activities, there is generally a lack of consistency in defining talent and talent management.

Even in the original *War for Talent* book itself, the term 'talent' was never explicitly defined, due to the belief that 'a certain part of talent eludes description; you simply know it when you see it'. This essentially defines talent as a charismatic X-factor which, as we discussed in Chapter 3, is most often found in extroverted, masculine and heroic leadership styles, which is not conducive to sustainable organisational team performance and, at worst, can to lead to unethical and potentially derailing behaviours. It is not surprising, therefore, to learn that Enron subscribed to this charismatic, intuitive and fixed mindset approach to talent management, thoroughly inculcated by their consultancy firm McKinsey. As many have argued since, this was instrumental in their board failure.

The CIPD's own 2018 definitions, though, are a good starting point, which is that talent consists of 'those individuals who can make a difference to organisational performance, either through their immediate contribution or in the longer term by demonstrating the highest levels of potential' and that talent management is therefore 'the systematic attraction, identification, development, engagement, retention and deployment of those individuals with high potential who are of particular value to an organisation'.

Within this definition are two ideas. Firstly, the definition provides us with clarity on what processes talent management involves. These are essentially all of the people elements in the life cycle of an employee, which in the talent management literature tend to include recruitment (or identification if internal to the organisation), induction, development, performance management and, ultimately, succession (hence the structure of the sections in this chapter).

The second idea implicit to the definition is the belief that talent is fixed: you are either talented or you are not and talent resides within only a certain number of people within an organisation such that only some can ever be 'high performers'. These are the enlightened few who you therefore must identify to bestow the benefits of talent management on. This is also the view of Blass (2007), whose definition of talent management is that of a perk for the best of the best.

However, over the last decade or so, there has been a backlash against this second paradigm of talent and talent management. The argument has been made that the assumption that only the top 10–20% of employees are talented is unfair, unethical, disrespectful and wrong. It is not surprising, the argument goes, that those in whom you invest will end up more successful, as this is a self-fulfilling prophecy.

Case study: Selection bias in junior ice hockey

The Canadian junior ice hockey leagues are a stark example of how context may predict 'talent' more than any particular time-specific assessment of individual competency. Gladwell (2008) describes the seemingly strange phenomenon of more than 40% of junior league players being born in the first three months of the year. This becomes more logical when we realise that the talent identification system in Canada kicks in at around eight years old, when the 'best' players receive special attention. However, 10–11 months difference counts for a lot in terms of maturity – both physically and in terms of skating and co-ordination skills – so naturally the 'most talented' are likely simply to be slightly older.

Therefore, although coaches believe they are always selecting based on objective ability, they are not aware that the contextual factor of birth month may bias their choices and blind them from seeing future potential in players born later in the year.

Those involved in talent management should not ask, 'How talented are you?' but instead pose the question, 'How are you talented?'

The argument that talent is contextually dependent rather than an inherent individual competence leads to a definition of talent management being one that recognises that everybody has some strength and therefore a potential role to play in the success of the organisation. This relative strength will only emerge as a talent in the appropriate context in the same way that an animal's form has adapted to its particular niche. It is about recognising an individuals' personal expertise and strengths and, where these are relevant to the organisation, enhancing these specific capabilities. Enhancing and supporting the positive then enables each individual to grow into the organisation and their potential role within it. As more senior roles become available, the individual to fill the role can be identified through their fit with the capabilities required for the role. This is borne out by various research that shows, for example, that organisations have the highest leader success rates when they fill the leadership roles internally. This is due to internal leaders having a greater fit and understanding of their context than external hires through having stronger and more extensive relational networks, feeling a greater commitment and purpose to the organisation and having more aligned values rather than simply a better track record and greater technical expertise. This has led to some suggesting there has been a shift from 'talent management to people management' with less focus on skills and more focus on a holistic approach to cultural fit. This fits more into the stakeholder approach and diversity and inclusion approach that we have discussed in Chapters 6 and 8.

Board talent management

The Chartered Governance Institute's 2014 study of company secretaries reported that:

> Our collective view was that ten years ago 50% of NEDs were poor. This has improved – boards are changing and becoming more effective. These days, our view is that's improved by 25%. So 75% of boards are performing, that means 25% still need developing.

Taking a 'talent as inherent in the individual' approach, one could argue that the improvement in non-executive director performance is due to boards recruiting and training more effectively. However, taking a more 'talent as an emergent quality from the stakeholder system' approach, we might argue that non-executive director improvement is more likely due to a combination of broader factors. These are the factors that we discussed in detail in Chapter 1, such as in enhancements of governance codes, increasing public scrutiny, greater stakeholder expectations, better appreciation of corporate social responsibility, increased stakeholder engagement and an increasing awareness of talent management processes themselves.

An example of governance code provision enhancement around talent management can be found in the FRC's 2018 UK Code of Corporate Governance, which states that a structured process for what we are defining as board talent management should be put in place as follows:

> The board should establish a nomination committee to lead the process for appointments, ensure plans are in place for orderly succession to both the board and senior management positions, and oversee the development of a diverse pipeline for succession.

The Code also stipulates that this process should be transparent in that:

> The annual report should describe the work of the nomination committee, including: the process used in relation to appointments, its approach to succession planning and how both support developing a diverse pipeline.

Over the following sections, we will explore the various elements of talent management:

- board director recruitment
- board director induction
- board director learning and development
- board director performance management
- board director succession

We will do this with a more systemic perspective on talent management by considering how external stakeholders are kept in mind throughout each of these processes.

This is important if we are to appreciate how talent management affects board dynamics, which we have previously defined as the 'interactions between board members individually and collectively, and how these influence, and are influenced by, their wider stakeholder system'. Before a nomination committee engages in the listed talent management processes, they must first understand the governance context they are working within and thus the specific board competencies that will then be required to build each talent management process around.

Board competencies

In 2010, the Chartered Professional Accountants of Canada produced an excellent resource entitled '20 Questions Directors of Not-for-profit Organisations Should Ask about Board Recruitment, Development and Assessment'. Interestingly (and perhaps taking a more systemic perspective), the first five questions are all context related and require answering before a board can begin to look at individual competencies and talent. The first five questions are as follows:

1. **What are the requirements for electing or appointing directors?**
   In order to answer this question, one must be cognisant of the governance requirements of one's country, sector or industry.
2. **What should the size and composition of the board be?**
   The answer to this question will need to strike a balance between the governance-based structural requirements of the board (such as how many and what ratio of executive or non-executive directors must it contain and from which stakeholder groups to be representative) and the constraints of group dynamics. For example, we know that as boards increase in size, individual

participation will decrease as will group cohesion, creating a very different board culture than one that is more compact.

3 **Do the board and its committees have mandates or charters?**
These documents will be important to the talent management processes of the board because they will define the scope of the tasks expected of the directors as a whole. The board mandate will clearly define how responsibilities are allocated between the board and the chief executive officer to prevent overlap or conflict. In addition, a committee charter, or terms of reference, will also be required for each committee to define the responsibility that the board delegates.

4 **Has the board established position descriptors for board roles?**
Each board role, including all directors, committee chairs, the senior independent director and the chair role itself and of course the role of any individuals that support the board, such as the company secretary, will require a clear description so that individuals, when recruited, fully understand what is expected of them in their role. The report provides a useful checklist for these director position descriptors. These are all part of clarifying the 'team task' that will greatly benefit the board dynamics cohesion and include expectations relating to:
- attendance and participation at meetings;
- preparation for meetings;
- communication outside meetings;
- committee service;
- contribution of skills and experience;
- ethical standards and fiduciary duty;
- participation in induction, development, organisation developmental and strategic planning sessions;
- availability to attend scheduled meetings and conference calls;
- chairing of meetings (for board and committee chairs); and
- governance, leadership and accountability expectations (for board and committee chairs).

5 **What skills and experiences does the board need in its directors?**
The answer to this question will be informed by board decisions on the current and future organisational strategy and potentially by the needs voiced by the management and staff of the organisation. These board skills and experience requirements will therefore be highly context specific, varying greatly from sector to sector and will depend on the current evolution of the organisation depending on where they are on the spectrum between start-up and liquidation.

It is only when we get to question six of the 20 questions checklist that a board is able to turn its attention to the specific behavioural attributes that are needed within each of the board roles. To emphasise the point, boards will only get their talent management right when they ground them in the needs of their specific environmental and stakeholder context, rather than simply relying on generic competencies or fixed ideas of director talent. Having said this, there are some transferrable director skills that may be relevant to the modern boardroom, in addition to contextual needs, and thus questions six and seven are as follows:

6 **What personal qualities and behavioural skills does the board need in its directors?**
7 **What skills, experience and personal qualities should board, and committee, chairs have?**

Although we introduced the concept of board role competencies in Chapter 3 as part of the 11 Cs model of governance, we will now answer these two questions in more detail below in relation to the CEO and other executive directors, the non-executive directors, the chair (and in so doing, the committee chairs) and the senior independent director.

Chief executive officer and other executive director competencies

Unsurprisingly, based on the importance of the chief executive officer role to an organisation, there is an extensive commentary on what constitutes an effective chief executive officer. This is in addition to the structural compliance considerations that are purported to contribute to chief executive officer effectiveness within a governance set-up. There exists a biased archetype that boards consider to be the ideal company executive – a charismatic six-foot tall white man, with a degree from a top university, who is a strategic visionary making an unstoppable and linear career trajectory demarcated by an ability to make near-perfect decisions under incredible pressure. This archetype is lived out when we look at the lists of chief executives in post in most developed economies. However, although this archetype fulfils the majority of chief executive and executive roles, it does not necessarily predict success. Therefore, although there are many 'top 10 attributes of successful CEOs' lists, it is important to turn to those resources that are most evidence-based.

One such example resource is the CEO Genome Project, a 10-year study of some 17,000 C-suite executive and 2,000 chief executive officers from all major industries and company sizes. This study blows the archetypal chief executive officer construct out of the water and should make boards better equipped when considering their leadership choices. For example, while boards gravitate towards charismatic extroverts, introverts are found to be slightly more successful. Similarly, a chief executive's educational background (supposedly a key component of their professional capital) was not correlated to performance. Worryingly, although boards are more than twice as likely to select a candidate that seems highly confident, this trait, again, has little connection to their future success.

Instead, the research found four behaviours (from a list of 30 competencies) that, if a person was to excel in two or more, seemed to distinguish higher-performing chief executives from weaker candidates. These behaviours were the deceptively simple, yet eminently developable, attributes of decisiveness, the ability to engage stakeholders, adaptability and reliability. These attributes were all explored in more detail in Chapter 5 on decision making (decisiveness), in Chapter 6 on stakeholder conversations (the ability to engage with stakeholders and reliability in relation to trust building) and in Chapters 10 and 14 (adaptability).

This research is another good example of how the assumed individual demographic factors that board members are most often primarily selected for are not actually those that eventually predict their success.

Non-executive director competencies

Like their executive counterparts, there are also many compliance guidelines, consultancy reports and research studies that have looked at what constitute the key attributes of non-executive directors.

In terms of specific behavioural attributes, rather than more technical and demographic requirements, Dulewicz and Gay (1997) found (in a study of 713 UK company directors) that, although the importance ratings differed by firm size and by executive and non-executive director, some competencies were rated highly across all demographics. These were, not surprisingly, somewhat similar to those noted for chairs and included 'integrity', 'change-orientated', 'listening' and 'judgement'.

Similarly, Ingley and Van der Walt (2001) identified 36 generic factors that influence the selection of directors in their sample of 157 New Zealand non-executive directors, noting the importance of 'strategic vision' and 'leadership'. Further, Canadian board expert Richard Leblanc also finds that there are some 15 key non-executive director behavioural attributes that boil down into five overall components: a strategic and advisory orientation; a monitoring and oversight orientation; analytical and thinking skills; an effective interpersonal and social style; and integrity and loyalty.

Finally, from a US perspective, Northwestern University Professor Simon Wong (2011) suggests that great directors are all able to exhibit the following mindsets and behaviours:

1 Think like an owner.
2 Know their companies.
3 Be prepared to 'roll up their sleeves'.
4 Take charge of their priorities.
5 Hire a collaborative CEO.
6 Protect their authority and independence.

One broad trend that has been noted recently is that effective non-executives are now seen less as the monitoring supervisors of the executive management and more their strategic partners, who are willing and able to take their role as joint leaders of the organisation's endeavours. This collaborative and systemic team leadership orientation of the board is asking non-executives to step up in their mindsets and skillsets beyond board consultation to organisational leadership.

Chair role competencies

It is the chair, as leader of the board, who has the most opportunity to influence the dynamics that are key to the board's effectiveness. Thus, the personal attributes and subsequent effectiveness of the chair are vital. As Leblanc (2010) has commented: 'In essence, the skills possessed by this individual may be the most important contributing factor as to whether or not a board is effective.' This assertion has been measured quantitatively by a 2012 Korn Ferry report, which found that 92.9% of directors questioned believed the 'quality of the chairman' was the most important characteristic of boards that have effective conversations.

How are chairs performing currently? This is difficult to judge and there is likely to be a normal distribution of performance in practice. However, there does seem to be an issue to do with how different directors might answer this same question. For example, some recent research from Andrew Kakabadse (2018) suggests a significant difference between how chairs and non-executive directors view chair performance compared to how executive directors view chair performance. On a scale of one to nine, executive scores averaged around two points lower on all views measured for the chair such as 'encourages open debate', 'raises sensitive issues', 'promotes teamwork', 'encourages feedback on his/her performance' and 'acts as a role model for others'. This suggests not only that many chairs have a rose-tinted opinion of themselves, but also that their lack of skill is probably resulting in low trust between non-executive and executive directors.

Following our appreciation of a contextual approach to talent management and competency identification, the role of a chair will need to be somewhat different depending on the choice of board structure. This will be led by cultural demographics such as which country, which sector, which organisational type and of which lifecycle stage the organisation belongs to. For example, in the UK, a chair's role is that they run the board while the chief executive officer leads the enterprise. However, in the US, the chair often also holds the chief executive officer role and leads both the board and the enterprise. In Australia, the chair role is delineated jointly and determined along with the chief executive officer.

If we take the UK chair role as an example, we see that the latest version of the FRC Code informs us, through Principle F, that:

> The chair leads the board and is responsible for its overall effectiveness in directing the company. They should demonstrate objective judgement throughout their tenure and promote a culture of openness and debate. In addition, the chair facilitates constructive board relations and the effective contribution of all non-executive directors, and ensures that directors receive accurate, timely and clear information.

This clearly outlines the broad outcomes required of the chair, but is less specific on how the chair might then achieve this. The Financial Reporting Council's Guidance on Board Effectiveness is also similarly opaque in its guidance on the role of the chair:

> The chair is pivotal in creating the conditions for overall board and individual director effectiveness, setting clear expectations concerning the style and tone of board discussions, ensuring the board has effective decision-making processes and applies sufficient challenge to major proposals. It is up to the chair to make certain that all directors are aware of their responsibilities and to hold meetings with the non-executive directors without the executives present in order to facilitate a full and frank airing of views.

What personal attributes must a chair have to achieve these outcomes? There are many idiosyncrasies, but some common best practices have been identified. Overall, chairs must be team builders who encourage challenge, contribution and consensus. In their research findings from the 2006 UK Non-executive Director of the Year Awards, Dulewicz et al. found that outstanding chairs have a high level of integrity and show high ethical standards. They spend significant time mentoring, developing and advising their colleagues. They are team builders and are empathetic. They encourage contributions from fellow directors and achieve consensus, yet they challenge and probe colleagues, especially the executive directors. Finally, they have an acute critical faculty and a critical thinking ability.

Other research similarly confirms that integrity, a strong leadership ability and an overall skill in building relationships are key. Research from Directorbank of 430 chairs and directors from over 900 boardrooms especially noted the qualities of patience, the ability to listen and supportiveness. One critical factor that these skills therefore enable is the understanding of the difference between their role and that of the chief executive, such that the outstanding chair does not try to run the business themselves. As one of the study's high-profile chairs, Charles Holliday (Chairman of Bank of America), summarised, a high-functioning chair should know:

> How to get groups to work together, how to listen, how to lead an effective meeting, how to keep your mouth shut and let others talk. It's leading teams when they don't really quite have to do what you say.

However, an ineffective chair can be marked out by attributes such as a tendency to dominate their board with a confrontational style, a failure to keep the board on course to make decisions, limited articulation and listening skills, insufficient interest or involvement in the business and poor leadership abilities.

Although the above commentary has applied directly to the chair of the board, chairs of each of the board committees will require similar competencies for them to successfully facilitate their unique mix of executives and non-executive to achieve their committees' mandate. It is also noticeable that many of the qualities noted of effective chairs are also those discussed in relation to the wider pool to governance professionals.

Senior independent director competencies

A variety of governance criteria guide the role of the senior independent director (SID). Provision 12 of the 2018 FRC Code, for example, states that:

> The board should appoint one of the independent non-executive directors to be the senior independent director to provide a sounding board for the chair and serve as an intermediary for the other directors and shareholders. Led by the senior independent director, the non-executive directors should meet without the chair present at least annually to appraise the chair's performance, and on other occasions as necessary.

However, the above description is of a senior independent director's role during 'normal' times on the board. Their role gains greater prominence during times of disruption when the board is undergoing signs of stress either externally, such as during a takeover bid, or internally, such as when there is a dispute between the chief executive and the chair.

Therefore broad leadership skills, relationship-building skills (such as empathy) and the ability to show personal resilience to manage calmly stressful situations are key role-specific behavioural competencies. As one senior independent director of several FTSE 100 companies stated in a Legal and General/Zygos Partnership report (2017):

> If a SID does their job well, you should never notice. When things are going well it can feel like there's nothing to do, but you need to keep your lines of communication open.

The senior independent director role has only existed formally since it appeared in July 2003 in the UK Combined Code following the January 2003 Higgs Review recommendations. This means the evidence-based understanding of the role is still evolving. Overall, the thinking thus far is that the role requires behavioural competencies similar to those of the chair. In addition, the senior independent director requires the ability to manage the paradox of having the competence to understudy for the chair in moments of crisis, but being able to avoid conflict such that they act in competition for the 'top' position.

General director competencies

To answer fully questions six and seven posed earlier from the Chartered Professional Accountants of Canada guidance, all directors will ideally need to show the range of evidence-based leadership attributes that were described in detail as part of the board attributes quadrant from the 11 Cs model in Chapter 3.

These include the general leadership competencies of emotional intelligence and a humble leadership style, partnered with the more future-thinking twenty-first-century attributes of agility, cultural and digital intelligence and personal resilience, in addition to appropriate levels of commitment in terms of personality, style, mindset and growth mindset and intrinsic motivation – all while not exhibiting overly derailing 'dark side' attributes – as well as a strong ethical character.

The Institute of Directors has published a director competency framework that may also provide some guidance on general competencies across all board directors. The framework has three dimensions – director knowledge, skills and director mindset – which each include a set of core competencies and actionable standards that can be used for assessment and personal and professional development. There are significant overlaps between the competency framework and the competencies that are listed in the personal attributes quadrant of the 11 Cs framework.

However, perhaps because the Institute of Directors framework is in line with the current perspective on talent management – that is, it views talent (as the CIPD does) as inherent to an individual – it is perhaps missing some more of the emergent and transferrable future system requirements that governance professionals are increasingly required to express. For example, it is surprising not to see a core competency for digital intelligence, as this is one that is increasingly required in modern boardrooms. Further, the requirement for cultural intelligence and international experience at board level has recently been described by the global search firm Egon Zehnder as the 'new must have in global boardroom talent' (2017). Based on rapid change and increasing demands, it is also surprising not to see some versions of agility and personal resilience in their framework. One of the top five talent challenges of board executives in the Association of Executive Search and Leadership Consultants (AESLC) 2017 report that was mentioned earlier is the challenge of 'a mismatch of current talent and future strategies'. It seems that the Institute of Directors' current framework falls prey to this mismatch and, while articulating past and present director requirements, places less weight on emerging future stakeholder requirements. As the AESLC study also notes:

> Leaders of tomorrow will have to flourish in a global environment of heightened uncertainty and lightning fast speed. As a result, the leadership competencies required to lead over the next decade, prioritise agility, emotional intelligence, lateral thinking, cultural acumen and comfort with uncertainty. Leadership teams of tomorrow will also be reflective of the diversity of thought required to drive innovation and growth in a changing business environment.

A positive contribution and good decision making from board directors will come firstly from them having the right knowledge, skill sets and mindsets. The FRC Guidance on Board Effectiveness (2018) provides some questions for the nomination committee, to help ensure they are considering the appropriate director competencies for the board. These questions are as follows:

- Have we assessed what skillset is required for the board and its committees?
- Do we reassess the make-up of the board as a result of emerging trends?

- Do we take account of the technical skills and knowledge required by the committees when recruiting members?
- How often is a skills audit undertaken and are we keeping up with the pace of change?

If we are to take a more systemic view on talent management, we must also recognise that the broader contextual view is required and therefore talent competencies will only be talent in the current context of the board. This context will be defined by, and must be inclusive of, a diverse range of external stakeholders' perspectives. As the Egon Zehnder report (2017) also notes, there is the 'growing expectation that director qualifications align with the company's specific challenges and goals. The directors of a high-performing board can no longer merely be generally "impressive"—they must provide management with informed and experienced insight on specific critical issues'.

Moreover, these 'issues have multiplied significantly. This reflects a complex business environment where the evaporation of geographic boundaries and the emergence of new markets, faster and better technology and new business models, create sizable opportunities and increased risk'.

When it comes to defining the appropriate competencies for one's board, as the FRC's guidance also states: 'with input from shareholders, boards need to decide which aspects of diversity are important in the context of the business and its needs'.

Board recruitment

The FRC's Guidance on Board Effectiveness clarifies that the nomination committee is responsible for:

> Board recruitment and will conduct a continuous and proactive process of planning and assessment, taking into account the company's strategic priorities and the main trends and factors affecting the long-term success and future viability of the company.

Recruitment is obviously a vital aspect of board talent management. There must be a clear process, drawing in the expertise of those around the board, such as HR specialists, governance experts, as well as members of the nominations committee and, where appropriate, third-party advisers and recruitment experts.

What process is chosen will very much depend upon the organisation's talent management perspective. The outdated charismatic perspective, arising from the 'war for talent' paradigm, will take as its starting point that the competencies of an effective board director are dictated mostly by the board director demographic factors that we discussed in Chapter 3. As we showed in that chapter, these demographics have historically been the pre-eminent information used with which to make recruiting decisions; however, there is very little evidence that they have any impact on board outcomes. The charismatic talent management process will therefore likely include using existing senior and board-level contacts and networking with fellow educational alumni as a way to search for prospective candidates. It may then involve initiating a standard selection process involving unstructured interviews that do not account for potential unconscious bias. This is likely to result in the selection of candidates who will be homogenous in their diversity to the other board members, hence the proliferation of the similar demographics that exist in many large organisations' boards today. This may give rise to a board culture that is defined by a working group of consultant-style directors who may add useful information but who are competitive and 'over-boarded' individualists ('Well, there is a war for my talent after all!') characterised by large egos and who therefore have the potential to create significant board conflict, or, at worst, derail unethically.

Although this caricature paints a bleak picture, it has, and continues to be, played out in the many high-profile corporate governance failures that we see. This is why an awareness of talent management philosophy and process is highly relevant to the governance professional as it has a significant bearing on board dynamics.

As a way of solving these issues, the prevailing talent management perspective has a different starting point. Director talent is identified through showing competence in current best practice knowledge, skills and personal attributes. The nomination committee's awareness of these competencies enables it to establish new director profiles and search for prospective candidates through a much broader range of mechanisms than just the 'demographic echo-chamber' of personal contacts, potentially including agencies and formal advertising. After identifying and shortlisting potential directors, the committee will engage in a due diligence process, which may involve matching a candidate's competencies against the director profile competency matrix. Candidates will then be approached and asked to complete a competency-based interview. There is also the potential for a significant vetting process, which may include detailed CV checks, reference checks, professional background checks, personality profiling (in particular the Hogan derailment profiles) and multiple interviews in different settings. Once candidate suitability is confirmed, they can then be nominated for election and appointed. This is likely to lead to a board director having the potential to be both highly expert and empathetic and who can therefore become a valued and cohesive team member. However, if broader stakeholder considerations have not been taken into account in relation to the director's appointment, they may lack wider perspectives and so could unwittingly promote groupthink and decision-making bias.

Therefore, how might the emerging systemic perspective to the board recruitment build on the competency-based process just described? A 2017 The Chartered Governance Institute report, entitled 'The stakeholder voice in board decision-making: strengthening the business, promoting long-term success', provides some principles for consideration in the recruitment process. The report introduces the principle that:

When recruiting any director, the nomination committee should take the stakeholder perspective into account when deciding on the recruitment process and the selection criteria.

The report suggests two broad approaches that a board could consider: either to reserve one or more board positions for directors drawn from a stakeholder group, such as the workforce, and/or to extend the selection criteria and search methods for non-executive directors to identify individuals with relevant experience or understanding of one or more stakeholder groups.

This is more likely to ensure not only that candidates with appropriate individual board competencies are selected, but that they are the right people in the context of the current board dynamic.

In addition, adding in some more leading-edge recruitment methodologies, such as using 'blind' applications (which screen out any biodata to further reduce unconscious bias), social media and digital data assessment (to screen a person's digital reputation in addition to their real-life one) and being interviewed by/meeting a variety of key stakeholders beyond just the nomination committee or their future board peers as part of the selection, may enhance the systemic nature of an effective board director recruitment process.

When adopting any of these processes to build a board that is diverse in character, experience or competencies, the board must first recognise the need for, and benefit of, this diversity. Secondly, it must consciously decide to take an approach that builds diversity, purposefully ensure that the appointment process can deliver the stated objectives and subsequently supports it once candidates are appointed through effective induction.

Board induction

The board induction is often the point in the talent management process that those outside the board become more involved. Often the induction is delegated to various individuals based on a programme of requirements. For example, an introduction to the administration and governance of the board is most frequently the responsibility of the company secretary. Other board support may take responsibility for introductions to the operations of the business, the financials and the strategy. Delegating this to fellow board members, both executive and non-executive, as well as the wider board support network, has the dual advantage of supporting knowledge sharing as well as creating an opportunity for the individual to build up a network within the organisation through one-to-one interactions.

When done well, board induction can transform from a process into part of an ongoing networking, mentoring or coaching relationship which is focused not just on providing task knowledge of governance, board and committee process and risk that the board thinks the new director needs to know, but also on supporting the more behavioural, emotional, motivational, relational and resilience aspects of what the new director uniquely might want and need. Those individuals supporting the board or seeking a future career goal of joining a board can benefit from being part of this process, particularly when the newly appointed director is a non-executive director with experience from other boards that they can impart and share with others outside the board, as well as in their interactions with fellow board members.

What does good practice board induction look like? First of all, not all organisations see it as necessary, so the first criterion is to do one rather than not. Over time, good practice has developed into board inductions taking more of a formal structure. As Long (2005) notes:

> The process of induction is recognised across sectors as an increasingly important requirement for non-executive directors. In many cases, induction onto listed boards has become formalised and thoughtful in order to maximise effectiveness and raise risk awareness.

Formal board inductions will typically include sharing director role descriptions, the board and committee mandates/charters, the directors' fiduciary responsibilities, the organisation's key governance information and relevant overview details of the organisation (including its past and current main activities, customers, projects and strategic priorities). Emotionally intelligent individuals working alongside the board will also support the new director by providing more behaviourally and psychologically focused information about the personalities and current cultural patterns that exist in the boardroom, without adding personal opinions as to the individuals themselves so that the new appointee isn't prejudiced ahead of making their own judgements of their new colleagues.

Beyond this, a more systemically orientated induction will include a focus on relationship building with key board stakeholders. The Chartered Governance Institute report on the stakeholder voice in board decision making is an excellent resource for giving advice on how this might be operationalised. As the report says:

> An understanding of the company's key internal and external stakeholders should therefore be an integral part of the induction process.

The induction, therefore, takes on a more cultural and values-led exploration rather than simply being a transaction of information. As the Financial Reporting Council's Guidance on Board Effectiveness also recommends:

> A non-executive director should use these conversations to better understand the culture of the organisation and the way things are done in practice, and to gain insight into the experience and concerns of the workforce.

One useful method of doing this, it suggests, is in:

> Partnering a non-executive director with an executive board member (which) may speed up the process of them acquiring an understanding of the main areas of business activity, especially areas involving significant risk.

To give some sense of how important this broad stakeholder and cultural induction process is, The Chartered Governance Institute report suggests that 'at least 10 days be set aside for this in the first year following the director's appointment'.

Board learning and development

Approaches to learning and development

One helpful model that provides a framework for thinking about how board learning and development can be structured is the 70/20/10 model, which was created by learning expert Charles Jennings. This model first makes the distinction between formal and informal learning. When directors are asked, 'What learning and development do you need?', they will usually reflect on the formal opportunities for development and training that might be offered. These are typically done in a classroom setting or as part of the academic course and may involve set texts and recommended reading. Although this is often what we exclusively consider as learning development, Jennings suggests that this 'just in case' formal training-type learning only constitutes around 10% of our total learning. The other 90% is made up of 'just-in-time' informal learning. This is constituted of mentoring and coaching conversations, which make up a further 20% to one's learning. However, overwhelmingly the greatest contributor to our learning is the on-the-job experiential learning, which constitutes 70% of all learning, according to the model.

Board development

How are boards doing in terms of learning development? Some are progressing, while some are still dismissive of formal development and unclear about its benefits.

Instead of focusing on the more formal approaches, board development and learning might best be supported through a board's informal learning. The shift from formal learning to mentoring and coaching is reflected in some research by the Corporate Executive Board in 2009, which asked the question of its senior level respondents, 'What drives leadership bench strength in organisations?' The research started out with the assumption that external executive education and classroom training, which tended to receive the greatest amounts of investment, would develop leaders the most. However, this only accounted for 23% and 48% of ratings of being the best type of development, respectively. Leading the way by some margin, with a rating of 93%, was 'coaching provided by a leader's direct manager' as the best method of leadership development.

The latest thinking on leadership development, though, suggests that this does not go far enough. Research undertaken by Henley Business School in 2006, entitled 'Tomorrow's leadership: the necessary revolution in today's leadership development', found that the majority of leadership development was not fit for purpose in that it was currently:

- not aligned enough to the strategic agenda of the organisation;
- spending too long on skills and knowledge and not enough time on shifting mindsets;
- not evaluating leadership development in terms of the impact it has on creating value for the organisation and its stakeholders; and
- overly focused on providing individual development for those in the most senior roles and not focused enough on collective leadership and the leaders of the future.

The report goes on to suggest some 'green shoots' of tomorrow's leadership development being interventions such as:

- challenge-based learning that is about real challenges in cross-functional teams and involves stakeholders;
- deep immersion training;
- systemic team coaching of intact teams;
- secondments and peer consultancy across the organisation and in the stakeholder ecosystem;
- shadowing;
- co-created personalised learning journeys; and
- self system awareness, such as developing agility and resilience.

Many of these approaches to leadership development reflect the various themes that we discuss in the text – for example, systemic team coaching in Chapter 14, engagement with the stakeholder ecosystem as mentioned in Chapter 6 and the development of twenty-first-century leadership competencies discussed earlier in this chapter and also in Chapter 3.

Real-world experience, supported by experts inside and outside the organisation acting as coaches/mentors, is the emerging systemic approach to effective board learning and development. In addition, the chair's approach and skill, and the equivalent competence of the committee chairs, will be important.

Board performance management

The performance management of individual directors often occurs as a natural consequence of the yearly board evaluation but it may also be a separate process that is delivered at a rhythm that is either more or less frequent than this. Regardless, those around the board will usually be significantly involved in the process which has, depending upon how it is delivered and what principles it is underpinned by, significant influence on the dynamics surrounding the board and therefore its ongoing performance.

Performance management overview

Performance management is how organisations set goals, evaluate work and determine development needs. The CIPD notes that performance management will reflect the organisation's values and align individual and team goals to organisational vision and strategy. More recently, this has been reworded to reflect a company's purpose and all the associated actions that are identified, Board effectiveness as a whole is often focussed on their success in delivering against purpose.

In the 'war for talent' paradigms of talent management, a common practice was what has come to be known as the 'rank and yank' technique. This was characterised by a typically annual assessment and forced normal distribution of team members (that is, they could all potentially be performing well against benchmarks outside of the team) such that the bottom 10% were exited and the top 10% were bonused and/or promoted. Popularised by Jack Welch in General Electric (GE), this was a common practice in many large organisations until relatively recently. However, there was no evidence base for this brutal process and, when it was studied in detail, was actually found to reduce overall performance and engagement mainly through the significant anxiety, ill-feeling and team conflict that it would often produce. This practice has now largely been abandoned by most organisations, GE included.

The approach that has replaced it is the now ubiquitous yearly or half-yearly competency-based assessment, often completed as a 360-degree feedback exercise by one's line manager, one's peers and one's direct reports and also through self-report. Although it is currently considered best practice, many organisations are reassessing whether this is something that they should continue. In its attempt to be rigorous, the practice often becomes an onerous, time and cost-heavy tick-box paper process. Moreover, recent research shows that it is actually fatally flawed by the problem of 'idiosyncratic rater effects' such that performance ratings reveal significantly more about a rater's biases than they do about the ratee's actual performance. In addition, there is the problem of the whole performance management process conflating what should essentially be separate activities. When one begins to understand that performance management is actually two things which have different needs – performance measurement or assessment on the one hand and performance development on the other – then we recognise it may be possible to design a better overall performance management process than what is currently standard practice.

Assessment

The assessment of board directors can be done either as a whole or individually, and is often delivered as part of the annual board evaluation. We go into more detail around what the objectives of the assessment can be, who will be evaluated, what will be evaluated, who will be asked, what techniques will be used, who will do the evaluation and what will be done with the results in Chapter 12 on board evaluation.

Briefly, though, individual directors may be assessed on the fulfilment of their role description, the contribution of specific skills and a diverse outlook and their personal attributes. Ideally, this should be done in a way that is simple and fair, values-based, unbiased and efficient. The competency-based methodology is sometimes none of these things: in recent years, some organisations have been turning to the idea of a 'performance snapshot' which is a much simpler and potentially more effective assessment process.

Development

Best practice in the development or 'performance acceleration' aspect of performance management is defined as a frequent (approximately every two weeks) 'check-in' conversation that is mainly appreciative, strengths-based, career-focused and delivered in a coaching style. We will explore how an individual outside but alongside the board, such as a company secretary or HR professional, may best perform these types of conversations with board directors in greater detail in Chapter 14 in their role as board 'team coach'. However, we will briefly mention here two of the key skills of a coaching approach: supporting great goal setting and delivering effective feedback.

Helping individuals set effective or 'well-formed' goals can hugely increase a person's likelihood of achieving those goals. Many people have heard of the acronym SMART, which provides guidance on how to set good goals. This originated from pioneering research conducted by Locke and Latham in the late 1960s and stands for making goals specific, measurable, achievable or agreed, realistic and time-based (that is, they have a deadline associated with them). Simply helping to support someone to make their goals SMART has been shown to increase performance dramatically.

However, to ensure that a goal is fully well formed, one also needs to consider why a goal exists and how it can be achieved as well as what it is. Thus, good practice in goal setting is about first clarifying one's performance goal, the 'what' using SMART, and then also the outcome goal to provide the motivation and 'why', in addition to the many process goals that one would need to achieve the performance, that provide clarity, belief and a focus on 'how'. In a coaching-orientated performance management check-in, one might help a coachee build motivation and more fully understand the desired outcome by repeatedly asking a questions such as 'And what would achieving this goal give you?' and/or 'What is the benefit of that to you or others?' Similarly, to enable someone to develop greater belief and focus through clarifying process goals, a coach may ask questions such as 'And how might you do that?' or 'What would be your first step to achieving that?'

In addition to supporting a person to set goals, providing effective and actionable feedback is a complementary coaching skill that enables people to understand where their current behaviours are in relation to their goal. Some best practice feedback recommendations are as follows:

1 All feedback is potentially useful – therefore re-label 'positive' feedback as 'motivational' (for confidence) and 'negative' feedback as 'developmental' (for competence).

2 Research shows that high-performing teams require at least three pieces of motivational feedback for every one piece of developmental feedback.
3 Don't do the 'feedback sandwich' (praise/criticise/praise). The message gets confused.
4 Instead, give motivational feedback immediately after the event and developmental feedback once emotion has reduced and in time ready for next event, i.e. 'feed-forward'.
5 Use words such as 'I appreciate...' for motivational and 'I encourage...' for developmental.
6 Provide feedback on specific behaviours ('When you said/did x...') rather than identity ('You are really good/bad at...').
7 Provide examples.
8 Let people know about common reactions to feedback (i.e. a pattern of shock, anger, denial, rationalisation, acceptance and then renewed action) so they can notice their own reaction and, in so doing, move to acceptance and renewed action more quickly.
9 Emphasise that feedback is 'true' from another person's perspective, but that this also does not mean it is *the* truth. We can choose how we respond in a way that benefits both ourselves and others.
10 When setting up a written feedback process, confidentiality can be maintained by using an online process or through using a third-party provider. Explain that feedback will be anonymous and how the feedback will be used at the end of the collection process.
11 If you are the team leader, role-model feedback good practice by asking for and giving feedback regularly, sharing your feedback with the team and asking for their support to continue developing and listening and saying 'thank you' when receiving it.
12 Even bearing in mind all the above points, giving feedback often reinforces status differences, creating parent–child rather than adult–adult relationships and conversations. Therefore, first ask people what they think and use feedback as a last resort.

How these two coaching skills of supporting well-formed goals and providing effective feedback play into the overall coaching approach will be discussed further in Chapter 14.

Remuneration

A final key component of the performance management aspect of board talent management, and one which is linked to initial goal setting and corresponding assessment, is board director remuneration. This has historically been a thorny issue and has received significant media and compliance attention. It is not the intention of this section to go into detail around director remuneration; instead, we will simply notice some patterns in relation to the past, present and future approaches to talent management that relates to it.

Much of the media attention on financial reward is due to the fact that boards have often been driven by the 'war for talent' philosophy, as the board is unsurprisingly always considered as significant talent. They are, therefore, under this paradigm, required to be rewarded handsomely and often induced to join an organisation through significant short-term rewards that hard-nosed contract bonus clauses might provide. There are many problems with this approach, not least the 'gaming' and unethical behaviours it is likely to engender.

The current best practice on reward is, on the contrary, that it should be more aligned to long-term outcomes. The current UK Code of Corporate Governance provides significant detail on how this might be done, summarising an effective approach as embracing clarity, simplicity, risk, predictability, proportionality and culture. The governance thought leader and one-to-one coach to Canadian chief executive officers, Richard Leblanc, provides an example of how, during his coaching assignments, he helps restructure the remuneration approach to link chief executive behaviour to pay incentives:

> Frequently, I find the CEO has little incentive to change, as most of the pay metrics are financial and short-term in nature. In CEO coaching assignments, I normally restructure the CEO's pay package to include non-financial metrics such as leadership, employee engagement, customer satisfaction, company culture, CEO succession planning, and/or board relations, or a combination of the above. Indeed, now, 75% of the value of a company are leading intangible measurements, such as the ones I mention, so pay metrics should reflect this. People behave the way you pay them. Boards often make the mistake of incentivizing aggressive, even unethical behaviour. CEO pay should be tied explicitly, unambiguously, to ethical conduct.

A future-focused approach to remuneration may recognise and appreciate that the research on extrinsic rewards unequivocally finds that they lead to negative outcomes and, in many cases, lower performance. If we can also link performance more to intrinsic motivation and cultural values – such as the universal human needs of autonomy, belonging, competence and purpose or meaning – then board directors will be motivated more by these pull factors than needing the push that inflated reward often clumsily provides.

A systems perspective to board performance management

One final reflection on performance management is the emerging thinking around the systems perspective to performance management in line with our approach taken in this text to board dynamics. A systems perspective challenges the whole paradigm and contends that there is actually little benefit in assessing individual director performance, as it is largely influenced by systemic factors rendering one's own competence to being a largely insignificant illusion. This seems quite shocking – as all paradigm shifts initially do – but the perspective has some clout behind it.

W. Edwards Deming, the management thinker and inspiration behind the original Honda 'Lean' methodology that rejuvenated Japan's economy in the 1950s, wrote: 'the system that people work in and the interaction with people may account for 90 to 95% of performance'.

Like a board that recognises its internal dynamics are largely a reflection of the broader context the board is part of, this perspective completely alters the quality of performance management conversations. With this perspective, a board talent manager, through coaching conversations with directors, can have a significant impact both on the board dynamic inside the boardroom and also on how the board interacts with key stakeholders. This approach also increases the likelihood of a key boardroom behaviour: appropriate challenge.

This approach can therefore develop a similar valuing of boardroom cognitive conflict and diversity in the service of the stakeholder system, rather than staying quiet to protect one's position.

Board succession

Board succession is the final aspect of the board talent management process. This is serious business, as the whole page and five sections on board succession in the FRC's Guide to Board Effectiveness attest.

In fact, due to high-profile chair and chief executive officer exits that have left companies high and dry with no obvious successor, the Code now requires listed companies to describe publicly their approach to succession planning and how it supports the development of a diverse pipeline in their annual report. The importance of effective board succession planning is that it acts as an insurance policy to reduce the risk of unplanned board exits. It is also a process that may reduce the potential for board conflict due to political jostling for future board positions.

In light of this, the role of the company secretary and others around the formal board is often to manage the process formally, but also informally to soften the politicking through sensitive facilitation and light mediation as necessary. This is another example of the board supporters' complementary task and people-orientated roles that they must be capable of moving between fluidly.

The talent management processes involved in board succession are similar to those described earlier in terms of board recruitment, such as the mapping of current and future board requirements. The FRC's Guidance for Board Effectiveness also counsels that succession plans should consider three time horizons:

- **contingency planning** – for sudden and unforeseen departures;
- **medium-term planning** – the orderly replacement of current board members and senior executives (e.g. retirement); and
- **long-term planning** – the relationship between the delivery of the company strategy and objectives to the skills needed on the board now and in the future.

The Guidance also makes the point that 'succession plans can also help to increase diversity in the boardroom and build diversity in the executive pipeline'. This highlights the more general point that the way the board approaches talent may influence the organisation but that the organisation may equally influence the board. For example, the board may need to up its game in terms of talent management to bring itself up-to-date with good practice that already exists within the rest of the organisation. Indeed, the board's approach to talent management can be an opportunity to lead emerging systemic best practice and, in so doing, to role-model this to their organisational and external stakeholders.

Conclusion

The individual sitting alongside the board has a key role to play as a 'talent manager' to the board, ensuring that the talent within the boardroom is effectively developed and that new recruits are a positive addition to the membership. Given the importance of the board and its leadership team in the success of an organisation, having effective talent management at this senior level is clearly a priority.

There are three main approaches in the evolution of talent management: the past 'war for talent' approach, the current 'competency-based' approach and the emerging 'systemic' approach. Required board role competencies will depend on a board's context, but there are some recognised preferences and core expectancies.

What are the key aspects of board talent management? In order that board talent management is systemic, a board must first understand: the governance requirements of their country, sector or industry; the size and composition required of their board; the board and committee mandates/charters; the established position descriptor for board roles; and the skills, experiences, personal qualities and behavioural abilities that board directors need. Once these competencies are clarified, there will need to be a strategic process for board director recruitment, board director induction, board director learning and development, board director performance management and board director succession.

There are various process options for board recruitment, induction, learning and development, performance management and succession, which will be driven by the underlying talent management approach adhered to by the organisation. The board's approach to talent management can both be informed by, and an opportunity to role-model to, board stakeholders. It can also serve to create a clear expectation for, and principals of, talent identification, engagement and promotion for the organisation as a whole.

It should remembered that, while the deliverables in the roles may be different, the core competencies and expectations of a board member are the same whether the individual is an executive or non-executive director. Getting a board that works well as a team, with the various competencies and talents evidenced across the team, can lead to a highly effective board. As can be seen from this and previous chapters, having each board member considered in isolation does not in and of itself deliver an effective board. Talent management needs to be considered as a part, and as a whole, when creating an effective board. Board moves, whether planned or implemented from need, impact on the board as a whole. Add into this the opportunity to widen diversity in a board when board recruitment is needed and the matrix of needs to address can become complex to ensure that the best individual at the time for the role is recruited. No longer is it sufficient to replace like for like, or to appoint board members through the chair's and board members' immediate network of connections.

How do you and your organisation leverage the opportunities that succession planning, recruitment, induction and training can provide to the effectiveness of your board both now and in the future?

12 – Board evaluation

The individual as a board consultant

Although individual director and board performance may already be addressed at specific times, such as when issues arise, during re-nomination or as part of coaching and mentoring, the process of board evaluation is increasingly recognised as a key set piece opportunity to positively influence the functioning of a board.

Although accountability for a successful board evaluation will ultimately lie with the chair as leader of the board, the responsibility for delivering the board evaluation in practice often lies with others sitting outside but aligned to the board, such as the company secretary, members of the HR department or individual members of the remuneration or nomination committee. The Corporate Secretaries International Association report 'Global board evaluation practices and trends', published in March 2018, reported that of the 84% of board evaluations that were facilitated internally in their global sample of 380 cross-sector organisations, individuals outside the board, most specifically the company secretary, led the board evaluation around half of the time. The role of internal board consultant, therefore, is a key requirement of any modern governance professional wanting to deliver an effective board evaluation successfully.

What does a skilful board consultant look like? Consulting thought leader Peter Block suggests that an effective consultant is (ironically) not one that takes on the role of expert, positioning themselves as more knowledgeable than the client and who dispenses their wisdom from on high. Nor is the successful consultant, on the opposite end of the spectrum, the one who takes on the role of being just a 'pair of hands', scurrying around at the bidding of the client with no voice of their own. Instead, the successful, or 'flawless' as Block terms it, consultant is one who takes on the role as an equal collaborator, such that the three primary goals of consulting, either internally or externally to one's organisation are to:

1. establish a collaborative relationship;
2. solve problems so that they stay solved; and
3. ensure attention is given to both the technical problem and the client relationships.

There are five classic phases that a consultant, and therefore any individual acting internally in a role as board evaluator, will need to negotiate. These are:

- Phase 1 – entry and contracting.
- Phase 2 – discovery and dialogue.
- Phase 3 – feedback and the decision to act.
- Phase 4 – engagement and implementation.
- Phase 5 – extension, recycle or termination.

The entry phase is key to set the appropriate role expectations and tone. In this phase, some of the issues that an individual will need to navigate are negotiating what exactly the chair wants from the board evaluation, coping with mixed motivation across the boardroom for the process and dealing with potential concerns about confidentiality, exposure and the loss of control. More broadly, as they move through the phases of consulting around an evaluation process, they will need to tread a careful line between facilitating the process enough to create structure and momentum, while also ensuring that the board feels like the individual is collaborating enough so that directors feel joint ownership of the project. This has significant implications for individual implementation of any changes as a consequence of the themes and feedback that emerge.

Having set the scene for an individual's role as a board consultant in the process, we will now step back and turn our attention to the current context of board evaluation among the board's various stakeholders.

The current board evaluation landscape

Evolving corporate codes

A well-defined system for board evaluation is required by many of the existing corporate governance codes for firms around the world. For example, the Principles of Good Corporate Governance and Best Practice Recommendations in Australia, the Final NYSE Corporate Governance Rules in the US and the Preda Code in Italy all make specific recommendations for periodic board and director evaluation.

The situation in the UK is no different. The Financial Reporting Council has charted the evolution of board evaluation through its codes and guidance over the years. In January 1998, the Hampel Report first recognised the possibility of a UK requirement for introducing formal procedures to assess both a board's collective performance and also that of the individual directors. The report did not go so far as to make a firm recommendation, but did note that many UK boards were already using evaluation in the interest of continuous improvement.

It was only in July 2003, after the Higgs review of the roles and effectiveness of non-executives, that the FRC's Combined Code on Corporate Governance first outlined actual provision for board evaluation, with the main principle that 'the board should undertake a formal and rigorous annual evaluation of its own performance and that of its committees and individual directors'. This Code also gave suggestions of good practice, including how to evaluate and what questions to ask.

There were no substantive changes in the Combined Codes of June 2006 and June 2008, but the June 2010 Code, in response to the 2009 Walker Review findings and now called the UK Corporate Governance Code, was the first to recognise the importance of external evaluators, stating in one of its core provisions that:

> Evaluation of the board of FTSE 350 companies should be externally facilitated at least every three years. The external facilitator should be identified in the annual report and a statement made as to whether they have any other connection with the company.

In 2011, the FRC published its Guidance on Board Effectiveness that took care to be 'neither prescriptive nor exhaustive'. However, in the September 2012 UK Corporate Governance Code, the FRC added a supporting principle that provided more direction than previously on areas to evaluate:

> Evaluation of the board should consider the balance of skills, experience, independence and knowledge of the company on the board, its diversity, including gender, how the board works together as a unit, and other factors relevant to its effectiveness.

The latest 2018 edition of the aspects of board evaluation required by the Code defines the evaluation Principle as:

> Annual evaluation of the board should consider its composition, diversity and how effectively members work together to achieve objectives. Individual evaluation should demonstrate whether each director continues to contribute effectively.

It also details two further evaluation provisions as follows:

> There should be a formal and rigorous annual evaluation of the performance of the board, its committees, the chair and individual directors. The chair should consider having a regular externally facilitated board evaluation. In FTSE 350 companies this should happen at least every three years. The external evaluator should be identified in the annual report and a statement made about any other connection it has with the company or individual directors.
>
> The chair should act on the results of the evaluation by recognising the strengths and addressing any weaknesses of the board. Each director should engage with the process and take appropriate action when development needs have been identified.

While the latest principles and provisions above are now relatively concise, the accompanying guidance document on board effectiveness published by the FRC in 2018 provides extensive direction on how to deliver a board evaluation successfully over three pages and 11 guidance notes. Some of these notes will be shared as supporting advice in the later sections of this chapter.

Organisational use of board evaluation

Having established that board evaluation is now required by most country governance codes, what is the extent of evaluation actually going on in companies? Over the past 20 years or so, a story has emerged that somewhat mirrors the evolution of the governance codes.

In the early 2000s in the US, for example, only a third of companies formally evaluated the board on a regular basis, while only a fifth evaluated individual directors (data from Korn/Ferry International research based on a survey of 2,041 board members). The reasons why evaluations were not being undertaken included issues such as board discomfort, being thought of as potentially disruptive to the team, worried about evaluations being used as a political tool, and so on.

However, even as evaluation increased over time in the US, generic 'boilerplate' reporting and non-specific disclosures became the norm. This may have been due to a view that evaluation is overly burdensome and time-consuming, that evaluation results could contain evidence of improper conduct and could be subsequently used in civil or criminal proceedings, or that if boards fail to respond to evaluation recommendations then stakeholders may become dissatisfied.

More globally, the Company Secretaries International Association published a report in March 2018 on the global board evaluation practices and trends. This study included 380 responses from governance professionals and both executive and non-executive board directors from 18 countries and all sectors. Their headline finding was that, over the 12 months leading up to survey completion, only 57% of organisations represented had performed an evaluation, 35% had not and 8% had been uncertain. Some of the reasons given for not performing an evaluation included the following:

- It was not required by regulation and the board was not convinced of the benefit.
- It was conducted only every third year.
- It was something the organisation has never considered.
- Although the board knows about evaluations, it has not been completed because the board does not fully appreciate the importance of board evaluations.
- Costs associated with an evaluation.

The report concluded that because: 'in many instances, the reason given for not completing an evaluation was that it was not required by regulation, thus seemingly a large number of companies… do not yet believe in the fundamental benefits of evaluation even when not mandatory or strongly suggested'.

Similarly, the UK take-up of evaluation practice has also been somewhat slow, superficial and sensitive. The reasons for this include:

- directors remain either unprepared or unconvinced of the benefits gained from evaluation;
- they are conscious of the difficulties concerning independent judgement and objectivity;
- there are worries about the transparency and clarity of process; and
- personal bias and existing sensitivities within the board.

The Institute of Directors' (2009) submission to the Walker Report argues that: 'although board evaluation has become more widespread amongst larger companies in recent years, evaluation techniques vary in rigour and objectivity'. However, recent years, with encouragement from government reviews and guidelines from regulators and other official bodies, have enabled a more professional evaluation process and sector to develop.

In January 2021 The Chartered Governance Institute published their 'Review of the effectiveness of independent board evaluation in the UK listed sector', which was carried out at the request of the UK Government Department of Business, Energy and Industrial Strategy. Statistically, this report noted that 'in their annual reports published in 2019, 38% of FTSE 350 companies reported that they had carried out an externally facilitated evaluation the previous year. Extrapolated over the three-year period within which the Code expects such reviews to be carried out, this suggests nearly full compliance. By comparison, only 37.5% of listed companies across Europe carry out an externally facilitated evaluation at least every three years'.

Annual reports issued in 2020 identified that 32 different individuals and organisations had been used the previous year. By comparison, 51 different reviewers had been used in 2012, which might perhaps suggest that some of the less well qualified reviewers have been 'weeded out' or rather that a few large providers had captured the market.

There is quite a high level of concentration, combined with a 'long tail' of reviewers with only one or two FTSE 350 clients. Two organisations undertook 40% of all externally facilitated reviews in the FTSE 350 in 2020, with one of them responsible for more than one in four of all such evaluations. However, as noted in the 2019 Grant Thornton report on application of the Code, 'previous market leaders are conducting fewer evaluations and smaller players are getting more, including two newcomers that each picked up several evaluations this year'.

In the author's interview research on the current status of board evaluation (Cross, 2013) in the UK, one industry expert summarised the then current status of board evaluation which can still be extrapolated forwards as

> It is used but people often buy into the quick fix rather than a longer-term journey. Having a rerun of the same instrument keeps people engaged and

honest. It is important to emphasise that insight and good intentions doesn't make a transformation.

Case study: Board evaluation at the top 10 UK companies

In 2010, the Australian Council of Superannuation Investors investigated the extent of evaluation in UK listed companies. They found that the top 10 UK companies reviewed all followed a similar pattern in their disclosure on board evaluation, demonstrating the strong influence of the Code. Most companies disclosed:

- that an annual evaluation is carried out and was carried out the previous year;
- that it was led by the chair (or a committee) and/or facilitated by an independent expert;
- that the process involved a questionnaire and/or interviews;
- a list of topics covered by the process;
- that the information was collected and reported back to board; and
- the conclusion – usually a statement that the board was performing effectively.

Two of the 10 companies went on to describe the outcome in terms of actions for improvement.

Some other case examples are as follows:

- **Royal Dutch Shell** – annual internal board evaluation led by the nomination and succession committee. There is a structured interview process described in detail with steps for continuous improvement of the board to meet the operational and strategic challenges of the company in the wake of the global financial crisis.
- **HSBC** – annual board evaluation conducted by the chair and an independent consultant. The evaluation examined eight key areas: board role and responsibilities; oversight; board meetings; information received; support for the board; board composition; working together; and outcome and achievements. Conclusions drawn were that the board and its committees were functioning effectively.
- **GlaxoSmithKline** – board evaluation comprised a questionnaire and interviews conducted by an independent consultant. Feedback to the board included a written report. Details of the actions resulting from the evaluation are provided.
- **Tesco** – regular board self-evaluation with a questionnaire prepared by the chair and company secretary. Interviews were also conducted, with results confirming a good performance by the board.

Board evaluation providers

> If evaluating boards of directors was a product, the 'evaluation' would be just beyond the product launch stage.
>
> (Goffee and Jones, 2005)

The above quote was written soon after the FRC's Combined Code made provision for internal board evaluation, but before it requested external evaluation. In parallel with the Code developments and the increasing company emphasis on evaluation, practitioners have also begun to offer their services to boards as evaluators. There are currently four types of external provider of board evaluation offering a mix of either face-to-face or online services:

1 independent consultancies, e.g. Boardroom Review, Bvalco, Garrett Learning Services, Board Evaluation and CS Skills Centre (serving the charity sector), etc.;
2 search firms, e.g. Egon Zehnder, Hanson Green and Wickland Westcott, etc.;
3 auditors, e.g. Deloitte, Ernst & Young, KPMG and PWC, etc.; and
4 governing bodies, e.g. the IoD and The Chartered Governance Institute, etc.

One issue has been a lack of common understanding of what 'good' evaluation and 'good' evaluators look like, as experience is often accumulated within consulting firms rather than in the public arena. This has led to a lack of providers to match demand and inconsistent quality. The suggestion is also that practitioners need to focus more on the behavioural elements that are accounted for within board dynamics.

As well as a focus on what providers do, there is also a debate about who they are and the professional standards they keep. Following the FRC's 2018 Code guidelines, any external provider must make a public disclosure about their connection, if any, to the company. This will hopefully ensure a reasonable degree of independence and should (but currently does not always) preclude those who provide other services, such as search agents who assist in the recruitment of directors and the remuneration consultants or indeed consultancies evaluating direct competitors.

Beyond disclosing name and independence, qualification and remuneration should be published in an external provider's statement. The Institute of Directors, in responding to the Walker recommendations, has gone further in terms of professionalisation and is calling for a 'Standardised Independent Governance Analysis' to be carried out by appropriately trained and accredited personnel.

The FRC's 2018 Guidance on Board Effectiveness provides some useful direction on what to take into account when selecting an external evaluator. Some of their advice is that the chair needs to:

- be clear what the board evaluation will offer – each provider will have a different method and experience, with cost and approaches varying greatly across providers;
- evaluate the skills, competencies and references of each individual involved in the evaluation against a specification agreed with the board;
- be mindful of existing commercial relationships and other conflicts of interests and select an evaluator who is able to exercise independent judgement; and
- agree with the evaluator the objectives and scope of the evaluation, expected quality, value and longevity of service and communicate this to the board.

Even before considering which external evaluator to appoint, the board, chair or company should be clear on their purpose for the evaluation. The Chartered Governance Institute's board evaluation report published in January 2021 noted that there are broadly two schools of thought, informed by different views on the purpose of evaluation, which in turn inform views and expectations about how the evaluation should be carried out and what it is expected to achieve. They are:

1 that the purpose of evaluation is to inform a continual process of self-improvement, which might include making changes to the board, and that disclosure should provide evidence of a robust process and a willingness to act on the outcomes. By doing so, the board can provide some reassurance to shareholders and others that it takes its responsibilities seriously and is endeavouring to carry them out to the best of its ability; or
2 that the purpose of evaluation is to provide an assessment of whether the board is or is not effective, in either absolute or relative terms, and that the purpose of disclosure is to provide assurance as to the future performance of the board and company.

However, an independent board evaluation should not be seen as an assurance function, as doing so would result in board evaluation becoming a backwards-looking compliance exercise that generates little value. Equally, it may reduce the board's willingness to be open with the reviewer and could raise unrealistic expectations as to the ability of the review to prevent future failings. It should be noted that engaging a third party does not transfer the board's responsibility to take action to improve its own performance; nor is it the role of external reviewers to provide an absolute rating or ranking of the board's current effectiveness (either to the board itself or to its regulators, shareholders or other stakeholders) or to provide guarantees or assurance as to the board's future effectiveness. The benefit of engaging an independent board reviewer instead derives from their ability to bring greater objectivity and fresh insights to the process. It also enables the company to signal to its shareholders and other stakeholders that the board takes its responsibility for continuous improvement seriously, although this benefit only materialises if there is sufficient transparency throughout the process and about the outcomes.

Board evaluation interest from shareholders and investors

Investor interest in human capital information is increasing. There is a post-financial crisis recognition of the link between board performance and company performance, however complex that link may be. But as the area is immature, investors are seeing this more as a reason to 'screen out' rather than 'select in' to their investment portfolio.

What information are investors using about board, and does this include them looking at board evaluation? Switzer and Cao (2011) found that the Rotman/Clarkson Canadian Board Shareholder Confidence Index ($CCBE^2$) was associated with higher firm performance (measured by Economic Value Added). One of the $CCBE^2$ variables is the extent to which a company implements regular and formal evaluation processes for the board and each of its individual directors, based on the disclosure of details regarding the evaluation processes. Therefore, the growing interest of shareholders and investors in the results of board evaluation may provide a further reason for undergoing the process.

How to conduct board evaluations

As board evaluation has developed, the practice has reduced the breadth of processes implemented although there remain various approaches and levels of quality and robustness.

Case study: The Royal Bank of Scotland's evaluation reporting

The FSA (now superseded by the Financial Conduct Authority) looked at the reporting of board evaluation as a response to the financial crisis. The Royal Bank of Scotland in particular received its scrutiny. In its 2011 report, the FSA noted that the evaluation reporting:

> did not identify a failure on the part of the Board as the box-ticking affirmation... and evidence base suggests that the RBS Board's composition and formal processes met acceptable standards.

How then, should boards be evaluated? Kiel and Nicholson's (2005) board evaluation framework (see Figure 13) does an excellent job of providing a structure to aid thinking through the process of evaluation. Their framework is essentially a list of seven questions that, although the combined answers may be quite different, will require agreed resolutions regardless of board type. They noted that, in relation to the importance of this type of process thinking, 'boards often neglect the process of engagement when undertaking evaluations... In short, the process is as important as the content'.

This echoes the need to act as a board consultant who places emphasis on the relationship as well as the task such that one maintains one's role as an 'adult–adult' collaborator without straying into a more 'parental' expert role.

Figure 13 Board evaluation framework (Nicholson and Kiel, 2005)

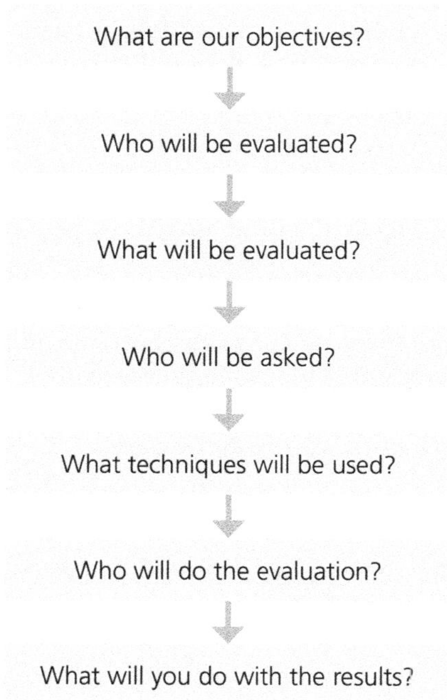

What are the objectives of board evaluation?

This first question enables the evaluation to be fit for purpose. For example, the traditional 'board-to-market' reporting is to create compliance accountability, whereas a 'board-to-board' evaluation may focus more on improving board functioning such as described by Sir Bryan Nicholson, the former Chairman of the FRC:

> Evaluation is essential to improving a company's performance – you cannot begin to address your weaknesses unless you know what they are.

Therefore, good board evaluation will first include some clear consultancy with key stakeholders, starting with the chair, to clarify the objectives of the evaluation which will then drive more strategic answers to the subsequent questions.

Various benefits have been associated with board evaluation. These benefits are to the individual directors themselves, the board as a group and the organisation as a whole. These can include some or all of the following (following Kiel and Nicholson, 2005):

Leadership

- Demonstrates commitment to improvement at an individual level.
- An effective chairperson using a board evaluation demonstrates leadership to the rest of the board.
- Demonstrates long-term focus of the board.
- Sets the culture and tone of the organisation.

Role clarity

- Clarifies duties of individual directors as well as committee roles.
- Sets a board norm for roles.

Teamwork

- Encourages individual director involvement.
- Develops commitment and a sense of ownership.
- Builds trust between board members.

Accountability

- Ensures directors understand their legal duties and responsibilities.
- Sets performance expectations for individual board members.
- Focuses board attention on duties to stakeholders.
- Ensures the board is appropriately monitoring the organisation.
- Improves corporate governance standards.

Decision making

- Identifies areas where director skills need development.
- Aids in the identification of skills gaps on the board.
- Improves the board's decision-making ability.
- Clarifies strategic focus and corporate goals.
- Improves organisational decision making.

Communication

- Builds personal relationships between individual directors.
- Improves board–management relationships.
- Builds trust between board members.
- Improves stakeholder relationships.

Board operations

- Saves directors' time.
- Increases effectiveness of individual contributions.

- Ensures more efficient meetings.
- Ensures an appropriate top-level policy framework exists to guide the organisation.

Many of the above themes are those that have appeared in other areas of the text in relation to board dynamics. Therefore, one general benefit of board evaluation is that it will support the measurement and ongoing improvement of board dynamics.

The question 'what are the objectives of the board evaluation' will usually be asked in the Phase 1 'entry and contracting' stage. At this stage, individual concerns and reservations about the process maybe encountered from individuals, even though directors may agree that an evaluation would be useful in principle.

This is therefore to be expected, embraced and inquired into, rather than railroaded over to ensure smooth passage to a fully bought-into Phase 2 of 'discovery and dialogue'. To ease anxieties, it may be prudent to provide answers to issues around data management and anonymity, external disclosure and implementation of recommendations. As a director of a national charitable organisation mentioned (Leblanc and Lindsay, 2010):

> Who gets the results? ... There needs to be clarity here... There needs to be clarity on how the data is used, who gets it, at what level, especially the qualitative data.... Otherwise, there is no trust.

The FRC's 2018 Guidance on Board Effectiveness recognises the importance of this trust and buy-in process created through a collaborative approach to board consulting in their guidance as follows:

> To ensure a more valuable review, the chair will need to ensure full cooperation between the company and the evaluator, including full access to board and committee papers and information, to observe meetings, and meet with directors individually.

Importantly, board evaluation should not be commenced with a set expectation of the results and outcome and should not merely be seen as a check box to justify continuation with no change. A board evaluation that embraces an outcome that can be positive for board effectiveness thereafter, as well as supporting individual growth and development, can be very powerful in its application. In contrast, a tick-box exercise that is solely in place to meet the principles of the code is unlikely to have delivered a cost-effective outcome.

Who is to be evaluated?

One key choice is whether the board should simply be evaluated as a group or whether the process should extend to individual directors. Although board-as-a-whole evaluation is excellent as a familiarisation tool for inexperienced boards, one disadvantage is that group evaluation may give only limited insight into performance problems. This is sometimes not recognised by directors, who may see individual evaluation as a challenge to their personal egos, the collegiate culture or even their independence. However, if they can agree to at least trial the process, then there is usually a recognition that individual director evaluation can be extremely beneficial. One particular time when individual evaluation is more likely is when directors stand for re-election.

If this is a first attempt at evaluation or there is some significant individual sensitivities around evaluation, it is recommended to evaluate the board as a whole first. One exception to this may be to evaluate the chair's role specifically, being such a key individual in board performance.

In general, though, four groups may be the subject of evaluation:

1. **board evaluation** – this is the most frequent type and involves assessments of effectiveness, structures, operational/design processes and cultural dynamics;
2. **committee evaluation** – similar to the board assessment but at each committee level;
3. **board and committee chair evaluations** – against board-approved role descriptions and performance indicators; and
4. **individual director evaluations** – either self, peer or key stakeholder assessments against board-approved role descriptions and performance indicators.

The majority of board evaluations review the competencies, capabilities and expertise of the individual directors and their high level interaction as a board. Few, if any, evaluate the effectiveness of the board as a collective delivering against the purpose of the company, the shareholder expectations and stakeholder deliverables. As this area of expertise develops further, and stakeholder engagement and company purpose become more widely discussed, board evaluations may see a benefit from appointing a provider that delivers more than the equivalent of an examination assessor.

What will be evaluated?

Once clear overall objectives and then a rationale for who will be evaluated have been made, the next task to consider is what factors to evaluate. Structural compliance factors, which are often easily visible and disclosed in annual reports, are one popular answer to the question. However, as recent corporate failures have shown, living up to the 'formal' standards is not enough. Thus, the factors chosen to be evaluated are those that are largely captured by all the quadrants of the 11 Cs model outlined in Chapter 1.

At a minimum, the evaluation should include some measure of the board's performance against its agreed mandate (the 'board tasks' discussed in Chapters 4 and 6). The evidence-base also strongly suggests including some behavioural factors, but the choice will very much depend on what the evaluation objectives are. If the objectives are not clear, a generic question set such as those in the following case study may be a useful starting point. Some of the team factors mentioned in Chapter 14 using a team coaching assessment perspective may also be useful to pull out issues in relation to the board dynamic.

Case study: Guidance on reviewing charity governance

The Charity Commission and The Chartered Governance Institute jointly produced templates for trustee and staff review. The 'Charity Governance questionnaire' comprises a limited number of open-ended questions and a range of statements that respondents are asked whether they agree with or not, by ranking from one to five.

The questions are a mix of structural and behavioural and, in this case, focus on the board's functioning as a whole rather than on individual trustee competence. Figure 14 shows a list of the questions used as an example of a simple written board evaluation methodology that could be complemented with other techniques such as qualitative interviews and meeting observations.

Figure 14 Example of a charity governance questionnaire (Charity Commission/The Chartered Governance Institute)

Please rank the following statements 1–5 as detailed below:

1 strongly disagree
2 disagree
3 neither agree or disagree, or do not know
4 agree
5 strongly agree

1. The board sets the strategic direction for the charity.
2. The board understands its role and legal duties.
3. The board acts collectively and all trustees participate in its work.
4. Trustee meetings are focused on the board's core roles not operational activities.
5. The trustees meet sufficiently frequently to fulfil their role and duties.
6. There are effective monitoring systems in place for the work delegated by the board.
7. The trustees, collectively and individually, challenge the information presented to the board.
8. The trustees undertake a regular skills audit to identify their collective strengths and highlight gaps in knowledge.
9. The trustees have articulated a clear strategy, vision and mission to the charity's staff, volunteers, beneficiaries and supporters.
10. The charity benchmarks its activities.
11. The charity complies with all appropriate legal and regulatory requirements.
12. What one thing would you introduce to improve the work of the trustees?
13. What issues relating to the charity's activities and governance keep you awake at night?
14. What aspects of the charity's governance are you most assured by or confident in?

What should we evaluate when considering the effectiveness of individual chairs and directors? Leblanc and Lindsay (2010) suggest three criteria:

1 **Fulfilment of their role description** – this will include attendance, meeting preparation and participation, understanding of governance role, committee service, etc.
2 **Contribution of specific skills and diverse outlook** – directors will have been selected strategically based on a current organisational requirement.
3 **Personal attributes** – these will include level of empathy, humility, ability to ask questions and inquire, ability to advocate appropriately, likelihood of derailment, etc.

If the objective of the board evaluation is simply compliance, then data around only the first of these criteria will be collected. If the focus of the board evaluation is more around strategy, talent or diversity, the second criterion is more important. However, if the focus of evaluation is more about board dynamics and board performance, then the third criterion will also become vital to assess. We have discussed all of these in Chapter 3.

If we take a systems perspective in board evaluation, there is perhaps less importance placed on individual evaluation but more on evaluating the board as a whole and also including as much key stakeholder feedback in the process as possible, as we shall now discuss.

Who will be asked to evaluate?

The vast majority of board and director evaluations ask the board themselves as the sole sources of information. However, there are a number of other groups external to the board that may be rich sources of feedback. Who is asked must be driven by the evaluation objectives; for example, if the evaluation is based upon building internal and external reputation, then management or outside parties such as major customers may be asked to provide feedback. It will also be important to keep in mind the potential drawbacks of asking specific groups for information – for example, external experts may provide useful benchmarking or best practice insights, but may not understand company context fully.

Therefore, spending some time outlining key stakeholder groups (perhaps using stakeholder mapping techniques) and aligning to the evaluation objectives may be useful activities in developing an appropriate board evaluation process.

What techniques will be used?

There are a variety of quantitative and qualitative board evaluation techniques that differ in their rigour and the rationale for using them. These include:

- informal open discussions or structured self-evaluation groups;
- benchmarking against recognised practices and codes of governance;
- standardised evaluation schemes or questionnaires; and
- participant observation and analysis.

While standard benchmarking questionnaires tend to focus on assessing structural elements of board governance, more invasive but effective participant observation techniques (often coupled with document analysis and facilitated by external independent evaluators) can reveal the board dynamics through analysis of what actually occurs, rather than what directors think or say occurs. In practice, most boards will explore a range of techniques to uncover different performance issues and to keep the evaluation process fresh and interesting.

Case study: Guidance on reviewing charity governance continued
The Charity Commission/The Chartered Governance Institute charity review includes a 'checklist of information to be provided by the charity to the reviewer' document.

This checklist provides an example of the type of document analysis that may be done as part of a board evaluation. The list is shown in Figure 15.

Who will facilitate the evaluation?

Evaluation is most often undertaken internally as a self-evaluation. As we mentioned at the start of the chapter, the Corporate Secretaries International Association report 'Global board evaluation practices and trends', published in March 2018, reported that board evaluations in their global sample were done internally 84% of the time. These evaluations can be undertaken by a variety of stakeholders:

- The senior independent director and/or chair of the board and/or company secretary could evaluate the board as a whole, board committees and/or individual directors.
- The nominating committee (or, alternatively, independent directors) could evaluate the board as a whole, other board committees and/or directors (as in many banks, e.g. Goldman Sachs, Merrill Lynch, UBS, Deutsche Bank, HSBC, Barclays, London Stock Exchange, ABM AMRO, ING Group, Credit Suisse Group and Citigroup).

Directors could evaluate themselves (and each other by peer review) and/or the board as a whole.

Board members could also utilise the tools and systems used by the wider organisation when undertaking employee evaluations: this has the added advantage of having a single consistent approach. This can be particularly beneficial when aligning director roles, responsibilities and deliverables to the workforce.

Although these may be based on in-depth contextual knowledge and are usually low cost, they are also potentially subjective and self-serving. Two key problems with internal assessments are transparency and capability. As the board decides on the evaluation process, evaluates its own members and prepares the

Figure 15 An example of document analysis – 'Checklist of information to be provided by the charity to the reviewer' (Charity Commission/The Chartered Governance Institute)

Suggested documents to be reviewed:

- names and roles of the people who will be attending the review meeting;
- copies of the completed trustee questionnaire;
- an up-to-date copy of the charity's governing document, along with any bye-laws, rules or standing orders;
- any non-statutory or 'glossy' annual report you may have available for the most recent year;
- governance policies, e.g. code of conduct;
- an organisation chart for your charity;
- minutes covering the last two financial years or as many as possible if less than that;
- minutes of the last two general meetings (if held);
- details of any quality system used;
- a completed Internal Financial Controls (CC8) checklist: (www.charitycommission.gov.uk/publications/cc8.aspx);
- documentation showing implementation of the policies and procedures you covered in the CC8 checklist;
- a copy of any key planning documents, such as business or strategic plans;
- a list of committees and their terms of reference;
- copies of any auditors' management letters issued in the last two years, if available;
- details of any significant events in the life of your charity in recent years, including:
  - a significant increase or decrease in activities, income or expenditure;
  - a change in the senior management of the charity;
  - a restructuring of the charity and its operations; and
  - examples of serious challenges for the administration of the charity tackled by the trustees.

final report on its own performance, such involvement may be perceived as a lack of transparency. Board evaluation is also difficult to conduct and directors may lack competency in, and time for, appropriate execution. In this case, appointing an independent external evaluator may ensure greater objectivity.

There are two approaches to the role of external board evaluator. One is the facilitation role of a trusted adviser (perhaps someone who the board potentially already knows, such as the firm's legal counsel, auditor or executive search firm) who provides the board with evidence and information with which to judge itself more objectively. The other approach is to appoint an expert specialist consultant who is more independent and technically skilled and who actively appraises the board according to competencies determined between the consultant and the board (or board's representative).

The choice of who undertakes the board evaluation will be based on a combination of the factors listed above and will, again, need to align with the evaluation objectives.

What will you do with the results?

What is reported and to whom will also depend upon the reasons driving the evaluation in the first place. If increasing board effectiveness is the original rationale, then findings may be shared first with the chair and then the board as a whole for subsequent discussion, with personal feedback being discussed in one-to-ones with individual board members.

However, if accountability, reputation management and organisational transparency are the main reasons for the evaluation, then information may also be shared with external stakeholders, such as shareholders. Disclosure is a sensitive aspect of board evaluation, so an appropriate balance between company fears and shareholder requests needs to be struck. In addition to these considerations, evaluation results are also increasingly required to be included in company annual reports. For example, Principle J of the 2018 UK Code recommends that:

> The annual report should describe... how the board evaluation has been conducted, the nature and extent of an external evaluator's contact with the board and individual directors, the outcomes and actions taken, and how it has or will influence board composition.

One powerful technique, if individual evaluations have been undertaken, is for the board to have a facilitated discussion about their own feedback. This can have a tremendous impact on board cohesiveness and trust, as well as awareness of individual differences. Again, this needs sensitive handling and will most likely require the chair to go first as a role model. This process can also be paralleled with the chairs of committee coming together to share peer feedback to understand better what effective chairship might look like. Most behavioural and personality type tests can also provide collective feedback for the team as a whole. These can provide insights into fellow personalities and preferences, particularly in terms of communication and interaction. If board members are receptive to this it can be invaluable in understanding why discussions may fail to gain traction with all participants, as well as how different communication techniques between individuals may have different outcomes.

Beyond sharing, any under-performance might be dealt with through developmental plans including mentoring or coaching. Supporting a director in relieving themselves of some of their responsibilities or taking a leave of absence may also be short-term practical options. An under-performing chair, due to psychological bias known as the 'fundamental attribution error' discussed in Chapter 6, may not fully acknowledge any particularly critical feedback. This may be a very difficult situation to handle, but it is one where a trusted adviser – such as the company secretary – in association with the senior independent director and perhaps the chair of the governance or nominations committees, may confront the chair with specific mention to their role terms of reference.

The main thrust of this section is that board evaluations seek to identify poor performance or lack of fit in any one director. When embraced positively, they can also increase effective interaction between the existing members and identify areas where the board composition may benefit from additional members. In the majority of cases, board appointments at their outset introduce additional knowledge, expertise, diversity and contribution to the board. Over time, this difference may not be as obvious both to the individual and their fellow board members. The board evaluation can be an opportunity to reinforce the reasons why each of the directors were appointed and what expertise they bring to discussions. By focusing on these positives, subsequent discussions may encourage greater use of this independent knowledge.

Board evaluation – moving towards best practice

The current state of board evaluation is mixed. Although board evaluation is occurring at a more frequent rate, most probably due to compliance requirements, its quality is in general erring towards poor or formulaic in approach an application.

A number of restraining forces are holding back development, such as a chair's ego and defensiveness, the organisational status quo, time, poor perceptions of board evaluation practice and cost, all of which may currently be stopping boards from undertaking evaluation. However, there are also some driving forces that might be most important in moving board evaluations towards better practice in future. Examples include having an enlightened chair, generational changes (younger generations are more used to giving and receiving feedback as a matter of course at work), having a particular performance issue, evolutions in the governance codes, peer pressure, the emergence of good board evaluation practice and stakeholder pressure. Further, there is certainly a shift in appreciation of the need to include board dynamics factors in board evaluation.

The fact that governance codes are evolving in relation to board evaluation is a good thing. The FRC's Guidance on Board Effectiveness is one particularly useful resource, which, if followed, will help raise standards of practice. The chair's role is obviously vital, as guidance note 116 summarises:

> The chair is responsible for making sure the board gets the most from an externally-facilitated board evaluation and should ensure it is not approached as a compliance exercise.

Furthermore, the Guidance provides a checklist for the chair (or indeed any other individual that may be responsible) such that they are:

> More likely to find the board evaluation process more valuable if:
>
> - its recommendations are constructive, meaningful and forward-looking;
> - there is a clear set of recommendations and actions and a time-period for review of progress against agreed outcomes by the evaluator with the board;
> - it includes views from beyond the boardroom, e.g. shareholders, senior executives who regularly interact with the board, auditors and other advisors and the workforce;
> - it includes peer reviews of directors and the chair plus feedback on each director;
> - good practice observed in other companies is shared;
> - the evaluator observes the interaction between directors and between the chief executive and chair;
> - there is a robust analysis of the quality of information provided to the board;
> - feedback is provided to each individual board member; and
> - the board is challenged on composition, diversity, skills gaps, refreshment and succession.

The 2018 Corporate Secretaries International Association report is also a useful resource to consult to support boards moving towards good practice. The report's five key takeaways are as follows:

1. The governance professional plays a critical role in the board evaluation process, such that they should 'stay abreast of board evaluation best practices'.
2. Use appropriate technology to assist affordability, insight and efficiency through, for example: questionnaire templates; continuity databases to compare year-to-year results; benchmarking data to compare with other boards; digitally secure platforms; database software to track completion and send reminders; automated basic reporting with options to generate visual summaries; and alignment with other technological advances.
3. Ensure the evaluation is concluded with a formal report. Although it was found that this is expected of external facilitation, it was not often true of internally facilitated processes, leading to lack of potential for comparisons and key remedial actions being lost.
4. Take accountability for the co-ordination of remedial actions and continuous performance discussions – as the saying goes, 'Weighing the pig doesn't make it fatter!'
5. Challenge the company to report transparently and openly (in the way that many global codes are now requesting).

A final insightful summary of the state of board evaluation was made by former British politician and Cabinet member, Patricia Hewitt (Senior Independent Director at BT between 2009 and 2014), in a Tomorrow's Corporate Governance report:

> There is not much self-evaluation in government, at least amongst politicians. In my experience, Cabinet and Cabinet sub-committees do not ask themselves 'how are we doing?' or engage in annual evaluations. So, after ten years in government, I was struck by just how much self-evaluation there is already in corporate boardrooms. We all know the importance of critical reflection when it comes to improving performance, whether for individuals or for teams. It is no different for the quality of conversation in the boardroom. Without that critical reflection, boards risk groupthink, blind spots and sub-optimal decision-making. Of course, board chemistry is vital in facilitating a good conversation. Sir David Walker was absolutely right, in his recent review of corporate governance, to highlight board dynamics and group psychology, which are not always given enough weight in board evaluations and follow-up.

Even though the practice of board evaluation does seem to be in its early days, the increasing understanding of its benefits, the key roles that governance professionals play and a board dynamics perspective give hope that we are slowly but surely moving towards better practice.

Conclusion

There is an evolving requirement for board evaluation as part of the evolution of corporate governance codes of practice, specifically in terms of externally facilitated evaluation and increasingly on factors associated with board dynamics.

Board evaluation practice is rapidly developing in terms of what companies are reporting, the development of providers of external expertise, investor interest and reporting on its application. So, what is the current state of board evaluation in the UK? There is an increasing awareness, usage and rigour; however, the area is by no means yet mature, standardised or, indeed, professionalised. More companies are beginning to complete evaluations – both internally and externally driven – a trend that has been catalysed by organisational scandals and governance code requirements. Providers are beginning to meet the demand, but currently follow no externally recognised benchmarks of quality; shareholders and investors are also gaining an interest in the behavioural aspects of boards, which is also driving the trend to more evaluation and more rigour. Current literature on how to conduct a board evaluation suggests that seven key questions should be posed and answered in order to conduct evaluation with rigour.

There are various benefits of board evaluation to the organisation, the board and to individual directors, which include benefits to leadership, role clarity, teamwork, accountability, decision making, communication and board operations. Some of the key decisions to make within the seven main areas of consideration include: whether to deliver the evaluation internally or engage external support; whether to evaluate the board (and/or any board committees) as a whole and/or also to evaluate individual directors; whether solely to ask directors to self-assess or whether to also include stakeholders in providing board feedback; whether simply to evaluate structural board elements or to include behavioural aspects; and whether to communicate results just to the board or to share results with the wider stakeholder community.

Although the current state of board evaluation is mixed, it is evolving towards better practice. An individual's role and the emphasis on board dynamics are two key aspects to consider. Aligned to the contents of other chapters such as those on diversity and board practicalities and the benefits of having an effective means of assessing the board becomes more important. The key is to encourage the use of board evaluation in the same way that individual and team assessments throughout organisations to improve effectiveness have now become commonplace.

A final note taken from The Chartered Governance Institute board evaluation review published in January 2021 the impact of any board performance review depends as much – if not more – on the attitude of the board as it does on the ability of the reviewer. The board appoints the reviewer, sets the terms of the review and decides how to respond to the findings. The role of the external board reviewer is to identify and highlight any issues that the board should consider; the role of the board is to take appropriate action to address them; and the role of shareholders and other stakeholders is to hold the board to account for the effectiveness of those actions.

All of these require a willingness from all concerned in the process to embrace the benefit that a constructive board performance review can provide.

Assuming that you now recognise how beneficial a board evaluation is, what are the key decisions that need to be taken into account when considering how to design and deliver a board evaluation for your organisation?

13 – Cultural differences in boardroom dynamics

The governance professional as cultural diplomat

In today's complex global business environment, we will work with, and be required to influence, peers and stakeholders with different backgrounds, values and assumptions. The board environment, although often censured for its lack of cultural diversity, has shown some evidence of change in recent years. Through the combined forces of media scrutiny, shareholder voice, increasing governance compliance and a greater awareness of the benefits, there is a trend for boards to become more diverse in some areas.

For example (although there is certainly still more work to do), female participation in FTSE 150 boards as of 2018 accounted for 25.5% of directorships, which is up from 10.6% 10 years previously. In contrast, the DiversityQ FTSE100 Board Diversity Report 2020 noted that there is still some way to go when measuring ethnicity, with board composition across this group being only 6% male BAME and 3.8% female BAME. It noted that there are just 99 senior BAME directors at board level, comprising 19 executive directorships and 80 non-executive directorships.

Conversely, the number of 'foreign directors' (defined as those who are not from the nationality of the company country) on FTSE 150 boards is relatively healthy, currently at 32.3% (up 31.8% over the last 10 years). Again, taking a global perspective, this figure is similar to Germany (31%) and Belgium (31.2%), compares favourably to the more inward-looking US (7%) and Italian (9.4%) board averages, but poorly to the Netherlands (57%) and Switzerland (59%).

As we discussed in detail in Chapter 8, which explored diversity in the boardroom and a board's diversity reflecting its stakeholders, we are also fundamentally interested in the connection between culture and performance that a diverse dynamic can bring. A variety of studies, as well as a wealth of anecdotal evidence, suggest that diverse teams tend to perform either better or worse than homogenous ones, with more performing worse than better. However, those multicultural teams that do perform at high levels can have results that exceed even their own expectations. These teams are characterised by acceptance, the nurturing of difference, cohesion and high innovation as they adapt with pace to their changing environment due to their increased information arising from their broader team awareness. The natural question is: how do such high-performing culturally diverse teams achieve their success?

Di Stefano and Maznezski (2000), in their research on global diverse teams, answer that: 'the key to unlocking creative synergy was in the team's interaction processes – how they understood, incorporated, and leveraged their differences'.

This chapter will consider an individual's role as cultural diplomat – a key figure in or alongside the boardroom who can not only mediate the likely conflict that cultural diversity and its associated cognitive conflict can bring, but also enhance the board dynamic by supporting individual directors on the board as a whole to appreciate and leverage their unique strengths and perspectives. This is only possible for an individual if they have an appreciation of what it means to develop cultural awareness and knowledge of how the different varieties of culture, such as organisational, sector and country cultural differences, might play out in the boardroom.

As we discussed in Chapter 6, in relation to stakeholder conversations, to understand and influence board dynamics is to appreciate how the wider system can affect, or be affected by, the board's culture and conversation. Having an appreciation of the systemic lenses, in particular 'lens five' (the stakeholder interfaces) and 'lens six' (the 'wider systemic context' defined by the acronym PESTLE: political, economic, social, technological, legal and environmental) is therefore important to appreciate. These lenses are the arena of cultural intelligence.

As we touched on in relation to board competencies in Chapter 11, the global search firm Egon Zehnder has described the requirement for cultural intelligence and international experience at board level as 'the new must have' (2017). This requirement is also reflected in the The Chartered Governance Institute's 2018 Competency Framework for Governance Professionals, which identifies one of its global areas of essential knowledge as 'strategy and culture'. Within this competency is the core understanding requirement of knowledge in 'the psychology of the organisation, the types of behaviours that may be exhibited and the impact of these behaviours on others' and also 'organisational and especially boardroom dynamics, understanding that different people have different motivations'.

The framework suggests that, once these core understandings have been established, an individual can 'contribute to discussions on strategy, risk and culture internally and amongst professions and peers' and, when they are excelling, a governance professional is able to 'provide effective support for the chair through deep understanding of issues of boardroom dynamics and the interpersonal skills necessary to be the trusted adviser of all in the boardroom'.

Developing both the skill and knowledge as a cultural diplomat is a vital psychological, social and cultural competency through which an individual can influence the board dynamic.

Cultural development

Culture and cultural variety

In Chapter 7, which looked at culture in the boardroom, we introduced the concept of culture by first sharing how it is colloquially defined as 'the way we do things around here'. We then unpacked the concept with greater rigour, following the thinking of Edgar Schein and his model of culture existing on three levels: the surface level of artefacts and etiquette, the middle level of espoused values and the deeper level of basic underlying assumptions. We recognised that culture is defined as both the shared values and beliefs that a group has and also as the consistent patterns of behaviour which these give rise to. This understanding set us up to look at the different ways that specifically board cultural patterns have been conceptualised, how they are shaped and how to influence them.

We also identified the concept of 'cultural variety', which recognises that there are cultures within cultures such that an individual's culture is multifaceted and has several levels. Having touched on the level of social class in Chapter 3, and having explored gender, generational and ethnic cultural differences in detail in Chapter 8 on board diversity, in this chapter we will look at how to conceptualise and influence the further key cultural varieties that influence the board dynamic: company culture, sector culture, vocational culture and country culture. However, before we can build an understanding of these remaining cultural varieties, we must first understand what constitutes the skill of cultural intelligence and how cultural sensitivity is developed.

Stages of cultural development

An excellent starting point to appreciate one's current level of cultural awareness is provided by the developmental model of intercultural sensitivity created by Milton Bennett, an American sociologist. The model also has an associated 60-item test to measure intercultural sensitivity at an individual, group or organisational level. As Bhawuk and Brislin (1992) note:

> To be effective in another culture, people must be interested in other cultures, be sensitive enough to notice cultural differences, and then also be willing to modify their behaviour as an indication of respect for the people of other cultures. A reasonable term that summarises these qualities of people is intercultural sensitivity, and we suggest that it may be a predictor of effectiveness.

The developmental model is based on six core orientations towards cultural differences which represent predictable stages of becoming more interculturally sensitive. Bennett contends that such sensitivity is not necessarily natural (as indicated by the many high-profile cultural clashes at board level and at international level by widespread oppression and conflict) and so this sensitivity must be learned. Thus, there are particular skills required to develop along each aspect of the continuum, which are based on clinical observations of more than 20 years of people making transitions across cultural boundaries. We will comment briefly on each stage in turn.

Stage one – denial

This stage is characterised by an individual not perceiving cultural difference at all or, perceiving it only in broad categories such as 'foreigner' or 'minority' (the well-known Japanese term 'gaijin' or 'alien' is relevant here). A person at this stage may make well-meant but naïve observations and benign stereotypes, as well as superficial statements of tolerance. Behaviour that is perceived as different to one's own culture may be expressed as incompetence and evidence of a deficiency in intelligence or personality. There is a tendency to think that culturally different people are less 'real' and therefore to be disinterested in them at best, or hostile and dismissive of them at worst. People at this stage may say or think something like, 'As long as we all speak the same language there is no problem'. Competencies to develop at this stage might include the ability to gather appropriate information about culture, the initiative to explore subjective culture and the ability to recognise differences, especially in concepts of trust, communication, friendliness and co-operation.

Stage two – defence

In this stage there is a recognition of cultural difference, but also a tendency to polarise it as 'us and them', whereby typically the 'us' is superior and the 'them' is inferior. This stage is characterised by people feeling threatened by cultural difference and so tending to be highly critical and blaming of cultural difference for the general ills of society (think about the politics and public sentiment leading up to Brexit and Donald Trump's election as US president as two good examples). People in this stage may say or think things like, 'I'm making a big effort with them but they are still rude with me, they should make more of an effort' or 'You have to be careful with them as they are deliberately trying to get a better deal at our expense'. Competencies to develop through this stage might include the discipline to maintain personal control, the ability to manage one's own discomfort and anxiety and patience.

Stage three – minimalisation

In this stage, there is the recognition of some superficial differences, such as eating customs (equivalent to the surface level 'artefacts' in Schein's cultural model), while holding a view that all humans are essentially the same. This stressing of a universal cross-cultural similarity reduces one's feeling of defensiveness such that people in this stage are much more tolerant of superficial cultural diversity. However, this stage also obscures deeper cultural differences, which may include the dominant culture's false assumption of equality. In this stage, people might say or think something like, 'When you get to know them, they are just like us' or 'If people are honest, some values are universal and we are all human'. Competencies to develop in this stage may include developing knowledge about intercultural communication processes, remaining open minded, knowing more about one's own culture, developing listening skills and the ability to be non-judgemental in interactions.

Stage four – acceptance

An attitude of cultural acceptance is one when one views one's own culture as just one of a number of equally complex worldviews. The acceptance stage is also characterised by curiosity and being respectful towards cultural difference, albeit without easily adapting behaviour to different cultural context. Typical things people may say or think at this stage include, 'Concepts of good and bad only exist in a cultural context – there are no universals'. Competencies to develop at this stage may include learning culture-specific knowledge, developing the ability to differentiate and create cultural categories, the ability to perceive a wide range of contextual factors, respect for others, values and beliefs, tolerance of uncertainty and ambiguity.

Stage five – adaptation

When one reaches the cultural sensitivity level of adaptation, one is able to develop communication skills and alternative behaviour for the different cultural context. This involves intercultural empathy such that a person can shift perspective to understand and be understood across cultural boundaries. The other person is perceived as equal, but with a different reality. This stage is characterised by generation of authentic behaviour in the alternative culture, which is indicative of intercultural communication competence. Typical things people might say or think at this stage include, 'To solve disputes with my culturally different colleagues, I'm going to have to change my approach' or 'I communicate with people from my culture and people from their culture differently to take into consideration the difference in the way we each show respect'. Competencies to develop at this stage include empathy, risk-taking skills, problem-solving skills and flexibility in social and communication style.

Stage six – integration

This stage is characterised by the internalisation of bi-cultural or multicultural perspectives. One would be able to conduct sophisticated cross-cultural mediation and be seen as a dynamic 'in-between', moving in and out of different cultures. Typical things people might say or think at this stage are, 'I truly enjoy participating fully in both of my cultures and feel at home in both' or 'Working with them has helped me significantly improve my decision-making ability so that I now have multiple ways of seeing the same issue'. Competencies to develop at this stage include a culturally sensitive sense of humour, the ability to take on leadership roles and the ability to switch identity according to cultural context.

The first three stages of the developmental model – denial, defence and minimisation – comprise the 'ethnocentric' phases of the model. Ethnocentrism is defined as the 'act of judging another culture based on preconceptions that are found in values and standards of one's own culture'.

One general point of reflection is that this text and even this chapter on cultural differences is itself bound by assumptions of a mainly English-speaking, UK-based and psychologically orientated cultural system and value set. Therefore, it is important to appreciate that what is considered best practice and thought leading here may be very different to what other cultural approaches to board dynamics may believe.

The final three phases of the model – acceptance, adaptation and integration – comprise the 'ethnorelative' phases: that is, they perceive other cultures as separate and valid alternatives that are no better and no worse than one's own. This echoes the definition we presented of diversity at the start of Chapter 8, which is the concept of valuing everyone as individuals. As the phase of acceptance is the entry point into ethnorelativism and includes the recommendation to develop culture-specific knowledge, I would assume that those of you who are reading this chapter are at least at that stage, having had enough interest in developing your cultural sensitivity to get to this point. However, it takes diligence to progress from acceptance to adaptation, or even integration, as we are evolutionarily hard-wired to seek out similarity rather than difference. Our social networks, for example, by their very nature create similarity as this is what develops stronger connections – a principle of network theory called 'homophily' which often results in the homogenous board diversity that is present in the absence of conscious effort to maintain broader searches in board talent management. The governance professional, board support or company secretary can be a useful board conscience and monitor of the levels of ethnocentrism that might naturally creep back into a board's talent management approach if diversity is seen as a pet project rather than integrated into the core values of board function.

Cultural intelligence

Cultural intelligence (CQ) builds on the concept of emotional intelligence, while incorporating the capability to interact effectively across cultures. It was introduced as a concept in the early 2000s, has been applied to both business and military settings, and is measurable using academically validated assessments which have consistently been shown to demonstrate that CQ is an accurate predictor of performance in multicultural settings. In governmental negotiation and diplomacy settings, it has been associated with the concept of soft power that we introduced in Chapter 10.

In their influential *Harvard Business Review* article (2004), Earley and Mosakowski observed that an individual with high emotional intelligence grasps what makes us human and at the same time what makes each of us different from one another. An individual with high cultural intelligence can somehow tease out of other persons' or groups' behaviours those features that would be true of all people and all groups, those particular to this person or this group, and those that are neither universal nor idiosyncratic. Therefore, they define cultural intelligence as 'an outsider's seemingly natural ability to interpret someone's unfamiliar and ambiguous gestures the way that person's compatriots would'.

They go on to propose that cultural intelligence can be developed in three ways. This is done firstly through improving one's cognitive CQ, which is knowledge about cultures, including facts and cultural traits. Secondly, one can develop physical CQ, which is specific skills to manage oneself and one's social interactions. Thirdly, one can develop one's emotional or motivational CQ, which includes the awareness one has of oneself and others.

Earley and Mosakowski created a simplified questionnaire to assist individuals in diagnosing their cultural intelligence in relation to these three different CQ facets. The questions, and how to rate oneself, are as follows:

Rate the extent to which you agree with each statement. (1 = strongly disagree, 2 = disagree, 3 = neutral, 4 = agree, 5 = strongly agree)

Cognitive CQ

- Before I interact with people from a new culture, I asked myself what I hope to achieve.
- If I encounter something unexpected while working in a new culture, I use this experience to figure out new ways to approach other cultures in the future.
- I plan how I'm going to relate to people from a different culture before I meet them.
- When I come into a new cultural situation, I can immediately sense whether something is going well or something is going wrong.

Physical CQ

- It's easy for me to change my body language (for example, eye contact or posture) to suit people from a different culture.
- I can alter my expression when a cultural encounter requires it.
- I modify my speech style (for example, accent or tone) to suit people from a different culture.
- I easily change the way I act when a cross-cultural encounter seems to require it.

Emotional/motivational CQ

- I have confidence that I can deal well with people from a different culture.
- I am certain that I can befriend people whose cultural backgrounds are different from mine.
- I can adapt to the lifestyle of a different culture with relative ease.
- I am confident that I can deal with a cultural situation that is unfamiliar.

Earley and Mosakowski's research indicates that an average of less than three for each facet suggests an area calling for improvement, while an average of greater than 4.5 reflects a true cultural intelligence strength.

Multicultural teams

Thus far in this section we have considered intercultural sensitivity and cultural intelligence from a one-to-one interpersonal standpoint. Research from Jeanne Brett, a professor of dispute resolution and organisations at Northwestern University's Kellogg School of Management et al. (2006) considers how to manage multicultural teams whose members come from different nations and backgrounds and thus have the potential for conflict. It highlights a variety of multicultural team challenges, such as including differences in communication style (direct Western styles versus indirect non-Western – such as Japanese – communication styles), trouble with accents and fluency, differing attitudes towards hierarchy and authority and conflicting norms for decision making. They articulate four strategies that the most successful teams and leaders they interviewed used for dealing with these challenges. These are:

- **adaptation** – acknowledging cultural gaps openly and working around them;
- **structural intervention** – changing the shape of the team;
- **managerial intervention** – setting norms early or bringing in a higher-level manager; and
- **exit** – removing a team member when other options have failed.

They note that adaptation is the ideal strategy as this enables the team to solve its own problem with minimal outside input and therefore also learn from the experience for the benefit of future team performance. For the adaptation strategy to work, team members must be exceptionally aware and also willing to invest time to negotiate a common understanding.

Having now developed some appreciation for what the research and evidence base suggests are the required skills to become culturally sensitive and intelligent as an individual and in support of multicultural teams, we will now provide some knowledge to conceptualise the remaining cultural varieties that a cultural diplomat may require, beginning with company culture.

Company culture

We have defined culture more generally but not yet company culture more specifically. One definition that has been used in the governance literature is from the King IV Report on Corporate Governance for South Africa (2016), which includes the Hofstede Centre (2016) definition of company culture as:

> The way in which members of an organisation relate to each other, their work and the outside world in comparison to other organisations.

Corporate culture has also been defined more prosaically by Kevin Craine in 'Corporate culture and document design strategy' as:

> Providing the human glue that can rally the collective energy of your company towards improvements and accomplishments, or it can be the glue that fastens your organisation to the way things have always been.

Deal and Kennedy's model of corporate culture (1982) provided an early conceptualisation of the components and types of culture that exist in organisations. (We are using the terms company, organisational and corporate culture here interchangeably, only using the term corporate culture as this is the term used by the Deal and Kennedy model.) Their model incorporates five elements as follows:

1 **The business environment** – these are the PESTLE elements that we have described previously, around which an organisation will orientate. They may influence specific cultural cycles, for example, in terms of technology change or customer demand.
2 **Values** – these are at the heart of corporate culture. Successful companies are most clear about these so that senior leaders and managers can publicly reinforce them.
3 **Heroes** – these are the personifications of an organisation's values, the role models against which employees can compare the behaviours. Heroes are like the visionary leaders in Kotter's leadership framework, such as figureheads like Richard Branson, whose purpose is to symbolise the company to the outside world.
4 **Rites and rituals** – these are the ceremonies and routine behaviours that reinforce the culture such as the common initiations for new employees or the traditional annual retreat.
5 **The cultural network** – this is the rumour mill that exists in an organisation, the informal coalitions and gossip that exist to spread information about values, behaviours and heroic myths.

Deal and Kennedy's second main contribution to our conceptualisation of corporate culture is in their framework that identifies four types of corporate culture that the above five elements support. These four types are created by the combination of two key dimensions, the risk attached to the company's activities and the speed of feedback to employees. This creates the following four organisational types:

- **The 'tough guy' culture** – this is characterised by high risk and quick feedback and is entrepreneurial and individualistic. Companies with this culture follow a cycle of boom and bust and are opportunistic.
- **The 'work hard, play hard' culture** – this is characterised by low risk but quick feedback on success. This culture is where an individual works alone, but has a supportive team – such as a high-volume sales company.

- **The 'bet-your-company' culture** – this is found in high-risk, long-term industries such as oil and aerospace businesses, which require significant technical expertise.
- **The 'process' culture** – this is characterised by low risk and low feedback. It typifies the public sector and traditional retail banks which prioritise status and the conduct of work.

Both Deal and Kennedy's five cultural elements and their four cultural types provide an individual with some sense of what it feels like within different organisations. For example, a culturally sensitive and intelligent individual will recognise the culture shock that may be felt when entering a new organisational culture. The 2018 Chartered Governance Institute report entitled 'Organisational culture in sport: assessing and improving attitudes and behaviour' considers the current cultures of international and domestic national governing bodies of sport and provides guidance on better appreciating and influencing a positive culture. The report advises that there are a number of places to look for evidence of an organisation's culture, which include:

- measures of organisational success against declared objectives;
- policy documents, risk registers and board minutes;
- staff turnover, planned and unplanned;
- board turnover and succession planning;
- board attendance and activity;
- board evaluation reports and governance reviews;
- regulatory involvement;
- audit reports, letters and annual returns;
- staff surveys and exit interviews;
- stakeholder surveys, particularly if benchmarked over time;
- impact assessments;
- results of whistleblowing and complaints processes; and
- the organisation's cultural reporting.

Based on our broad understanding of culture from Edgar Schein, this evidence list seems quite formal and perhaps represents either artefacts or documents which might reveal the espoused values of the culture, rather than indicating what the deeper embedded culture actually is within an organisation. Following Deal and Kennedy's model, therefore, it may also be useful, in addition to these more formal artefacts, to tap into the informal aspects of the culture through an exploration of the organisation's metaphors and stories. One method of doing this is to create focus groups and workshops to record employees' answers to some of the following questions.

Imagine that your organisation is an organised religion:

- List five core beliefs and give examples of each.
- What's the worst sin someone can commit? What's the punishment for committing it?

- Who is the most spiritually advanced leader in your organisation and why? What sermon does he or she preach?
- What parable is repeated most often from the organisational 'bible' (e.g. told over lunch in the restaurant, at the coffee machine or in the pub)?
- What types of activities are most like rituals? What do they say about what is important in this religion?

Mergers and acquisitions

The culture of an organisation becomes central when two companies are merged, or an acquisition takes place. Different sectors have different cultures, for example media versus accounting. Unless the strategy is to diversify into another sector, most organisational mergers take place in the same sector. However, this does not automatically ensure that it is a merger of two similar cultures. The history of the organisations, the individual leaders and the culture percolating down from the board will have set the tone for the organisational culture. Often the organisation that is acquiring is more dynamic and driven than the company they are acquiring. In contrast, an organisation that has been acquired may have lost its way and plateaued in its growth and, as a result, have a culture that reflects this more static state.

On average, 70% of mergers fail and of these, approximately 30% fail as a direct result of a lack of cultural integration. Culture is one of the areas with least focus before, during and after a merger and, even where the cultures seem to be similar, the differences are often too great to overcome. This may be due to a difference at leadership level, but may equally be throughout the two organisations.

Culture in mergers may affect the new combined organisation in a number of ways, including:

- **Decision making:** different styles of decision making, such as dictatorial versus consensus, may delay or derail significant decisions at a time when rapid decisions are needed, for example, the appointment of leaders across the combined company.
- **Leadership style:** employees may not want to remain in a company with a changed style, particularly those in senior positions where they are closest to the leaders.
- **Strategic focus:** particularly where an organisation may see the merger as the solution, the combination of two divergent leadership teams may result in 'strategic lethargy' – an inability to capitalise on the benefits of the combined organisation, or an unwillingness to implement new strategies.
- **Ability to change:** a static organisational style may not be able to change quickly enough to embed the benefits of the merger.
- **Internal communication:** styles of communication between functions and teams may need to be rebuilt based on a new combined culture. For example,

one culture may prefer face-to-face whilst the other may prefer written communication. While those preferring written communication may seek to have an audit trail, those preferring verbal communication may see this as a sign of lacking trust.

- **Defining success:** recognition of personal success may be different and changes may not be welcomed, for example, being team-focused versus individual-focused or monetary drivers versus career promotion.

A global organisation working across countries may already work in a way that embraces the benefits of multiculturalism. However, where they are strategically acquiring to expand into a new country, the acquired organisation may not be culturally aware in the same way and may struggle to become part of a country-diverse organisation. Sending leaders from the global organisation into the newly acquired local company may be embraced by the local leadership team but may have a negative effect further down the organisation. This may impact on the success of the integration, the profitability of the acquired company and the strategic benefit of the international expansion.

Case study: Daimler Benz and Chrysler's culture clash

In 1998, Daimler Benz, the German car company, purchased the US company, Chrysler, for $36 billion. Daimler Benz had succeeded by responding to an affluent market and catered to the elite class. However, the US market opportunity was more geared to competing solely on price. The cultural differences of the two markets to which the companies catered, in addition to the differing country cultures, proved a difficult divide to bridge. Working together was extremely difficult for the two brands. Co-ordination, trust and teamwork was heavily lacking and the union failed as a result. In 2007, Daimler Benz sold Chrysler to Cerberus Capital Management for $650 million. Clearly, when two companies are so diverse, from language to market and beyond, one needs to more carefully consider the implications – the 'cultural due diligence' – before signing on the dotted line.

Sector culture

Organisations working in different sectors may experience common patterns that are very different from those in other sectors. The competing values framework created by Cameron and Quinn (2006) (see Figure 17) is extremely useful in providing an insight into how particular underlying values of organisations combined to create a sector culture dynamic (rhe competing values framework is actually an excellent model that can be used as a template for organisational culture too, but we will apply it to sector culture differences for our purposes).

Figure 17 The Competing Values framework (Cameron and Quinn, 2006)

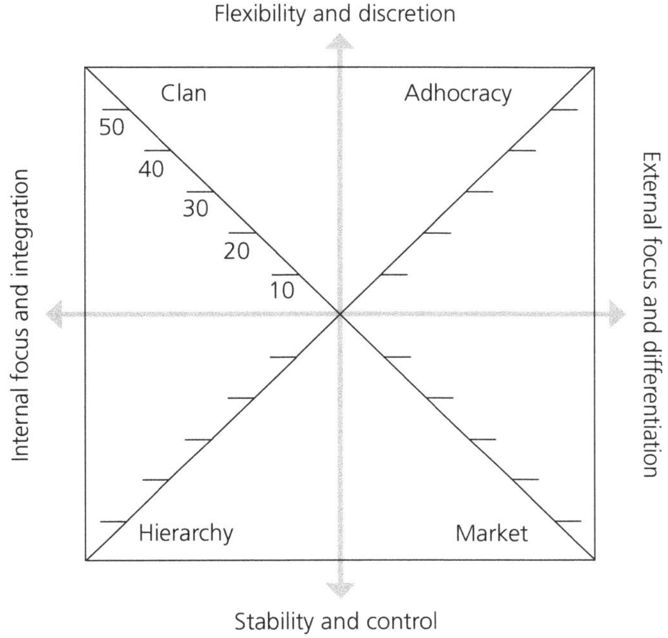

The framework is a four-box model which is defined by two axes. The horizontal axis delineates whether an organisation has more of an internal focus or an external focus and the vertical axis splits into those who focus more on stability and control of their current situation versus organisations who focus more on flexibility and discretion and are therefore more future focused. The combination of these axes creates four competing quadrants as follows:

- **Hierarchy culture – internal/current:** This culture is very formalised structured and focuses on efficiency at low cost. Success in this culture is about high standards, risk awareness, efficient structure and compliance. An excess of this culture, however, can lead to perfectionism, risk aversion, being procedurally rigid and excessively bureaucratic.
- **Clan culture – internal/future:** This culture feels like a friendly place to work where people share personal details. Commitment is high and there is a concern for customers and people. The organisation places a premium on teamwork, participation and consensus. Success in this culture is defined by feeling committed, collaborative, talent-focused and well-being orientated. However, an excess of this culture leads to a lack of challenge, groupthink, non-value adding development and a feeling of excessive cosiness.

- **Adhocracy culture – external/future:** In direct tension with the hierarchy quadrant, this culture is dynamic, entrepreneurial and a creative place to work, where people are prepared to take risks. Growth is about gaining unique and new products and services. The organisation encourages individual intuition and freedom. Success in this culture is about being growth-orientated, leading-edge, responsive and innovative. However, an excess of this culture can lead to being unfocused, excessive risky behaviours and feeling chaotic.
- **Market culture – external/current:** In direct tension with the clan culture, this culture is results-orientated and the major concern is about getting the job done. People are competitive and goal-focused and there is an emphasis on winning. The culture values sales and market share as well as status and reputation. Success is defined as achieving, being task-focused, having goal clarity and feeling high energy. An excess of this culture can lead to burnout, being obsessed with the numbers and being destructively competitive.

Using the competing values framework, we might naturally notice that particular sectors are more likely to be associated with one of the four quadrants cultures. Therefore, some of the sector culture differences using the framework, and what this might look like in terms of the board dynamic, are as follows:

- **Listed companies:** Due to the short-term quarterly shareholder reporting requirements, these organisations will often fit into the Market quadrant. Examples of market culture sectors include retail, corporate finance and FMCG. These sectors are increasingly being bound by compliance necessities, but are more likely to attract status-driven derailing personality types. They are usually under more media scrutiny and can include directors with other board commitments due to the core value of status in this type of culture. This leads to more sector stress and burnout, less of a focus on teamwork and more challenging and directive leadership styles. However, as there is a requirement for practices such as evaluation in listed companies, there may be opportunities to engage the cultures in these sectors in more reflective and developmental practices. For those that do take this opportunity, there is the potential for significant benefit.
- **Privately owned companies, SMEs, start-ups:** These types of more entrepreneurial sectors are more likely to fit into the Adhocracy culture defined by the competing values framework. Boards will be smaller and more comprised of executives rather than non-executive directors. The chair and the chief executive officer may be the same person and there is potentially not yet any formal company secretary position. The board may be unintentionally built more around fostering the owner/founder's ego rather than challenging thinking. Although the culture may fight against it, there would be great value in including some level of process in this organisational culture and board.

- **Public sector, formerly public-owned companies, utility, logistics organisations:** These naturally fall into the Hierarchy culture with their emphasis on efficiency and internal accountability. The boards of these organisations will typically be larger representative boards, which may mean that directors act more as individual experts and so always caveat opinions in line with their political representation, which can stifle debate. Furthermore, the focus on more process and being less risk-averse means that it is often difficult to challenge.
- **Charity sector:** This sector often falls into the Clan culture on the competing values framework. As charity work may often be unpaid or lower paid, the emphasis is more on a values-based commitment, which may come from a strong sense of belonging and association with a greater cause.

Case study: easyJet's business culture shift

The airline easyJet was founded in March 1995 by Stelios Haji-Ioannou. It has gone from being a start-up with just two planes through to profitability and successful flotation within a five-year timeframe. It is now a large organisation with a turnover in excess of £1 billion. In essence, it has shifted its culture from being a start-up adhocracy to one that is now a combination of a low-cost sales-based market culture serving customers day-to-day and a hierarchy culture which logistically ensures airline safety and efficient operations. As Haji-Ioannou stated in 2005:

> I think the only way to start a company is with a very strong entrepreneurial culture, usually led by a single individual. But very few people of that nature make it all the way through to leading a major plc. I think there needs to be a change at some stage, with more process-oriented professional managers coming in to strike the balance between risk management and entrepreneurial drive... As the founder, I have stepped aside a bit and allowed professional management to run it on a day-to-day basis, despite the fact that I retain a significant shareholding. Observing this culture change is one of the most amazing transformations to see; some companies do it well, while others do it less well. Some things become easier; others become worse.

One final use of the competing values framework is in how it can raise awareness of vocational culture differences between people who work within the same sector and organisation. One's vocational culture is determined by one's professional career and the values and beliefs that underpin that particular profession. These can often be mapped onto the Competing Values framework. For example, the finance, sales and operations professions fall naturally into the Market culture, the human resources function would usually fit in opposition to this as a Clan culture, the marketing function is normally experienced as an Adhocracy culture and a finance function would naturally feel like a Hierarchy culture.

Country culture

Theories of country culture

The final perspective on culture to consider, and the one which most people first think of when we use the word culture, is that of country culture or nationality. This is a significantly researched area with a number of leading authorities including Geert Hofstede, Fons Trompenaars and Charles Hampden-Turner and Edward T. Hall. These researchers have focused on cultural orientations in the form of scales and dimensions to understand cultural differences. These cultural orientations help us think about the degree to which international peers have similar or different values, attitudes and expectations as a group; they also help us to describe these differences and similarities and also to consider how an individual is similar or different to any generalisable country culture. We will now provide a brief overview of each of these leading cultural thinkers' theories, as well as their main dimensions.

Geert Hofstede's cultural dimensions

This is probably the most well-known classification of cultural dimensions and was created through research that Hofstede completed while working internationally with IBM. The original five dimensions are as follows:

- **Power distance** – the extent to which the less powerful members of organisations and institutions (like the family) expect that power is distributed unequally and whether there is a respect for hierarchy versus more equality and flat structures (e.g. Saudi Arabia and India versus Australia and the UK).
- **Individualism** – this is the self-focus of a culture. It is opposed by collectivism, the degree to which individuals are integrated into groups.
- **Masculinity** – masculinity and its opposite, femininity, refer to the distribution of roles between the genders and the cluster of gender characteristics that are valued.
- **Uncertainty avoidance** – this deals with the society's tolerance for ambiguity versus their need for clarity (e.g. Sweden versus Japan).
- **Long-term orientation** – this refers to the value of persistence and ordering relationships by status, as well as the value of thrift and respect for tradition.

Fons Trompenaars and Charles Hampden-Turner cultural dimensions

This framework is also well known and researched and has overlaps with Hofstede. The dimensions they classify to diagnose culture, and the associated question each dimension asks to classify, are as follows:

- **Universalism versus particularism** – what is more important, rules or relationships? (e.g. Canada and the US versus Egypt and Saudi Arabia.)
- **Individualism versus communitarianism** – do we function in a group or as an individual? (e.g. Australia and the US versus Mexico and Pakistan.)

- **Neutral versus effective** – do we display our emotions? (e.g. Japan and the UK versus Italy and Spain.)
- **Specific versus diffuse** – how far do we get involved?
- **Achieved status or ascribed status** – do we have to prove ourselves to receive status or is it given to us?
- **Time orientation** – do we do things one at a time or several things at once?
- **Internal versus external orientation** – do we control our environment or work with it?

Edward T. Hall's cultural dimensions

Hall developed the concept of a high context culture (communication is not always obvious by what is said, e.g. Saudi Arabia, Brazil and India) versus low context culture ('I say what I mean and I mean what I say', e.g. Germany and America) between implicit and external communication styles. He also coined the term 'polychronic' to describe the ability to attend to multiple events simultaneously, as opposed to 'monochronic' individuals and cultures who tend to handle events sequentially (e.g. Italy versus Germany).

Implicit in the idea of cultural orientations is the idea of 'tendencies and marginality'. This is a critical concept, as we are always dealing with individuals: although they may be typical in some basic beliefs and orientations, they are unlikely to fully reflect the average. Further, we need to understand the extent to which our own values conform to the tendencies in a home culture and how the tendencies in other cultures are a valid alternative to our own culture's approach to similar problems and issues. It is important to recognise that our own comfort or tolerance levels will be tested the more distant another person is from our own orientation.

Country culture differences in the boardroom

It is useful to look at specific examples to bring the above frameworks to life and create actionable insight for those wanting to apply the theory.

One useful action is to look online for the country culture norm data that is produced around cultural dimensions. For example, Hofstede has norms for most countries in the world on the dimensions. If we take the UK as an example, we see that, through Hofstader's lens, the top three orientations are individualism, masculinity and indulgence. In terms of individualism, the UK records a score of 89 and is among one of the highest scores globally, beaten only by some of the countries it spawned (including Australia and the US). This accounts for the stereotype of the British person being private and 'strong enough' to think for themselves, that is, the 'stiff upper lip'. The high masculinity score also indicates that the UK is a society driven by competition, achievement and success as compared to a more feminine society which values quality of life as a sign of success (for example, Scandinavian countries). At the other end of the spectrum, Britain has one of the lowest rankings for its power-distance orientation, which is an indicator of a society that believes that inequalities among people should be minimised. This is the British sense of fair play, which drives the belief that people should be treated in some way as equals.

Another interesting example of how the cultural dimensions play out in relation to some of the themes associated with board dynamics is Japan as regards to leadership style and feedback. According to Hofstede's database, Japan ranks number one of 53 national cultures on the uncertainty avoidance orientation, such that it is a culture which has an extremely low tolerance for ambiguity. How this plays out in terms of leadership characteristics can be seen in the results of a study that asked leaders from different cultures to say to what extent their leaders and managers need to be experts or should delegate thinking and decisions. Unsurprisingly, Japanese managers ranked being expert the highest out of all nation states, at around 80% agreement that a manager should be completely knowledgeable. This is not surprising, as one way to avoid uncertainty is to try to be an expert in all aspects of the work of one's team. The coaching approach to leadership discussed in Chapter 10, and explored in more detail in Chapter 14, is a much more difficult behaviour for a Japanese leader to grasp and to feel comfortable in enacting. Similarly, this has implications to how one might provide or receive feedback. As the Japanese are a highly collectivistic culture, conflict is avoided for the sake of social harmony. Therefore, a request for direct feedback may be seen as shocking or even offensive.

One final example of how cultural difference might play out in the boardroom is around the issue of punctuality. It is incredible to notice the amount of variability and nuance between country cultures, which if unappreciated and not accounted for, has the potential to create significant intercultural team conflict. Based on their cultural orientations, here are a number of illustrative differences between country cultures in relation to punctuality (sourced from mrgamez.com):

- South Korea – a lot of value is placed on punctuality and being late is a sign of disrespect.
- Malaysia – saying you will be five minutes late usually means an hour and being late is an accepted norm that does not require an apology.
- China – it is not considered late if you arrive within 10 minutes of the agreed time.
- Japan – if a train arrives more than one minute after it is scheduled, it is considered late.
- Mexico – it is not uncommon for people to turn up half an hour late for a scheduled meeting.
- Germany – in Germany, you are expected to arrive at least 10 minutes early for any scheduled meeting.
- Nigeria – if a meeting is scheduled at 1pm, that means the meeting will start any time between 1pm and 2pm.

- Brazil – when making a social appointment, you are not required to be there on time. Unless the phrase 'English time' is used, which means you have to be punctual.
- Ghana – most meeting times are considered to be flexible, even if an exact time is given. It can very often mean at any point during the day.
- Greece – punctuality is not considered that important, but foreigners are still expected to turn up on time for meetings. Socially, you should be at least 30 minutes late.
- Russia – patience is considered a very important quality in Russian culture, but punctuality is not. As a foreigner, you are expected to be on time, but do not expect the same, or an apology, from your Russian counterpart.

As we noted in Chapter 9, in relation to meeting design characteristics, being punctual with start and end times created better perceptions of meeting value. However, this was likely to be culturally based research. Spending time discussing process and ground-rule behaviours, such as being explicit and contracting around simple things such as timing expectations, is vital – rather than simply cracking on with the task of the agenda and hoping that everyone is on the same cultural page.

Case study: Quite the language barrier

The former Chair of the *Financial Times* and former Director for People at Pearson plc, Sir David Bell, has worked in many international business environments and has a number of stories to tell about cultural differences. One of his stories shows that the impact of just one word can be incredibly significant, even for those who speak the same language. As Bell recounts,

> Years ago, the American man who was then running our education business came to England to talk to some of his people. They had done some work for him and he said to them, 'I think that was really quite a good piece of work'. Afterwards, he said to me, 'David, I told them I thought it was quite a good piece of work and they all looked really depressed'. I said, 'That, Larry, is because the word "quite" means one thing in English-English and a different thing in American-English. In American-English, if you say "quite good" it means "very good". In English-English, it means "awful"'... The bigger and more international you are as a business, the more you have to be thinking all the time: how are we going to make people from very different cultures understand that they're all part of the same company? That is a real challenge.

With this appreciation of country culture difference and how to classify them, as well as similar knowledge about organisational, sector and vocational culture dimensions, an individual can become more culturally attuned to the subtle cultural dynamics that may be playing out between individual board members and with the board culture as a whole. This will enhance their invisible leadership 'smart power' influence and also their potency as 'team coach' – a role that we shall explore in more detail in the next chapter.

Conclusion

In a progressively diverse organisational and board environment, an individual with board influence increasingly needs to play the role of cultural diplomat to mediate potential conflict and facilitate effective board function. In order to do this, both cultural sensitivity and cultural intelligence are required, though not necessarily in equal measure, and they can both be developed and improved over time.

Knowing and understanding the culture of an organisation, both through its current state and the organisation's history that has developed it, is invaluable when looking at the effectiveness of both the organisation and the board. Company culture can be described using Deal and Kennedy's five cultural elements and their four cultural types, which highlight tensions between organisational risk-taking and speed of feedback. Sector and vocational culture can be diagnosed using the Competing Values framework, through its values tensions of internal versus external focus and current versus future focus. Country culture can be understood through the lenses of various bipolar cultural dimensions which, when combined, illuminate the reasons why different cultures behave as they do.

What are the country and organisational culture differences of which individuals need to be aware? The area of cultural difference in the boardroom can be bewildering to the uninitiated. However, to help make sense of behaviours different to one's own, country culture can be understood through a number of general dimensions. For example, Hofstede identifies differences in terms of power distance, individualism, masculinity, uncertainty avoidance and long-term orientation. Similarly, organisational or sector cultural differences can be understood through the competing values of short-term versus long-term focus and internal versus external focus. Armed with these frameworks, one is more able to accept, adapt and integrate cultural differences in order to become more culturally sensitive and build culturally intelligence.

Alongside digital abilities, international experience is a frequent requirement for new board members of large companies. The reflection of this to board composition and cultural awareness is clear. However, there is no advantage in appointing a single individual to the board – board diversity – if the culture of inclusion to enhance the board conversation is not present. As has been shown, cultural awareness has many layers that need to be reflected in an effective board. An individual within or alongside the board can either openly or informally ensure that these differences are embraced to the benefit of the collective board and the organisation as a whole.

Do you have a culturally diverse board? If so, is this cultural difference consciously recognised? If not, are you aiming to have one in the near future, or considering how a culturally diverse board could be beneficially implemented?

Whatever your stage of cultural diversity at board level, how can cultural differences across all their forms be embraced for the benefit of your organisation as a whole?

14 – Developing behavioural agility

The internal board team coach

The highly competent twenty-first-century corporate governance professional has the agility to move beyond simply being a technical expert to also embrace the skillsets and mindsets of being a behavioural expert. This is perhaps new ground for many company secretaries to tread. The Chartered Governance Institute's 2014 report entitled 'The company secretary: building trust through governance' – which can equally be applied to other roles aligned to the board beyond the company secretary – reported that:

> Respondents also note a gap between discretionary technical skills, which can be learned, and softer social interactions requiring practice and experience. The latter skills, they feel are currently absent from professional qualifications.

This chapter focuses on some of these 'softer social interactions' and relationship competencies that an internal team coach needs to facilitate – not only tasks, but also the people who are performing those tasks. These skills are generally appreciated as being key requirements of both the board chair and committee chair, as well as the senior independent director as a chair understudy; however, The Chartered Governance Institute report and other recent commentary generally acknowledges that these social skills are also now vital for governance professionals too. In fact, by developing and applying these skills, individuals working close to the board both add greater value to board effectiveness and also enhance their own contribution and career aspirations through being visible, supportive and encouraging.

In a meta-analysis of 50 studies, Burke et al. (2006), found that the impact of team leadership on performance is significant – being up to 31% predictive of performance outcomes. Their research noted that the best team leaders have both a task and person focus. The most effective task behaviour for successful team leaders is something they called 'boundary spanning' with stakeholders, which accounted for 24% of the team effectiveness variance. This boundary-spanning competency is related to how much a leader can connect and relate with stakeholders outside their own team. It is something that more professionals acting alongside leadership teams are being called on to do more of in a modern board environment, rather than be solely inwardly focused on technical matters.

The research found that the highest person priority focus was the behaviour of 'empowerment', which was defined in terms of being effective at coaching, feedback, facilitation and having consultative and participatory styles. This accounted for up to 22% of the team's effectiveness. These studies highlight the need for individuals aligned to leadership, including the company secretary, to be a key invisible leader holding 'power behind the throne', to develop the personal agility to be task and person-focused.

This agility to shift from being a technical content expert to a more behavioural and relational process expert with a person focus is what we are generically defining in this chapter as being a *team coach*. In Chapter 10, we saw that the coaching style has significantly more sustainable positive outcomes than many other more heroic leadership styles, and in Chapter 4, we noted that team coaching was one of the six conditions that senior leaders can put in place to develop great leadership teams.

In their research on global senior leadership teams, Ruth Wageman et al. (2007) found that all teams needed an expert team coach to become high performing, especially when they get stuck and have difficulties in improving their ability to become more effective and make better decisions together. The chair is often the natural holder of the team coach position; however, both coaching and participating in discussions is often difficult to do. Furthermore, the chair also has a dependent performance management responsibility in the boardroom, which can sometimes conflict with effective coaching. Therefore, independent external or semi-external team coaching, such as that provided by the individuals alongside the board, may be important as a support for the chair.

The term 'team coach' is used here to describe the behavioural approach to supporting the board as a team, both as a group of individuals and collectively. This general term is made up of a subset of various roles which the competent professional will also have the agility to shift between. These roles include being an expert one-to-one coach, a board mentor, a systemic team coach, a board facilitator, a governance supervisor, a relationship mediator and even, on occasion, a boardroom counsellor. The following sections will delve into each of these various roles that make up the overall team coach competency – highlighting why they are important, what behaviours and attitudes underpin them and some practical tools for how to apply them. We will give more attention to the mindsets and skillsets of the one-to-one coach, as most of these overlap with all the other team coaching roles. We will also highlight how the other roles are similar or different to coaching and how their boundaries may sometimes overlap, giving rise to potential ethical challenges.

One-to-one coach

The case for coaching

The concept of coaching as one of the pre-eminent leadership styles has gained in prominence in most organisations and sectors over the last few decades. As we saw in Chapter 10, the coaching leadership style, along with the visionary leadership style, significantly outperforms the more neutral and directive styles that have been the standard paradigms of leadership over the last century.

Coaching as an empowering leadership style is backed up by many research studies and practical examples. For example, Lorinkova et al. (2012) performed an experiment with 60 teams, comparing those led by a directive style and those led by a more empowering leadership style. They found that, in the early stages of team performance, the directive style wins out, setting off the blocks at a quicker pace. However, over time, the empowering style begins to catch up and outperform the directive style. As the researchers concluded:

> When teams have an extended timeline or must be able to adapt to complex and changing environments over time, an initial and continuing empowering leadership style may be most appropriate.

It is certainly true that a boardroom context has more extended timelines compared to most other organisational groupings and must be able to adapt to complex and changing environments over time. Therefore, those formal board leadership positions, such as the overall chair and the committee chairs, as well as the more, behind-the-scenes professional individual style of leadership, would be best served in the long run by the empowering leadership style.

When it comes to making the case for coaching from a senior leader testimonial point of view, there is no shortage of high-profile business leaders who sing the praises of being coached. This contention was found to hold true of the company more broadly when Google embarked on some work codenamed 'Project Oxygen' in 2009 to find out what was true of managers of their most successful teams. Based on being in a hi-tech industry, their working hypothesis had always been that the best leaders and managers were those with significant technical expertise. However, after 'Googling' themselves and gathering more than 10,000 observations about managers across more than 100 different variables from performance reviews, feedback surveys and other reports, they found that the most predictive behaviour was actually 'being a good coach'. This was defined as 'providing specific, constructive feedback and balancing the negative and the positive' and 'having regular one-to-ones, presenting solutions to problems tailored to your employees' specific strengths'. Surprisingly, they also found that having technical skills so that you can help advise the team came last in priority of the top eight competencies that they published. Happily, the skill of coaching was also found to be able to be developed such that, the year after the research findings were published, Google was able to show a statistically significant improvement in manager quality for 75% of their worst-performing managers.

The 2014 The Chartered Governance Institute report on the new roles of the company secretary quoted one response on coaching as: 'I coach executives on how to present to the board.' However, when we consider how an individual may apply one-to-one coaching in their role, this statement might be expanded to something like: 'I coach both executive and non-executive directors on how to be effective in their role'. This will often involve the 'quiet word' outside of the boardroom in a less formal environment. It may link to some of the issues discussed in Chapter 11 around talent management, such as supporting a director's development during induction or over the course of their tenure and helping with their performance management and potential succession conversations; it may be useful to help directors with their decision making, especially to check and unpick bias, or to support a director who is struggling to cope and having a dip in their resilience, as we shall discuss further in Chapter 15.

What is coaching?

The origins of coaching as we know it today in organisations are rooted in the humanistic psychology movement emanating from the West Coast of America in the 1970s. Influenced by Carl Rogers' approach to counselling and his emphasis on an unconditional positive regard in therapy, the then-tennis coach, Timothy Gallwey, experimented with various coaching approaches on his clients, described in his seminal book *The Inner Game of Tennis*. Gallwey's insight was that learning, performance and, in fact, the enjoyment of a skill could be accelerated when one helped a coach remove any psychological interferences to their latent potential. In the early 1980s, Gallwey began training people in his questioning techniques and applying his methods to business settings. One of these early adopters was Sir John Whitmore, who is generally recognised as one of the early pioneers of business coaching methods. Whitmore provides a useful definition for coaching: 'unlocking a person's potential to maximise their own performance. It is helping them to learn rather than teaching them'.

The coaching approach has now gained a significant global following and has spawned an industry of evidence-based research. Although there are now various offshoots and styles of coaching itself, there are a number of generally recognised core skills and mindsets that underpin the above definition.

These core coaching skills are:

- building a trusting coaching relationship;
- asking effective questions and listening to/noticing responses;
- supporting effective goal setting; and
- providing effective feedback.

These core skills are underpinned by an attitude known as the 'coaching mindset'. This is rooted in a humanistic psychology approach that fundamentally believes in the positive potential of every individual.

We discussed goal setting and feedback in detail in Chapter 11; however, we will touch on the coaching mindset and building coaching relationships below, as well as outlining good practice options for effective coaching questions.

Coaching mindset

The coaching mindset holds the belief in the potential of the person that we are coaching such that, with appropriate support and challenge, they will be able to find answers within themselves to the questions that they are asking rather than be dependent upon others.

One test to see if one is adopting a coaching mindset in any conversation is to notice the percentage of open questions that one is asking, as these presuppose that someone can offer an answer. Although we may think that we are helping by continuously dispensing directive advice and expertise when people come to us with an issue or dilemma, what we are actually doing is setting ourselves up in an uneven parent–child dynamic, which reinforces a coachee's incompetence, does not build their confidence or belief, does not stimulate deep learning or consequential retention and promotes dependence on the coach to answer any future problems that the individual may have. Although it sometimes feels good for our ego to be needed for our expertise, always being in a directive mindset also means we become a bottleneck, which can significantly slow down organisational decision making.

A belief in someone's potential is similar to the growth mindset that we discussed in Chapter 4 and also relates to the psychological trait of optimism about oneself and others that relates to resilience, as we shall discuss in Chapter 15. A person who holds these mindsets is able to make a distinction between current performance and potential, recognising that one does not predict another and can appreciate that potential is unknown and therefore perhaps quite a significant distance away from current levels of performance.

Case study: The four-minute mile and the power of belief

A classic case that highlights the power that belief has on performance is that of Roger Bannister breaking the four-minute mile. In 1946, the Swedish runner Gunnar Haag had set the world mile record at four minutes and one second, a time that stood for the next nine years. Due to the record's longevity just outside of four minutes, a general consensus emerged that it was not physically possible for the barrier to be broken. For example, in 1953, the *Journal of Exercise Physiology*, one of the pre-eminent evidence-based sports science journals at the time, reported that:

> The human being is incapable of covering a mile distance in less than four minutes. The oxygen-carrying capacity required (within the human skeletal and muscular setup) is simply not possible.

Similarly, the running community had also developed a fixed mindset about the body's capacity to break the four-minute mile. The best runner at the time, John Landy, was quoted in 1953 as saying:

> 'I've given up on it (breaking four minutes). Haag was a freak and he didn't get that close, I'm starting to believe it can't be done'.

However, Roger Bannister, at the time a medical student at Oxford, was quoted as saying:

> Scientists have proven that it's not possible to run a sub-four-minute mile but I don't listen to that kind of talk, thoughts like that have a way of sinking into your feet.

With this uncharacteristic belief in his own and other runners' potential, and training only 30 minutes a day with new methods around his academic timetable, Bannister went on to set a new world record of 3 minutes, 59.4 seconds in 1956. What was most interesting, though, was what happened next. Bannister had not only physically broken the four-minute barrier but he had also broken the mental barrier, such that John Landy then went on to set a new world record a whole second and half quicker only 46 days later and countless other athletes then went on to break four minutes in the following few years.

If you don't believe that the person you are coaching can improve and change, then don't coach them. Instead, work on your own mindset first, perhaps by being coached yourself. The good news is that it is possible to train yourself to shift from a fixed mindset to a growth mindset, improving the performance of those you are coaching based simply on the shift in your own attitude towards them.

Building coaching relationships

In previous sections of the book, we have discussed the importance of building trusting relationships as a key component to developing a high-performing board team. We framed trust as something that develops as one transforms the level that one communicates at from ritual and cliché, to facts and information, to discussing personal beliefs and attitudes and, finally, to disclosing one's emotions and feelings. We also recognised that trust can be represented as an equation, such that it is equal to credibility plus reliability plus intimacy, all divided by a self-focus (note that a self-focus is the antithesis of the coaching mindset that we have just discussed above). We also noted that, of these equation components, intimacy best predicts high levels of trusting relationships.

It is these levels of relational intimacy, which are also a foundational skill to developing in a one-to-one coaching relationship – indeed, in any of the team coach roles that we are discussing in this chapter. For example, in one study of successful therapeutic relationships, therapists were first asked for the reasons why those particular relationships had been so successful. The therapists mostly answered that it was because their expertise and models of therapy best suited those clients with whom they had had the best outcomes. However, when the researchers asked the recipients of the successful therapy for their reasons, the clients unanimously agreed that it was the quality of relationship that they had mutually built over time that predicted the therapy's success.

How is it possible to build a successful relationship, coaching or otherwise? Simply, it is to spend time treating people like human beings rather than 'human doings', as one does when we see another person simply as instrumental in achieving our particular task. This requires empathy (as we have discussed being measured by the 'Reading the Eyes in the Mind' test online) and spending time talking to people about what really matters to them.

Case study: The Timpson test

Timpson is a British multinational retailer specialising in shoe repairs, key cutting and engraving, as well as dry-cleaning and photo processing. It has over 1,300 outlets in the UK and Ireland and was founded in 1865 by shoemaker William Timpson and his brother-in-law Walter Joyce. It is still family owned and has been run, from 1975 until recently, by Sir John Timpson.

Timpson's philosophy is that 'if you treat people well, it is blindingly obvious that they will do a good job' and the company has been in the top 10 of the *Sunday Times* Top 100 Best Companies to work for every time it has entered. One mechanism they use to operationalise this philosophy is what they call the 'Timpson Test', something that every manager needs to pass to attain and stay in their role. The test requires a manager to know a range of personal details about every member of their team such as their age, partner's name, children's names/ages/schools, their last and next holidays, their main hobbies, their career history, their health record and so on.

This test essentially forces Timpson's managers and leaders to have more trusting conversations and empathise with their staff and is a challenge to all of us who are in similar leadership and coaching roles.

One final point to make about building a trusting coaching relationship is that, regardless of the quality of the relationship, there must also be an appropriate quantity of interactions for a relationship to be built. Research from former Gallup employee Marcus Buckingham (2016) suggests that we need to have a meaningful check-in with a team member around every week, or every two weeks at most, to enable us to support their performance and drive their engagement. If check-ins slip to once every three weeks, then the quality of relationships and therefore performance and engagement are found to drop significantly.

This empathetic approach to coaching and understanding the board members as individuals can be reflected into listening, questioning and being open-minded to individuals' different drivers and priorities. Understanding these drivers can enable any individual to be more effective in their relationships with others, supporting a more productive output from the relationship. Ask yourself if there are any professional relationships where you don't know much about the individual. You may believe this is because they are a private person who doesn't share their thoughts frequently outside of formal meetings. Could it be because you haven't asked, or they haven't been given the opportunity to share?

Effective coaching questions

When people complete training courses on coaching skills, they often mistakenly leave with the impression that coaching is all about asking rather than telling. It is certainly true that there is significant power in simply listening to what someone says and then asking a question about it, as a way of both showing belief in that person's potential and as a key tool in building a trusting relationship.

Coaching is more accurately described as being about raising awareness and generating responsibility in the person you are coaching. We may sometimes need to be directive when someone is unconsciously incompetent – that is, they don't know what they don't know – to gain quick wins and or in situations where immediate health and safety or other significant risk is concerned. We would ultimately want directors to be empowered and to take responsibility for governance themselves rather than this being the sole preserve of the governance professional. Questions therefore become our default coaching approach. It is true that those in most professions need, when transitioning to a coaching approach, to reset their baseline percentage of ask-to-tell from telling around 90% of the time to asking around 90% of the time, based on a shift to a belief in potential mindset. This is sometimes difficult to do having been schooled and rewarded for being an expert for much of our career. However, with practice it is entirely possible to develop the ability to feel comfortable shifting one's style to suit the conversational need. This agility will be hugely rewarded in how one is then able to accelerate the independent learning and decision making of those who are coached.

In addition to asking great effective coaching questions, there is also, of course, a need to notice and listen to a coachee's responses rather than breathlessly battering them with volleys of questions. This is where silence also becomes a useful tool to allow people to fill the gap with their thinking, potentially providing space for a more considered, systemic (rather than symptomatic) reflection. Noting the importance of listening, the CEO of Best Companies, who produce the annual 'Best Companies to Work For' lists in conjunction with the Sunday Times, stated that 'if a company wanted to make a difference in its workplace, the one single thing it could do is just start listening to people more'.

It is also important to pay attention not just to the words that are said, but also to the tone that is used, the body language that is associated with those words (which may be incongruent with them) and also what is not mentioned and left unsaid. All of this noticing is useful material to inform one's next question or feedback reflection.

If we agree that questions are important as the default method of communication in coaching as a way of raising awareness and generating responsibility, then what types of question are there and how are these best utilised in a coaching conversation? Here are some general pointers:

- **Open questions** – these are the default question type to use in coaching as they are most likely to help a coachee raise awareness of their issue. If a coach has their own solution in their head and is therefore unconsciously shifting to 'expert' mode, it is likely that open questions will cease to be used and we will naturally try and direct our coachee to our solution by using closed questions, e.g. 'Have you thought of x?' Therefore, practice and feedback in open questions can be useful to notice and correct when this happens.

- **Closed questions** – although perhaps subservient to open questions in coaching, they are useful at certain points such as when checking, e.g. 'Am I right in saying that these are your options?' and, at the end of coaching, e.g. 'So, have you committed to this?'
- **'Why' questions** – these are useful for opening people up to recognise the reasons for events being as they are. However, 'why' questions come with a health warning. Asking too many 'why' questions in a row may make someone feel like they are under interrogation and may move the discussion into more of a counselling conversation.
- **'What' questions** – these are the Swiss army knife of open coaching questions. They help someone explore their current reality in detail and are a useful substitute for why questions.
- **'How' questions** – these are very useful to move us forward to where we want to go and are therefore voiced in coaching when considering options and actions. However, be careful not to move to 'how' questions too early. It would be recommended to wallow in 'what' questions for longer, rather than forcing people to solve problems too early in coaching conversations.

Coaching has been described as a 'conversation with a purpose'. One useful coaching model which gives coaching direction is the GROW model. This has been adopted by many organisations as their default method of coaching. GROW stands for goal, reality, options and will and denotes different types of questions that one can ask in a coaching conversation. Coaching may naturally begin with goal questions such as, 'What do you want?' or 'What would you like to talk about?' and then move to reality questions such as 'What is currently happening?', 'Who is involved?' or 'How much is this happening?'

The conversation may then naturally shift to options questions such as, 'What could you do?', which provide a bridge from one's current reality to one's goal. A coaching conversation may be completed by will questions such as, 'What will you do?' and 'What can you commit to?', which help the coachee clarify actions they are going to take following the coaching. Although presented here somewhat linearly, the GROW model is more of a cycle, so that a coaching conversation can jump around the model and need not be followed too tightly. One recommendation is to spend the most time on goal questions, and then revisit them often, as coaching conversations will result in the goal shifting to something more meaningful as the coaching progresses.

Another useful framework is the recently developed 'Coaching Habit 7 Questions' from Australian coach Michael Bungay Stanier. He suggests that coaching can be hugely effective in only a 10-minute conversation using the following seven questions:

1. **What's on your mind?** This question enables a coach to get straight to business informally and non-aggressively.
2. **And what else?** This question is intended to be repeated to enable the coachee to develop more ideas and possibilities beyond an initial answer that they may have already considered.
3. **What's the real challenge here for you?** This question enables the coach to help the coachee appreciate the underlying issue rather than the symptom of their issue.
4. **What do you want?** Similar to the grow model's goal question, this simple question helps people voice their goal instead of the coach assuming what it might be, and also enables the coachee to feel empowered.
5. **How can I help?** This shows support. It is especially useful if someone is feeling overwhelmed with the topic that there they are discussing.
6. **If you are saying yes to this, what are you saying no to?** This question is known as the strategic question and gives lets people appreciate that it is possible to say no to things, which comes with a great sense of relief.
7. **What was most useful for you?** This is a wrapping-up question that encourages the coachee to identify the real point of the conversation and provide constructive feedback on the process.

These questions all map onto the GROW model (except perhaps the last one, which is more of an evaluation question); however, one point to notice here is that the questions start in reality before clarifying the goal in question four. They are also all open questions and six out of the seven are 'what'-initiated open questions.

One word of caution in using pre-defined questions: their over-use can become detrimental if they become seen as part of a pre-determined process rather than a supportive discussion. In one organisation, those that had been on the leadership development programme were easily singled out because they used one particular question that otherwise was not part of the general business conversation. Those who had not been on the programme, and were therefore unaware of its origin, found its use by their leaders and line managers as a challenging but beneficial question. Those who had been on the course used it as a beneficial part of their leadership toolkit, while equally recognising it as a badge of honour earnt through nomination for, and attendance at, the leadership programme. The question was 'What do you propose?'

Coaching trends

A number of coaching trends have emerged in recent years. At its broadest level, one trend has been that more and more organisations are providing coaching to their staff. We know, for example, that successful organisations provide 20% more coaching to employees than companies that perform less target this coaching away from talent development, leadership development and manager coaching to generating an overall culture of engagement.

Beyond one-to-one coaching, there is also a trend towards the recognition and proliferation of systemic team coaching which we will discuss in more detail in a later section of this chapter. This is due to the recognition of the more systemic nature of an individual's behaviour such that a team coach might have a wider impact on a greater number of individuals with a broader coaching remit. Not only this, but team coaching can provide better value by providing coaching support to more people in less time.

Another recent trend of one-to-one coaching is in coaching resilience. This is not surprising, bearing in mind the increasing workplace demands that are being placed on people, as we shall discuss in Chapter 15. In association with this, more senior leaders are receiving coaching support, as we can see in the examples of CEO coaching at Google and Microsoft. Indeed, chief executive officer coaching in order to support their resilience, combining the last two of these trends, is now becoming recognised as a potential new role of the chair.

Mentoring

The case for mentoring

Mentoring has many of the key benefits of coaching, as well as an overlapping mindset and skillset. In fact, one of the international governing bodies of coaching also has the word 'mentoring' in its title, being the European Mentoring and Coaching Council, showing how (sometimes confusingly) similar the two disciplines are. Many of the organisational benefits of coaching are mirrored in mentoring, as highlighted in a Deloitte (2012) report noting that retention was 25% higher in companies that engage in mentoring.

Mentoring is a skillset that may be useful to governance professionals to support executives and non-executives alike, as well as developing professionals who are a few steps below them on the professional ladder.

What is mentoring?

Professor David Clutterbuck, one of the co-founders of the European Mentoring and Coaching Council, has defined mentoring as:

> Offline help by one person to another in making significant transitions in knowledge, work or thinking... A mentor is a more experienced individual willing to share knowledge with someone less experienced in a relationship of mutual trust.

As we can see from this quote, there are similarities and differences between mentoring and coaching. Both modalities focus on a learner's thinking; both coaches and mentors use their experience to craft powerful questions; both see advice giving as permissible (but not as a first resort); both have a duty of care towards the coachee/mentee; and both base their communication on a mutually trusting relationship.

However, there are some key differences between mentoring and coaching. A mentor is more likely to make introductions and to develop a mentee's networks; they are more likely to explain organisational politics; and they are more likely to be someone who has previously trodden the path and hence has inside knowledge in the area within which the mentee is currently working. A coach, however, is more likely to provide feedback, is more likely to engage in a shor- or medium-term contract that is formalised and defined, and they are therefore more often likely to be entering into a paid relationship with a coachee.

Michael Heath (2012) has created a useful classification of four types of mentor that a governance professional may find themselves enacting to support board members. These four types are positioned in a four-box model created by the axes of 'need for task expertise' (either low or high) and 'need for facilitative expertise' (either low or high) as follows:

- **Buddy mentor:** The low need for facilitative expertise/low need for task expertise type is the buddy mentor, who is useful for a settling-in process. This may be the role that an individual plays during a director induction. The mentoring role here is defined by teaching the buddy mentee things that are essential to transitioning into the new director role or, indeed, into the new organisation. This type of mentoring is valuable in the first few months when the individual can provide nuggets of information on how to do things, where issues of conflict might be, how to best work with the chair and other directors, etc. It is a useful role that a non-executive director could provide to a fellow non-executive director, or an experienced non-executive director could provide to a newly promoted executive director.
- **Expert mentor:** The low need to facilitate expertise/high need for task expertise creates the expert mentor type. In this role, a mentor's job is not to focus on personal issues but to be more technical and situation-specific. A company secretary may use expert mentoring when they put their hat on as a governance expert to teach a new director their responsibilities or to share the appropriate governance response to an existing director. Similarly, an executive director with specific responsibilities, such as a finance director or HR director, may share specific technical knowledge as a means to increase a fellow director's understanding in a particular area. This type of mentoring is furthest from the coaching mode in that the expert, when brought specific concerns, will give concrete answers on what is to be done to save a director time in working out a situation themselves. It is essentially a teaching role and best done outside of the boardroom on a one-to-one basis if it is given in the spirit of support.

- **Attached mentor:** The high need for facilitative experience/high need for task expertise mentor type is the attached mentor, also known as the 'knowledgeable friend' type. In this role, the mentor can be both an authority and a sounding board and can play an internal sponsoring role. This is the classic mentoring role whereby a mentor can use their skill in asking questions to enable thinking, but also can provide organisational and subject matter knowledge if required to aid a mentee's thinking. Advice, therefore, will be offered when it is clear that the mentee cannot find their own solution.
- **Detached mentor:** Finally, the high need for facilitative expertise/low need for task expertise dynamic is the detached reflector mentor type. This style of mentoring is the most non-directive and is more similar to a classic coaching style, whereby a mentor may support directors with broad issues beyond the technical. They will use their experience to challenge and help the mentee widen their perspective and explore options as they would using a coaching approach, such that they are facilitators of the mentee's thinking.

As can be seen from the above types, there is a significant overlap between being a governance expert, a mentor, a coach, or indeed, any combination of these. What is most important is that the individual who is using these approaches understands what approach they are using at any time and whether that is most appropriate stance for the conversation and situation in which they find themselves.

The question to ask is, 'What does this person most need from me right now?' The answer may vary from moment to moment, hence the need for agility to fluidly transition between roles.

Trends in mentoring

Mentoring, especially in North America, has often been seen as a sponsoring mechanism whereby one acquires a 'trophy' senior leader as a mentor to enable accelerated climbing up the organisational greasy pole. However, in recent years, mentoring has been seen as less about sponsoring and more about personal and career development. Within this paradigm, and with relevance to boards in relation to the issue of diversity, there has been a significant drive to provide mentoring for high-performing women so that they might gain both the career and personal learning benefits that mentoring can often bring.

However, in some recent research looking at 4,000 executives who have received mentoring, it was found that men's mentors were more senior. There was also a correlation between getting promoted if one had had a mentor in the two years previously for men but no correlation for women. This led to the study concluding that women, when they can access mentoring support, are 'over-mentored but under-sponsored' and the authors recommending that, although acknowledging a recent shift in mentoring from sponsoring to development, this should not be the case for mentoring high-performing women.

A second key trend in mentoring is the concept of reverse mentoring. This is when usually younger and less senior employees mentor older and more senior leaders in a particular competency that they have, most commonly related to technology and digital skills. Reverse mentoring may be offered to senior leaders on the use of social media as a method of stakeholder communication and engagement. If nothing else, this reverse mentoring enables those in senior positions to have visibility of the wider organisation and, potentially, the views of consumers, if they are mentored by an individual that reflects their customer base.

Systemic team coaching

The case for systemic team coaching

In the last few years, team coaching has become one of the biggest trends in coaching. According to the Riddler and Sherpa reports on the coaching industry, team coaching is currently the fastest-growing form of coaching globally. Apart from having greater reach and therefore being more time- and cost-efficient, team coaching is increasingly being seen as a necessity for senior leadership teams. As we have discussed, the research of Ruth Wageman et al. found that team coaching, going beyond just multiples of one-to-one coaching support to board executives, was a vital enabler of high-performing senior leadership teams globally. This perspective is supported by research from a Henley Business School report on 'Tomorrow's leadership and the necessary revolution in today's leadership development'.

Systemic team coaching – that goes beyond just traditional teambuilding, away days and workshops that tend to look only the at internal team dynamics – is the most fruitful approach to team coaching as this can impact on and is affected by all team stakeholders. This is in line with our original definition of board dynamics: the 'systemic team coach' approach, out of a variety of approaches that have emerged, seems best suited for employment by the individual.

What is systemic team coaching?

Systemic team coaching is an approach to team coaching which was coined by Professor Peter Hawkins in his 2017 book *Leadership Team Coaching*. It draws on a number of disciplines including individual one-to-one coaching, group coaching approaches such as the action learning set approach, teambuilding, team facilitation, inter-team coaching and organisational development. Systemic team coaching is defined by Hawkins et al., John Learly-Joyce and Hilary Lines from the Association of Executive Coaching (2018), as:

> A process of coaching the whole team both together and apart, over a designated period of time to enable it to:
>
> - align on common purpose;
> - collaborate and learn across diversity;

- develop collective leadership;
- achieve performance outcomes;
- engage effectively with their key stakeholders groups; and
- jointly transform the wider business.

Based on everything that we have discussed so far in terms of board dynamics, this approach to supporting a board – which we might call 'systemic board coaching' – seems entirely relevant as a role that an individual sitting alongside the board, or a non-executive within the board, may play. These are some of the important characteristics of systemic team coaching and how they may relate to this individual:

- The coaching happens over a period of time, not in a one-off workshop – the individual, therefore, may be ideally positioned to support as a team coach as they experience the board over a continuous period of time, often as the most tenured attendee or supported of board meetings.
- Systemic team coaching requires the core skills of a one-to-one coach and much more besides. We have discussed the core skills of one-to-one coaching as: having belief in potential, the ability to build trusting relationships, to ask questions and listen well, to provide effective feedback and to help support a great goal setting. A great team coach will also be an effective group facilitator and understand the dynamics of how people work in teams.
- In systemic team coaching, the coaching objective needs to be created by the team. This is important to ensure all members of the board team feel committed and engaged to the process.
- Surprisingly, the team leader (in this case, the chair) is not the client of the systemic team coach – instead, the stakeholder system and wider community that the board is serving is the key client, also described as the 'stakeholder of tomorrow'. This is the higher client purpose that an individual as a systemic team coach can pivot around.
- Systemic team coaching goes beyond simply improving internal boardroom dynamics – as we discussed in Chapter 6, this approach pays as much attention to what is happening outside the team, the 'boundary spanning', as to what is happening inside the team board.
- Systemic team coaching will involve coaching the board together and also one-to-ones – one-to-one coaching helps individual board directors identify how they can best contribute to the board's shared goal which would have been worked out initially in a cohesive team context.
- Systemic team coaching can be useful at different moments in a team's evolution depending upon their current challenge – a new board or a new chair are ideal times to introduce team coaching approaches, as these are occasions when a team may need to revisit their collective goals and relationships.

Systemic team coaching disciplines and interventions

Historically, team coaching has either focused on the strategic off-site, where teams come to get together to discuss and reconsider their purpose and goals for the year ahead, or supported the team through team-building events, whereby personality profiles and team games are used to reveal and improve the team relationship dynamics. These are certainly key aspects of team coaching but they miss out the vital external stakeholder perspectives that should drive a team's agenda.

The systemic team coaching five disciplines model, developed by Peter Hawkins (2014) (see Figure 18) captures a broader remit of what constitutes a high-performing team.

Figure 18 The systemic team coaching five disciplines model, developed by Peter Hawkins (2014)

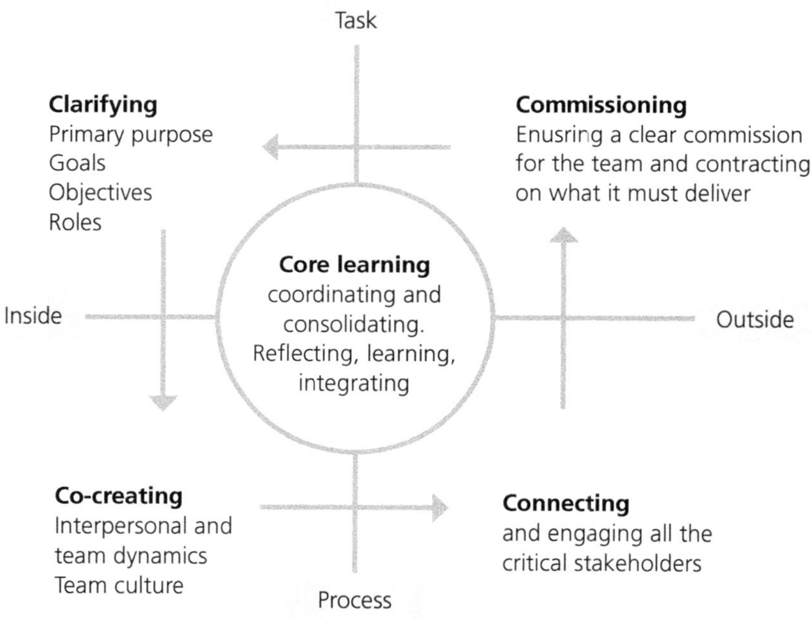

His framework has two dimensions, inside or outside the team and task or people function, which combine to produce a four-box model (the framework has also been developed into a team diagnostic which can help teams evaluate their current function and provide guidance on where to develop in the future). Together, these dimensions create the first four disciplines, with an additional fifth discipline in the centre:

Discipline one – commissioning (task focus/outside the team)

This discipline focuses on what stakeholders expect of the team and requires the team to iteratively contract with them on what the team is required to deliver. There are many teams, and boards, that merrily work away without always being clear what their external stakeholders fully expect of them, and are then surprised when those stakeholders provide negative feedback on their performance.

In order to help with commissioning, the systemic team coach may facilitate stakeholder interviews, stakeholder mapping, roleplay, focus groups or other desktop strategic research to help the board team better clarify their commission.

Discipline two – clarifying (task focus/inside the team)

Having agreed what stakeholders require of them, the team will then need jointly to clarify, agree and commit to how it will execute on this expectation together. This will involve them considering their shared purpose, vision, strategy, objectives, systems and processes, roles and responsibilities and values.

There are many models and exercises that a team coach can use to support in the clarifying stage of systemic team development such as developing a team charter, vision/mission/values activities, utilising a SWOT analysis, etc. For example, Jim Collins, the author of *Good to Great*, has an excellent vision framework resource on his website.

Case study: Team success in cycling

The former Performance Director of British Cycling, and subsequently general manager of Team Sky/Team Ineos/Ineos Grenadiers, Sir David Brailsford, has achieved an incredible amount of rapid success in the world of cycling both on the road in the Tour de France and on the track at the Olympic Games. This is partly due to the precision and clarity that he brings to his team development.

This clarity is formalised in a number of ways, including in the 'Team Sky Rules', a set of rules and expectations that were written on a poster inside the team bus.

Discipline three – co-creating (people process focus/inside the team)

This is where a team coach can support a team in working together to deliver their joint endeavour. In a board's case, it is equivalent to the boardroom dynamics and team culture that we have discussed in detail in Chapter 4. Some models and exercises that are useful to support a team in this discipline include psychometric tools and personality types such as the MBTI and Belbin team roles, Lencioni's 'five dysfunctions of a team' framework, Tuckman's developmental model and so on.

Discipline four – connecting (people process focus/outside the team)

This is where the team needs to engage with all their key stakeholders and be tuned into the broader organisational and environmental culture within which they exist. The role of the team coach in this discipline is to support the team in preparing to communicate with outside stakeholders. Exercises that can be used to do this include stakeholder mapping, interviews, role-plays and even the empty chair technique (mentioned in Chapter 9).

Discipline five – core learning

This is where the team is encouraged to stand back and reflect on its own performance to consolidate on successes and learn from mistakes. The board evaluation is an obvious set piece of core learning that an individual from within or alongside the board is often responsible for and can deliver in a team coaching role.

However, core learning is also an ongoing process such that a team coach may consistently invite feedback from key stakeholders and encouraging honest conversation internally between board members, both during and between board meetings.

In summary, the skills and methodology of systemic team coaching provide opportunities for the coach to improve the board dynamics and therefore governance performance of a board team. Although the role of team coach may ideally be played by an external coach, certain aspects at certain times may be part of the remit of an individual alongside or within the board. They may be taken on both through formal appointment or, more frequently, through the individual adopting this role informally as and when the opportunities arise.

Facilitator

The case for facilitation

The Chartered Governance Institute's 2014 report 'The company secretary: building trust through governance' shares some research by Kakabadse and Kakabadse, which found that:

> More than 33% of top teams are divided on mission, purpose, vision and strategy of the organisation, leading to dysfunctional political behaviour at senior levels, which permeates the organisation and becomes part of the culture of the enterprise.

The report suggests the supportive individual's role (which, while specifically focused on the role of the company secretary in this report, can be extended to other board support functions) centrally involves 'independent and sensitive facilitation which teases out deep-rooted issues, non-political truths, honest opinion and novel ideas'. The report goes on to suggest that:

> The majority of respondents in this study agree that the company secretary is ideally placed to align interests, facilitate dialogue and negotiate at different organisational levels.

One of the respondents noted that, beyond their task knowledge, an individual can 'value-add in terms of facilitative skills, guiding the business through complexities... truly nurturing and managing relationships between people'. Another respondent noted that the role is all about facilitating relationship management:

> It's part of your diplomatic skills... Social awareness, people skills, tact, trust... You can influence how that happens and help people get to where they want to get too... So you have a facilitating role.

The competency of facilitation seems to be a key requirement of the value-adding, behaviourally orientated, people-focused twenty-first-century governance professional.

What is facilitation?

At its simplest, facilitation can be defined as the process of designing and running a successful meeting. In Chapter 9, we discussed in detail the key design characteristics that a meeting facilitator, in the board's case often the responsibility of the company secretary, must be mindful of in order to set a meeting up for success. A more detailed and descriptive definition is usefully provided by the Institute of Cultural Affairs, which defines facilitation as:

> The act of making something easier. In group work, the facilitator works with people to help them have a conversation, come to agreement, or plan for the future. In general, the facilitator acts as a trusted and neutral outside voice, making decisions about the process the group goes through but allowing the group to focus on and control the content of the discussion. The facilitator is a gentle guide, making it easier for the group to have that discussion.

This idea of an individual being a 'gentle guide' to make board work 'easier' is certainly part of the people-orientated role that an individual can be called on to play. Schwarz (2002) describes the role of a facilitator when working with the group as:

> A process in which a person who is acceptable to all members of a group, substantively neutral, and has no decision-making authority, intervenes to help a group improve the way it identifies and solves problems and makes decisions in order to increase the group's effectiveness.

The independence and lack of decision making which characterise the company secretary's role in the boardroom, as well as other individuals working alongside but outside the board, positions them perfectly to play a continuously facilitating role both between, and during, board meetings.

In addition, a non-executive director may also be a facilitator in support of the chair as, while they have a decision-making authority, they have no executive role outside of the board and their emphasis can be purely on board effectiveness.

When skilled in facilitation, a non-executive board member can be highly beneficial in encouraging board discussions.

Facilitation skills and interventions

There are numerous approaches and tools available that can guide and improve competency in facilitation. The intention here is to provide some of the most well-known, as well as those that may be most relevant for an individual informally or formally taking on this role within the boardroom setting.

Heron intervention styles

John Heron, one of the pre-eminent pioneers of modern facilitation, articulated six categories of intervention that a facilitator may choose to employ. Of these six, three are more 'push', being prescribing, informing and confronting, and three are more 'pull', being catalytic, cathartic and supporting. We will consider each intervention briefly in turn:

- **Prescribing** – this facilitation intervention is when one gives directions, advice and recommendations. It is useful if expertise is asked for, when guidance is needed, if a participant is unable to direct themselves or if there are ethical guidelines. Some verbal examples of prescribing might include, 'I recommend this process', 'I suggest that you do it this way' and 'Have you talked to the chair about this?' The skill in prescribing is knowing how to do it well (such as how to voice well in terms of team dialogue), whether in fact to prescribe at all, to be clear in giving instructions when prescribing, to explain why when prescribing and to ensure that one plays to an individual's intrinsic motivations. Some traps to avoid in prescribing are when one gives unwanted advice, when prescribing means that one is taking over and imposing solutions, when one overdoes prescribing and creates dependency, when one hesitates when firmness is actually required and when one over controls an aspect of a conversation.
- **Informing** – this is when we give information and knowledge during a conversation or meeting. It is useful to show where to find extra help and information, to supply appropriate facts and data, to explain what is happening and to share one's own experiences as appropriate. This informing role is one often played by the more experienced mentor. Some examples of informing might include, 'You can find the information in this particular code of governance', 'These are the three key things that you need to know about your fellow directors' and 'We have an important deadline coming up on this particular date.' The skills of informing are to present information clearly, to check for understanding, to invite and handle questions and to judge how much information to give. Traps of informing, are around overloading, not structuring the information well enough and not saying why something is important.

- **Confronting** – this intervention concerns raising awareness and challenging assumptions and is a key skill required of all board directors as we have discussed elsewhere in the text. It is useful to show the consequences of particular actions, to challenge people to rethink assumptions, to raise awareness of other stakeholders' perceptions and to boost confidence by affirming success if an overly negative comment has been voiced. Some verbal examples of confronting might include statements such as 'Are you all assuming that this behaviour would be considered ethical by all stakeholders?' or 'Are you aware of the impact of your behaviour on other board directors?' The skills of the confronting intervention are to know when would be appropriate to confront, to be able to ask direct questions, to give constructive feedback, to challenge defensive excuses and to give space to those confronted so that they may reflect. Some traps in the confronting intervention might be that one acts too much in the parental style, one makes character judgements and generalisations rather than confronting on specific behaviours, confronting on a trivial issue and not ensuring that confronting provides the possibility of a win–win or at the very least the opportunity to save face.
- **Cathartic** – this intervention is about helping release emotions that block progress and is useful when meeting participants are afraid of risk of failure, when they feel incompetent, when they feel frustrated, demotivated, angry or upset, or if, on the contrary, people feel overly excited, joyful or pleased. Examples of cathartic interventions might be, 'How are you feeling about this?' and 'I have the impression that you don't agree with this'. The skills of the cathartic intervention are to actively listen, to use effective questions, to show empathy, to feed back what you are perceiving and generally to create a supportive climate. Some traps that might interfere with an appropriately executed cathartic intervention could be talking too much and not listening, making it hard for people to express their emotions, spending too long in their emotions, sympathising too quickly rather than empathising and denying or criticising another's feelings.
- **Catalytic** – this is when one intervenes to promote expansive and self-directed conversations. It is useful to help people achieve a deeper level of understanding, to achieve a broader discussion, to encourage people to take more responsibility and to promote motivation and commitment. Some examples of a catalytic intervention might be, 'What is the real challenge that we are facing here?' or 'What would you do differently next time?' The skills required of catalytic interventions include asking a wide range of questions, being able to reflect back and paraphrase, to refrain from inputting one's expertise and to be comfortable with conversational silence. Some traps may be including too many closed questions, structuring a conversation too soon, following what you find interesting in a conversation and not clarifying a conversation's goals enough. This catalytic style intervention is also similar to the coaching and

mentoring style, which can help transform thinking by raising awareness and generating responsibility.

- **Supporting** – this final intervention is about validating and building self-confidence and is useful when morale is low, to encourage risk taking, to reward success and to validate people's contributions in a conversation (especially introverted personality types). Some verbal examples of a supporting intervention might include, 'Your questions in that board meeting were fantastic', or 'I'm confident that you will make a big success of this role'. The skills required of supporting are to be able to express appreciation, to share your own mistakes and to apologise when necessary. Some traps within the supporting invention are to come across as patronising, to show support using the words 'yes, but', to overdo supporting so it feels false, to hold back on appreciation due to one's own inhibitions and to send mixed signals.

Overall, the use of Heron's intervention styles must be accompanied by a clear awareness of one's own preferences, an awareness of where one's meeting participants are at any particular stage and also one's awareness of the process that one is facilitating. Competence in using the six intervention styles is all about selecting the right intervention at the right time and moving elegantly from one intervention to another, so that one can balance more authoritative styles – which are usually more appropriate at the start and ends of discussion – with more facilitative styles that support generative dialogue and learning during the meat of a conversation or meeting.

Contracting and ground rules

In Chapter 9, we were introduced to research that showed that the inclusion of meeting agreements at the start of a meeting correlates with more positive meeting perceptions. Meeting agreements, also known as contracting or ground rules, are a key tool in a facilitator's armoury which can significantly influence the outcome of the meeting.

One framework for effective contracting comes from the psychological theory of transactional analysis, which describes the three Ps of contracting. The first of these are the 'practicalities', which provide the participants with protection. Practicalities of the meeting are vocalising and agreeing the meeting basics such as start and end times, the existence and presence of breaks, access to refreshments and toilet facilities, health and safety announcements, wifi access and any other more basic needs that meeting participants may have. If these basics are missed, then this can create significant agitation in meeting attendees if, for example, they need to leave early for a flight but have not shared this at the start of the meeting.

The second area of contracting concerns the 'professional' aspects, which create permission around what is and is not to be included in the meeting and also what may or may not be shared outside of the meeting. In terms of a board meeting, the professional aspects of contracting will concern what the stakeholders' expectations are of each board meeting and what levels of confidentiality, or indeed transparency, there will be for the conversations.

The final contracting area is the 'psychological' contract, which concerns how the group needs to be to work well together as a high-performing team. The author and consultant Peter Block often poses four questions to meeting participants at the start of meetings, which encourage them to consider how they are going to choose to act. These questions, which can also be used as a process review at the end of the meeting, are as follows:

- How valuable an experience do you plan to have?
- How engaged do you plan to be?
- How much risk are you prepared to take?
- How interested are you in other people's experiences?

One of the most powerful tools to create a psychological contract is for meeting participants to agree on ground rules. The organisational psychologist Roger Schwarz suggests that ground rules are a tool to set meeting culture by enacting a set of core values and assumptions to guide behaviour. He contends that good meetings will have the core values of transparency, curiosity, accountability, informed choice and compassion, which underpin nine behavioural ground rules for effective groups to enhance how they work together. These ground rules are as follows:

1. state views and ask genuine questions
2. share all relevant information
3. use specific examples and agree on what important words mean
4. explain reasoning and intent
5. test assumptions and inferences
6. jointly design next steps
7. focus on interests, not positions
8. discuss undiscussable issues
9. use a decision-making rule that generates the level of commitment needed

The person setting the agenda, or those inputting into it, might use these as a starting point for discussion when a board contracts around how they plan to work together.

Process breaks

A process break is a moment of 'time out' during a meeting to review how well a group or team are working together to achieve their stated task. Process breaks are especially useful with highly task-focused teams who may often get stuck due to unintended behavioural issues and conflicts. For example, when something seems unspoken or there is some surprising eruption of emotion from one particular director, a process break may be enacted to understand what is going on. This tool therefore gives teams permission to speak about more attitudinal and emotional aspects of their dynamic rather than simply factual aspects and can themselves build trust, as well as reducing stress and conflict. They work best when the use of them is included in the initial contract so that they do not come as a surprise. Process breaks become less required and less frequent once teams become more self-aware and can self-regulate.

Mindful meetings

The idea of 'mindful meetings' has arisen out of the more mainstream recent interest in mindfulness that will be discussed in more detail in Chapter 15 as a method of building resilience. There are many online toolkits for how to lead mindful meetings . The essence of a mindful meeting is that it is one that infuses mindfulness practices and emotional intelligence into an effective meeting structure to reduce interference and support better individual and team functioning. We know that teams with high levels of empathy are higher performing, so this approach certainly has a well-evidenced underpinning. Mindful meetings may include set-piece moments such as:

- encouraging individuals to do a mindful self-check before entering the meeting space, such as simply breathing three times mindfully to check in with one's mental and emotional state;
- inviting everyone to take a minute to arrive. This might include inviting people to be silent for one minute before the meeting begins to gather their thoughts, to consider their responsibilities and to empathise with the many stakeholder expectations that they have going into the meeting;
- performing a quick check-in of 30 seconds to see how people are feeling (which may also serve as a brief process check); and
- periodically asking questions such as 'Is there anything that is getting in the way of you being fully present? If so, is there something that can be done quickly to resolve that?'

All the above facilitation techniques may encourage participants to be less distracted and more mindful throughout the meeting. One practical application of this is to ask all participants to turn off or pocket their mobile phones or, at least, to disclose if they are expecting a time-restricted call or email that cannot be ignored during the expected time of the meeting. Too frequently, board members are distracted by their technology and lose the thread of the discussion or believe that, because the current topic is not their primary responsibility or area of expertise, that they can be less present. In contrast, it is often in these discussions that the contribution of the less technical or connected can provide the meaningful comment or question that has a considerable impact on the outcome.

The check-in

Inspired by the aviation industry's improved safety record through the employmeny of checklists, and the more recent benefits that surgeons have also gained from a similar practice, organisations are also now more frequently beginning meetings with some kind of a 'check-in'.

This could simply be going round the room asking people to confirm their name, their role or what they are hoping to bring to the meeting. This short and simple process fulfils various functions. Firstly, it enables everybody to feel like they are part of the meeting, having voiced at least one thing, meaning that they are much more likely to voice something later as the meeting continues. Secondly, and most importantly, it reduces the status hierarchies within the room as everybody has democratically been allotted equal time and space to voice something at the start of the meeting. Thirdly, depending on the check-in choice, an appropriate tone can be set such that a cohesive culture can be set into motion.

Case study: Let me introduce myself

As detailed in his book *The Checklist Manifesto*, American surgeon Atul Gawande pioneered the use of checklists to improve outcomes in the operating room. Surprisingly, and most notably, it was found that by simply allowing everyone to introduce themselves by name before surgery, the average number of complications and deaths dropped by a massive 35%.

However, when he attempted to roll out the ideas into a greater number of operating theatres, he received significant resistance from 20% of doctors, who saw the idea of running through a checklist before surgery as a waste of time. However, they were soon convinced to change their mind with the question, 'If you were to have an operation, would you want the checklist?' After raising this question, compliance rates jumped to 94%.

Positivity

Positive psychology advocates that we are more creative, less stressed, more confident, make better decisions and in general perform better both individually and in teams when we are building on strengths and noticing what is working rather than what is not.

In meetings, this translates into methods that attempt to draw people to more positive emotions in order to engender psychological safety, growth mindsets and more quality dialogue. For example, an effective question to ask at the start of the meeting (taken from a solution-focused approach) is, 'What are your best hopes for this meeting?' Similarly, a facilitator may include in the check-in a request for each person to share a highlight or something they are proud of since they last met.

Other supporting roles

In addition to the more significant one-to-one coaching, mentoring, systemic team coaching and facilitation roles that an agile individual may find themselves needing to flex between, there are also some other supporting roles that they may also be called upon to play from time to time (or that individuals may want to have in their armoury no matter what primary role they play). These are the supervisor, mediator and counsellor roles.

Supervisor

An experienced individual may at times need to support the competency-building of directors other colleagues who are developing as professionals. Within this capacity, they may take on the role of 'governance supervisor'. In many other professions, there is often a regulatory expectation that supervision is inherently part of good practice. However, even in the absence of this, supervision can be useful to support the practice of other governance professionals.

Governance supervision aligned to the board can be defined as:

> a structured formal process for directors or governance professionals, with the help of a knowledgeable supervisor, to improve the quality of their governance, to grow their governance capacity and to support themselves and their governance practice.
>
> (adapted from Hawkins and Schwenk, 2006)

Proctor (1987) has suggested that there are three functions of supervision. These are: the 'normative' function, where a supervisor advises the supervisee on ethical behaviour; the 'formative' function, where a supervisor supports a supervisee is learning in their particular field of practice; and the 'restorative' function, whereby a supervisor provides emotional support for the supervisee.

Mediator

According to the CIPD, the annual cost of conflict at work in the UK alone in 2012 was estimated at £24 billion. Further, 25% of line managers' time was absorbed simply managing conflict within their role. As we have discussed previously in the text, tension and challenge is a necessary requirement and likely eventuality of an effective, diverse and cognitively conflicting board. However, when this boils over into personality and relationship conflict, the skills of mediation may be necessary. Due to their relative independence, an individual functioning outside the board (or within it as a non-executive director) may be ideally positioned to help mediate when relationship conflict arises in the boardroom.

The skillset of mediation is similar to those required for coaching, mentoring and facilitation, but the structure is more formal and may require some training to enable competence or external mediation if the issue is beyond the internal individuals comfort zone. Although this more formal mediation may be beyond a person's remit, some understanding of the process may be useful to provide more informal mediation support.

Counsellor

The skillsets of a trained counsellor also overlap with coaching, mentoring and facilitation skills. This include the need to build a trusting relationship, to ask effective questions, to listen well and show empathy and to be both supportive and appropriately challenging. Because of their trusted position in an organisation, individual directors may seek out the support and advice of individuals aligned to the board on issues that go beyond the technical. These conversations may border on counselling conversations, within which directors may express significant and potentially disabling emotion about a particular subject, either work or non-work related.

Helping someone to talk through an emotional barrier may be appropriate and within one's remit and skillset; however, an individual needs to know where to draw the line and feel comfortable referring someone if the issue seems too significant for them to support. The conversation might then turn to how a person can find that support, which is more of a rational topic and therefore safer ground, but will still show appropriate empathy and support to help the person move forward.

Team coach competence

It may seem surprising to describe an individual who works in and around the board as the board's team coach and to suggest that they must be competent and agile enough to perform in, and elegantly move between, all of the roles discussed in this chapter. However, it is highly likely that an individual may already be playing many of these roles at any one particular time. It is just that they have not labelled themselves as such and that they are perhaps already somewhat unconsciously competent.

One's attitude towards these roles is perhaps a more central requirement than perfecting all of the technical skills. Having said this, some kind of structure within which to develop further can be useful. Therefore, some recommendations for developing competence as a team coach might include the following:

- Assigning time to self-coach by reflecting on one's practice, journalling, etc.
- Employing one's own coach, mentor or supervisor, be it a professional paid coach or a peer and/or to become part of a group coaching process such as an action learning set.
- Learning more about the team coaching roles through literature, podcasts, seminars and conference sessions and becoming part of a governing body such as the International Coaching Federation, the European Mentoring and Coaching Council or the Association for Coaching.
- Investing in becoming fully qualified through a reputable training organisation, for example, the Association of Executive Coaching in the UK and Ireland.

Conclusion

A twenty-first-century governance professional and board supporter must not only provide governance task expertise, but must also be behaviourally agile and perform the role of team coach. Their role as team coach will involve key activities such as one-to-one coaching, mentoring, systemic team coaching and facilitation and also, potentially, supervision, mediation and counselling.

Within this, the one-to-one coach role requires a mindset that believes in the potential of the person being coached as well as the skills to build trusting relationships, ask effective questions, provide feedback and support goal setting. The coaching mindset and the skillset needed to be effective in this role are important to develop as they overlap and, although there are differences, they are shared by the other 'team coach' roles.

Similarly, an individual may be required to mentor directors and adapt their style depending on requirements based on the four types of mentoring: buddy, expert, attached and detached. While acting as either a coach or a mentor and applying one or the other depending on the circumstance, the systemic team coach must also attend to all five disciplines of the team: commissioning, clarifying, co-creating, connecting and core learning. In addition, supervision, mediation and counselling roles may be required at particular times. Identifying all these functions, recognising their differences and applying the most appropriate at each time is a skill that can be developed over time through practice and is an invaluable skill in the toolkit of a governance professional.

Separately, the facilitation role is key in meeting design and delivery and requires agility to move between different types of intervention. What are some of the tools available to individuals as a board facilitator? Before a meeting even starts, a facilitator can use design characteristics to set the meeting up for success (see Chapter 9). While facilitating, one can be aware of and moderate one's style to suit the situation, either pushing more through prescribing, informing and confronting and/or pulling more through being catalytic, cathartic and supporting. Specific interventions such as contracting on meeting ground rules, using process breaks, incorporating mindful practices and using check-ins and the influence of positivity are some further tools that one might choose to employ.

There are many ways to develop 'team coach' competence, including self-reflection, being personally coached or mentored, self-tutoring or through a variety of formal learning activities. It's a case of choosing the method that works best for you.

Throughout your career, and earlier in your formal education, who are the individuals that have supported, coached and mentored you to be the best you can be? How can you replicate this for others in your current situation?

How could your board benefit from discussions being facilitated, or individuals being mentored or coached? How could this be implemented to best effect?

15 – Maintaining personal resilience

The requirement for resilience

The individual as a corporate athlete

The focus of the book so far has been on what board dynamics is and how an individual, beyond their technical expertise, can positively influence these dynamics. These are external-facing roles associated with leading others and leading the governance of the organisation. The focus of this chapter turns inwards, to the individuals' personal leadership and enquires into how they function as a 'corporate athlete'. Any professional individual can only continue to deliver sustained performance if they are first able to look after and pace themselves. Board membership is often made up of driven, ambitious individuals who possess an innate self-confidence and self-belief. As a result, those individuals working within and alongside boards need to be resilient.

If an individual acting at a senior level or in a supportive role is able to maintain their own resilience, but also understand the components of resilience more generally, they are then also able to support others in building their resilience. As discussed in Chapters 3 and 11, resilience is a key competency of board directors. This is emphasised by Michael Willis et al, in their 2015 book *The Resilient Director: Building an Effective Board*, where they state:

> Resilience can be a critical survival skill in the boardroom. The ability to hang on in there and see things through, can be a board saving skill, as resilient directors persevere and do not admit defeat, even at times when problems are not being properly addressed. The status quo is being too easily accepted. Resilient directors face up to the harsh realities of the boardroom and seek to change them, and this requires an ability to play the long game, not to admit defeat, and to live on the edge of the social dynamic of the existing culture of the board, however dysfunctional that may be.

In their 2017 paper, 'The chairperson buffering role in turbulent environments', Dr Filipe Morais et al. from Henley Business School suggest that one of the new roles for the chair is in supporting the resilience of their chief executive officer. This is particularly true, they found, when there was significant disruption in the business in situations such as hostile bids, strategic turnarounds, large restructurings and reputational crisis.

Extending this thinking, we can see that other professional individuals can also play an important supporting role for maintaining or developing the resilience of both the chief executive officer and the chair as part of their role. As Morais indicates, this can also importantly be achieved while maintaining their independence.

The level of the stress problem

Why is it that resilience has recently emerged as a highly prominent and widely regarded key twenty-first-century leadership competency? As we introduced in Chapter 3, there is a contention that the world is becoming more volatile, uncertain, complex and ambiguous. Although historians point to the fact that every generation believes that theirs is the one within which the pace is accelerating quicker than others, there is a broad perception that the Fourth Industrial Revolution that we are currently living through is creating the most challenging living and working conditions that we have seen. For example, although there are significant benefits of modern technology, there are also challenges associated with it. A Chartered Management Institute report suggested that with high connectivity we also see higher levels of stress: those who struggle to switch off from work and check email more report lower personal productivity and job satisfaction and experience more frequent stress.

More than two-thirds of people who rate themselves as less than productive say that technology has made it harder to switch off from work. But it is not just technology that is increasing the pace of our world. There are also increasing levels of customer expectation associated with digital advances. For example, the public sector is now expected to deliver services in the same way as the Amazons and Apples of this world and, unsurprisingly based on their structures which often discourage innovation, are not currently living up to this challenge.

What is the impact of this increasingly challenging world? Using North America as an example, we can see that stress is now linked to all six leading causes of death: coronary heart disease, cancer, lung ailments, accidents, liver disease and suicide. Further, 75–90% of all doctor visits are currently for stress-related conditions. Within the workplace, there is a suggestion that companies are now facing an employee burnout crisis. In a recent Gallup study of nearly 7,500 American employees, 23% reported feeling burnt out at work very often or always, while an additional 44% reported feeling burnt out sometimes. Job burnout has accounted for an estimated $125 billion to $190 billion in healthcare spending each year. The report suggested that the primary drivers of job burnout included unfair treatment at work, unreasonable deadlines, unmanageable workload, lack of support from managers and, as mentioned above, the added stress of having to respond to emails and texts outside of office hours.

In the UK, the CIPD reported 131 million working days were lost to sickness absence in 2016, which equates to 6.3 days per person per annum. This figure has increased year on year since 2013.

More recently, the impact of COVID-19 on the workplace, and the downstream working conditions it has necessitated, has significantly increased work-related stress. Those in the healthcare industry are obvious candidates, but there has been heavy reporting of increased levels of stress in those who are now forced to work from home. Anecdotal reporting indicates that less downtime, and the removal of non-family social interaction that the communal workplace provides for during the working day, have exacerbated stress and feelings of isolation. The forced use of technology to enable continued connectivity has also meant that digital stress is now more prevalent across all ages.

This is the context and backdrop against which boards and individuals are working, which highlights the urgent need to develop personal resilience.

Case study: The tragic results of board conflicts

Possibly one of the biggest wake-up calls associated with the potential stress at board level was the 2013 tragedy in Switzerland which saw two board directors commit suicide within weeks of each other. In his suicide note, Pierre Wauthier, the 53-year-old chief financial officer of Zurich Insurance Group, wrote that he'd been driven to desperation by his chair's overbearing style which had created a relationship so toxic that suicide seemed a logical escape.

Similarly, the Swisscom chief executive officer Carsten Schloter, 49, who had committed suicide five weeks earlier, had been experiencing intense conflict with the arrival of the company's new president, Hansueli Loosli, in mid-2011. Commentators put Schloter's decision to take his own life down to this conflict, the constant work demands that he was facing in his role and also to personal difficulties, including his separation from his wife a few years previously. Two months before he committed suicide, Schloter told a Swiss newspaper how he felt strangled by these demands, commenting that 'when you permanently check your smart phone to see if there are any new emails, it leads you to not find any rest whatsoever. I find it increasingly difficult to calm down'.

The stress response

The first essential step towards greater personal resilience is to develop a finely tuned awareness of how stress is triggered, how you experience it and how stress impacts on your behaviour. Most stress and coping models from the literature identify three core elements: the demands that are placed on an individual, an individual's appraisal of those demands, and the responses that the individual has to that appraisal. We will look at each one of these in further detail.

Demands

As we touched on above, there are a variety of increasing demands that people may be facing within organisations and boardrooms today. These may be linked to work overload, work conflicts, relationship issues or other work environment stressors such as poor shift patterns, lighting and physical challenges. However, these work demands may be compounded by other issues that may be creating a demand outside of the workplace at home or in one's community. In addition, stress theory also takes account of whether a person is currently undergoing major life events or is currently going through, or has in the past been the subject of, personal trauma or abuse. In isolation, these demands may be manageable by individuals; however, they may create a different demand proposition in combination, as we saw in the above case study.

Those supporting the board – such as a company secretary, head of HR, executive assistant or strategy adviser – may face a number of specific demands within their role. For example, they must maintain their independence to balance different parties' interests. They must manage a range of dilemmas and tensions, such as those that may naturally occur between the non-executives and company executives, while maintaining trust with both sides. Furthermore, the demand of increasing workload may come into play as their role becomes more significant due to increasing requirements and the recognition of the need for them to become involved in behavioural issues on top of technical ones. All of these often arise within the context of being unsupported and not fully understood or appreciated for the understated role that an effective professional often plays.

Appraisal

Stress theories suggest that the combination of demands that are currently being placed on an individual are then perceived by the individual as either *opportunities* or *threats*. It seems strange that we are suggesting that stress may be perceived as an opportunity; however, there is a concept called 'eustress', which is defined as stress that has a positive impact on an individual. In fact, we know that all organisms need some level of stress for them to thrive. It is only when this stress is perceived as overly demanding that it can have negative consequences.

What might be perceived as an opportunity to one person may actually be perceived as a threat by someone else. For example, when major organisational changes are announced, we know that different people have different responses based on such factors as their genetics, their level of development and maturity, their life experience and training and their personality types. This is good news as, although some aspect of our appraisal systems will remain fixed, our ability to increasingly view demands as opportunities for growth is able to be enhanced through a variety of methods that we shall discuss later in the chapter.

One example of this difference comes from the field of how one experiences trauma. Although the concept of post-traumatic stress disorder – the stress that occurs as a consequence of significant and negatively appraised demands in one's life – has received much attention in recent years, there is also an accompanying condition known as post-traumatic growth. This is the personal development that occurs when a person is able to find the (however unlikely) positive benefits of going through a significantly traumatic life event. In fact, those people who are the most resilient are the ones who have come through the most difficulties in life.

Response

Once our brain has appraised something as a threat, our sympathetic nervous system goes into action, resulting in a number of initial physiological responses. The irises of our eyes narrow, our blood vessels contract, our heart starts beating faster, our adrenal glands release adrenaline and our body generally prepares for one of three responses: fight, flight or freeze.

Our evolutionary appraisal mechanism is, as a species, slightly weighted towards appraising demands as threatening. This is unsurprising, as there would have been an obvious statistical benefit in responding to a twig snapping as if it were a predator rather than a friend approaching because of the existential cost of getting the interpretation wrong. The nature of our modern world is such that we are constantly bombarded with potential threats but, even though they are no longer life-threatening, our brain cannot tell the difference and so creates the same physiological stress response. This constant level of bodily stress is the reason why the number of people suffering from burnout and stress-related illness has exponentially increased.

Being in this constant state of high alert eventually leads to a number of negative cognitive, physical, emotional and behavioural symptoms. At the cognitive level, we might experience our stress in terms of memory problems, poor judgement, indecision, attention deficit, inefficiency, brain fog and self-doubt. In terms of physical symptoms, we might experience our stress in terms of chest pain, high blood pressure, immunosuppression, bodily aches and pains, indigestion or irritable bowel syndrome, or skin problems. If we are more prone to experience our stress symptoms as emotional, we may experience them in terms of increased likelihood of depression, irritability, fatalistic thinking, cynicism, frustration, panic and anxiety. Finally, we may notice stress symptoms that are behavioural, which may include behaviours such as increased isolation, demotivation, insomnia, hypersomnia, increased alcohol/stimulant intake and a loss of sense of humour. As you can see, a number of these relate specifically to some of the issues we have discussed in the book around board dynamics, such as poor judgement and indecision; however, all of these symptoms can negatively affect senior leaders' ability to perform well over time.

These responses are normal and can be successfully coped with when an individual understands what coping mechanisms they have at their disposal. They can implement these with appropriate awareness and support. However, the individual must first recognise the symptoms that they are experiencing and be able to identify the source of the stress that is causing the symptoms.

Case study: Lloyds Bank's 'high-profile sick leave'

António Horta-Osório, a Portuguese banker, was appointed as the chief executive officer of Lloyds Bank in March 2011. In November 2011, he went on temporary leave due to exhaustion, which *The Evening Standard* labelled the most high-profile sick leave in the City. The following month, he announced that he was ready to return to work.

He has publicly acknowledged how his efforts in restoring Lloyds Bank's fortunes in 2011 almost shattered his mental health. He has since become a strong campaigner for employers to implement mental health and resilience schemes at work and to raise the profile of mental health generally so as to reduce its stigma.

Defining resilience

The resilient individual

The word 'resilience' has become a common term in the organisational and human resources lexicon. The current thinking is that personal resilience is now a required core competency of the twenty-first-century leader. For example, the UK-based global retailer Tesco includes resilience as one of its five core leadership skills (along with collaboration, empathy, responsiveness and innovation).

Many definitions currently exist for resilience, the majority of which usually include some version of the concept of 'bouncing back' (with some more marketing-orientated commentators having even coined the term 'bounce back-ability'). A slightly more precise and evidence-based definition to introduce for our purposes comes from the American Psychological Association (2019), which defines resilience as:

> The process of adapting well in the face of adversity, trauma, tragedy, threats or significant sources of stress – such as family and relationship problems, serious health problems or workplace and financial stressors. It means bouncing back from difficult experiences.

This definition nods to the fact that much of the resilience literature and research historically emanates from studies of childhood trauma, post-traumatic military populations and communities who have suffered from natural disasters. However, the more recent literature has expanded to include more 'normal' populations and has started to focus on both the family and work environments within which resilience might occur.

Although the 'bounce back' term is often used as a helpful shorthand into understanding resilience, there has been a recent critique that this does not capture the full extent of the term. For example, Jenny Campbell, chief executive officer of the UK company the Resilience Engine, describes the resilience dynamic as having three stages that we move through. These are the 'break down', the 'break even' (which encompasses the idea of coping to bounce back and which she contends much of the UK workforce plateaus at) and then the more aspirational 'break through' phase. This final stage captures the idea that there is a level of resilience that can propel one to becoming even more resourceful, adaptable and energised than one might have been before facing the sources of stress. This is similar to the concept of 'post-traumatic growth' that we mentioned earlier, in line with the research that the most emotionally mature people are those who have developed their innate and learned resilience to navigate significant life demands successfully.

In partnership with the Academy of Executive Coaching, Campbell published a survey on the demand for resilience in the workplace in November 2018. With a sample of over 200 respondents, the headline finding was that 82% of people acknowledged that their demand for resilience is currently high. However, only 10% of respondents agreed that this demand was manageable for them. This suggests a significant current need to support people to increase their resilience resourcefulness in the workplace. This will help those people shift, as Campbell suggests, from simply oscillating in a repeating pattern between break-down and break-even, such that they might be more likely not just to bounce back but, in addition, achieve a breakthrough.

The resilient board member

There is currently very little research or information on resilience in the boardroom. Similarly, there is also paltry specific advice on how to develop resilience in the boardroom apart from the recent book, *The Resilient Director* by Michael Willis et al. (2017), which explores director resilience as we have defined it in its first chapter. The authors contrast resilience with what they call 'compression' as a consequence of stress which, at board level, has a number of causal factors that include the following:

- Life as a director can be lonely and largely unsupervised, whereby each director has to find their own way of being and behaving.
- Managing and being part of a team that often has difficult personalities that can be a destructive force in the life of the board.
- Being part of the board that has unrealistic expectations of itself, its members and its chair, which can lead to disillusionment at best, or personal and organisational breakdown at worst.
- Poor board processes or processes that are offered in ways that are inaccessible, inappropriate, or even not available at all such as induction, evaluation, performance management, mentoring, etc., such that the learning board is not yet a reality.
- A failure to review the work of the board, especially if this does not compare well with the increasing role of accountability found within the rest of the organisation.

In relation to the individuals outside the boardroom, there is a growing realisation of the need for the competency of resilience in effective governance professionals. The Chartered Governance Institute's 2018 Competency Framework for Governance Professionals defines one of the core values enabling good governance as being 'purposeful'. Within being purposeful is the sub-value of resilience. The framework defines four levels of competency proficiency being 'entry', 'emerging', 'established' and 'excelling', such that a governance professional who is established 'shows resilience when dealing with powerful personalities and emotions and demonstrates perseverance in the face of challenges'. Further, a governance professional who is highly competent and perceived as 'excelling' will be 'solutions-driven and demonstrates tenacity, resilience and persistence in reaching the right decision'.

Building resilience

Now that we have a clear understanding of the need for resilience in the boardroom based on the demands that exist and we also have an appreciation of how the symptoms of stress can occur, it is now time to turn our attention to how to build resilience, both in theory and in practice, and to see how this has been applied in organisations in recent years.

Resilience in theory

There are a variety of theories of resilience. This section will describe two of those that have emerged from the evidence that have been applied practically in organisations.

Based on the stress model above, we can see that all resilience techniques must affect one or more of these three aspects of stress. We can intervene by reducing the demands, which is known as 'problem-focused coping'; we can find ways to change our perception of the demands that still exist, which is known as 'appraisal-focused coping'; or we can develop coping strategies to deal with the symptoms of stress, broadly known as 'emotion-focused coping'. All aspects of resilience can therefore be located in one or more of these areas of coping.

One of the most evidence-based and well-known frameworks for resilience is the 'Resilience Prescription', created by the academics Stephen Southwick and Dennis Charney, who have studied resilient people for more than 20 years. Their samples have included Vietnam prisoners of war, special forces instructors and civilians who have dealt with challenging experiences like medical emergencies, abuse and trauma. In their book, *Resilience: The Science of Mastering Life's Greatest Challenges*, they describe their 10-point prescription which summarises their research on what resilient people have in common. These characteristics are:

1 looking after your physical condition;
2 developing and training regularly in multiple areas (emotional, mental, moral, physical, etc.);
3 a positive attitude and optimism;
4 developing coping strategies and making use of them;
5 developing cognitive flexibility and learning to reframe;
6 facing your fears;
7 having actively found resilient role models;
8 recognising and developing your signature strengths;
9 a strong personal moral compass and sense of purpose; and
10 establishing and nurturing a supportive social network.

The most resilient individuals were found to have had all of these 10 attributes in common, which enabled them to negotiate their significant demands successfully. How one cultivates each of these can be done in many ways and the following section will provide a number of pointers to doing this.

The second framework for resilience is the 'i-resilience' model developed by Professor Ivan Robertson and Sir Cary Cooper. This model has an associated validated personality questionnaire that has been completed by over 150,000 individuals and is accessible for free online through the developers' website (see 'Useful references'). The i-resilience model has four aspects:

1 **Confidence** – having feelings of competence, effectiveness in coping with stressful situations and strong self esteem.
2 **Social support** – building good relationships with others and seeking support... rather than trying to cope on their own.
3 **Adaptability** – flexibility in adapting to changing situations which are beyond our control... [and the ability] to cope well with change and recover from its impact quicker.
4 **Purposefulness** – having a clear sense of purpose, clear values, drive and direction [to] help individuals to persist and achieve in the face of setbacks.

As you might notice, there are a number of overlaps between the i-resilience framework and the Resilience Prescription. However, the i-resilience framework is mentioned here as it has specifically been tailored to organisations, has a validated measure and is slightly simpler to grasp.

Any professional individual might be interested to use these models (and their associated diagnostics) as a way to raise their own self-awareness of their current levels of resilience in their role or in their life more broadly. They might therefore be able to focus on natural strengths to build on and also potential weaknesses to mitigate against. Assessing and sharing director self-perceptions, as part of board one-to-one or team coaching, can also be a useful process so that others can either provide peer feedback or be more appreciative of the relative strengths and weaknesses in their board team.

Resilience in practice

There are numerous practical methods that have been used to develop personal resilience. The range of techniques presented is by no means exhaustive, but does provide a useful and evidence-based starting point to cope with demands, reframe thinking or manage stress symptoms. Similar to the progression of psychology introduced in Chapter 4, the techniques are separated out into behavioural (or physical) approaches, cognitive approaches, humanistic approaches and social approaches.

Physical

The physical approaches to resilience can either operate as a method of building resilience to prevent stress in the first place, or as an antidote to stress when it arises. They can be divided into three topics, following Tom Rath's excellent book on the same subject, *Eat, Move, and Sleep*.

Interestingly, all of the principles and approaches associated with healthy nutrition, exercise and sleep largely aim to recreate the conditions that we evolved with on earth over millions of years. This 'ancestral approach' to physical health suggests that it is mostly the side-effects of our modern lifestyles, which have only existed for the last century or so, that are creating the current chronic health epidemic and associated reduced physical resilience. Ironically, it is now modern technology, through various tracking devices and self-quantifying apps, which is providing greater individual insight and impetus to develop this aspect of our resilience.

Eat

Although many diets are professed to be the answer, based on our genetic variation and differing lifestyles there is perhaps no one diet or way of eating that fits every individual. However, there are some broad evidence-based principles that are generally agreed across all nutrition professionals. Firstly, one should attempt to limit as many stimulants as possible, particularly sugar and caffeine, to reduce the body's natural stress response spikes throughout the day. Some practical suggestions are as follows:

- Limit sugar-based drinks (this includes diet varieties and fruit juices).
- Decrease the percentage of simple carbohydrates in the diet (often found in processed foods, cereals and baked goods).
- Although there are mental and physical benefits to caffeine consumption, limit to two or three cups a day before 2pm.
- Drink smaller cups of caffeinated drinks, or perhaps introduce decaffeinated or herbal drinks as a replacement.
- Introduce a physical 'movement snack' to substitute the chemical stimulant fix in a normal sweet snack.
- Consider intermittent fasting once a week to reset one's insulin sensitivity and satiety reflex.

Secondly, it is advisable to reduce the level of toxins, irritants and inflammatory foods that one consumes. This would include foods that have gluten (such as bread, cereals and pasta), those from genetically modified origins, those that have industrial seed oils in them (such as sunflower oil) and heavily refined food more generally. Finally, some ancestral principals for eating are to include as many whole foods, that is, those that need no label (like a fruit, a bean, a nut, an egg or a vegetable) as possible, to buy local seasonal and organic foods where possible, to consume grass-fed meat and dairy, free range poultry and eggs and wild rather than farmed fish that are lower in mercury (being salmon, mackerel, anchovy, sardine and herring, the so-called smaller, SMASH fish).

Move

Southwick and Charney's 'Resilience Prescription' research describes exercise as the 'magic bullet' to resilience. There is a significant amount of evidence that shows that low levels of physical activity lead to a greater likelihood of experiencing stress, poorer psychological wellbeing and the likelihood of reacting to stress more extremely when it occurs.

The impact of taking up physical activity has been shown to be equivalent to receiving cognitive behavioural therapy and is now prescribed medically for those diagnosed with mental illness. More generally, exercise has been shown to combat the 'stasis syndromes' such as obesity-related diseases, heart disease and various cancers.

However, the research does not suggest that we define 'exercising' as committing a block of time every day in one's diary or indeed to subscribing to a gym membership. More practically, the research suggests that we gain all the resilience benefits of exercise by building it into our day and moving more whenever we can. For example, parking at the other end of the car park, taking the stairs rather than the lift and using one's bike to commute when possible are some lifestyle methods of incorporating exercise without having to schedule it into one's calendar. In addition to moving more for aerobic benefits, we also need to challenge our muscular system regularly. However, rather than pumping iron in the gym (which is great if practical and enjoyed, of course), one can build the habit of doing a few simple bodyweight exercises while waiting for the kettle to boil.

If one is interested in committing to something more formal and organised, the recommendation is that this should be fun, social and, if possible, outside to get the psychological benefits of sunlight and nature. The recent explosion in the NHS 'Couch to 5K' initiative, outdoor bootcamp sessions and Saturday morning parkruns is testament of this.

Sleep

Historically, pushing through and working all hours has been seen as a badge of honour in organisational life. For example, there was considerable press reporting of former UK Prime Minister Margaret Thatcher's need for only four hours' sleep per night.

However, sleep is now increasingly being seen as the secret weapon in corporate performance. The impact of either a lack of sleep or poor sleep is incredibly significant on our ability to be resilient the next day and on our resilience and well-being more generally. Our bodies are just not evolved to cope with the lack of quantity and quality of sleep that most people are getting on average in recent years. One worrying statistic is that in 1942, the average American adult got 7.9 hours sleep per night, whereas in 2018 this had dropped to only 6.5 hours. This 20% drop in only 80 years is causing significant stress issues in the global developed working population. In the naturally controlled experiment of the clocks changing in spring and autumn, we find that with one hour of lost sleep, the incidence of heart attacks the following day goes up by a staggering 24% in spring, but with the gain of one hour in the autumn, the instance of heart attacks drops by 21%.

One particular statistic that is relevant to board directors is the impact of a lack of sleep on one's emotional intelligence – one of the key criteria to building collaboration in teams. A 2015 study found that those who report less than 6.5 hours of sleep the previous night score significantly lower on subjective emotional intelligence compared to those who report over eight hours' sleep the previous night. This means that the quality of sleep the night before a board meeting may be one of the key predictors of the success of the meeting the following day. Some practical steps to improve on sleep are:

- Keep a consistent routine of sleeping hours (even on the weekend, as 'catching up' on sleep is not possible mentally or physiologically).
- Ensure one is at the right temperature when going to bed (around 19°C is advised, which is perhaps slightly lower than one might think). Core body temperature can be reduced by having a shower or bath in the evening, which, paradoxically, draws heat out of the body as it attempts to cool itself.
- Commit to light hygiene by turning house lights down in the evening or replacing bright bulbs for lower lumens and warmer non-blue wavelengths; limit screen use within an hour of sleep; if screens are necessary, turn them to night modes or purchase blue blocking glasses or use blue-blocking apps such as Iris or f-lux.
- Stop caffeine intake after 2pm.
- Limit alcohol intake before bed (this may help one get to sleep, but the sleep will be of significantly lower quality).
- Consider using melatonin to aid sleep, especially to combat jet lag, rather than using over-the-counter sleeping pills (like alcohol, these result in unconsciousness rather than quality sleep cycles).

Cognitive

When someone goes on a resilience training course, flicks through a resilience blog article or picks up the latest resilience book, they are most likely to find recommendations for the cognitive approaches to building resilience. This section will detail these components under the generic sections of being able to re-frame, inoculate, build belief and actively cope. The first three of these support individuals to shift their appraisals of environmental demands away from being threats and towards them seeing them as opportunities. On the contrary, active coping resilience tools are mostly used as a way to deal with stress symptoms in a planful way.

Reframing

We know that taking a more positive view on life, being hopeful and optimistic, is associated with a great number of improved psychological outcomes. On the contrary, pessimism is a maladaptive behaviour in most situations. There is research that shows that pessimistic life insurance agents make fewer sales attempts, are less productive and persistent and are more likely to quit than their more optimistic peers. Similarly, pessimistic students get lower grades, relative to their aptitude tests and past academic record, than optimistic students.

Pessimists are often very good at what has been termed 'crooked thinking' – that is, they are very good at catastrophising ('I just know it's going to be a disaster'), overgeneralising ('We never deal with change well here'), discounting the positive ('Nothing went right'), negative predictions ('I will never be able to meet that deadline'), mind-reading ('My team look bored, they're not interested in what I'm saying'), black-and-white thinking ('If we don't win this client opportunity, we'll go out of business') and taking things personally ('They said my time management could be improved, but I'm useless'). In general, pessimists are likely to tell themselves that bad events are permanent, pervasive (that is, universal) and personal (their own fault). Optimists, on the other hand, are able to see the exact opposite. They can perceive bad events as temporary, having a specific cause rather than being universal and not their fault.

It is sometimes useful, however, to be pessimistic. For example, pessimism in lawyers is often seen as a plus, as they are able to defend clients against what might seem far-fetched eventualities. However, this comes at a high price, as lawyers are around 3.6 times more likely to suffer from depression and are more likely to end up getting divorced than the average profession. Governance professions may also benefit from targeted pessimism in order to notice and articulate potential risk. However, the skill here is in being able to deploy pessimism only in specific situations while working and living life more generally as an optimist.

Although optimism is somewhat determined by one's genetics, it is possible to develop. Rather than just forcing oneself to think more positively, though, optimism is developed by first noticing one's thoughts and language, possibly through self-reflection, coaching and feedback, and then, secondly, disputing those thoughts. This is the essence of a cognitive behavioural therapy approach. In this age of technology and in the absence of engaging in full-blown therapy, evidence-based and accessible digital solutions such as the WOOP app are useful resources.

Inoculate

The most widely known stress inoculation method, perhaps the one that is most recommended to develop one's resilience, is the practice of mindfulness. This is the 'psychological process of bringing one's attention to experiences occurring in the present moment'. It can be developed through the practice of meditation, which is often recommended as a timed daily practice, or one can develop and practice mindfulness as one progresses through one's daily activities.

A strand of mindfulness called 'mindfulness-based stress reduction', developed by American professor of medicine John Kabat-Zinn, has its roots in Buddhist spiritual teachings, but itself is secular. This and another approach called 'mindfulness-based cognitive therapy' have been shown to have positive outcomes in supporting those with depression, for example, and, more broadly, mindfulness has been used in various aspects of society, including in schools, business and even government. Companies such as Google, Apple and Procter & Gamble currently offer mindfulness coaching and resources to improve both employee well-being and performance and hundreds of MPs in the British Parliament, for example, have recently received mindfulness training.

Significantly, perhaps, for the boardroom population, mindfulness has been correlated with more emotional regulation and ethical decision making. Unsurprisingly, there are many resources on mindfulness including apps that can be used to support one's practice such as Andy Puddicombe's Headspace (which has been credited by many Olympic athletes), Oak and Waking Up.

Beyond mindfulness, there are a number of more physical methods of stress inoculation which train the brain and body to notice stress but not be caught up in it. These include:

- cold therapies, such as cold water dowsing and cold showers/baths (as advocated by the Dutch resilience guru Wim Hof);
- heat therapies, such as the use of saunas which has been shown to have significant health benefits in the Finnish populations that habitually use them;
- breath-holding, which has been popularised by divers and the surfing community; and
- fasting, which has been found to have many physical and psychological benefits.

Build belief

Self-belief can be separated into the two distinct but related concepts of self-esteem and self-confidence (one of the key components of the i-resilience framework). Self-esteem is defined as 'how we value ourselves as a human being', is developed over time and is less likely to change based on current demands. Self-confidence, however, is 'the trust that we have in ourselves to deliver in specific circumstances'. This is more easily and immediately influenced by external conditions. There are four main methods of developing both self-esteem and self-confidence. These are as follows:

1 **Acknowledge one's performance accomplishments** – in order to build self-esteem, ask questions such as, 'What have I achieved?', 'What am I most proud of?' and 'What attributes do I have that enabled me to achieve these?' To build self-confidence, rather than noticing what is missing and not achieved on the to-do list at the end of the day or in a meeting, ask, 'What's better today and what have I achieved?'
2 **Use others' success vicariously** – find a resilient role model and recognise that they may have been in the position that you currently find yourself in. Ask yourself 'What could I learn from them and what would they do in my situation?'
3 **Verbal persuasion** – use positive affirmations to act as if you are resilient or have already achieved the outcome.
4 **Emotional arousal** – when feeling a lack of confidence, change your emotional state by using techniques such as physically moving or listening to energetic music.

Active coping

The final toolkit of cognitive resilience are those active coping methodologies that are practical methods to reduce cognitive anxiety and the feeling of being overwhelmed that are often symptoms of negative reframing. Some examples of simple techniques include the following:

- **Morning routines** – starting the day proactively and with a positive intent can make a huge difference to the rest of one's day. Morning routines that involve some light physical activity such as walking or stretching, some positive mental activities such as meditation or journaling, or even something simple as making your bed (which sets one's brain onto a more positive trajectory) have been found to be extremely positive for one's mental well-being.
- **Time management** – stopping to write down everything that is in one's head, especially before sleep, is a useful and researched way to reduce mental rumination. The urgency and importance matrix, whereby one allocates all one's jobs into one of four boxes, is a very useful simple tool to recognise that one may be unduly worrying about things that are urgent but not important and enables one to focus back on what is important.
- **Assigning uninterrupted 'deep work' time** – once one's important tasks are recognised, timetabling and protecting time to work on these tasks has been shown to be incredibly mentally liberating. Ensure that notifications are turned off and that one stays in uni-task mode rather than multitasking

(which has been shown to be detrimental to one's resilience) by using time-boxing techniques such as the 'Pomodoro method'.

Humanistic

In Chapter 4, we introduced the humanistic approach to psychology as one that acknowledges and studies the whole person and their healthy potential and which focuses on topics such as creativity, empathy, motivation and meaning. The humanistic techniques to build resilience include those mentioned by both the Resilience Prescription and the i-resilience frameworks. These can be synthesised into the three areas of applying one's 'signature strengths', developing one's moral compass and finding greater meaning and purpose in daily activities.

Signature strengths

The concept of signature strengths was developed by Professor Martin Seligman, one of the world's leading thinkers on resilience and former president of the American Psychological Association. The concept is based on the acknowledgement that we each have different abilities which, if fully realised through our actions, will enable us to become both resilient and able to perform at sustainably high levels.

Seligman's 'Values in Action' inventory is a psychological assessment measure which is designed to identify an individual's profile of signature character strengths. There are 24 character strengths, which cluster into six areas: wisdom/knowledge, courage, humility, justice, temperance and transcendence. A self-assessment on this online test followed by a combination of personal reflection, coaching and/or boardroom peer discussion can raise awareness and generate actions that may have a positive impact on one's future resilience.

Moral compass

We have discussed the development of an ethical character in the boardroom in some detail in relation to competencies in Chapter 3 and also ethical culture in Chapter 7. One of the aforementioned key thinkers on corporate ethics is Professor Roger Steare, who has developed an assessment of corporate ethics called MoralDNA. This assessment helps an individual become more aware of one's moral character in relation to one's ethic of obedience, ethic of care and ethic of reason, in work and in life in general.

Beyond using this assessment, there are a number of practical habits that one can deploy to develop one's moral compass. Of particular note is the tool of 'gratitude journaling', whereby individuals capture what they are grateful for every morning and/or evening. The use of gratitude journals over time not only correlates with spiritual and moral wellbeing but also has been shown to be associated with better sleep, a less depressed mood, less fatigue and even lower levels of physical inflammatory biomarkers. The *Five Minute Journal*, available both in physical book form and as a digital app, is a good resource for those who want to apply the practice.

Meaning

In the same way that the best practice of high-performing teams includes the development of a strong and compelling team purpose, developing clarity around one's own individual meaning and purpose also has significant benefits for a variety of positive physical and mental outcomes, including resilience.

The development of meaning has been formalised as a therapy, known as logotherapy, developed by Viktor Frankl, who recounts his own experience of resilience through purpose as a World War II prisoner of war in his seminal book *Man's Search for Meaning*. Frankel's philosophy is summarised in the Nietzsche quote, 'He who has a why to live for can bear almost any how.'

A more recent application of the same philosophy as related to organisations is found in Simon Sinek's 'Start With Why' TED talk and process, which outlines how to discover and develop one's purpose, through either guided individual reflection or peer coaching support.

Social

The final method of developing one's resilience is underpinned by the recognition that we have evolved as social animals and we therefore need other people in our environment to be fully human. Research has shown that social connections with other people releases oxytocin in our bodies, which is calming and stress reducing, and that this happens as much when we are giving others help as receiving help. In recent years, social support has become recognised as potentially the first place to start in building one's resilience. As the American Psychological Association notes, 'Many studies show that the primary factor in resilience is having caring and supportive relationships within and outside the family.'

In a board or work context, this may mean giving or receiving coaching and mentoring support, being involved in an action learning set or community of practice and attending either formal events such as conferences or informal work gatherings. Outside of work, social support may involve guarding time with one's family, developing hobbies that take you into different social groups and connecting through travel or volunteering. Although it may seem a luxury to engage in social connection time, research is unequivocal about the fact that it is vital as a way of improving functioning and performance.

For example, a recent study explored whether rotas in a large call centre should be either more efficient, such that there was no overlap between shifts and people never met peers in coffee breaks, or less efficient but more social. Paradoxically, it was found that average customer call time went down (even though customer satisfaction remained stable), boosting productivity and saving the company millions of dollars when overlapping coffee breaks were factored into the rota design. All this occurred because of informal social sharing, which also had the impact of reducing employee stress levels which, not surprisingly, resulted in less turnover.

Resilience programmes

The concept of resilience is now so pervasive that it is highly likely that most large organisations in the private, public and not-for-profit sectors have now engaged with resilience in some capacity. At one end of the spectrum, large organisations, such as the retail giants Tesco and Sainsbury's, have chosen to name resilience as a leadership competence that will then be fully integrated into talent management processes, including selection, induction, performance management and development.

However, as yet, the concept of resilience and the systematic development of resilience capabilities in the boardroom is considerably underdeveloped. It is therefore a significant opportunity for governance professionals first to role-model resilience by developing their own capabilities, but then also to lead and support the development of directors in the boardroom as the service of enhancing governance through board dynamics. But what might these programmes of resilience look like?

One useful resource to answer this question is the recent systematic review on resilience training in the workplace from Professor Ivan Robertson et al., published in 2015. The study identified 155 published peer-reviewed articles since 2003 on resilience training and selected only 14 of these for their robustness to examine the validity of the outcomes they found for resilience training. The 14 studies included programmes that varied in length from a single 90-minute session to workshops running over a period of three months and included online programmes as well as those that incorporated 2.5-day face-to-face retreats and group workshops supported by one-to-one coaching.

Positive psychology approaches, such as those mentioned in the humanistic section above, and cognitive behavioural therapy were the most commonly used resilience approaches; however, mindfulness and biofeedback technology-led programmes were also used. The study concluded that resilience training may provide benefits for subjective wellbeing outcomes such as stress, anxiety, depression and negative emotional responses. It also showed significant positive effects on self-efficacy and reduction in participant fatigue after resilience training. One study also reported an increase in participant anti-thrombin levels after training (anti-thrombin is an anticoagulant which helps prevent thrombosis) and a reduction in the stress hormone cortisol. The systematic review concluded that, for resilience training to be effective, an organisation needs to be clear on what they mean by resilience and then to design interventions that build from that definition. Further, although there appeared to be no one best method of developing resilience, the authors advised that some element of one-to-one coaching or ongoing support is likely to create better outcomes.

Case study: Lloyds Bank's mental health resilience programmes

As mentioned in an earlier case study in this chapter, the chief executive officer of Lloyds Bank, António Horta-Osório, is now an advocate for raising awareness of mental health issues at work following his own personal high-profile experience of burnout.

Not surprisingly, Lloyds is a role model for developing resilience programmes that both support people who have experienced, or are currently experiencing, poor mental health and building the resilience capacity of employees so that they are less likely to experience these issues in the first place. Some of the interventions that they have used are as follows:

- Sharing personal experiences on their intragroup website by publishing stories of colleagues who have experienced poor mental health so as to normalise the phenomenon.
- Implementing an employee assistance programme helpline to provide advice on coping with anxiety, mindfulness and dealing with self-control.
- Launching a colleague social media competition to share top tips for improving mental well-being at work which has since turned into a continuous live conversation, including over 2,000 colleague entries.
- Developing a leadership programme called 'optimal leadership resilience' which covers nutrition, heart monitoring, sleep management, mindfulness, psychological testing and analysis. Initially created for the group executive committee and the top 200 senior leaders, the programme has also been extended to the next 2,000 group leaders.
- Increasing private medical cover available for mental health conditions to be equal to that for physical conditions.

A resilient board dynamic

So far, we have considered resilience from an individual perspective. As we know from the concepts described in Chapter 6, our behaviours can be as much influenced by the systemic context within which we find ourselves as they are by our own individual physiology and psychology. We will consider briefly how the broader board dynamic may be influencing an individual's resilience, including that of board directors, looking particularly at the key individual relationships that a senior individual has and also the broader board culture in which they are working.

Relationships

As we have seen, supportive relationships are one of the primary factors in maintaining resilience. However, because maintaining independence and discretion is key to many senior roles, this is often difficult to achieve internally within an organisation. As one respondent mentioned in The Chartered Governance Institute's 2014 report on the role of the company secretary:

> It can be the loneliest job in the organisation... You have to have the strength of character and professionalism to stand alone if need be and do what you believe is right... Regardless of others around you trying to push or influence... and regardless, to an extent, of what you believe, (if) it is the strategy of the board.

Developing high-quality relationships may also be somewhat compromised, depending upon an individual's reporting structure. Rather than reporting directly to the governing board, individuals may find themselves reporting into an executive function, including chief executive officers, chief operating officers, chief financial officers/finance directors, legal teams and perhaps company owners (often in smaller organisations) in a dual reporting line. These reporting lines may not be ideal: they can contribute to a significant amount of role conflict and excessive or mixed demands placed upon an individual, who may feel that their main role is compromised.

The quality of relationship that an individual has with the chair of the board of directors, moderated by the chair's leadership style, is perhaps one of the greatest factors in the requirement for, or the development of, resilience in any role associated with the board. This was especially highlighted by the Swiss case example at the start of the chapter. As Sir Cary Cooper writes in the Chartered Management Institute's 'Quality of working life' report (2016):

> The thing that is causing people to get ill at work and adversely affect their quality of working life is line managers who are not socially and interpersonally skilled – they don't have the soft skills that are needed.

Even though the demands of an individual's role may be significant, they will be more manageable with appropriate levels of support from their line manager, in this case, the chair. They may have all the individual resilience tools in their armoury; however, these will simply become a sticking plaster over a continually open wound created by poor chair understanding and support. As one of the respondents in The Chartered Governance Institute report notes, 'when a relationship with the chairman is not working, you leave... And it may or may not be of your choosing.'

The resilient board

One final consideration which will dictate the level of individual and board director resilience is the extent that the board culture itself engenders resilience. The board culture will be explained by the patterns of board relationships and whether the board 'team tasks' are appropriate to support resilience. We touched on the research of resilient teams in Chapter 4 and employing this information is a useful starting point. Further, the concept of creating a resilient environment has been researched by Professor Peter Heslin, an associate Professor at the University of New South Wales, based in Sydney, Australia. Heslin writes that:

> Many people think good management is about doing more with less. The result is that people are having to work harder and constantly produce more, with less administrative support. Managers and employees alike are being seriously squeezed... The most effective businesses work out how to lower the heat in the kitchen and understand the benefits of treating their people well. Yes, there are important strategies that an individual can learn to do, but ultimately, leaders should pride themselves on creating environments that foster resilience.

How, then, can a board create an 'environment that fosters resilience'? Robertson and Cooper (2017) describe six essential conditions of well-being which are required to do this in organisations, which will for our purposes enable the creation of a 'well board'. These are as follows:

1. **Resources and communication** – ensure that there is reduced pressure by providing appropriate resources and information. For example, ensure board packs are distributed with ample time and include appropriate information so that it is that is easy to digest. More generally, ensure that there is continuous formal and informal 'check-in' communication between board members.
2. **Control and autonomy** – ensure that there are as few limitations on how the director job is done as possible to enable freedom to make appropriate decisions. This can be ensured through fully clarifying roles, expectations and boundaries through the induction process, by creating opportunities for input before meetings around agendas and after meetings to review meeting processes.
3. **Balanced workload** – ensure that there are peaks and troughs in workload, that deadlines and unsociable hours are managed and that work–life balance challenges are worked through.
4. **Job security and change** – manage the pressure from change and uncertainty about the future of the board through regular updates on governance changes.
5. **Work relationships** – identify whose role it is to facilitate and, if necessary, mediate, the potentially high-pressure relationships between board directors, as well as with employees and with other key stakeholders.
6. **Job conditions** – strive to improve work conditions and the boardroom environment, drawing on the factors mentioned in Chapter 9, even in the absence of tangible pay and benefits true of director roles in some sectors.

Conclusion

There is an increasing need for resilience in the modern workplace to manage stress for all individuals in the workplace. This includes the twenty-first-century governance professional, who must begin to see themselves as a 'corporate athlete'.

Resilience is defined as the ability to bounce back from adversity, with resilient individuals exhibiting a number of key physical, mental, emotional and social attributes that they have acquired from both nature and nurture. There are a variety of resilience techniques that can be learnt and applied to one's work and life.

Companies are increasingly implementing resilience programmes to support employee wellbeing and performance. However, these have not reached the boardroom in any meaningful way, despite the breadth of reporting on workplace wellbeing and the reported increase in levels of stress.

What are the options for developing a more resilient board? Most starting points for developing resilience will focus on the development of individual resilience through training in cognitive techniques, such as reframing and mindfulness. Initial research has shown that this approach may work to some extent, but it is by no means the full picture. Other options may therefore be to: role-model and share information/stories about resilient behaviours to educate others; focus on training other drivers of personal resilience (such as physical health, building belief, active coping processes, building on strengths, developing gratitude, reframing one's 'why' and building social connections); employ and encourage more supportive leadership styles; and develop an environment that fosters resilience (through regular communication, supporting autonomy, balancing workload, reducing uncertainty, enhancing relationships and improving basic job conditions).

In addition to individual competencies, tools and techniques, the resilience of any individual working alongside or with the board is also influenced by their personal role structure, their chair's style and relationship, their interaction with other board members and by the culture of the board.

There is no corporate or personal prize given for ignoring signs of stress in ourselves or our colleagues. The global pandemic has also identified the differing ways that stress can affect us all with the move to home-working replacing the stresses of office working and commuting with significant work–life conflicts. Being able to recognise stress, and then build a personal form of resilience, is crucial to each individual. Being able to identify and empathise with the challenges of others, and to provide meaningful support, will create benefits for the wider business. As the experience of a multitude of high-profile leaders has shown, the impact of stress on both work and non-work life can be considerable. If it is not addressed at an early stage, stress in leaders and board members may permeate through an organisation's culture, damaging the bottom line, the reputation and, ulimately, the whole future of the organisation.

What are your options for building personal resilience, identifying stress in others and providing support to your colleagues? How can your organisation learn from others and the wider business world, especially after the onset of COVID-19 restrictions and the resultant increase in stress?

Conclusion

The aim of this book was to introduce the theory of boardroom dynamics with examples of its practical application. The intention was to provide a foundation of broad knowledge on the topic while introducing thought-provoking examples and questions on its application in the real environment.

The topic of boardroom dynamics and all its component parts has increased in discussion and dissemination in recent years, especially when aligned to the effectiveness of a board and the impact that an ineffective board can have on the health and success of an organisation.

Throughout this book, we have touched on both the dynamics within the boardroom itself and the board as a collective, as well as the dynamics in play between the individual members of the board themselves. With a greater understanding and recognition of these various elements, as well as a conscious acceptance of their influence, a board and the individuals in and around it can create greater harmony and success.

From the effects of cultural differences, to diversity, psychology and governance structures, the task has been to introduce the concepts in a clear way so that readers can identify them in play within their own organisation. By recognising each element, the potential benefits of what is already in place can be enhanced, whilst negative factors can be minimised or addressed.

We have also recognised the considerable influence of individuals working alongside the board, whether as governance professionals or in other similar roles. Their potential role as an invisible leader and/or team coach (where the team is the board) has enormous potential to support, create or influence a highly effective board. Individuals fulfilling this role may undertake this either consciously or unconsciously. Even if not in the role of an 'invisible leader', the ability to identify that role in others and recognise its importance is invaluable.

When looking below the board, the dynamics between a management team can also make a significant difference. Larger organisations will recognise this in the differences seen between different offices or, in a retail scenario, stores. Even with the same overall leadership, strategy and culture, the dynamics in play within the management teams of two different offices, locations or stores will result in different levels of success. If it can be clearly seen at this level, consider the difference that a highly effective board can make to the overall organisation.

Throughout this book, we have introduced practical applications of the theories we have described. Equally, practical aspects were introduced where they have a direct impact on the board and its effectiveness. Elements such as the physical environment and meeting design were presented and explained in the context of boardroom interactions and success. Decision making in all its forms, as well as tools aligned to decision making, were discussed and developed in detail. This is crucial: a board that is incapable of making decisions will be ineffective, no matter what dynamics are in play between members and within the board room.

Equally, the stakeholders of an organisation were considered, recognising the development of wider stakeholder engagement as an increasingly important phenomena beyond simply treating the shareholder as the only stakeholder. Across the chapters the input from, and communication to, stakeholders was directly and indirectly introduced to emphasise the importance of the board delivering success for all concerned.

Finally, it should be noted that dynamics within a boardroom are not the responsibility of any one person. The expectation is that all those connected to a board will strive to deliver success. The knowledge and understanding provided by this text should form a part of the reader's understanding of the breadth of the topic. Its application is a duty for all concerned for the benefit of the whole organisation. By recognising and applying the most relevant elements, the reader may also gain personal benefit in their own career.

Having gained this knowledge and understanding of the broad range of topics aligned to boardroom dynamics and the interplay between individuals the final question for consideration is:

How will you apply this knowledge to your own career as well as within the organisation you work for?

Directory of web resources

American Psychological Association
www.apa.org

Centre for Evidence-Based Management
www.cebma.org

Chartered Institute of Professional Development
www.cipd.co.uk

Cognitive Bias Codex
https://betterhumans.coach.me

Good Judgment Project online course
https://good-judgment.thinkific.com/courses/Superforecasting-Fundamentals

Hofstede Country Culture Insights
www.hofstede-insights.com

Implicit Association Test
https://implicit.harvard.edu/implicit/uk

Index of Common Board Problems
www.chamber101.com

Institute of Business Ethics
www.ibe.org.uk

Jim Collins
www.jimcollins.com

Punctuality around the world
www.mrgamez.com/punctuality

RobertsonCooper Ltd (2019). i-resilience questionnaire
www.robertsoncooper.com/iresilience

Social Intelligence test
https://socialintelligence.labinthewild.org/mite

Spencer Stuart
www.spencerstuart.com/research-and-insight/ukbi-2018

Glossary

Board culture – the repeating patterns of the board dynamic.

Board dynamics – the interactions between board members individually and collectively and how these influence, and are influenced by, their wider stakeholder system.

Boardroom dynamics – the interactions between board members individually and collectively in the boardroom.

Coaching – unlocking a person's potential to maximise their own performance. It is helping them to learn rather than teaching them.

Cognitive bias – a systematic pattern of deviation from norm or rationality in judgment.

Cohesion – the tendency for a group to be in unity while working towards a goal or to satisfy the emotional needs of its members.

Collective intelligence – shared or group intelligence that emerges from the collaboration, collective efforts and competition of many individuals and appears in consensus decision making.

Competency – a cluster of related knowledge, skills and attitudes that affect a major part of one's job (a role or responsibility), that correlates with performance on the job, that can be measured against well-accepted standards and that can be improved via training and development.

Counselling – the process of assisting and guiding clients, especially by a trained person on a professional basis, to resolve especially personal, social, or psychological problems and difficulties.

Cronotype – the behavioural manifestation of underlying circadian rhythms of myriad physical processes.

Cultural intelligence – an outsider's seemingly natural ability to interpret someone's unfamiliar and ambiguous gestures the way that person's compatriots would.

Cultural sensitivity – being interested in other cultures, sensitive enough to notice cultural differences and then also willing to modify behaviour as an indication of respect for the people of other cultures.

Culture – a pattern of shared basic assumptions that was learned by a group as it solved problems of external adaptation and internal integration, has worked well enough to be considered valid and, therefore, to be taught to new members as the correct way to perceive, think and feel in relation to those problems.

Diversity – valuing everyone as individuals.

Emotional intelligence – the ability to identify and manage one's own emotions, as well as the emotions of others.

Ethnocentrism – the act of judging another culture based on preconceptions that are found in values and standards of one's own culture.

Evidence-based practice – the conscientious (effort), explicit (clarity) and judicious (critical and quality) use of the best available evidence from multiple sources to increase the likelihood of a favourable outcome.

Facilitation – a process in which a person who is acceptable to all members of a group, substantively neutral and has no decision-making authority, intervenes to help a group improve the way it identifies and solves problems and makes decisions in order to increase the group's effectiveness.

Governance supervision – a structured formal process for directors or governance professionals, with the help of the company secretary as supervisor, to improve the quality of their governance, to grow their governance capacity and to support themselves and their governance practice.

Group – two or more people who interact with one another, share similar characteristics and, collectively, have a sense of unity.

Groupthink – overriding desire for consensus and unanimity, leading to poor decision making, in cohesive groups due to suppression of internal dissent and consequent inadequate evaluation.

High performing team – a team that possesses unique and expert level knowledge, skills and experience related to task performance and adapt, coordinate, and cooperate as a team, thereby producing superior or at least near optimal levels of performance.

Human capital – the sum of knowledge, skills and experience and other relevant workforce attributes that reside in an organisation's workforce and drive productivity, performance and the achievement of strategic goals.

Learning agility – a mind-set and corresponding collection of practices that allow leaders to continually develop, grow and utilise new strategies that will equip them for the increasingly complex problems they face in their organisations.

Mediation – a dynamic, structured, interactive process where a neutral third party assists disputing parties in resolving conflict through the use of specialised communication and negotiation techniques.

Mentoring – help by a more experienced individual willing to share knowledge with someone less experienced in a relationship of mutual trust to help them make significant transitions in knowledge, work or thinking.

Mindfulness – the psychological process of bringing one's attention to experiences occurring in the present moment.

Micro aggressions – words or actions that, although probably not noticed by the person enacting them, or even indeed by others around them, reinforce stereotypes and thus reduce the likelihood of viewing people according to their individual merits as opposed to the merits or otherwise of their stereotype.

Personality – the characteristic set of behaviours, cognitions and emotional patterns that evolve from our biology and our environment.

Professional capital – the functional, industry and executive management experience, as well as specific prior board directorships, that an individual candidate might bring.

Psychological safety – being able to show and employ one's self without fear of negative consequences of self-image, status or career.

Psychology – the scientific study of the mind and how it dictates and influences our behavior.

Resilience – the process of adapting well in the face of adversity, trauma, tragedy, threats or significant sources of stress – such as family and relationship problems, serious health problems or workplace and financial stressors. It means bouncing back from difficult experiences.

Social capital – the number and strength of one's personal connections that may include professional networks, alumni networks and social networks.

Systemic team coaching – a process of coaching the whole team both together and apart, over a designated period of time to enable it to align on common purpose, collaborate and learn across diversity, develop collective leadership, achieve performance outcomes, engage effectively engage with their key stakeholder groups and jointly transform the wider business.

Talent – those individuals who can make a difference to organisational performance, either through their immediate contribution or in the longer term by demonstrating the highest levels of potential.

Talent management – the systematic attraction, identification, development, engagement, retention and deployment of those individuals with high potential who are of particular value to an organisation.

Team – a small group of people with complementary skills who are committed to a common purpose, performance goals and approach for which they hold themselves mutually accountable.

Index

www.ingramcontent.com/pod-product-compliance
Ingram Content Group UK Ltd.
Pitfield, Milton Keynes, MK11 3LW, UK
UKHW021058130926
8556IPUK00046B/1216

9 781860 728